Autodesk®
Architectural Desktop 2004

A Comprehensive Tutorial

Autodesk®
Architectural Desktop 2004

A Comprehensive Tutorial

H. Edward Goldberg, AIA

Registered Architect

PEARSON

Prentice
Hall

Upper Saddle River, New Jersey
Columbus, Ohio

Library of Congress Cataloging-in-Publication Data
Goldberg, H. Edward.
   Autodesk Architectural desktop 2004: a comprehensive tutorial / H. Edward Goldberg.
     p. cm.
   Includes index.
   ISBN 0-13-113497-3
   1. Architectural drawing--Computer-aided design. 2. Autodesk Architectural desktop. 3.
AutoCAD. I. Title.

NA2728.G67 2004
720'.28'40285536--dc22

2003060429

Editor in Chief: Stephen Helba
Executive Editor: Debbie Yarnell
Managing Editor: Judith Casillo
Editorial Assistant: Jonathan Tenthoff
Production Editor: Louise N. Sette
Production Supervision: Lisa Garboski, *bookworks*
Design Coordinator: Diane Ernsberger
Text Designer: STELLARViSIONs
Cover Designer: Thomas Mack
Production Manager: Brian Fox
Marketing Manager: Jimmy Stephens

This book was set in Janson by STELLARViSIONs. It was printed and bound by Courier Kendallville, Inc. The cover was printed by Phoenix Color Corp.

Disclaimer:

The publication is designed to provide tutorial information about AutoCAD® and/or other Autodesk computer programs. Every effort has been made to make this publication complete and as accurate as possible. The reader is expressly cautioned to use any and all precautions necessary, and to take appropriate steps to avoid hazards, when engaging in the activities described herein.

Neither the author nor the publisher makes any representations or warranties of any kind, with respect to the materials set forth in this publication, express or implied, including without limitation any warranties of fitness for a particular purpose or merchantability. Nor shall the author or the publisher be liable for any special, consequential or exemplary damages resulting, in whole or in part, directly or indirectly, from the reader's use of, or reliance upon, this material or subsequent revisions of this material.

Pearson Education Ltd.
Pearson Education Singapore Pte. Ltd.
Pearson Education Canada, Ltd.
Pearson Education—Japan

Pearson Education Australia Pty. Limited
Pearson Education North Asia Ltd.
Pearson Educación de Mexico, S. A. de C.V.
Pearson Education Malaysia Pte. Ltd.

10 9 8 7 6 5 4 3 2
ISBN: 0-13-113497-3

I dedicate this book to the women I love,
my mother Lillian,
my wife Judith Ellen,
and my daughter Allison Julia.

Acknowledgments

I want to thank all the wonderful and dedicated people at the Building Systems division of Autodesk in New Hampshire for their professional assistance and for their friendship. Special thanks go to Julian Gonzalez, Bill Glennie, and Dennis McNeal on the ADT 2004 team.

I want to acknowledge Sara Ferris and Lara Sheridan at CADALYST magazine for being so wonderful to work with.

I want to acknowledge Art Liddle, past editor of CADALYST, who introduced me to this excellent program.

How to use this book

This book has been organized into three main parts: "Getting Started," "Sections and Tutorials" (typically made of several tutorial "exercises" that illustrate commands), and "Putting It All Together," which uses the knowledge gleaned from the Sections and Tutorials to create a building.

The exercises in this book are designed to be tutorials in most of the major commands and routines used in operating Autodesk Architectural Desktop 2004. Rather than require the student to read a great deal of verbiage and theory, this book uses the hands-on method of learning, with each exercise guiding the student through the typical use of the commands for a subject. It is intended that the student perform the exercises first before attempting to use the program to design a building. It is also intended that the student perform the sections in the order presented as the sections often add information for later exercises. Even if a student understands a particular command, it might still be helpful to complete that exercise either to gain new insight or to compare operator strategy. This book assumes a general knowledge of standard AutoCAD or AutoCAD LT up to Release 2000i. Students without knowledge of Paperspace and Modelspace will be at a very great disadvantage. It is also important that the student have a good understanding of the Windows® operating system, and be able to quickly navigate the various navigation trees in that system.

Because buildings are so complex, and the variations are so numerous, 3D CAAD (Computer-Aided Architectural Design) programs such as Autodesk Architectural Desktop are not inherently easy to use, and have, in my opinion, never been a program for the computer or CAD novice. Because of this complexity, one can become very frustrated when first approaching the multitude of commands even though the programmers have gone to great effort to make this software user-friendly.

This author believes that a good operator follows several fundamental working procedures.

- Use the fewest number of keystrokes for a particular operation. Do not use the full typed name of a command if the command can be performed with a letter alias.
- Use the space bar on the keyboard while operating the program instead of the Enter key except when inserting text.
- Use a strategy of operating this program as you would play a game of chess, thinking several moves ahead, and never moving backwards unless absolutely necessary.

Walk-through

Autodesk® Architectural Desktop 2004
A Comprehensive Tutorial

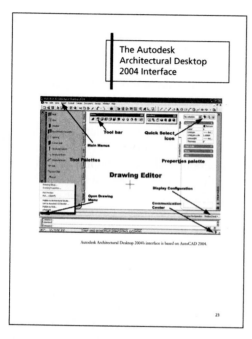

Part I—Getting Started sections provide essential information, preparing users for the guided tutorial on Autodesk Architectural Desktop 2004, including Definitions, Concepts, Abbreviations, and more.

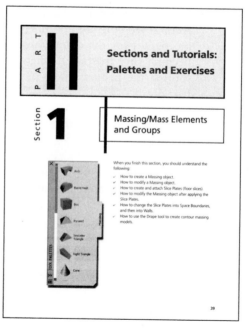

Part II—Sections and Tutorials presents Tool Palettes in the order in which they are commonly used.

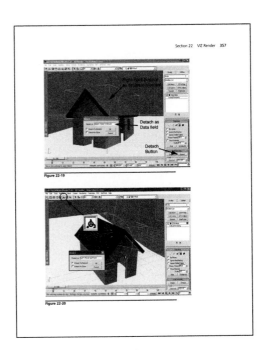

Figure 22-19

Figure 22-20

Numerous walk-throughs and hands-on activities teach commands and routines in relation to the production of architectural drawings.

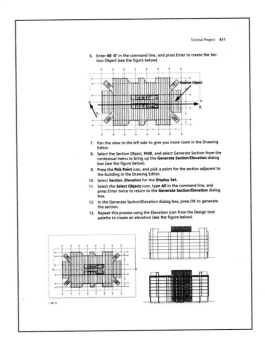

6. Enter **60'-0"** in the command line, and press Enter to create the Section Object (see the figure below).

7. Pan the view to the left side to give you more room in the Drawing Editor.
8. Select the Section Object, RMB, and select Generate Section from the contextual menu to bring up the **Generate Section/Elevation** dialog box (see the figure below).
9. Press the **Pick Point** icon, and pick a point for the section adjacent to the building in the Drawing Editor.
10. Select **Section_Elevation** for the **Display Set.**
11. Select the **Select Objects** icon, type **All** in the command line, and press Enter twice to return to the **Generate Section/Elevation** dialog box.
12. In the Generate Section/Elevation dialog box, press OK to generate the section.
13. Repeat this process using the Elevation icon from the Design tool palette to create an elevation (see the figure below).

Part III—Putting It All Together uses the knowledge gleaned from the Sections and Tutorials to create a building.

Contents

How to Use This Book   vii

Walk-through   viii

PART I   Getting Started   1

Definitions   1

AEC Objects   1

Styles   2

Multi-View Blocks   2

Tool Palettes   3

Check Boxes   3

Radio Buttons   4

Contextual Menus   4

Concepts   5

The Mass Model   5

Space Planning   6

The Virtual Building Model   7

Questions and Answers about Autodesk Architectural Desktop 2004   9

Installing Autodesk Architectural Desktop 2004   15

Abbreviations   21

The Autodesk Architectural Desktop 2004 Interface   23

Tool Palettes   25

Bringing Up the Tool Palettes   25

Resizing the Palette   25

Auto-hide   26

Tool Palettes Properties   27

Deleting Tool Palettes   28

The Properties Palette   29

Bringing Up the Properties Palettes   29

Quick Select   30

The Content Browser   31

Bringing Up the Content Browser   31

The Open Drawing Menu   35

Drawing Setup   36

Publish to Architectural Studio   36

Link to VIZ Render   36

Publish to the Web   37

etransmit   37

P A R T   I I   **Sections and Tutorials: Palettes and Exercises**
39

Section 1
Massing/Mass Elements and Groups   39

Massing and Mass Modeling   40

Hands-On: Creating a Massing Object   40

Hands-On: Modifying a Massing Object   42

Hands-On: Creating and Attaching Slice Plates (Floor Slices)   47

Hiding the Slice Markers   48

Hands-On: Modifying the Massing Object After Applying the Slice Plates   48

Hands-On: Changing the Slice Plates into Space Boundaries and Walls   51

Hands-On: Using the Drape Tool to Create Contour Massing Models   52

Section 2
Space and Space Boundary Objects   55

Space Objects Properties Tool Palette   56

Hands-On: Creating a Spaces Tool Palette   57

Hands-On: Creating a Space Object and Labeling It with a Space Tag   58

Hands-On: Creating a Simple Space Plan with Space Objects   60

Hands-On: Applying Space Boundaries   64

Hands-On: Modifying Space Boundaries   64

Hands-On: Using the Space Auto Generate Tool   69

Section 3
Walls   73

Walls   73

Wall Objects Properties Tool Palette   74

Hands-On: Placing a Wall Object   75

Hands-On: Changing Walls by Dynamically Pulling on Grips   76

Hands-On: Creating Wall Sweeps   77

Hands-On: Creating Wall Endcaps   78

Hands-On: Using Plan Modifiers   80

Hands-On: Using Body Modifiers   82

Hands-On: Using the Roof/Floor Line Option   84

Hands-On: Using Interference Conditions   87

Hands-On: Cleanups   88

Hands-On: Editing Wall Styles   89

Section 4
Windows   95

Hands-On: Placing a Window Object Using Reference   97

Hands-On: Placing a Window Object Using Offset/Center   98

Hands-On: Changing Window Size with Grips   99

Hands-On: Adding a Profile   99

Hands-On: Moving the Window Vertically, Within the Wall,
and Along the Wall   101

Hands-On: Editing Wall Styles   102

Section 5
Doors   107

Hands-On: Placing a Door Object Using Reference   109

Hands-On: Placing a Door Object Using Offset/Center   109

Hands-On: Changing Door Size and Swing Location with Grips   110

Hands-On: Controlling the Door Swing Angle   112

Hands-On: Adding a Profile   113

Hands-On: Adding a Door Knob   114

Hands-On: Moving a Door Vertically, Within the Wall,
and Along the Wall   117

Hands-On: Editing Door Styles   118

Hands-On: Using the Materials Tab   119

Section 6
Curtain Walls   123

Hands-On: Creating a Curtain Wall Tool Palette   125

Hands-On: Placing a Curtain Wall   126

Hands-On: Setting Miter Angles in the Contextual Menu and Start
and End Miters in the Curtain Wall Properties Toolbar   126

Hands-On: Using Roof Line/Floor Line Selections in the Contextual Menu   128

Hands-On: Applying Tool Properties to a Layout Grid   130

Hands-On: Applying Tool Properties to an Elevation Sketch   132

Hands-On: Editing Grid in Place   134

Hands-On: Editing Curtain Wall Styles   137

Section 7
Door and Window Assemblies   141

Hands-On: Creating a Primary Grid   142

Hands-On: Creating a Door Style for Double Doors   144

Hands-On: Assigning Doors to a Door/Window Assembly Infill   144

Hands-On: Testing the Partially Complete Door/Window Assembly   146

Hands-On: Adding Sidelites   146

Hands-On: Sizing the Frame of a Door/Window Assembly   148

Hands-On: Removing the Sill of a Door/Window Assembly,
and Changing the Sidelite   149

Hands-On: Using the New Custom Door/Window Assembly   150

Section 8
Stairs   151

Properties Palette   152

Hands-On: Setting the AEC Object Settings for Stairs   154

Hands-On: Making a New Stair Tool Palette   155

Hands-On: Placing a Stair   155

Hands-On: Modifying the Stair with the Stair Grips   156

Hands-On: Changing Stair Styles   157

Hands-On: Adding a Stair Rail   158

Hands-On: Editing a Stair Style   159

Hands-On: Placing a Multi-landing Stair   160

Hands-On: Interference Conditions   162

Hands-On: Anchoring a Second Stair to an Existing Landing   163

Hands-On: Projecting a Stair Edge to a Polyline   164

Hands-On: Projecting a Stair Edge to a Wall or AEC Object   165

Hands-On: Generating a Polyline from a Stair Object   167

Section 9
Railings   171

Hands-On: Making a New Railing Tool Palette   172
Hands-On: Placing a Railing   173
Hands-On: Editing a Railing Style   173
Hands-On: Modifying Balusters   177
Hands-On: Adding a Railing to a Stair and Stair Flight   179
Hands-On: Adding a Railing to a Landing   180
Hands-On: Adding a Railing and Landing Support—Anchor to Object   181
Hands-On: Creating a Railing Using a Polyline   182
Hands-On: Editing a Railing Profile in Place   183

Section 10
Roof and Roof Slab Objects   187

Hands-On: Making a New Roof and Roof Slabs Tool Palette   190
Hands-On: Placing a Roof Object   190
Hands-On: Modifying a Roof Object   191
Hands-On: Editing a Roof Edge   193
Hands-On: Using Apply Tool Properties to Roof and Surfu   195
Hands-On: Converting to Roof Slabs   196
Hands-On: roofslabmodifyedges   197
Hands-On: Applying Tool Properties to a Roof Slab   197
Hands-On: Cutting a Hole in a Roof Slab   198
Hands-On: Adding Edge Profiles in Place   199
Hands-On: Creating a Roof Dormer   201

Section 11
Slabs and Slab Objects   205

Hands-On: Creating a New Slabs Tool Palette   207
Hands-On: Direct Mode and Direction   207
Hands-On: Projected Mode   208
Hands-On: Applying Tool Properties to: for Slabs   209
Hands-On: Cutting Slabs   210
Hands-On: Modifying a Slab Object   212

Section 12
Structural Members, Column Grids, Grids, and Anchors   217

Hands-On: Making a New Structure Tool Palette   219

Hands-On: Placing a Column and Column Grid   219

Hands-On: Modifying Structural Members   220

Hands-On: Creating a Round Composite Concrete and Steel Column   223

Hands-On: Adding Bar Joists   224

Hands-On: Labeling a Column Grid   227

Hands-On: Adding and Labeling a Layout Grid 2D   229

Layout Curves   230

Hands-On: Creating and Using a Layout Curve   231

Hands-On: Using a Wall as a Layout Curve   231

Hands-On: Layout Grid (2D)   232

Section 13
AEC Dimensions   235

AEC Dimensions   235

Hands-On: Setting the Text Style   236

Hands-On: Creating a Dimension Style   237

Hands-On: Creating an AEC Dimension Style   238

Hands-On: Using and Modifying an AEC Dimension Style   239

Hands-On: Dimensioning Doors and Windows
with AEC Dimension Styles   241

Hands-On: Adding a Manual AEC Dimension   244

Hands-On: Detaching Objects from AEC Dimensions   245

Hands-On: AEC Dimension Chains   246

Hands-On: The AEC Dimension Wizard   248

Section 14
Elevations   251

Hands-On: Making a New Elevation Tool Palette   251

Hands-On: Creating a Sample Building for the Elevation Exercises   252

Hands-On: Making an Elevation   254

Hands-On: Modifying and Updating the 2D Elevation   256

Hands-On: Subdivisions   257

Section 15
Sections   263

Sections   263
Hands-On: Making a Section Tool Palette   264
Hands-On: Creating a Sample Building   264
Hands-On: Placing the Standard Section Object   266
Hands-On: Generating the Section   267
Hands-On: Changing the Direction Arrow Appearance   268
Live Section Definitions   269
Hands-On: Creating a Sample Building for a Live Section   270
Hands-On: Creating a Live Section   272

Section 16
Mask Blocks   275

Hands-On: Creating a Custom Fluorescent Fixture Called New Fixture   275
Hands-On: Testing the New Light Fixture Mask Block   276
Hands-On: Using Create AEC Content to Place the New Light Fixture in the DesignCenter   279
Hands-On: Testing the New Light Fixture Mask Block from the DesignCenter   280

Section 17
Multi-View Blocks   283

The Chair   283
Hands-On: Creating the Autodesk Website Icon   283
Hands-On: Going to the Chair at the Nsight3D Website   284
Hands-On: Creating Content from a 3D Mesh   285
Hands-On: Creating a Multi-View Block   288
Hands-On: Testing the Multi-View Block   289

Section 18
Schedules and Schedule Tags   291

Hands-On: Making a New Schedule Tag and Schedule Tool Palette   291
Schedule Tags   292

Hands-On: Placing Door and Window Tags   292

Hands-On: Placing Schedules   295

Hands-On: Updating Schedules   296

Hands-On: Using Schedules to Locate Objects   296

Hands-On: Exporting Schedules to Databases   296

Hands-On: Creating and Using Custom Schedules   298

Section 19
The Detailer   307

Hands-On: Creating a 2D Building Section with the Detailer   307

Labeling a 2D Building Section with the Detailer   312

Section 20
The DesignCenter   315

Content   315

Hands-On: Using the DesignCenter to Create a Kitchen   316

Section 21
Drawing Management   325

The Drawing Management Concept   326

Hands-On: Using the Project Browser   326

Hands-On: Creating Constructs and Elements in the Project Navigator   329

Hands-On: Working with Constructs and Elements in the Project Navigator   331

Hands-On: Assigning Constructs and Elements in the Project Navigator   333

Hands-On: Creating Views in the Project Navigator   336

Hands-On: Creating Plotting Sheets in the Project Navigator   338

Section 22
VIZ Render   345

How Best to Learn to Operate VIZ Render   346

Hands-On: Making a Simple Scene   346

Hands-On: Using VIZ Render   349

Hands-On: Creating and Using Materials   355

Hands-On: Applying Materials   358

Hands-On: Creating and Modifying Materials   362

Hands-On: People and Trees   367

PART III Putting It All Together   373

Tutorial Project   373

Hands-On: The Massing Model   373
Hands-On: Rendering the Massing Model   378
Hands-On: Creating Slice Plates from the Massing Model   380
Hands-On: Setting Up the Project   382
Hands-On: Using Slice Plates from the Massing Model   383
Hands-On: Adding Stairs   386
Hands-On: The First-Floor Slab   386
Hands-On: The Column Structure   389
Hands-On: The CORE   393
Hands-On: The Second-Floor Walls and Slab   396
Hands-On: The Third-Floor Slab   399
Hands-On: Making the Second-Floor Stair Construct   400
Hands-On: Making the Fourth-, Fifth-, Sixth-, and Seventh-Floor Slabs   400
Hands-On: Making the Third-, Fourth-, Fifth-, Sixth-, and Seventh-Floor Walls   401
Hands-On: Making the Third-, Fourth-, Fifth-, and Sixth-Floor Stairs   401
Hands-On: Making the Third-, Fourth-, Fifth-, Sixth-, and Seventh-Floor Columns   402
Hands-On: Making the Second- through Seventh-Floor CORE   402
Hands-On: Creating a View (Showing All the Components Together)   402
Hands-On: Making the Roof Structure   404
Hands-On: Making the Roof Slab and Roof Cant   406
Hands-On: Making the Rooftop Structure   408
Hands-On: Adding the ROOF STRUCTURE.dwg and ROOF SLAB to Your VIEW   409
Hands-On: Making a Section and Elevation   410
Hands-On: Making SW Isometric and Elevation and Section Plotting Sheets   412

Index   415

Autodesk®
Architectural Desktop 2004

A Comprehensive Tutorial

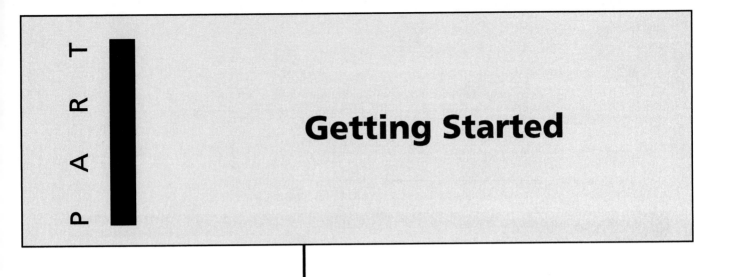

PART I

Getting Started

Definitions

AEC Objects

In Autodesk Architectural Desktop, AEC Objects are specific virtual architectural objects such as walls, doors, windows, stairs, and so on that are programmed to act and interact in the same manner as they would in the real world. These AEC Objects give Autodesk Architectural Desktop 2004 much of its power and productivity. They can usually be controlled parametrically through the Properties palette, which can be made to appear whenever that object is selected. Often one AEC Object will interact with another, as would happen when an AEC door is placed in an AEC wall. AEC Objects are often referred to as "intelligent architectural objects."

Styles

Styles are information contained in drawings (DWG), and control the parameters of AEC Objects. Because of the software programming, this information directly controls Autodesk Architectural Desktop 2004's basic drawing entities such as lines and circles. Since Styles do not contain any entities, they provide a very efficient method for controlling content within the program and a very quick transfer of that content over the Internet.

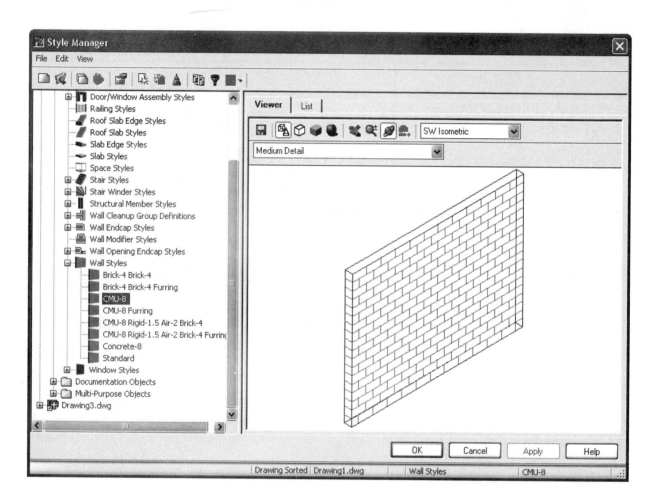

Multi-View Blocks

Although there is a plethora of AEC or programmed content, there is always need for specialized content. Here, Autodesk Architectural Desktop provides a variation on its standard "Block" system familiar to users of AutoCAD and AutoCAD LT. Multi-View Blocks allow the user to place content in one view and have the appropriate view of that content appear in other views at the same time. Although Multi-View Blocks don't have the intelligence, they can greatly increase productivity. Autodesk Architectural Desktop 2004 includes many routines that depend on Multi-View Blocks. An exercise in the creation of Multi-View Blocks is given in this book.

Tool Palettes

New to Autodesk Architectural Desktop 2004 are Tool Palettes. These palettes can be sized, renamed, modified, and moved. Most of the major architectural routines are represented as icons or pictures, and can be implemented by either dragging into or clicking in the Drawing Editor from these palettes. The developers of the program have replaced most of the standard toolbars and icons with this method in order to optimize the drawing environment for maximum productivity.

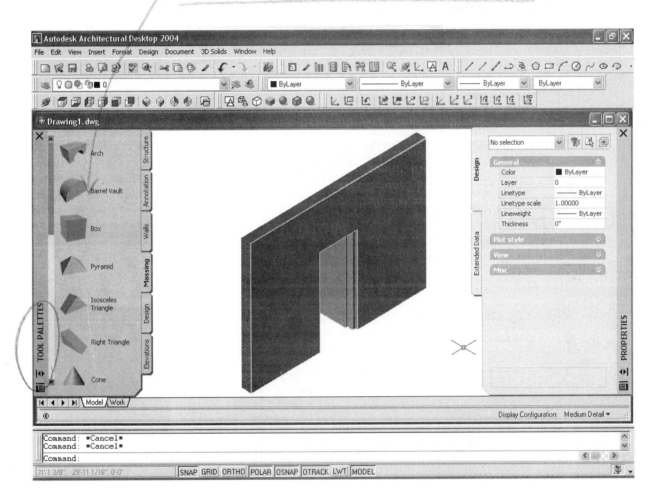

Check Boxes

Check boxes indicate the on or off state of available options. If they are in a group, several check boxes can be selected at the same time.

Radio Buttons

Radio buttons (the name comes from the button selectors on car radios) indicate the on or off state of available options. Only one button in a group of buttons can be chosen.

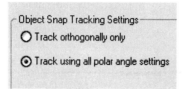

Contextual Menus

Contextual (Context-Sensitive) menus became popular when Microsoft introduced Windows 95. Autodesk Architectural Desktop 2004 makes extensive use of these menus to control options and subcommands of various components. Contextual menus are typically summoned by clicking the right mouse button on a specific object, entity, or spot in the interface. Through programming, the appropriate menu or "context" will appear for that object at that point in its command structure. As an example, clicking the right mouse button on a Door within a Wall will provide all the commands available for the door and its relationship to the wall.

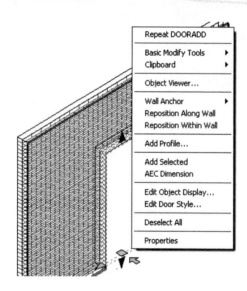

Concepts

As with previous versions of Autodesk Architectural Desktop, this new release uses three different concepts for eventually creating documentation. These concepts are the Mass Model concept, the Space Planning concept, and the Virtual Building concept. Of course, you can always operate Autodesk Architectural Desktop 2004 as a typical 2D electronic CAD drafting program, but that really negates the benefits of the Virtual Building features, and eliminates much of the intrinsic volumetric information endemic to the Virtual Building.

The Mass Model

The Mass Model concept is unique to Autodesk Architectural Desktop and is based on a modeling tradition called "massing model" used by many architects. In that system, the architect or designer makes a cardboard, wood, or clay "study model" of the building. These small models often show the relationship between parts of the structure while also indicating scale and the effect of light and shadow on the facades. Typically the architect would later create more sophisticated models while creating the construction documents.

In Architectural Desktop 2004 you can make very sophisticated virtual massing models. These massing models can then be sliced into "Floorplates" or horizontal sections from which walls can be automatically generated. These walls are the connection point between the massing model and the construction documentation in Architectural Desktop 2004.

Space Planning

The space-planning concept has been used by architects and designers for years. In this concept, rectangles and circles represent building program areas. The designer places these forms in relationship to each other to create "flow diagrams." Once established, the relationships are then used to help create the form of the structure. In Autodesk Architectural Desktop 2004, the developers have taken this one step farther by combining a 3D component to the relationships. Every space-planning object also contains information about floor-to-ceiling heights, and floor-to-floor heights. After the space planning has been completed, the space plan can automatically be converted into three-dimensional walls into which doors, windows, and so on can be added. The three-dimensional plan can then form the basis for construction documents. Additionally, it can be culled for space information that can be transferred to database programs.

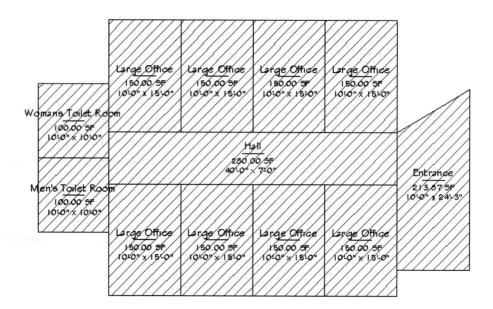

The Virtual Building Model

The Virtual Building or 3D model differs from standard electronic drafting in that components of a building are placed much as you would place objects in the real world. Instead of drawing lines and circles, you place doors, windows, walls, and roofs that can be parametrically controlled or modified, and simulate a real-world relationship. To this end Autodesk Architectural Desktop 2004 has a myriad of parametric tools. The Virtual Building concept has been the subject of much discussion by architects and designers and is generally accepted as the direction that CAAD is going. Autodesk Architectural Desktop 2004 and its previous releases have always been considered a leader in this trend.

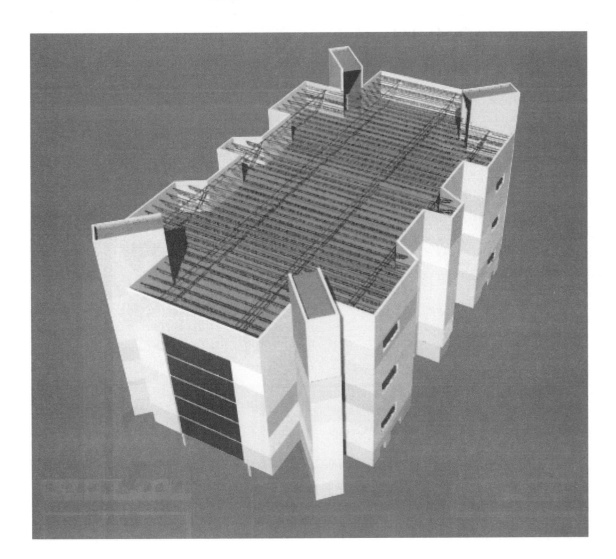

Questions and Answers about Autodesk Architectural Desktop 2004

The following information was taken from Autodesk press releases. The author has selected this information to answer questions that might be in readers' minds.

? What are the key areas of improvement in Autodesk Architectural Desktop 2004?

It has more than 300 enhancements that address

- Ease of use
- Drafting and design
- Construction documentation
- Drawing and level management
- Design visualization
- File sharing and collaboration

Key features include a streamlined user interface, customizable tool palettes, direct object manipulation, automated file and level management, and integrated photorealistic rendering and animation. These enhancements to Autodesk Architectural Desktop 2004 software offer more productivity, better coordination, and smoother collaboration and data exchange.

? Are Autodesk Architectural Desktop and Autodesk Revit files interoperable?

You can easily exchange design data (2D DWG files) between Autodesk Architectural Desktop and the Autodesk® Revit® building information modeler through their respective Export to AutoCAD features.

? What versions of AutoCAD does Autodesk Architectural Desktop software's Export to AutoCAD feature support?

This release supports Export to AutoCAD 2004 and AutoCAD 2000 DWG and DXF™ formats, as well as Release 12 DXF, making it possible for users of AutoCAD 2000, AutoCAD 2000i, AutoCAD 2002, and AutoCAD 2004 to open Autodesk Architectural Desktop 2004 files without using object enablers.

? What is the Autodesk AEC Object Enabler?

The Autodesk® AEC Object Enabler is a freely downloadable and distributable utility that gives an AutoCAD user functionality and design flexibility through the power of Autodesk Architectural Desktop objects. With the proper version of the AEC Object Enabler, any AutoCAD 2000, 2000i, 2002, or 2004 user can have full compatibility with Autodesk Architectural Desktop objects. For more information and to download the AEC Object Enabler, go to www.autodesk.com/aecobjecten.

? **Will Autodesk continue to develop Autodesk Architectural Desktop?**

Yes. With well over a quarter million Autodesk Architectural Desktop licenses world-wide, Autodesk plans to continue to develop and support the software through product updates as well as periodic extensions.

? **Why was the Drawing Manager introduced in Autodesk Architectural Desktop 2004?**

Earlier releases of Autodesk Architectural Desktop simply enabled you to continue to manage projects using existing standards for manually organizing file structure and xref relationships. While continuing to respect your practices and standards, this release of Autodesk Architectural Desktop introduces the new drawing management feature for users who want to take advantage of its automated project and level management tools.

? **Besides the Drawing Management feature, how has project coordination improved?**

Coordination has been improved through the addition of materials, a new feature that provides both graphic and nongraphic detail to your drawings for design, documentation, and visualization purposes. In addition, extended scheduling functionality enables you to tag through xrefs and schedule external drawings. Also, interoperability with Autodesk Building Systems improves coordination between disciplines.

? **How does VIZ Render differ from Autodesk VIZ?**

VIZ Render, Autodesk Architectural Desktop software's native visualization tool, uses some of the core technology developed in Autodesk® VIZ. Much of the photometric lighting and rendering technology from Autodesk VIZ 4 has been included in VIZ Render. There are, however, many differences between the applications. VIZ Render has been optimized to accept the data organization from Autodesk Architectural Desktop 2004 in a much more efficient way. The entire user interface has been revised and simplified to make the process of creating high-quality visualization more accessible. The guiding principle in developing VIZ Render was that Architectural Desktop is the model authoring application. You organize and build the model exclusively in Architectural Desktop and then seamlessly link to VIZ Render for image making.

? **Can I export VIZ Render files to Autodesk VIZ?**

Although VIZ Render can import files (MAX) from both Autodesk VIZ and 3ds max™ software, VIZ Render files (DRF) cannot be imported to Autodesk VIZ or 3ds max.

? **Is a network version of Autodesk Architectural Desktop available?**

Yes. Autodesk Architectural Desktop software uses FLEX*lm*® network license management. For more information, see "Platforms, System Requirements, and Network" later in this document.

Technology

? **What are intelligent building model objects?**

The ObjectARX® technology used in Autodesk Architectural Desktop enables you to create intelligent building model objects that know their form, fit, and function and behave according to their real-world properties. This technology improves software performance, ease of use, and flexibility in design. Intelligent building objects respond directly to standard AutoCAD editing commands in the same way that common AutoCAD drawing objects—such as lines, arcs, and circles—do, and yet they also have the ability to display according to context and to interact with other building objects intelligently. Object-based technology transforms ordinary geometry into intelligent building objects whose behavior models that of physical objects.

? **What is the significance of door, wall, window, and other building model objects?**

These intelligent objects improve design productivity and efficiency because custom objects (doors, windows, stairs, and other building elements) behave according to the specific properties or rules that pertain to them in the real world. Building objects thus have a relationship to one another and interact with each other intelligently. For example, a window has a relationship to the wall that contains it. If you move or delete the wall, the window reacts appropriately. In addition, intelligent building objects maintain dynamic links with construction documents and specifications, resulting in more accurate and valuable project deliverables that can be used to manage a building throughout its life cycle. When someone deletes or modifies a door, for example, the door schedule is automatically updated.

? **What is the significance of 3D in Autodesk Architectural Desktop?**

Because the objects in Autodesk Architectural Desktop describe real-world building components, both 2D and 3D representations can be created automatically and either one can be used to view or edit the model. This conveniently and smoothly integrates 2D and 3D functionality and allows exploration of design ideas within CAD in a fashion similar to the way architects and designers mentally envision their designs. For example, you can quickly and easily create 3D massing studies in the initial phases of the design process to explore multiple design scenarios. Or you can develop a floor plan in 2D and then immediately generate a perspective view of it in 3D. You can even use 3D to visually check for any type of interference in your design. Using 3D is not required in Autodesk Architectural Desktop. Object technology increases productivity and accuracy without the need to leave the 2D view. With Autodesk Architectural Desktop software you can incorporate 3D into your design process at your own pace.

? **Has 2D functionality been enhanced?**

Yes. Although Autodesk Architectural Desktop offers many new 3D features, the software's intelligent objects and architectural tools provide important benefits for 2D design development and construction documentation. You have all the functionality of AutoCAD 2004 plus architectural design and drafting tools. Therefore, you can create key project deliverables, such as plans and specifications, more efficiently and accurately.

Compatibility

? **Is Autodesk Architectural Desktop 2004 interoperable with other Autodesk products?**

Yes. AutoCAD 2004 is the foundation for an interoperable family of Autodesk products, including Autodesk Architectural Desktop 2004. Sharing the same database framework component—ObjectDBX™ for reading and writing drawing files—helps to ensure that the next generation of Autodesk products is interoperable with Autodesk Architectural Desktop 2004. These include industry-specific products such as Autodesk® Building Systems, Autodesk® Revit®, and the AutoCAD Autodesk Map™, AutoCAD® Mechanical, Autodesk® Mechanical Desktop®, Autodesk® Land Desktop, as well as software that address many industries such as Volo® View, Autodesk® Express Viewer, Autodesk® Raster Design, and Autodesk® OnSite View.

? Is Autodesk Architectural Desktop 2004 compatible with earlier releases of Autodesk Architectural Desktop?

Yes. Designs created in earlier versions of Autodesk Architectural Desktop easily migrate to Autodesk Architectural Desktop 2004. Files created in Autodesk Architectural Desktop 2004 need to be saved as 2D DWG files to be read by versions of Autodesk Architectural Desktop based on AutoCAD 2000, 2000i, and 2002 platforms.

? Will my third-party applications work with Autodesk Architectural Desktop 2004 software?

Your existing third-party applications may or may not be compatible with Autodesk Architectural Desktop 2004. Contact your independent software supplier for details. Autodesk has been working closely with members of the Autodesk Developer Network to ensure that your applications will be available for Autodesk Architectural Desktop 2004. For more information about the availability of third-party applications compatible with AutoCAD 2004, visit www.autodesk.com/partnerproducts.

? Is Autodesk Architectural Desktop compatible with Industry Foundation Classes (IFC)?

Yes, Autodesk Architectural Desktop is compatible with Industry Foundation Classes. However, you must download and install the IFC 2.x plug-in from G.E.M. Team Solutions. This plug-in will not be available until after it passes the second certification round by the IAI (Industry Alliance for Interoperability). This certification is currently scheduled for May 2004. For more information visit the G.E.M. website at www.team-solutions.de/ifc.

? Autodesk Architectural Desktop 2004 has AutoCAD 2004 as its foundation. Has the AutoCAD 2004 drawing file format (DWG) changed from the AutoCAD 2000/2000i/2002 products, as it did between AutoCAD Release 14 and AutoCAD 2000?

Yes, the AutoCAD 2004 DWG file format has been updated and is different from the 2000/2000i/2002 DWG file format. This new format is also the same DWG file format that is used in the latest releases of the Autodesk industry-specific products such as Autodesk Revit, Autodesk Architectural Desktop, Autodesk Building Systems, Autodesk Map, Autodesk Land Desktop, Autodesk Mechanical Desktop, and AutoCAD Mechanical software. To provide performance enhancements, smaller file sizes, presentation graphics, and drawing security, both the DWG and DXF formats required updates. However, you can still easily share files among design team members using AutoCAD 2000/2000i/2002 and AutoCAD 2004 software products. As in the past, this version of AutoCAD opens DWG files from all earlier DWG versions of the software (including AutoCAD Release 14) created by any Autodesk product.

? Can I run Autodesk Architectural Desktop 2004 side by side with other AutoCAD platform-based applications?

Yes, Autodesk Architectural Desktop 2004 can be installed side by side with any other AutoCAD 2000i, AutoCAD 2002, or AutoCAD 2004–based product. These products include Autodesk Architectural Desktop, Autodesk Building Systems,

Autodesk Mechanical Desktop, AutoCAD Mechanical, Autodesk Land Desktop, Autodesk Map, and AutoCAD LT® software.

Support and Training

What support is available for Autodesk Architectural Desktop?

You can learn about all support options from your local Autodesk System Center (ASC), reseller, or distributor. Support contracts are also available through the Autodesk Subscription Program. For support over the Web, visit www.autodesk.com/support.

What documentation comes with Autodesk Architectural Desktop?

Autodesk Architectural Desktop comes with the following online and printed documentation:

- *New Features Guide* (print)
- User's Guide (online help; compiled HTML help and PDF)
- Metric and imperial tutorials (compiled HTML help and PDF)
- ActiveX Reference (compiled HTML help)
- Installation guides (single user and network; compiled HTML help and PDF)
- Readme files (standard and Object Enabler)

Platforms, System Requirements, and Network

Following are the minimum hardware and operating system requirements for running Autodesk Architectural Desktop.

Description Minimum Requirement

Operating system Microsoft® Windows® XP (Professional, Home Edition, or Tablet PC Edition), Windows 2000 Professional, or Windows NT® 4.0 (SP6 or later) (Windows 95 and 98 are no longer supported.)

CPU Intel® Pentium® 4 or AMD K7 with 1.4 GHz processor

RAM 512 MB (1 GB recommended)

Free disk space, 650-MB free hard disk space, and 75-MB swap space

Display resolution 1024×768

If you want to fully benefit from all the new features in Autodesk Architectural Desktop 2004, such as materials and the new VIZ Render visualization capabilities, then a 1.4 GHz CPU or better is recommended.

Have there been any improvements to software deployment through network licensing?

Enhanced FLEX*lm* 8.3 software helps you get the full benefit from your Autodesk Architectural Desktop licenses. For example, with the new license borrowing feature you can install a time-limited license on your computer while disabling the license on the server for that same period. You can then run Autodesk Architectural Desktop without having a connection to the license server.

Is Autodesk Architectural Desktop being released as an English-only product?

No. This product will be released worldwide. Versions of this product will be available in a wide range of languages and with localized content in many countries. For information on product availability contact your local reseller or Autodesk Systems Center (ASC).

?   **Is subscription available for Autodesk Architectural Desktop?**

Yes, subscription is available in most countries around the world. The Autodesk Subscription Program is the easiest way to keep your Autodesk Architectural Desktop software up-to-date. For an annual fee, you get the latest versions of your licensed Autodesk software, a single lifetime contract number, convenient software management, and all the other great benefits of the Autodesk Subscription Program.

Users with subscription for the Autodesk Building Systems, Autodesk Architectural Desktop, and Autodesk Revit applications also receive important benefits, including use of Autodesk® Architectural Studio and the ability to transfer licenses between Architectural Desktop and Revit for a small fee. Visit www.autodesk.com/subscription or contact your Autodesk Authorized Reseller for more information about this pipeline to software simplicity. Autodesk Architectural Desktop subscriptions are sold by Autodesk Authorized Building Industry Solution Resellers on behalf of Autodesk. For added assurance subscription members also can choose to enroll in Autodesk Direct Online Support.

Installing Autodesk Architectural Desktop 2004

Autodesk Architectural Desktop 2004 ships with 2 CDs labeled 1 of 2 and 2 of 2. Installing Autodesk Architectural Desktop 2004 is relatively easy; the directions follow.

1. Insert the disk labeled 1 of 2 in your CD and close the CD tray.
2. If your Windows Operating system is set for **Autorun,** the CD will begin to self-load.
3. If the CD does not self-load, go to the next step.
4. In the Microsoft Windows Desktop, select the **Start** button, and pick the Run icon to bring up the Windows **Run** dialog box.
5. In the Windows **Run** dialog box press the **Browse** button, and select the CD drive letter (labeled ADT 2004a).
6. In the ADT 2004a directory on the CD drive, select Setup, and press the OK open button to return to the Run dialog box.
7. In the **Run** dialog box, press the OK button to start the installation process.

Be prepared to wait for several seconds until the main Autodesk Architectural Desktop 2004 screen appears. (See the figure below.)

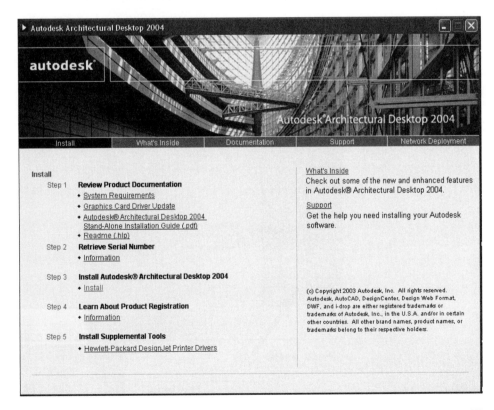

In the main Autodesk Architectural Desktop 2004 installation screen you can choose from several sources of information. It is a good idea to select each of these sources in order to make sure that you have met the correct hardware and operating system requirements for the program. If everything is OK, do the following.

8. Select the underlined word **Install** in **Step 3,** and wait several seconds until the **Autodesk Architectural Desktop 2004 Setup** dialog box appears. (See the figure below.)

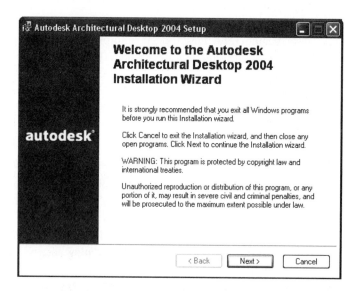

9. In the Autodesk Architectural Desktop 2004 Setup dialog box select the **Next** button to bring up the Autodesk Software License Agreement.

10. If you accept the agreement, select the **I accept** radio button, and press the **Next** button to bring up the **Serial Number** data field. (See the figure below.)

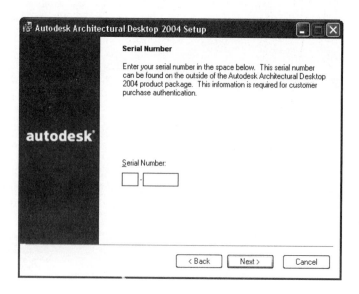

11. In the Serial Number data field, enter the serial number that comes with your copy of the program, and press the **Next** button to bring up the **User Information** data field. (See the figure below.)

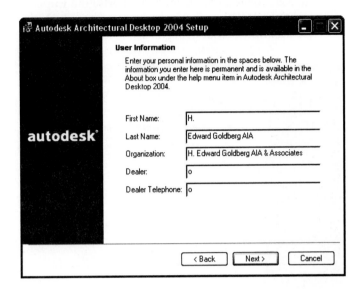

12. After entering your personal information, press the **Next** button to bring up the **Select Installation Type** radio buttons. (See the figure below.)

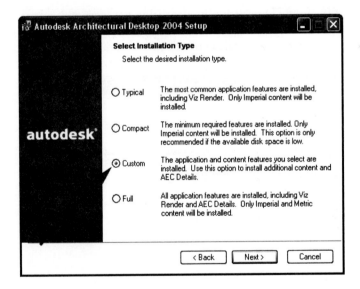

This author prefers the Custom radio button. The following information illustrates that use; if you prefer, you can select the **Typical, Compact,** or **Full** installation options.

13. After selecting the Custom radio button and pressing the Next button, the Feature dialog box will appear. (See the figure below.) For each feature that you want to install, activate the **Will be installed on local hard drive** field. Activate to install on the local hard drive the **Imperial** content, **VIZ render,** and **Details.** When finished selecting, press the Next button to bring up the **Destination Folder** dialog box.

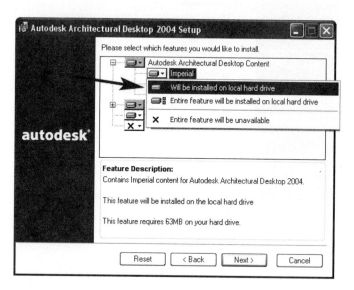

14. In the Destination Folder dialog box, accept the destination location (c:\Program Files\Autodesk Architectural Desktop 2004\by default) or change the location to suit your computer. (See the figure below.)

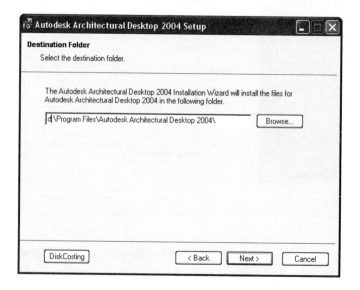

Note: Regardless of where you place the Autodesk Architectural Desktop 2004 program, it will always create a folder for keeping your project files on the **C** drive in the **My Documents** folder.

15. Press the Next button to bring up the **Choose a default text editor for editing text files** dialog box; accept the default text editor location, or browse to the location in which it exists, and check the Display the Autodesk Architectural Desktop 2004 shortcut on my desktop checkbox. (See the figure below.)

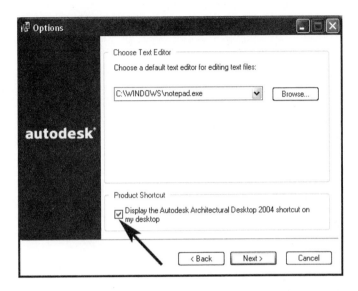

16. Press the Next button to bring up the **Are you ready to begin installation?** (just a last check) dialog box. (See the figure below.)

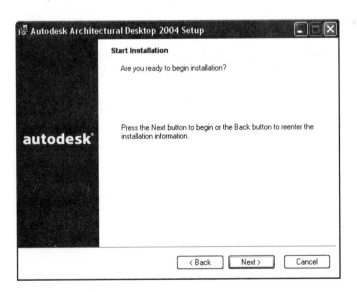

17. Press the Next button to start the installation.

Tip

After you have saved an Autodesk Architectural Desktop drawing, you can also start the program by dragging and dropping that drawing icon onto the Architectural Desktop icon. This will automatically start Architectural Desktop 2004 and bring up that drawing.

Abbreviations

In order to make this book easier to understand, shortcut abbreviations are often used. The following list codifies those abbreviations.

Please Read Before Proceeding

Activate a field   Refers to selecting a selection made up of a sentence

Activate a viewport   Refers to clicking in a viewport to make it the active viewport

ADT or ADT 2004   Refers to Autodesk Architectural Desktop 2004

AEC Objects   Refers to any Autodesk Architectural Desktop 2004 intelligent object such as walls, stairs, schedules, etc.

Ancillary   Refers to space between the ceiling and the floor above

Browse   Refers to searching through the file folders and files

Contextual menu   Refers to any menu that appears when an object or entity is selected with an RMB

Dialog box   Refers to any menu containing parameters or input fields

Display tree   Refers to Microsoft Windows folder listing consisting of + and − signs. If a + sign appears, then the listing is compressed with more folders available

Drawing editor   Refers to the drawing area where drawings are created

Drop-down list   Refers to the typical Windows operating system list with arrow; when selected, a series of options appear in a vertical list

DWG   Refers to an Architectural Desktop Drawing

Elevation view   Refers to Front, Back, Right or Left views, perpendicular to the ground plane

Layouts   Refers to drawing areas. All layouts except the Model Layout can be broken down into Paper Space viewports; more layouts can be added

Plan view   Refers to looking at a building from the Top View

Press the Enter button   Refers to any Enter button in any dialog box on the screen

Press the Enter key   Refers to the keyboard Enter key (the space bar will usually act as the Enter key except when entering dimensions, text, or numerals)

Press the OK button   Refers to any OK button in any dialog box on the screen

RMB   Refers to clicking using the **right** mouse button. This is most often used to bring up contextual menus

Tooltips   Refers to the information that appears when the cursor is momentarily held over an icon

Viewports   Refers to Paper Space viewports

The Autodesk Architectural Desktop 2004 Interface

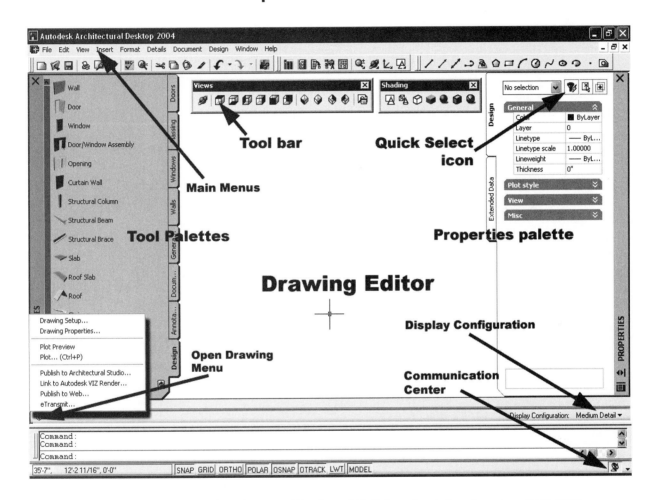

Autodesk Architectural Desktop 2004's interface is based on AutoCAD 2004.

Tool Palettes

Tool Palettes are brand new to Autodesk Architectural Desktop 2004. You use them to organize and make available all your desired tools and assets such as doors, windows, and walls.

Autodesk Architectural Desktop 2004 ships with seven default TOOL PALETTES and the PROPERTIES palette in place. These can be easily modified or deleted, or new palettes can be added.

Bringing Up the Tool Palettes

The Tool Palettes can be brought up by three methods:

a. Typing **toolpalettes** in the Command line.
b. By pressing **Ctrl + 3** on the keyboard.
c. By selecting the **Tool Palettes** icon.

Resizing the Palette

You can resize the tool palettes by moving your cursor to the cut corner at the bottom of the palettes. Your cursor will change to a "double arrow." Click, hold, and drag vertically and horizontally to resize, as shown in the figure below.

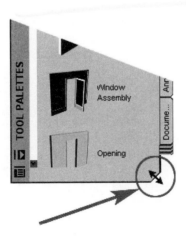

If you have more tool palettes than are showing, a "stair step" icon will appear at the bottom of the last tab name. (See the figure below.)

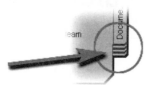

If you click on the "stair step" icon, a menu will appear that you can use to select all the tool palettes, as shown in the figure below.

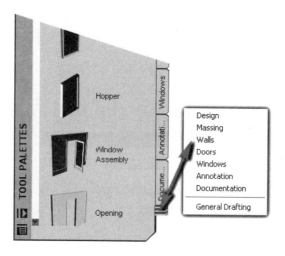

Auto-hide

Because the palettes cover some of the Drawing Editor, there is a control called Auto-hide that opens and closes the palette when the cursor is moved over its surface. The following figures show the icon used to turn Auto-hide on or off.

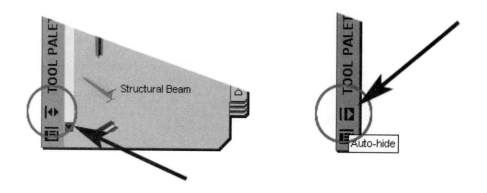

Tool Palettes Properties

The Tool Palettes Properties give access to options necessary to control the size, location, and appearance of the palettes. Tool Palettes Properties also allow for creation and renaming of palettes. (See the figures below.)

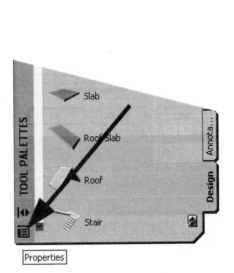
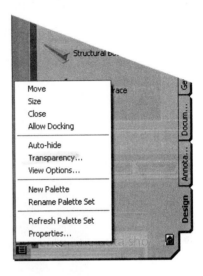

Allow Docking

    a.   Allows the palette to attach to the sides of the Drawing Editor.

Transparency

    a.   Makes the palette transparent, allowing entities on the Drawing Editor to be seen.

View Options

    a.   Changes the sizes of the Tool Palette icons, as shown in the figure below.

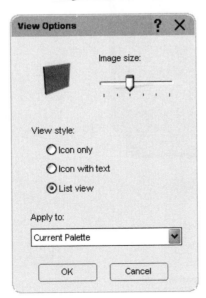

New Palette

a. Selection for creating new palettes.

Rename Palette Set

a. Selection to Rename the entire set of palettes.

Deleting Tool Palettes

To delete a palette, RMB on the **Tool Palettes** tab to bring up the **Delete Palette** option. (See the figure below.)

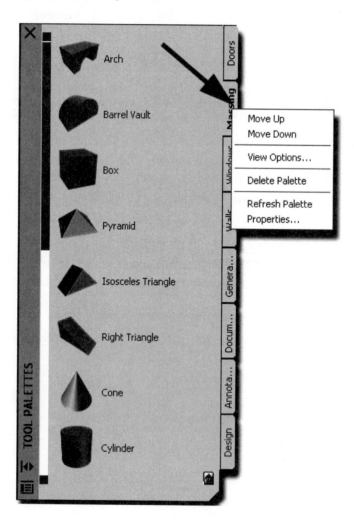

The Properties Palette

The Properties palette changes depending on the AEC Object or entity that is selected. All the properties of the selected object can be changed in this palette. The palette also contains the Quick Select Icon; this is very useful in selecting objects, especially when several objects are located together.

Bringing Up the Properties Palettes

The Properties palettes can be brought up by three methods:

a. Typing **properties** in the Command line.
b. By pressing **Ctrl + 1** on the keyboard.
c. By double-clicking any AEC Object or Entity (see the figure below).

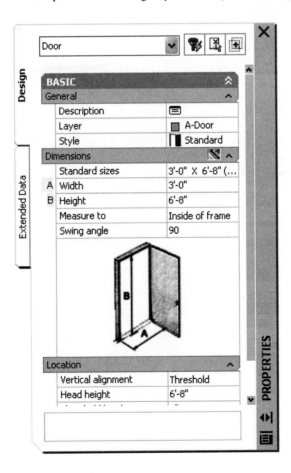

Quick Select

To use **Quick Select:**

a. Select the **Quick Select** icon at the top of the **Properties** palette (see the figure below, left) to bring up the Quick Select dialog box (see the figure below, right).

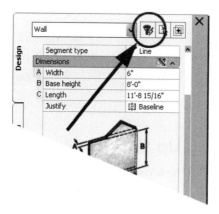
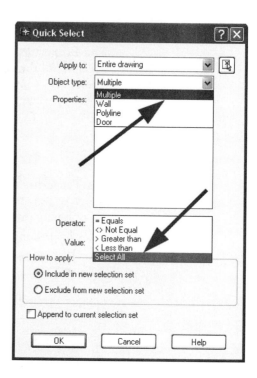

As you add content into the drawing, more object types will be available in the Object Type drop-down list.

The Content Browser

The Content Browser locates all your AEC tools such as walls, windows, and doors. You drag your tools into your Tool Palettes using AutoDesk's **idrop** technology. You can also drag AEC content back into your tool palettes to create new tools. After creating a new tool palette, it is a good idea to drag a copy of the tool palette back into the My Tool Catalog folder in the Content Browser to save a copy of the palette.

Bringing Up the Content Browser

The Content Browser can be brought up by three methods:

a. Typing **aeccontentbrowser** in the Command line.
b. By pressing **Ctrl + 4** on the keyboard.
c. By selecting the Content Browser icon (see the figure below).

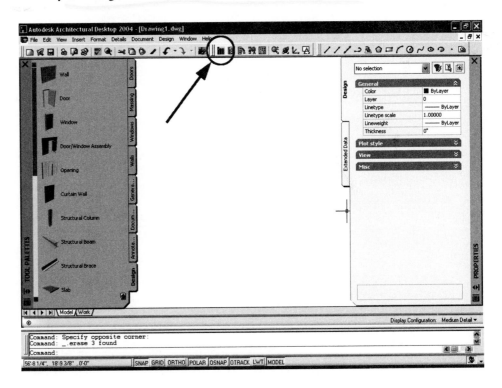

The Content Browser starts off with the Catalog Library, which contains several catalogs (see the figure below).

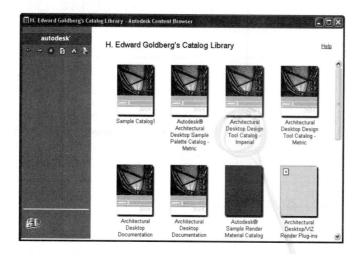

You drag content from the Catalog folders into your tool palettes, as shown in the figure below. (Make sure Auto-hide is turned off when you do this.)

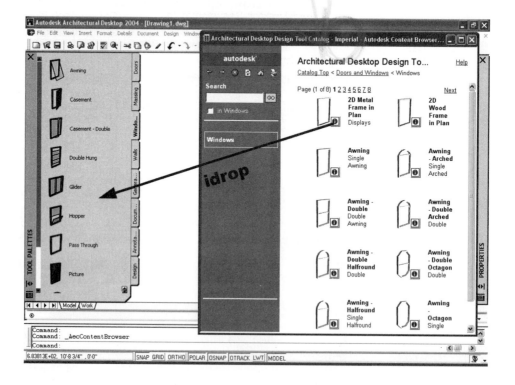

You can also create a tool by just by dropping an ADT object from the drawing to a tool palette, a style from Style Manager to a tool palette, or a piece of AEC Content from the Custom tab in the Design Center. (*Note:* Some objects use fixed images like the Schedule Tool, AEC Dimension Tool, and the Layout Object Tools.)

The following tool catalogs are supplied with the program:

Catalog Name	Contents
Autodesk® Architectural Desktop Stock Tool Catalog	A catalog that contains the standard, stock tools in Autodesk Architectural Desktop
Autodesk® Architectural Desktop Sample Palette Catalog - Imperial	A sampling of tools in imperial units for objects such as doors, walls, and windows
Autodesk® Architectural Desktop Sample Palette Catalog - Metric	A sampling of tools in metric units for objects such as doors, walls, and windows
Architectural Desktop Design Tool Catalog - Imperial	Content tools in imperial units for design and documentation of multiview blocks and symbols
Architectural Desktop Design Tool Catalog - Metric	Content tools in metric units for design and documentation of multiview blocks and symbols
Architectural Desktop Documentation Tool Catalog - Imperial	Content tools in imperial units for annotation and documentation
Architectural Desktop Documentation Tool Catalog - Metric	Content tools in metric units for annotation and documentation
Autodesk® Sample Render Material Catalog	Architectural render materials for use with Autodesk Architectural Desktop and Autodesk VIZ Render
My Tool Catalog	An empty tool catalog provided so that you can create your own tool set
Autodesk® Architectural Desktop Tutorial Palette Catalog	A catalog of the tools used in the metric-based Autodesk Architectural Desktop tutorial
Autodesk® Architectural Desktop Tutorial Tool Catalog	A catalog of the tools used in the imperial-based Autodesk Architectural Desktop tutorial
Architectural Desktop VIZ Render Plug-ins	Links to third-party plug-ins for Autodesk Architectural Desktop

You cannot add or remove items from the Autodesk-supplied tool catalogs, but you can create your own tool catalogs. You can also copy other tool catalogs and website links into your catalog library.

The Open Drawing Menu

The Open Drawing Menu icon is located at the bottom left of the Autodesk Architectural Desktop 2004 interface (see the figure below).

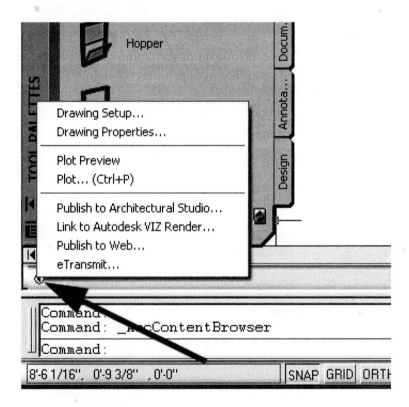

Drawing Setup

1. Drawing Setup brings up the Drawing Setup dialog box with tabs to set drawing units, Scale, layers, and Display. The Drawing Setup dialog box can also be gotten from the Format menu in the Main toolbar, as shown in the four figures below.

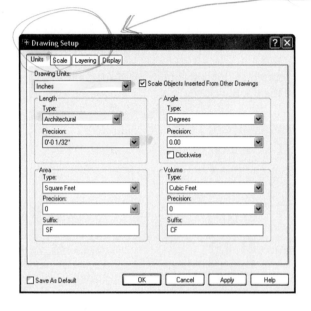

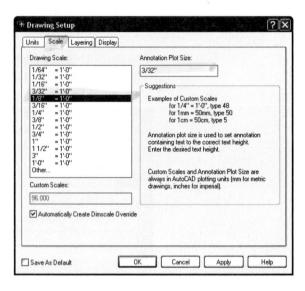

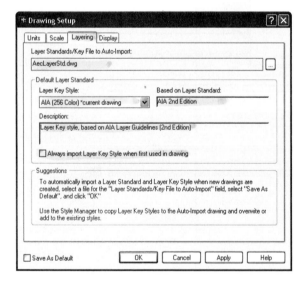

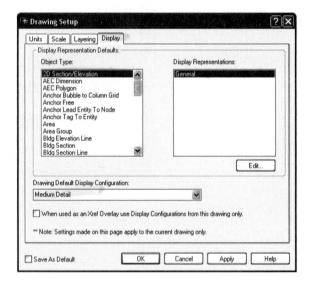

Publish to Architectural Studio

1. If you have Autodesk Architectural Studio and it is running, you can send your 2D and 3D information to that program.

Link to Autodesk VIZ Render

1. The VIZ render will give you access to photorealistic rendering plus animation. The process is described in the VIZ RENDER section of this book.

Publish to the Web

1. This provides an easy to use Wizard that creates an Internet Web page with **idrop** capability (see the figure below).

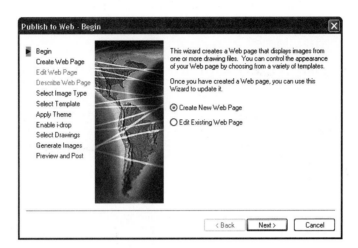

etransmit

1. This creates a compressed email package of your drawings with all necessary files. It also includes a transmittal (see the figure below).

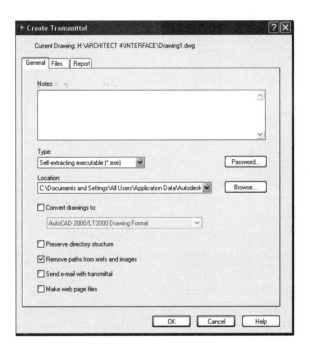

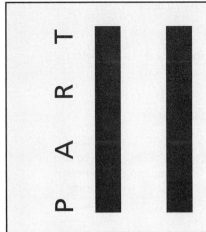

P A R T

Sections and Tutorials:
Palettes and Exercises

Section

1

Massing/Mass Elements and Groups

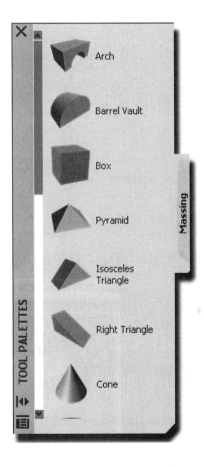

When you finish this section, you should understand the following:

- ✔ How to create a Massing object.
- ✔ How to modify a Massing object.
- ✔ How to create and attach Slice Plates (floor slices).
- ✔ How to modify the Massing object after applying the Slice Plates.
- ✔ How to change the Slice Plates into Space Boundaries, and then into Walls.
- ✔ How to use the Drape tool to create contour massing models.

Massing objects can be dragged or inserted either from the Design Tool Palette, or by typing **MassElementAdd** on the Command line.

Massing and Mass Modeling

Mass modeling is unique to Autodesk Architectural Desktop 2004. It replicates the system frequently used by architects on large buildings. The initial design studies for large buildings are often first modeled in clay or wood. These small models generally show the relationship between parts of the building while indicating scale as well as how light and shadow react with the facades. Mass modeling is meant to be a quick process, akin to the building blocks we all played with as children.

With Massing, Autodesk Architectural Desktop 2004 takes the concept of mass modeling one step farther. Not only can you model the concept, but also within the program, you can automatically take that model through to the document creation stage.

The Massing tool palette comes with 16 preconfigured Primitives (3D shapes). The Primitives can be dragged or inserted into your drawing from the tool palette. The size of the primitive can be preset or can be modified when inserting. This can be determined by selecting Yes or No from the Specify on Screen drop-down list in the Properties tool palette when inserting the primitive. Selecting and pulling on grips or changing parameters in the Properties tool palette associated with Massing can easily modify each primitive's size and shape.

After a Massing model has been created, floor slices can be created from the model. These floor slices can be used as a basis for area and space studies, or for eventually generating walls. It is this method that allows you to quickly model a building and electronically convert that model into construction documents.

The following exercises are designed to give you a hands-on feel for using the Massing feature of the program. After doing these exercises, I recommend that you explore all the Primitives, and try making new ones using the Extrusion and Revolution feature as well as the Convert to Mass Element tool that converts solid models and AEC Objects to Mass elements.

Hands-On

Creating a Massing Object

1. Start a new drawing using the Architectural Building Model and View (Imperial - ctb) template.
2. Change to the Work Layout.
3. Change to the NE Isometric View.
4. Select the Massing Tool Palette.
5. Drag the Box Primitive massing icon to the drawing area or click once on the Box icon and move your cursor to the drawing area. *Don't click in the drawing area yet!* Move your cursor to the closed Properties Toolbar to open it. (See Figure 1-1.)
6. When the Properties toolbar opens, notice a blue asterisk icon (settable option upon insertion) next to the **Specify on screen** option. Select **No** from the drop-down list (this will allow you to preset the Width, Depth, and Height of the box). Set the Width to 60′, Depth to 260′, and Height to 60′ (see Figure 1-2).

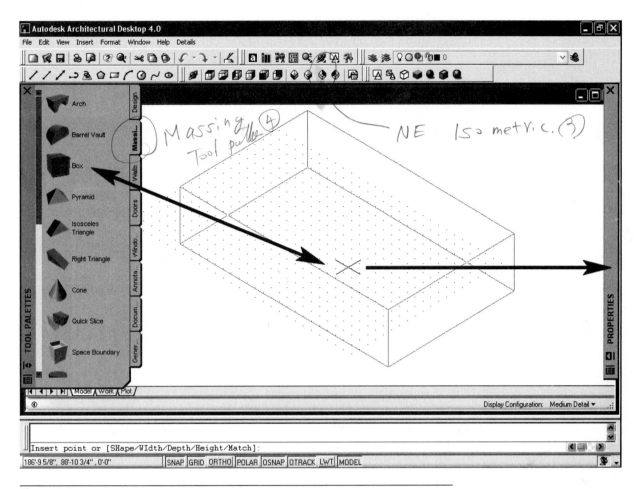

Figure 1-1

Figure 1-2

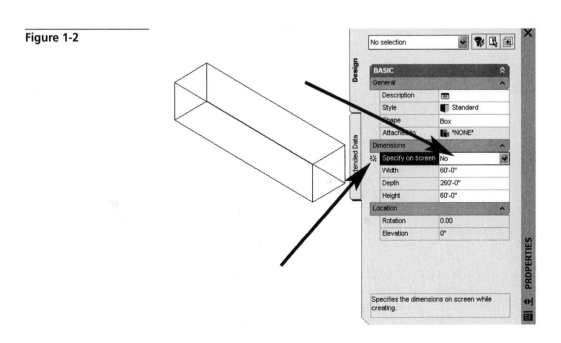

7. Once the size properties have been set, click to set the **BOX** primitive, and then press the Enter key on the keyboard twice to accept the default rotation and close the command. **Save this file.**

Hands-On

Modifying a Massing Object

1. Select the primitive to activate its grips, and then select **Free Form** from the **Shape** drop-down list to make the Massing box editable (see Figure 1-3).

!   **Note:** Before the Massing primitive has been changed to a Free Form, it can be adjusted in the standard ADT 2004 manner by activating grips and entering dimensions, or pulling on the grips.

2. Select the Free Form, and move your cursor over the "dot," right-mouse-click, and select Split Face from the contextual menu (see Figure 1-4).

You can recognize an editable Free Form shape because its grips will be changed to dots. Selecting the dots will select the faces of the Free Form Massing object (see Figure 1-5).

3. Set your OSNAP settings to Endpoint and Perpendicular.
4. Enter **fro** in the command line and click on the upper right corner of the face.
5. Move the cursor to the left along the top of the face, and then enter **80**′on the command line and press the Enter key.

Figure 1-3

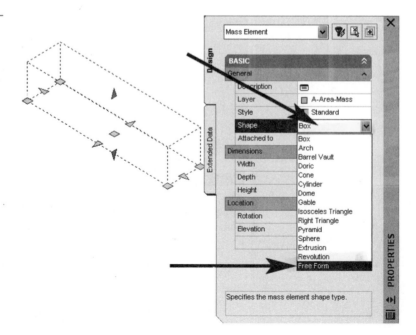

Figure 1-4

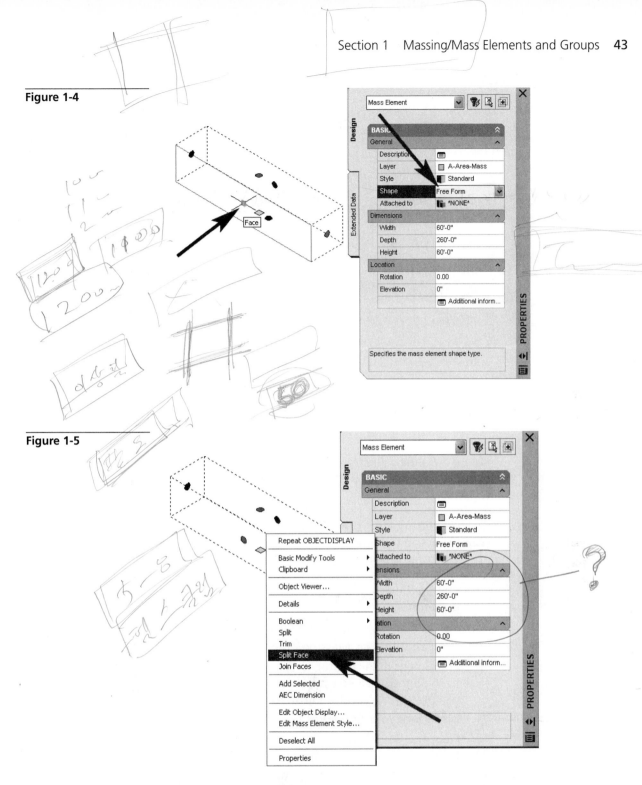

Figure 1-5

6. Finally, move your cursor down to the lower edge of the face until the Perpendicular Osnap icon appears, and then click to split the face. Press the Esc key to complete the command (see Figure 1-6).

Select the "dot" on the new face, and right-mouse-click to see your options when "pulling" on the face dot (see Figure 1-7).

Stop for a moment and look at the various ways that you can adjust a Massing object.

There are six adjustments that can be made to the faces. These are cycled by pressing the Ctrl key on the keyboard while moving your cursor.

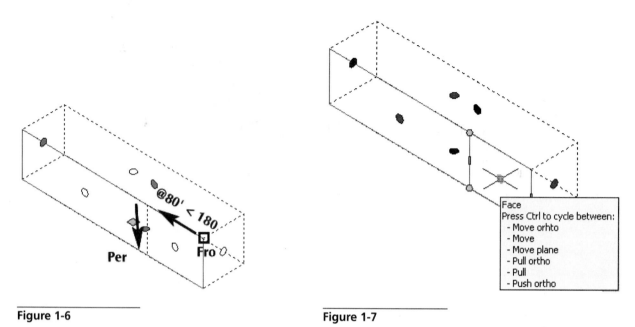

Figure 1-6

Figure 1-7

Figure 1-8 shows illustrations of different variations. It also illustrates moving edges. Pushing or pulling on the vertical tabs that appear at the edges can move these edges.

By using various primitives and adjusting them by splitting, pushing, pulling, and moving their faces, you can quickly create a mass model of your proposed building.

Now continue on to the next step in the hands on tutorial.

7. Pull on the dot and press the Ctrl key on your keyboard until the face pulls forward.

8. Enter 60′ on the command line and press the Enter key (see Figure 1-9).

9. Drag another Box Massing object into the drawing area.

10. This time, similar to Step 6, select **YES** from the drop-down list next to the **Specify on screen** option on the Properties Tool Palette. (This will now allow you to adjust your massing object while placing it.

11. Make sure your **End Point Osnap** is active.

12. Place the Box Massing object on top of the Massing object that has been modified previously.

13. With the new Box Massing object selected, right-mouse-click and select **Boolean > Union** from the contextual menu (see Figure 1-10).

You have now created a modified Massing object made from two Massing objects (see Figure 1-11).

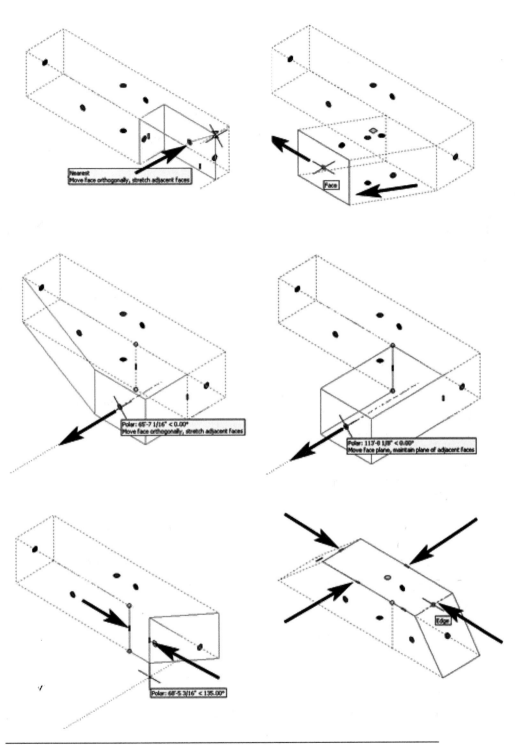

Figure 1-8

Figure 1-9

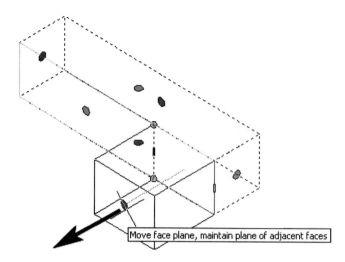

Move face plane, maintain plane of adjacent faces

Figure 1-10

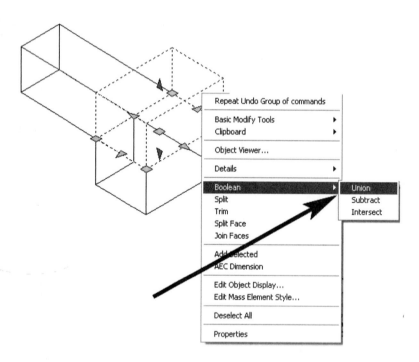

Figure 1-11

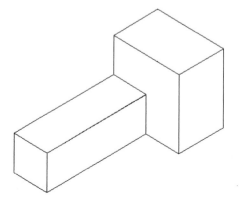

Hands-On

Creating and Attaching Slice Plates (Floor Slices)

1. Select the Massing tool palette, and select the Slice icon (see Figure 1-12).
2. Click in the Top viewport.
3. Enter 11 in the Command line and press the Enter key.
4. Select a spot near the massing model, and then place a second to create a rectangle. (*Note:* This rectangle is just a marker; make it big enough to be comfortable for you to see.)
5. Accept the default Rotation (0.00) and Starting height (0″).
6. Select all the markers with a window crossing, RMB, and select Attach Objects from the contextual menu that appears.
7. Select the Massing object that you created in the previous section and press the Enter key.

You have now created 11 Slice Plates (floor slices) in your Massing object (see Figure 1-13).

8. Change to the NW Isometric View and select the topmost Slice Marker.
9. RMB and select **Set Elevation** from the contextual menu.
10. Enter 115′ in the command line and press Enter **(note that the topmost Slice Plate moves upward).** Save this file.

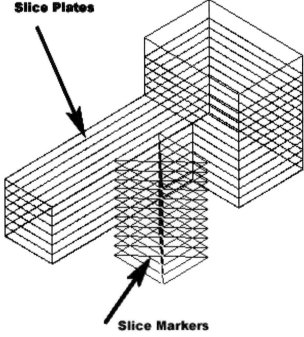

Slice Plates

Slice Markers

Figure 1-12   **Figure 1-13**

! **Note:** Slice plates can also be adjusted by selecting the Front View, and moving the Slice markers in the Y direction.

Hiding the Slice Markers

1. Select one of the Slice markers, RMB, and select **Edit Object Display** from the contextual menu that appears to bring up the Object Display dialog box.
2. Double-click on the word **General** to bring up the **Display Properties** dialog box.
3. In the Display Properties dialog box turn the Cut Plane and Outline visibility off, and then press the OK buttons on the dialog boxes to complete the command and return to the Drawing Editor.

Hands-On

Modifying the Massing Object After Applying the Slice Plates

1. Select another Box Massing object from the Massing tool Palette, and give it a 30' Width, 60' Depth, and 60' Height.
2. Place the new object as shown in Figure 1-14.
3. Select the original Massing object, RMB, select Boolean > Subtraction from the contextual menu, and select the new Massing object.

! **Note:** If you have trouble selecting the Massing objects because you keep selecting the Slice Plates instead, you can temporarily turn off the visibility of their layer.

4. Enter **Y** for Yes at the command line to erase the layout geometry.

Notice that the Slice Plates follow the new outline created by the Boolean subtraction (see Figure 1-15).

5. Using the Massing object modification techniques, modify the Massing object.
6. Create new Massing objects and Boolean them to the original object.

The Slice plates will always follow the Modified Massing object (Massing Model) (see Figure 1-16).

7. RMB in an empty space in the Drawing Editor, select Object Viewer from the contextual menu, and select the Massing object.
8. Turn on perspective and Flat shading to see the model (see Figures 1-17 and 1-18). **Save the file.**

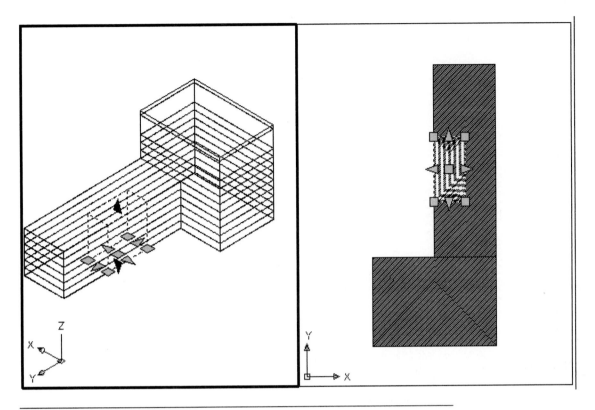

Figure 1-14

Figure 1-15

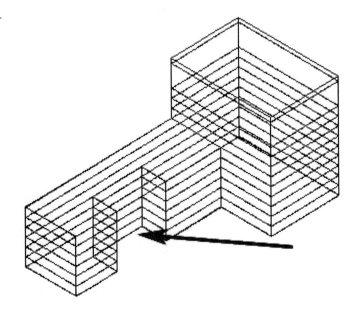

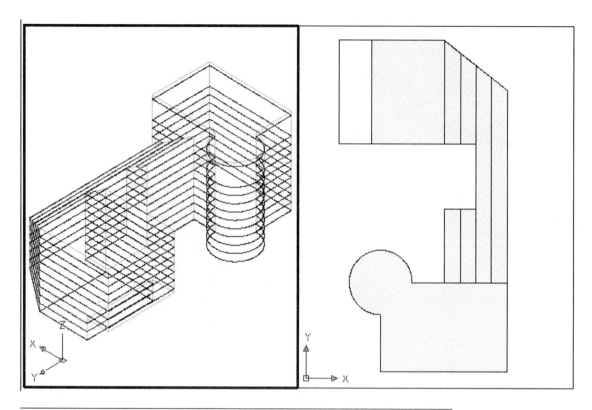

Figure 1-16

Figure 1-17

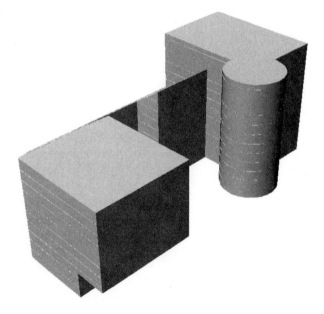

Figure 1-18

Hands-On

Changing the Slice Plates into Space Boundaries and Walls

1. Use the previous exercise's file.
2. Change to the **Model** Layout.
3. Change to SW Isometric View.
4. Select the **Content Browser** icon from the **Navigation** toolbar to bring up the **Content Browser.**
5. Select the **Autodesk Architectural Desktop Stock Tool Catalog > Architectural Object Tools > Page 2**, and drag the **Space Boundary** tool into your tool palette.
6. **RMB** on the Space Boundary tool and select **Apply Tool Properties > Slice** from the contextual menu that appears.
7. Select all the slices and press Enter.
8. Select the **Quick Select** icon from the Properties palette, select **Space Boundary** from the Object Type, **Select All** from the **Operator**, and press OK.
9. While the Space Boundaries are selected, open the Properties palette, and change the Base Height to 10'-0".
10. Select any other Slice and change its particular height to match your needs.
11. Select each Space Boundary, RMB, and select Convert to Walls from the contextual menu that appears.

The slices have now been converted to wall objects.

Hands-On

Using the Drape Tool to Create Contour Massing Models

1. Start a new drawing using the Architectural Building Model and View (Imperial - ctb) template.
2. Change to the Model Layout.
3. Change to the Top View.
4. Using the **Rectangle** tool from the **Draw** menu draw and modify until you get a drawing similar to that in Figure 1-19.
5. Select each modify rectangle, RMB, and change the elevation of each to 2'-0" increments with the smallest rectangle having an elevation of 12'-0".
6. Change to SW Isometric View (see Figure 1-20).
7. Select the **Drape** Tool from the Massing Tool Palette, select all the contours, and press Enter.
8. Select two opposite corners of the bottommost modified rectangle, and press Enter.
9. Accept the mesh size of 30, and press Enter.

Figure 1-19

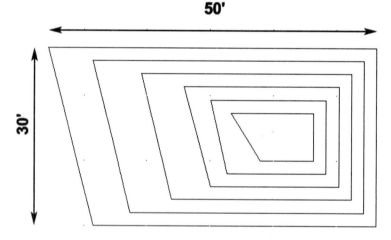

50'

30'

Figure 1-20

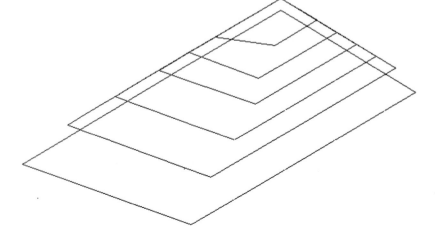

10. Enter 2'-0" in the command line for the base thickness and press Enter to complete the command.

11. Erase the modified rectangles.

12. Press the **Gouraud** icon in the **Shading** toolbar to shade the contour massing model (see Figure 1-21).

Figure 1-21

Section 2

Space and Space Boundary Objects

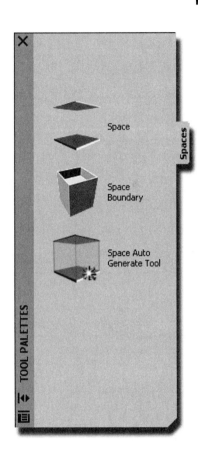

When you finish this section, you should understand the following:

- ✔ How to create a Spaces tool palette.
- ✔ How to create a Space object.
- ✔ How to create a simple space plan with Space objects.
- ✔ How to apply Space Boundaries.
- ✔ How to use the Space Auto Generate Tool.

Space objects and **Space Boundary objects** create a sophisticated but easy-to-use space-planning system.

Space objects can contain Property Set Data that can be automatically retrieved and read in AEC schedules. They also represent ceilings and floors in cut sections.

The **Space object** represents contained 3D space. It includes floor and ceiling thickness, floor to ceiling heights, elevation, and ancillary space heights. All the aforementioned attributes can easily be modified. The Space object does not contain wall information.

The **Space Boundary object** represents the area that contains space. It includes wall thickness and height, which can be modified through the Properties tool palette. The Space object does not contain floor or ceiling information.

Space Boundary objects can **Manage** the Space objects that they contain.

Space Objects Properties Tool Palette

Number	Name	Purpose
1	Style	Select available Space Styles
2	Space height	Floor to ceiling height
3	Floor boundary thickness	Floor thickness
4	Ceiling boundary thickness	Ceiling thickness
5	Height above ceiling	Distance above top of ceiling to top of wall (when Space Boundary or Wall is generated)
6	Specify On Screen	Change Length and Width by dragging on screen
7	Constrain	Constrains dragging of object to only Area, Length, Width, or None
8	Area	Preset area value of Space Object
9	Length	Preset length value of Space Object
10	Width	Preset width value of Space Object
11	Target Dimensions	Preset Space Object Style values
12	Rotation	Preset Rotation angle of Space Object
13	Elevation	Preset Elevation of Space Object

Hands-On

Creating a Spaces Tool Palette

1. Click on the Tool Palettes **Properties** icon at the bottom of the tool palette to drop the Tool Palette contextual menu.
2. Select New Palette and name it Spaces (see Figure 2-1).
3. Select the Contact Browser icon from the Main toolbar to bring up the Content Browser.
4. Select the Autodesk Architectural Desktop Stock Tool Catalog to open the next page.
5. At the next page, select Architectural Object Tools to open the next page.
6. Click on **Next** in the bottom right corner of the page to bring up Page 2.
7. Click on the **iDrop** icon and drag the Space, Space Boundary, and **Space Auto Generate Tool** onto your new Spaces tool palette.
8. Repeat this process selecting the **Architectural Desktop Documenta-tion Tool Catalog - Imperial > Schedule Tags > Room & Finish Tags** and dragging the **Space Tag** into the Spaces tool palette (see Figure 2-2).

You have now created and populated your own Spaces tool palette.

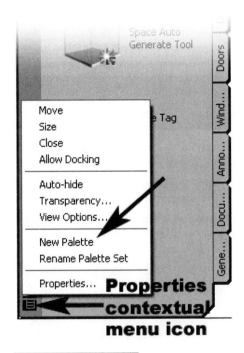

Figure 2-1

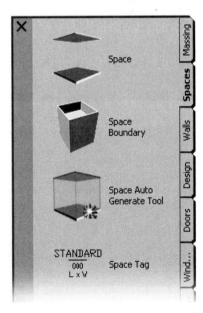

Figure 2-2

Hands-On

Creating a Space Object and Labeling It with a Space Tag

1. Start a new drawing using the Architectural Building Model and View (Imperial - ctb) template.
2. Change to the Model Layout.
3. Change to the Top View.
4. Select **Format > Style Manager** to bring up the **Style Manager** dialog box.
5. Select the **Architectural Objects** folder and double-click on **Space Styles**.
6. Create several new Space Styles and call them **Hall**, **Small Office**, **Large Office**, **Men's Toilet Room**, **Woman's Toilet Room**, and **Entrance**.
7. Click on the **Space** icon on the Space tool palette, and move your cursor over the **Properties** tool palette to open it.
8. In the Properties tool palette, set the following:

   a. Style = **Hall**
   b. Space height = **7'-0"**
   c. Ceiling boundary thickness = **2"**
   d. Floor boundary thickness = **4"**
   e. Height above ceiling = **1'-6"**
   f. Specify on screen = **Yes**
   g. Constrain = ***NONE***

9. Click in the Drawing Editor and press Enter twice to complete the command.

You have now placed a Space object called Hall.

10. Click on the **Space Tag** icon on the **Spaces** tool palette and select the Space object you just placed.
11. Press Enter to center the tag on the object and bring up the Edit Property Set Data dialog box.
12. Select the **Add property Sets** icon (Figure 2-3) to bring up the **Add Property Sets** dialog box (Figure 2-4).

Note: The **Edit Property Set Data** dialog box is where you enter information to be stored in the Space object.

The **Add Property sets** dialog box contains check boxes to determine if you wish to include room finish and/or room object information in the Space object.

13. In the **Add Property Sets** dialog box check the **RoomFinishObjects** and **RoomObjects** check boxes and press Enter to return to the Edit Property Set Data dialog box.

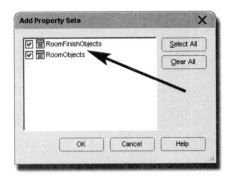

Figure 2-3

Figure 2-4

14. Stretch the Property Set Data dialog box to its full extent.

15. In the Edit Property Set Data dialog box enter the data shown in Figure 2-5.

! **Note:** The **yellow lightning bolts** in the Edit Property Set Data dialog box signify information that already exists in the Space object (see Figure 2-5).

Figure 2-5

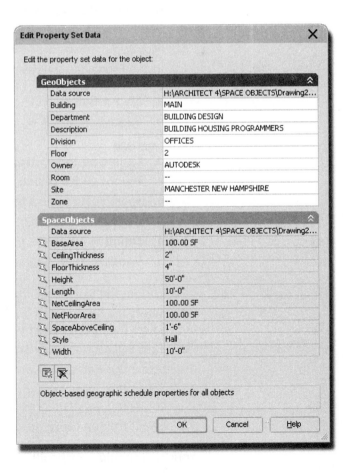

Figure 2-6

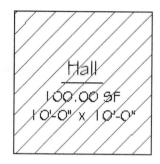

16. Press OK to complete the command and return to the Drawing Editor.

You now have a tagged space object (see Figure 2-6). Save this DWG.

Hands-On

Creating a Simple Space Plan with Space Objects

1. Use the previous exercise.
2. Change to the Model Layout.
3. Change to the Top View.
4. Select the **Space** icon from the **Spaces** tool palette you created.
5. Move your cursor over the **Properties** palette to open it.
6. In the Properties palette set the following:

    a. Style = **Hall**
    b. Space height = **9'-0"**
    c. Floor boundary thickness = **12"**
    d. Ceiling boundary thickness = **2"**
    e. Height above ceiling = **0"**
    f. Specify on screen = **No**
    g. Constrain = ***NONE***
    h. Length = **10'-0"**
    i. Width = **10'-0"**

7. Click in the Drawing Editor, and press Enter twice.
8. Select the **Space Tag** icon from the Spaces Tool palette you created, select the Space Object you placed in Step 7, and press Enter twice.
9. Turn **POLAR** on.
10. Select the Hall to activate its grips.
11. Select the right center grip, drag to the right (0°), enter 30'-0" in the command line, and press Enter (see Figure 2-7).
12. Select the top center grip, and drag in the 270° direction 3'-0".

Your Hall should now be 40' × 7' wide.

Figure 2-7

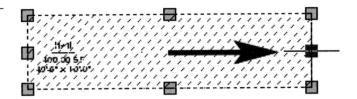

13. Again select the **Space** icon from the **Spaces** tool palette you created.

14. In the Properties palette set the following:

    a. Style = **Entrance**
    b. Space height = **12'-0"**
    c. Floor boundary thickness = **12"**
    d. Ceiling boundary thickness = **2"**
    e. Height above ceiling = **0"**
    f. Specify on screen = **No**
    g. Constrain = ***NONE***
    h. Length = **10'-0"**
    i. Width = **30'-0"**

15. Place the Entrance space as shown in Figure 2-8.

16. Select the Entrance space, RMB, and select **Divide Spaces** from the contextual menu that appears.

17. Drag a line across the Entrance space to create two spaces as shown in Figure 2-9.

18. Again select **Space** icon from the **Spaces** tool palette you created.

19. In the Properties palette set the following:

    a. Style = **Large Office**
    b. Space height = **7'-0"**
    c. Floor boundary thickness = **12"**
    d. Ceiling boundary thickness = **2"**

Figure 2-8

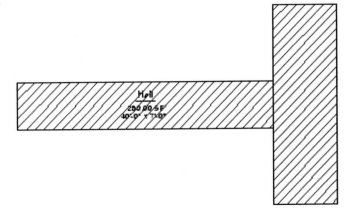

Figure 2-9

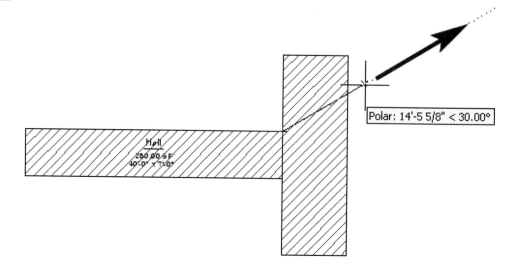

e. Height above ceiling = **0″**
f. Specify on screen = **No**
g. Constrain = ***NONE***
h. Length = **10′-0″**
i. Width = **15′-0″**

20. Enter **D** in the command line and press Enter until the insertion point of the Large Office space object is at the upper left of the object.
21. Snap the Large Office space object, the Hall, as shown in Figure 2-10.
22. Array the Large Office four columns to the right, and mirror it as shown in Figure 2-11.
23. Complete the space plan by adding the toilet rooms.
24. Select the Space Tag icon from the Spaces tool palette, select each space, and press Enter to continue placing each tag until all the space are labeled (Figure 2-12).

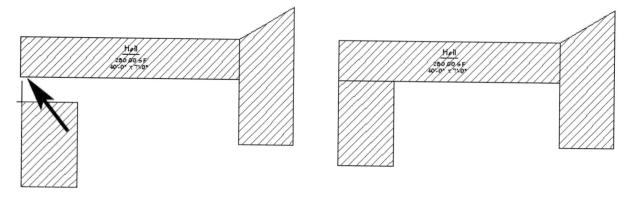

Figure 2-10

Figure 2-11

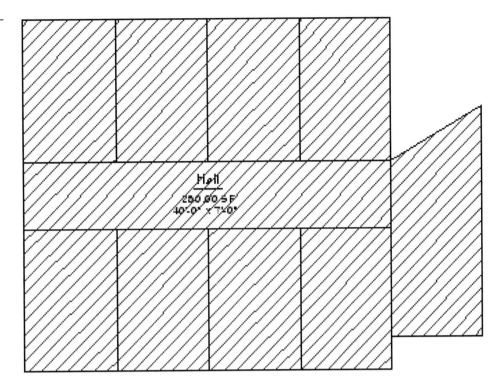

Figure 2-12

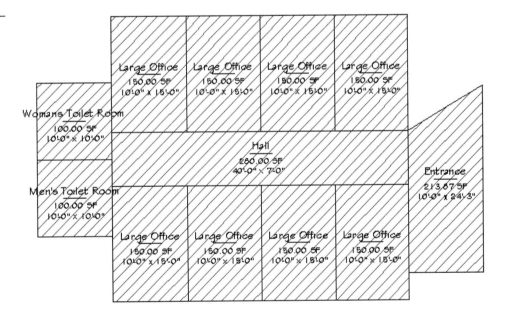

Hands-On

Applying Space Boundaries

1. Use the previous exercise.
2. RMB on the **Space Boundary** icon and select **Apply tool properties to > Space** from the contextual menu that appears.
3. Move your cursor over the **Properties** palette to open it.
4. Select the **Quick Select** icon; select **Space Boundary** from the **Object Type** drop-down list.
5. Choose **Select All** from the Operator drop down list, and press the OK button.
6. Again move your cursor over the **Properties** palette to open it.
7. Select **Solid** from the **Boundary type** drop-down list.
8. Press the ESC key twice to complete the command.

Space boundaries have been placed around the spaces (see Figure 2-13).

Figure 2-13

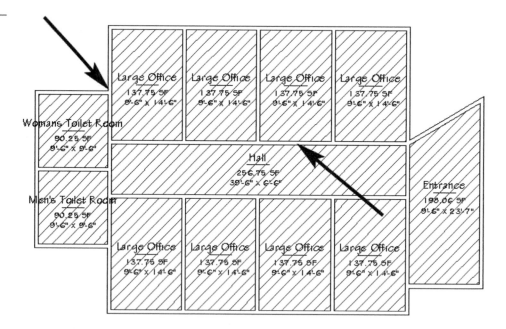

Hands-On

Modifying Space Boundaries

1. Start a new drawing using the Architectural Building Model and View (Imperial - ctb) template.
2. Change to the Model Layout.
3. Change to the Top View.
4. Select the **Space** icon from the **Spaces** tool palette you created.
5. Insert a space in the Drawing Editor with the following properties:

a. Style = **Standard**
b. Space height = **8'-0"**
c. Floor boundary thickness = **12"**
d. Ceiling boundary thickness = **2"**
e. Height above ceiling = **2'**
f. Specify on screen = **No**
g. Constrain = ***NONE***
h. Length = **30'**
i. Width = **30'**

6. Apply a **Space Boundary** to the space.
7. Using **Quick Select**, find and change the space boundary to **Solid** Boundary type, with a Width of 12".
8. Change to the SW Isometric View.
9. Double-click the space boundary to open its Properties palette.
10. Select **Ceiling stops at boundary** from the Ceiling condition drop-down list.
11. Enter **3'-0"** in the Upper extension data field, and press the Enter key.
12. Press the **Esc** key twice to clear the space boundary's grips (see Figure 2-14).
13. Select the space boundary again, and **RMB** anywhere in the Drawing Editor to bring up the contextual menu.
14. Select **Edit Edges** from the contextual menu.

Note: **Edit Edges** and **Add Edges** are the options Architectural Desktop uses to edit any segment of a space boundary.

15. Select the space boundary again, and **RMB** anywhere in the Drawing Editor to bring up the contextual menu.

Figure 2-14

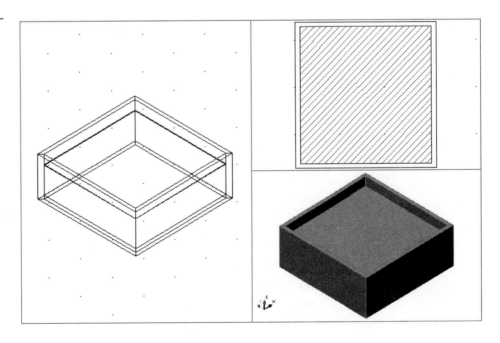

16.   Select **Edit Edges** from the contextual menu.

17.   Select the edge shown in Figure 2-15, and press Enter to bring up the **Boundary Edge Properties** dialog box.

18.   Select the **Dimensions** tab.

This tab contains controls for the Type, Width, and Justification of Space Boundaries.

19.   Select the **Design Rules** tab.

This tab contains controls for the Space Boundary Conditions at the Ceiling and Floors in relation to Spaces.

20.   Uncheck the **Automatically Determine from Spaces** check box.

This will disconnect the relationship of the chosen Space boundary segment from the adjacent space.

21.   Enter 8′-0″.

22.   Select the **Ceiling Stops at Wall** radio button, and press Enter.

The top of the space boundary segment is now 8′-0″ above the ceiling of the adjacent space (Figure 2-16).

23.   Change to the Top View.

Figure 2-15

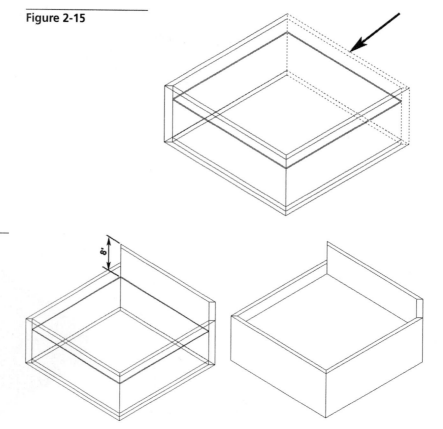

Figure 2-16

24. Select the space boundary, RMB, and select **Insert Joint** from the contextual menu that appears.
25. Select the midpoint of the leftmost space boundary segment.

Nothing will appear to happen, but a joint has been added. (If you change to SW Isometric, you can see the joint.)

26. Select the space boundary again and notice that two more grips appear on the leftmost segment.
27. Click and drag one of the new grips to the left (180°) 10'-0" and press Enter.

Notice that the Space Object fills the space. This is because the Manage spaces check box is checked (Figure 2-17).

28. Undo the command, and return to Step 27 of this exercise.
29. Repeat Step 27, but hold down the Ctrl button while dragging the grip.
30. Again Enter 10'-0" in the Command line and press Enter.
31. Double-click the space boundary again to open its Properties palette.

Notice that the space boundary drags a rectangular space out from the segment (Figure 2-18).
    Repeat this process inserting joints and pulling on different grips (Figure 2-19).

32. Double-click on the space boundary again to bring up its **Properties** palette.
33. Change the **Manage contained spaces** drop-down list to **No**.

This disconnects the intelligent linkage between the space boundary and the adjacent space object.

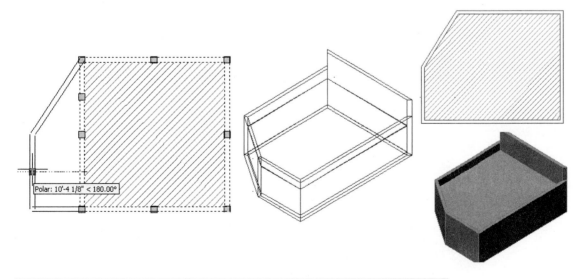

Figure 2-17

Figure 2-18

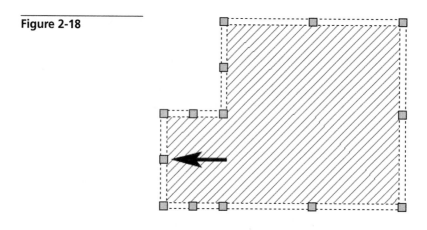

Figure 2-19

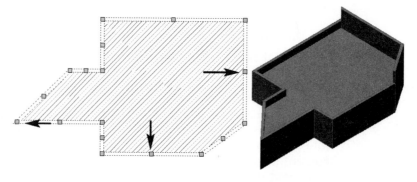

34. **RMB** anywhere in the Drawing Editor to bring up the contextual menu.

35. Select **Remove Edges** from the contextual menu.

36. Select the segment shown in Figure 2-20, and press Enter to complete the command.

37. Change to the Top View.

38. Double-click on the space boundary again to bring up its **Properties** palette.

39. Change the **Manage contained spaces** drop-down list back to **Yes** to electronically reconnect the space boundary and the space object.

40. Again **RMB** anywhere in the Drawing Editor to bring up the contextual menu.

41. Select **Add Edges** from the contextual menu.

Figure 2-20

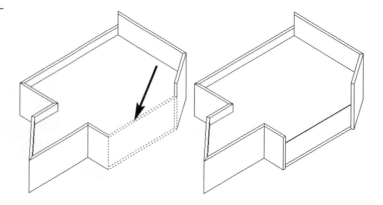

Figure 2-21

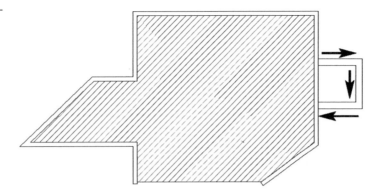

42. Move your cursor over the **Properties** palette to open it.

43. Set the Width to **18″**.

44.   Turn the Near and Perpendicular snaps on.

45. **Near** snap to the right-hand space boundary segment, and add three 10′-0″ segments returning perpendicular to the starting segment as shown in Figure 2-21. These new segments are now part of the original space boundary.

To add a Space object to the Added Edges, use the Space Auto Generate Tool, which is demonstrated in the following exercise.

Hands-On

Using the Space Auto Generate Tool

1. Start a new drawing using the Architectural Building Model and View (Imperial - ctb) template.

2. Change to the Model Layout.

3. Change to the Top View.

4. Select **Format > Style Manager** from the **Main** toolbar to bring up the **Style Manager** dialog box.

5. Create five new space styles and call them **A, B, C, D**, and **E**, respectively, and then press the OK button.

6. Using lines, polylines, and a circle, create the 2D drawing shown in Figure 2-22.

7. Select the **Space Auto Generate Tool** from the Spaces tool palette to bring up the **Generate Spaces** dialog box.

8. Select All linework from the **Selection Filter** drop-down list and press the OK button.

9. Select the four lines enclosing **A** and press Enter to open another **Generate Spaces** dialog box (see Figure 2-23).

10. Press the Properties icon to bring up the **Space Properties** dialog box.

11. Select the **Style** tab.

12. Pick the **A** style you created in Step 5.

13. Change to **Dimensions** tab.

Figure 2-22

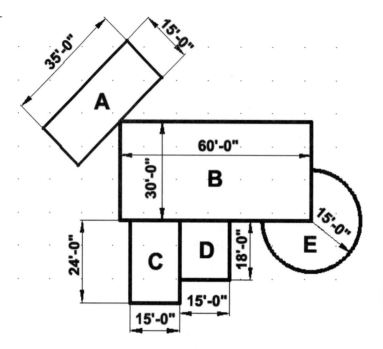

Figure 2-23

14. Set the following:

    a. Space Height = **9'-0"**
    b. Floor Boundary Thickness = **6"**
    c. Ceiling Boundary Thickness = **2"**
    d. Height of Space Above Ceiling = **2'-0"**

15. Press **OK** to return to the Generate Spaces dialog box.

16. Press the **Tag Settings** button to bring up the **Tag Settings** dialog box.

17. Check the **Add Tag to New Spaces** check box, select **Aec3_Room_Tag** from the **Tag Definition** drop-down list, check the Auto-Increment numerical properties check box, and set Increment to 1.

18. Press the **OK** button, and click inside the **A** enclosure you have selected.

19. Repeat Steps 9 through 18 for the enclosures B, C, D, and E, but change the **Space Height** and **Height of Space Above Ceiling** for each.

All the enclosures should now be labeled with incremental numbers.

20. Apply a **Space Boundary** to the spaces.

Figure 2-24

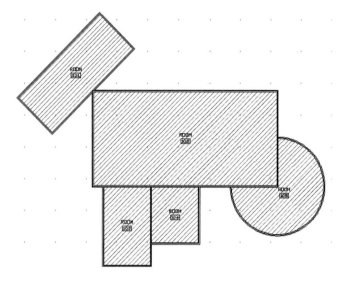

21. Using **Quick Select**, find and change the space boundary to **Solid Boundary** (see Figure 2-24).
22. Enter **space** on the Command line, and press Enter.
23. Enter **Q** (Query) on the Command line, and press Enter.
24. The **Space Information** dialog box will appear.
25. Change to the **Space Info Total** tab.

Here you will see the quantities and areas of each space (Figure 2-25).

26. Press the Create MDB button and save the file for use in a database program such as Microsoft Access.

Figure 2-26 shows a shaded perspective of the space plan created using the Space Auto Generate Tool.

Figure 2-25

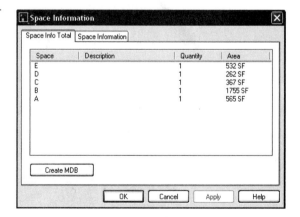

Figure 2-26

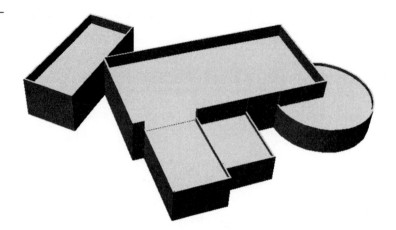

Section 3

Walls

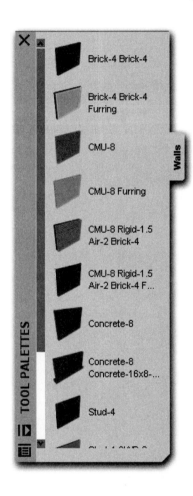

When you finish this section, you should understand the following:

✔ How to place a Wall object.
✔ How to change Walls by dynamically pulling on Grips.
✔ How to create Wall Sweeps.
✔ How to use Wall Endcaps.
✔ How to use Plan Modifiers.
✔ How to use Body Modifiers.
✔ How to use the Roof/Floor line option.
✔ How to use Interference Conditions.
✔ Cleanups—Applying 'T' Cleanup and Wall Merge
✔ How to edit Wall Styles.

Wall objects can be dragged or inserted either from the Design Tool Palette, or by typing **walladd** on the Command line.

Walls

Wall objects are the basis of all buildings; they enclose space and give the building its character. Because buildings require a vast variety of wall types and configurations, these objects have become very sophisticated in Autodesk Architectural Desktop 2004.

Figure 3-1

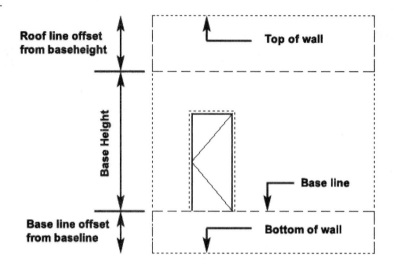

In order to understand how to use ADT 2004's Wall objects, one must first understand some basic ADT 2004 Wall object conventions. Among these conventions are Base height, Baseline, Roofline Offset from Base height, Floor line offset from Baseline, and Justification (see Figure 3-1).

Wall Objects Properties Tool Palette

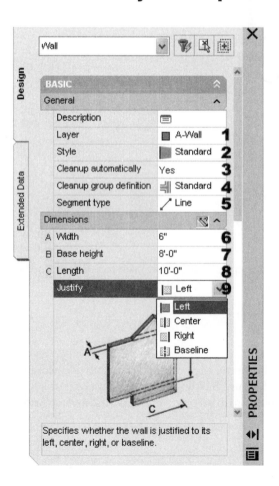

Number	Name	Purpose
1	Layer	Change this to place the wall on another layer
2	Style	Change this to change to another style such as 12" brick and block, etc.
3	Cleanup automatically	Change to Yes or No if you want the wall to join with similar components of intersecting walls
4	Cleanup group definition	Change to Style allowing Wall Cleanup between host and XREF drawings and/or allowing objects anchored to walls in other cleanup groups to be moved or copied to walls in this cleanup group
5	Segment type	Change to either Line or Arc to create linear or curved walls
6	Width	Set the width for *non*preset walls
7	Base height	Set a new Base height
8	Length	Set a new wall length
9	Justify	Change whether the wall is placed; this references from the left, center, right, or baseline of the wall

ADT 2004 contains controls and routines for modifying the shape of the wall itself. These include Wall Sweeps, Wall Endcaps and Opening Endcaps, Plan Modifiers, Body Modifiers, Modifications to the Roof/Floor lines, and Interference Conditions.

Hands-On

Placing a Wall Object

1. Start a new drawing using the Architectural Building Model and View (Imperial - ctb) template.
2. Change to the Model Layout.
3. Change to the Top View.
4. Select the Wall icon from the Design tool palette and drag your cursor over the Properties palette to open it.

Note: The blue asterisks are called "Add" icons and they represent properties that are available only when adding an object.

Here you will find all the size parameters that you can change upon insertion of a wall.

Figure 3-2

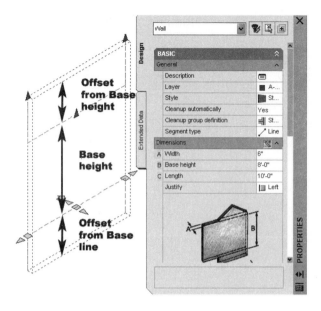

5. Set the following in the Properties palette:

   a. Style = **Standard**
   b. Width = **6″**
   c. Base Height = **10′-0″**
   d. Justify = **Left**
   e. Roof line offset from base height = **4′-0″**
   f. Floor line offset from base line = **-3′-0″**

6. Click in the drawing area and drag a 10′-0″-long wall, and click a second time to complete the command.

7. Change to SW Isometric View (see Figure 3-2).

Hands-On

Changing Walls by Dynamically Pulling on Grips

Example: Dynamically changing the Roof offset

1. Select the wall to activate its grips.
2. Move your cursor over the leftmost top grip, and notice the tool tip.
3. Select the grip and move your cursor upward.
4. Tab to change the magenta-colored dimension selection.
5. Enter 8′-0″ for the "overall dimension of the Roof offset," and press Enter to complete the command (see Figure 3-3).

Figure 3-3

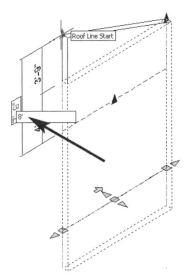

Hands-On

Creating Wall Sweeps

1. Change to Top View.
2. Select the **CMU-8 Furring** icon from the Walls tool palette, and drag your cursor over the Properties palette to open it.
3. Place a new wall with the following properties:

   a. Style = **CMU-8 Furring**
   b. Width = **9-1/2″**
   c. Base Height = **10′-0″**
   d. Justify = **Left**
   e. Roof line offset from base height = **0**
   f. Floor line offset from base line = **0**

4. Change to NW Isometric View.
5. Select the wall, RMB, and select **Sweeps > Add** from the contextual menu that appears to bring up the **Add Wall Sweep** dialog box.
6. Enter the following:

   a. Wall Component = **CMU**
   b. Profile Definition = **Start from scratch**
   c. New Profile Name = **TEST SWEEP PROFILE**

7. Press OK, and select a location on the wall for editing; a blue field with grips appears (see Figure 3-4).
8. Grab the lower grip of the blue field, drag it in the direction of 180°, enter 2′-0″ in the command line and press Enter (see Figure 3-5).

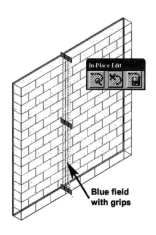

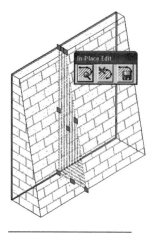

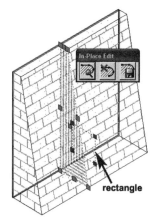

Figure 3-4   **Figure 3-5**   **Figure 3-6**

9. Select the **Rectangle** icon from the **Draw** menu and place a rectangle as shown in Figure 3-6.

10. Select the blue field, RMB, and select Add Ring from the contextual menu that appears.

11. Select the rectangle, enter **Y** (Yes) in the command line, and press Enter.

12. Accept Join in the command line, and press Enter.

13. Press the **Save All Changes** icon in the **In-Place Edit** dialog box to complete the command and create the new wall sweep (see Figure 3-7).

Figure 3-7

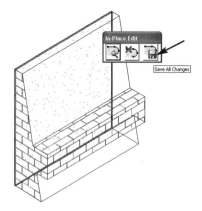

Hands-On

Creating Wall Endcaps

1. Clear the previous exercise.

2. Change to Top View.

3. Select the **CMU-8 Rigid-1.5 Air-2 brick 4 Furring 2** icon from the Walls tool palette and drag your cursor over the Properties palette to open it.

4. Place a new wall with the following properties:

   a. Style = **CMU-8 Furring**
   b. Width = **1'-5"**
   c. Base Height = **10'-0"**
   d. Justify = **Left**
   e. Roof line offset from base height = **0**
   f. Floor line offset from base line = **0**

5. Zoom close to the left end of the wall (see Figure 3-8).
6. Select the wall, RMB, and select **Endcaps > In-Place Edit** from the contextual menu that appears.
7. Select a point near the left end of the wall and a blue field will appear on the wall surface (see Figure 3-9).
8. Select the Topmost blue field (where brick is located) to activate its grips.
9. Move your cursor over the grips to activate their individual tool tips and select the leftmost grip labeled **Edge.**
10. Pull the left Edge grip to the left, enter 4 in the command line, and press Enter (see Figure 3-10).
11. Select the lower middle grip that is labeled **Edge** and pull it to the lower edge of the wall (see Figure 3-11).
12. RMB on the blue field and select Save as **New Endcap Style** from the menu that appears to bring up the New Endcap Style dialog box.

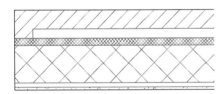

Figure 3-8

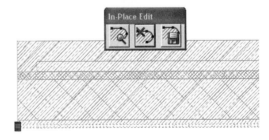

Figure 3-9

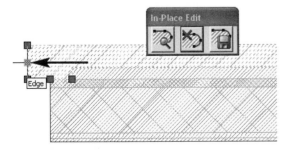

Figure 3-10

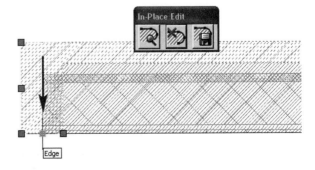

Figure 3-11

Figure 3-12

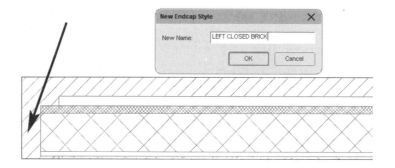

13. Give the Endcap the new name **LEFT CLOSED BRICK**, press OK, and then press the **Yes** button to save as wall style override to complete the new endcap (see Figure 3-12).

Hands-On

Using Plan Modifiers

1. Clear the previous exercise.
2. Change to the Work Layout.
3. Select the **CMU-8 Rigid-1.5 Air-2 brick 4** icon from the Walls tool palette and drag your cursor over the Properties palette to open it.
4. Place a new 10″-long wall in the Top View with the following properties:

    a. Style = **CMU-8 Furring**
    b. Width = **1′-3-1/2″**
    c. Base Height = **10′-0″**
    d. Justify = **Left**
    e. Roof line offset from base height = **0**
    f. Floor line offset from base line = **0**

5. Place an open polyline as shown in Figure 3-13.

Figure 3-13

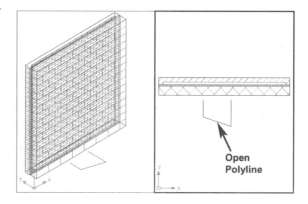

Open Polyline

6. Select the wall, RMB, and select **Plan Modifiers > Convert Polyline to wall Modifier** from the contextual menu that appears.

7. Select the Polyline, enter **Y** (Yes) in the command line, and enter **TEST WALL MODIFIER** in the **New Wall Modifier Style Name** dialog box that appears.

8. The **Add Wall Modifier** dialog box now appears. Press OK to end the command and add the Wall Modifier (see Figure 3-14).

9. To **Modify the Modifier,** double-click the wall to bring up the **Properties** palette.

10. Scroll down to the bottom of the Properties palette, and click on **Plan Modifiers** to bring up the **Wall Modifiers** dialog box (see Figure 3-15).

11. Place the dimensions shown in Figure 3-16.

12. Press OK and see the result (see Figure 3-17).

Figure 3-14

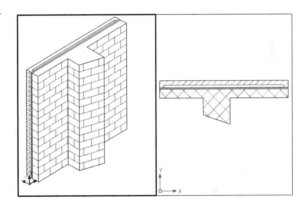

Figure 3-15

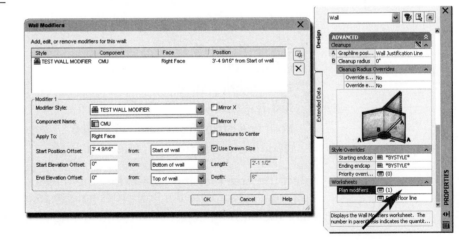

Figure 3-16

Figure 3-17

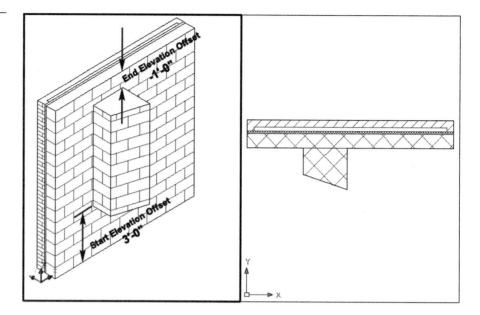

Hands-On

Using Body Modifiers

1. Clear the previous exercise.
2. Change to the Work Layout.
3. Select the **Wall** icon from the **Design** tool palette, and drag your cursor over the Properties palette to open it.
4. Place a new 10'-long wall in the Top View with the following properties:

    a. Style = **Standard**
    b. Width = **12**
    c. Base Height = **10'-0"**
    d. Justify = **Left**
    e. Roof line offset from base height = **0**
    f. Floor line offset from base line = **0**

5. Select the **Arch Massing** object from the Massing tool palette, and drag your cursor over the Properties palette to open it.
6. Place the Massing object with the following properties:

    a. Style = **Standard**
    b. Width = **2'-6"**
    c. Depth = **3'-0"**
    d. Height = **3'-0"**
    e. Radius = **1'-0"**
    f. Elevation = **2'-0"**

7. Place as shown in Figure 3-18.

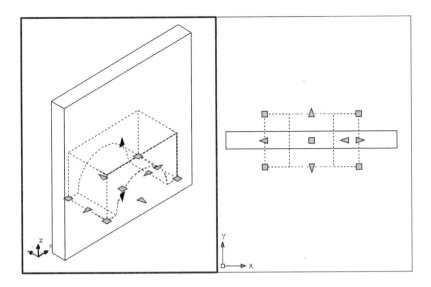

Figure 3-18

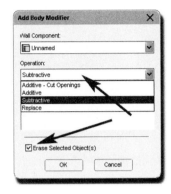

Figure 3-19

8. Select the wall, **RMB**, and select **Body Modifiers > Add** from the contextual menu that appears.

9. Select the Massing object and press Enter to bring up the **Add Body Modifier** dialog box.

10. Select **Subtractive** from the **Operation** drop-down list, and check the **Erase Selected Objects** check box (see Figure 3-19).

11. Finally, press the OK button to complete the command and add the Body Modifier (see Figure 3-20).

12. Insert a door in the wall and see how the Body Modifier affects the wall (see Figure 3-21).

Try the rest of the Body Modifier options for yourself.

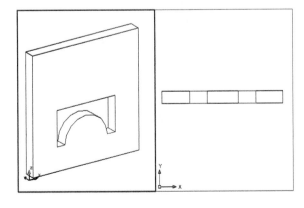

Figure 3-20

Figure 3-21

Hands-On

Using the Roof/Floor Line Option

1. Clear the previous exercise.

2. Select the **Wall** icon from the **Design** tool palette, and drag your cursor over the Properties palette to open it.

3. Place a new 10′ long wall in the Top View with the following properties:

   a. Style = **Standard**

   b. Width = **6**

   c. Base Height = **10′-0″**

   d. Justify = **Left**

   e. Roof line offset from base height = **0**

   f. Floor line offset from base line = **0**

4. Select the wall, RMB, and select **Roof/Floor Line > Edit in Place** from the contextual menu that appears to apply a blue editing field on the wall (see Figure 3-22).

5. Select the blue field, RMB, and select Add Gable from the contextual menu that appears.

6. Select the roof line—the wall adds a gable (see Figure 3-23).

7. Select the wall; the blue field reappears; RMB and select Add Step from the contextual menu that appears—the wall adds a step (see Figure 3-24).

8. Select the wall; the blue field reappears; RMB and select Add Vertex from the contextual menu that appears.

9. With the near Object Snap set, click on a point on the gable, and press Enter.

10. Select the wall again; the blue field reappears; an additional vertex will appear where you clicked.

11. Drag on the vertex to change the wall and click to change the shape of the wall (see Figure 3-25).

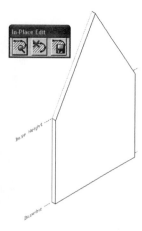

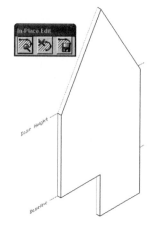

Figure 3-22   Figure 3-23   Figure 3-24

Figure 3-25

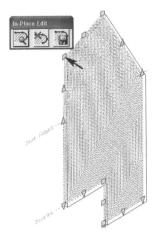

12. Select the blue field, RMB, and select Remove from the contextual menu that appears.
13. Click on the gable to remove it.
14. Change to the Front View.
15. Place a Polyline as shown in Figure 3-26—the Polyline does not have to be on the same plane as the wall, only parallel to the plane of the wall.
16. Press the **Save All Changes** icon in the **In-Place Edit** toolbar to complete the command.
17. Change to the SW Isometric view, and press the **Hidden** icon in the **Shading** toolbar (see Figure 3-27).
18. Double-click the wall you just edited to bring up its Properties palette.
19. Scroll down to the last field on the palette called **Roof/floor line.**
20. Click on the roof/floor line field to bring up the **Roof and Floor Line** dialog box (see Figure 3-28).

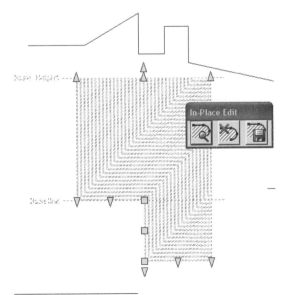

Figure 3-26

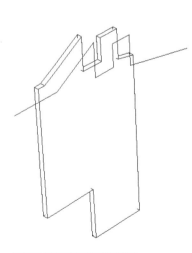

Figure 3-27

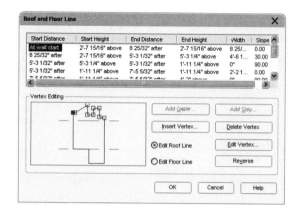

Figure 3-28

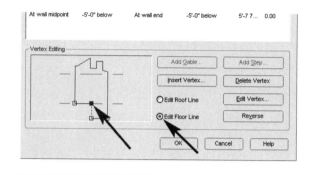

Figure 3-29

21. Select the **Edit Floor Line** radio button, and select the vertex shown in Figure 3-29.

22. In the Roof and Floor Line dialog box press the Edit Vertex button to bring up the **Wall Roof/Floor Line Vertex** dialog box (Figure 3-30).

23. Enter 3'-0" in the **Vertical Offset > Distance** data field.

24. Select the **from Baseline** radio button, press OK to return to Roof and Floor Line dialog box, then press OK to return to the Drawing Editor.

You have now modified the wall floor line through the Roof/Floor dialog boxes (see Figure 3-31).

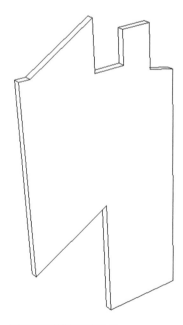

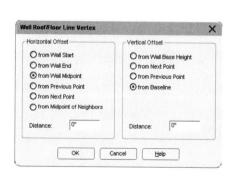

Figure 3-30

Figure 3-31

Hands-On

Using Interference Conditions

1. Start a new drawing using the Architectural Building Model and View (Imperial - ctb) template.
2. Change to the Model Layout.
3. Change to the Top View.
4. Place a standard 6″-wide **10′-0″**-high, **10′-0″** -long wall.
5. From the **Design** tool palette select the **Stair** icon, and place a **Standard**, **Straight 3′-0″**-wide stair with a height of **10′-0″** (Figure 3-32).

If you don't understand how to place stairs, see Section 8, "Stairs," for exercises on placing and modifying stair objects.

6. Select the wall, RMB, and select **Interference Condition > Add** from the contextual menu that appears.
7. Select the stair you placed, and press Enter.
8. Enter **S** (Subtractive) in the command line and press Enter.

The Interference area above the stair, and set in the stair properties palette, is removed from the wall (Figure 3-33).

9. Double-click the stair to bring up its Properties palette.
10. Scroll down to **Interference > Headroom height**.
11. Change the Headroom height to 4′, and notice the change in the interference condition in the wall (see Figure 3-34).

Wall Interference Conditions will work in concert with any intelligent ADT AEC Object.

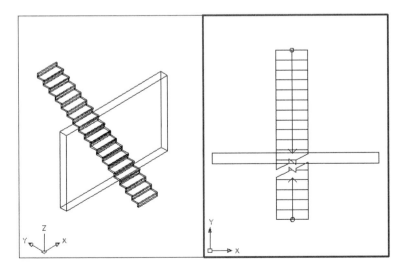

Figure 3-32

Figure 3-33

Figure 3-34

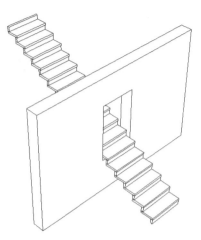

Hands-On

Cleanups

1. Start a new drawing using the Architectural Building Model and View (Imperial - ctb) template.

2. Change to the Model Layout.

3. Change to the Top View.

4. Place a standard 6″-wide **10′-0″**-high, **10′**-0″-long wall.

5. Select the walls, RMB, and select Add Selected from the contextual menu that appears.

6. Place another wall perpendicular to the first as shown in Figure 3-35.

7. Select the vertical wall segment, RMB, and select **Cleanups > Apply 'T' Cleanup** from the contextual menu that appears.

8. Select the horizontal wall to create the 'T' cleanup (Figure 3-36).

9. Add another vertical wall adjacent to the vertical wall; make the adjacent wall 24″ long and overlapping it (Figure 3-37).

10. Select the new wall segment, RMB, and select Add wall Merge Condition from the contextual menu that appears.

11. Select the first walls, and press Enter.

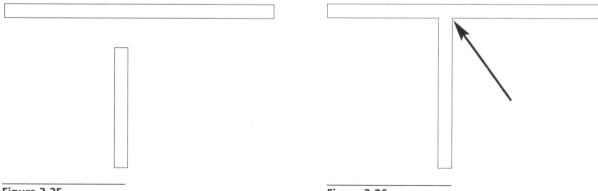

Figure 3-35   Figure 3-36

Figure 3-37

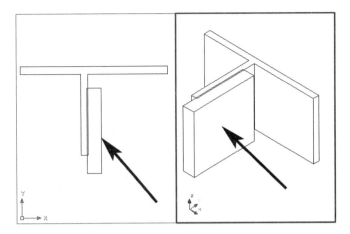

Figure 3-38

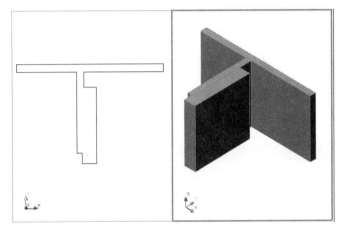

The wall is now merged into one wall, but the new segment can still be adjusted and moved separately (Figure 3-38).

Hands-On

Editing Wall Styles

Base Height, Baseline, Edge, and Floor Line Concepts (Figure 3-39)

In this exercise, you learn how to create a wall and foundation using the components shown in Figure 3-40.

Creating the Wall Style

1. Start a new drawing using the Architectural Building Model and View (Imperial - ctb) template.
2. Change to the Model Layout.
3. Change to the Top View.
4. Select Format > Style Manager from the Main toolbar to bring up the Style Manager dialog box.
5. Open the Architectural objects tree, select the Wall Styles icon, RMB, and select New from the contextual menu that appears.

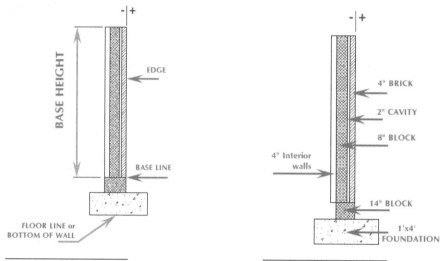

Figure 3-39

Figure 3-40

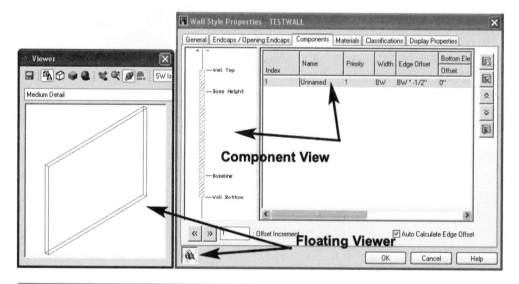

Figure 3-41

6. Rename the New Style to **TESTWALL,** and deselect it.

7. Double-click on the icon next to the name TESTWALL to bring up the **Wall Styles Properties** dialog box.

8. Select the Components tab, and open the Floating Viewer (see Figure 3-41).

Adding and Modifying Wall Components

On the Component tab, notice that the Edge Offset drop-down list reads BW* -1/2″. This means that the Edge Offset is set to be half the width of the Base Width (BW). (Base Width refers to any wall having a parametric or user-enterable width.) I normally set the Edge Offset to the outer edge of the total wall (Figure 3-42).

Figure 3-42

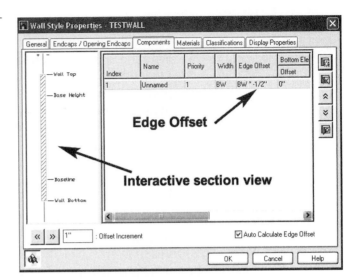

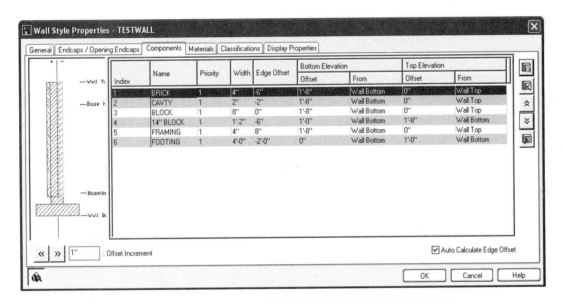

Figure 3-43

9. In the Wall Style Properties dialog box, click on the **Add Component** icon at the top right side of the Components tab, and add five components called **BRICK, CAVITY, BLOCK, 14″ BLOCK, FRAMING,** and **FOOTING.**

10. Set the settings for the Components as shown in Figure 3-43.

Note: Set the setting one component at a time and observe the result in the interactive viewer.

11. Change to the **Materials** tab.

12. Select the **Add New Material** icon to bring up the **New Material** dialog box.

13. Enter the name **BRICK SECTION**, and press the OK button to return to the Materials tab.

14. Activate the **BRICK** Component, and select **BRICK SECTION** from the **Material Definition** drop-down list.

15. With the BRICK component still active, press the **Edit Material** icon to bring up the **Material Definition Properties** dialog box (see Figure 3-44).

16. Activate the **General Medium Detail** Display Representation, check its **Style Override** check box, and press the edit **Display Properties** icon to bring up the **Display Properties** dialog box.

17. Select the **Hatching** tab.

18. Activate the **Surface Hatch** Display Component, select the Hatch icon in the **Pattern** column, and select **Brick_Running _C** pattern (Predefined Type).

19. Set the **Scale/Spacing** to 1", and Angle to 0.00.

20. Activate the **Layer/Color/Linetype** tab and turn the **Surface Hatch** to **Visible**.

21. Press the OK buttons to return to the Wall Style Properties dialog box.

22. Repeat the process for all the other components, creating the following materials for BLOCK, FRAMING, and FOOTING, respectively (see Figures 3-45, 3-46, and 3-47).

Figure 3-44

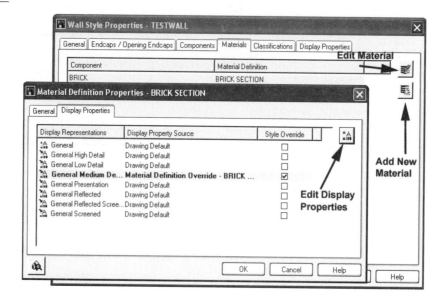

Block

Figure 3-45

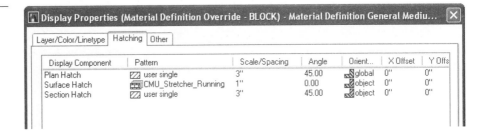

Framing

Figure 3-46

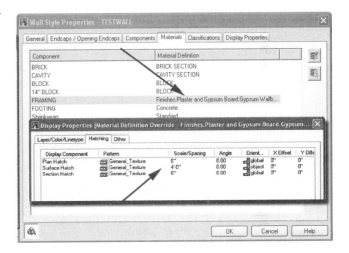

Footing

Figure 3-47

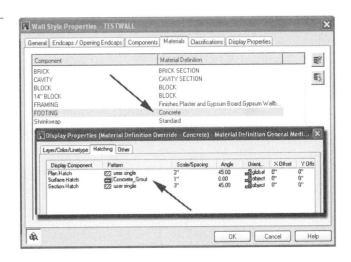

Figure 3-48

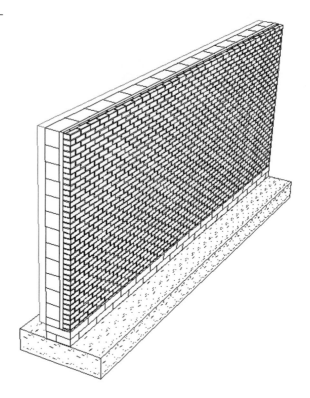

You have now created a new wall style. Place a wall with this new style (see Figure 3-48).

Windows

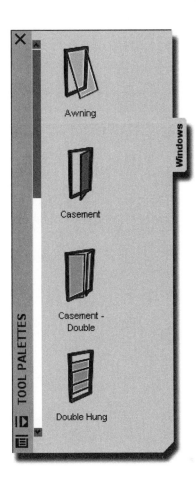

When you finish this section, you should understand the following:

✔ How to place a Window object using Reference.
✔ How to place a Window object using Offset/Center.
✔ How to Change Window Sizes with Grips.
✔ How to Add Profile.
✔ How to Move the window vertically, within the wall, and along the wall.
✔ How to edit Window Styles.

Window objects can be dragged or inserted either from the Design Tool Palette, by clicking RMB on a wall, or by typing **window add** on the Command line.

Number	Name	Purpose
1	Style	Change this to change to another style such as Casement, etc.
2	Standard Sizes	Select from a list of preset sizes
3	Width	Change width of window
4	Height	Change height of window
5	Measure to	Width and height are set to inside or outside of window frame
6	Opening percent	Set amount that window is open in model and elevation view
7	Position along wall	Set to **Offset/Center** or **Unconstrained**; Offset/Center automatically offsets a set distance from the wall ends, or inserts at center of wall
8	Automatic offset	Set to amount of offset when position along wall is set to **Unconstrained**
9	Vertical alignment	Set to **Head** or **Sill**; this will govern on insert
10	Head height	Set elevation for top of window if **Vertical alignment** is set to **Head**
11	Sill height	Set elevation for bottom of window if **Vertical alignment** is set to **Sill**

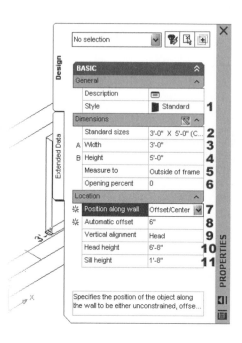

Windows can be placed directly into walls by right-clicking on the wall and selecting Insert > Window from the contextual menu, or by selecting from the Windows or Design tool palettes and pressing Enter.

Hands-On

Placing a Window Object Using Reference

1. Start a new drawing using the Architectural Building Model and View (Imperial - ctb) template.
2. Change to the Model Layout.
3. Set the Object Snap to End Point.
4. Change to the Top View.
5. Place a standard wall 10′-0″ long, 10′-0″ high, and 6″ thick. (See Walls section for information on how to place walls.)
6. Select the **Double Hung** icon from the Windows tool palette and drag your cursor over the Properties palette to open it.
7. Enter the following data:

   a. Style = **Double Hung**
   b. Width = **3′-0″**
   c. Height = **5′-0″**
   d. Measure to = **Outside of Frame**
   e. Position along wall = **Unconstrained**
   f. Vertical alignment = **Head**
   g. Head height = **6′-8″**

8. Select the wall and enter **RE** (Reference point) in the command line.
9. Select the left corner of the wall, move the cursor to the right (0°), and enter **3′** on the keyboard. Then press Enter to place the window 3′-0″ from the left wall corner (Figure 4-1).

Figure 4-1

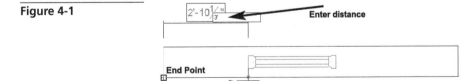

Hands-On

Placing a Window Object Using Offset/Center

1. Erase the window in the previous exercise.
2. Turn off all Object Snaps.
3. Select the **Double Hung** icon from the Windows tool palette and drag your cursor over the Properties palette to open it.
4. Enter the following data:

   a. Style = **Double Hung**
   b. Width = **3'-0"**
   c. Height = **5'-0"**
   d. Measure to = **Outside of Frame**
   e. Position along wall = **Offset/Center**
   f. Automatic Offset = **6"**
   g. Vertical alignment = **Head**
   h. Head height = **6'-8"**

5. Select the wall near the left end of the wall, click the mouse, and press Enter to complete the command and place the window.

The Window will be placed 6" from the left end of the wall (see Figure 4-2).

! **Note:** By pressing the tab key you can cycle the 6" dimension, and enter an overriding dimension.

6. Again, select the **Double Hung** icon from the Windows tool palette and drag your cursor over the Properties palette to open it.
7. Select the wall near the center of the distance left between the previous window placement and the right-hand wall end. Click the mouse, and press Enter to complete the command and place the window.

The Window will be placed at the center of the distance between the second window and the right end of the wall (see Figure 4-3).

Figure 4-2

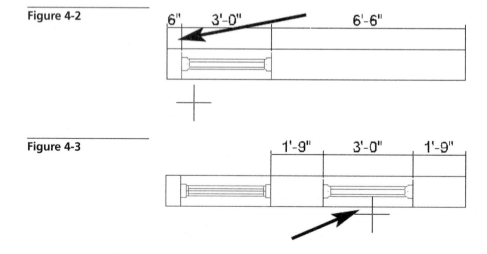

Figure 4-3

Hands-On

Changing Window Size with Grips

1. Select a window to activate its grips, and drag to the right (0°). If the window has sizes listed in its Window Styles Properties > Standard Sizes, it will snap at gray lines in plan. These are sizes listed in the aforementioned Properties (see Figure 4-4).

Figure 4-4

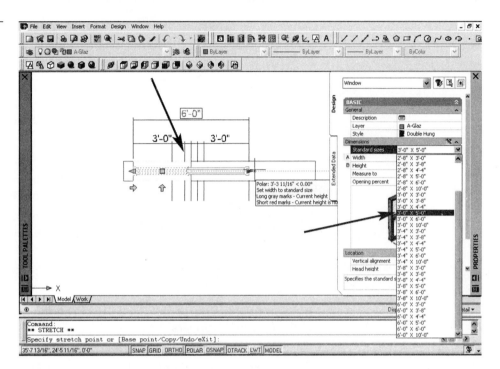

Hands-On

Adding a Profile

1. Erase the previous exercise.
2. Place a Standard wall 10'-0" long, 10'-0" high, and 6" thick.
3. Select the **Pivot Horizontal** icon from the Windows tool palette and drag your cursor over the Properties palette to open it.
4. Enter the following data:

   a. Style = **Pivot Horizontal**
   b. Width = **5'-0"**
   c. Height = **4'-0"**
   d. Measure to = **Outside of Frame**
   e. Position along wall = **Unconstrained**
   f. Vertical alignment = **Head**
   g. Head height = **6'-8"**

Figure 4-5

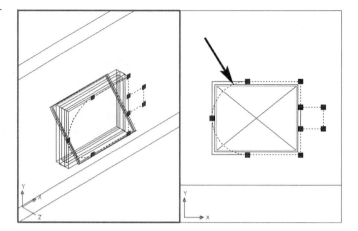

5. Place the window 2'-0" from the left edge of the wall.

6. Change to the Front View.

7. Place a closed Polyline as shown in Figure 4-5.

8. Select the window, RMB, and select **Add Profile** from the contextual menu that appears to bring up the **Add Window Profile** dialog box.

9. Select Start from scratch from the **Profile Definition** drop-down list, enter **TEST PIVOT WINDOW** in the **New Profile Name** data field, and press Enter.

A blue hatch field will appear on the window.

10. RMB on the blue hatch field and select replace Ring from the conceptual menu that appears.

11. Select the closed polyline that you created in Step 7 of this exercise.

12. Enter **Y** (Yes) in the command line, and press Enter to complete the command.

13. RMB on the blue hatch field and select Save Changes from the conceptual menu that appears (see Figure 4-6).

14. Mirror the window in the front view (see Figure 4-7).

Figure 4-6

Figure 4-7

Hands-On

Moving the Window Vertically, Within the Wall, and Along the Wall

1. Erase the previous exercise.
2. Place a standard wall 10'-0" long, 10'-0" high, and 6" thick.
3. Select the **Double Hung** icon from the Windows tool palette and drag your cursor over the Properties palette to open it.
4. Enter the following data:

   a. Style = **Double hung**
   b. Width = **3'-0"**
   c. Height = **5'-0"**
   d. Measure to = **Outside of Frame**
   e. Position along wall = **Offset/Center**
   f. Vertical alignment = **Head**
   g. Head height **= 6'-8"**

5. Place the window at the middle of the wall.
6. Change to the Front View.
7. Select the window to activate its grips.
8. Activate the square grip at the bottom of the window; a yellow dialog field appears (see Figure 4-8).
9. Press the **CTRL** key twice until the dialog field reads **Perpendicular move vertically**.
10. Press the **Tab** key until the data field turns magenta in color.
11. Enter 3'-6" in the command line and press Enter.

The window will move vertically and be 3'-6" above the wall baseline.

12. Activate the square grip at the bottom of the window again.
13. Drag the grip to the right until the yellow dialog field appears.
14. Enter 3'-0" in the command line and press Enter.

Figure 4-8

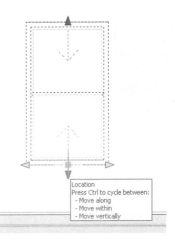

The window will move horizontally 3'-0" in the direction that the grip was moved.

15. Enter 3'-0" in the command line and press Enter.
16. Change to the Top View.
17. Activate the square grip at the center of the window.
18. Press the **CTRL** key once until the dialog field reads **Perpendicular move within width**.
19. Move the grip vertically.
20. Enter 2" in the command line and press Enter.

The window will move vertically within the wall 2" in the direction the grip was moved. Save this file.

Hands-On

Editing Window Styles

1. Use the precious exercise.
2. Change to the Front View.
3. Select the window, RMB, and select Edit Window Style from the contextual menu that appears to bring up the Window style properties dialog box.
4. Select the **Dimensions** tab.

This is where you set the **Frame Width** and **Depth.** Check the Auto-Adjust check box if you want the frame depth to match the wall in which it has been inserted.

The **Sash Width** and **Depth** plus the **Glass Thickness** are also located in the Dimensions tab.

5. Select the **Floating Viewer** icon at the lower left corner of the Window Style Properties dialog box to bring up the Viewer.
6. In the Viewer, select the Gouraud Shaded icon in the top Viewer toolbar (see Figure 4-9).

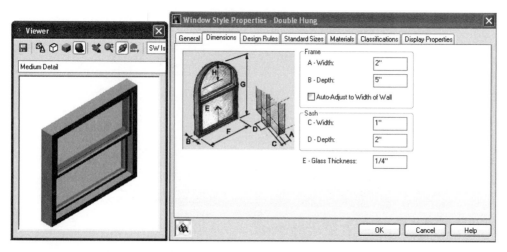

Figure 4-9

7. Enter the following data in the entry fields:

   a. Frame Width = **1**″
   b. Frame Depth = **12**″
   c. Sash Width = **4**″
   d. Sash Depth = **4**″

Press Enter after entering the last data field, and note the change in window in the Viewer (see Figure 4-10).

8. Reset the data fields to the following:

   a. Frame Width = **2**″
   b. Frame Depth = **5**″
   c. Sash Width = **1**″
   d. Sash Depth = **2**″

9. Select the **Design Rules** tab.
10. Select the **Predefined** radio button; select **Round** from the **Predefined** drop-down list, and **Awning-Transom** from the **Window Type** drop-down list.

Note the change in window in the Viewer (see Figure 4-11).

11. Select the Use Profile radio button, and select **TEST PIVOT WINDOW** from its drop-down list (TEST PIVOT WINDOW was the profile created in Step 9 of "Adding a Profile" in this section).

Note the change in window in the Viewer (see Figure 4-12).

12. Change to the **Standard Sizes** tab.

The Standard Sizes tab is where standardized windows are entered. These sizes allow you to change windows interactively as shown in the following exercise.

Figure 4-10

Figure 4-11

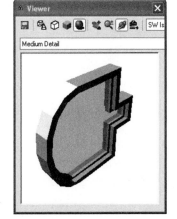

Figure 4-12

13. Press OK to close the **Window Style Properties** dialog box.
14. Change to the Top View.
15. Double-click on the window to bring up its **Properties** palette.
16. Set the Style to **Double Hung**, and allow the palette to close.
17. Select the window's right arrow grip, and drag it to the right.

You will see a yellow dialog field explaining the gray and red marks that appear above the window. These marks are "snap" points corresponding to the preset width sizes set in the Standard Sizes tab of the Window Style Properties dialog box (see Figure 4-13).

18. RMB on the window again and select **Edit Window Style** from the contextual menu that appears.
19. Change to the **Materials** tab.
20. Activate the **Frame** field, and click on the **Material Definition** drop-down list (see Figure 4-14).

Four preset materials are shipped with the program. If you need more materials, you need to add and edit a new material.

21. To add and edit a new material, press the **Add New Material** icon at the right side of the materials tab.
22. Enter a new name for the new material in the **New Material** data field that appears, and press OK.
23. Activate the New Material field in the **Material Definition** column, and select the **Edit Material** icon above the Add Material icon to bring up the **Material Definition Properties** dialog box.

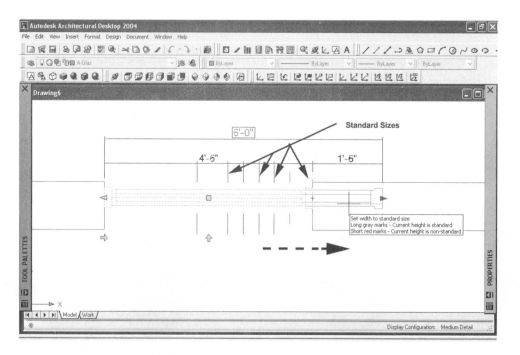

Figure 4-13

Figure 4-14

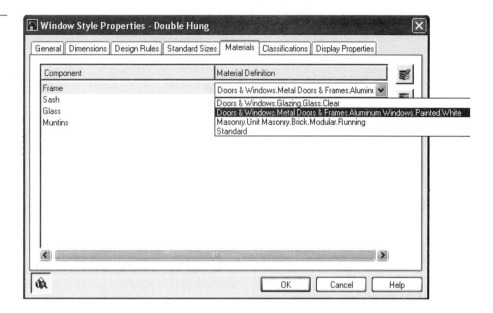

24. Check the **Style Override** check box for the **General Medium Detail** Display Representation to open the **Display Properties** dialog box.

25. Select the **Other** tab (see Figure 4-15).

In the **Other** tab you can control the placement of hatches on surfaces, and Browse for materials made in the VIZ Render module (see Figure 4-16).

26. Press the OK buttons until you return to the Window Style Properties dialog box.

27. Change to the **Display Properties** tab.

28. Select the **Elevation** field.

29. Press the **Edit Display** icon at the upper right side of the Display Properties tab to bring up the **Display Properties** dialog box.

30. Select the **Muntins** tab.

31. Press the **Add** button to bring up the **Muntins Block** dialog box.

Figure 4-15

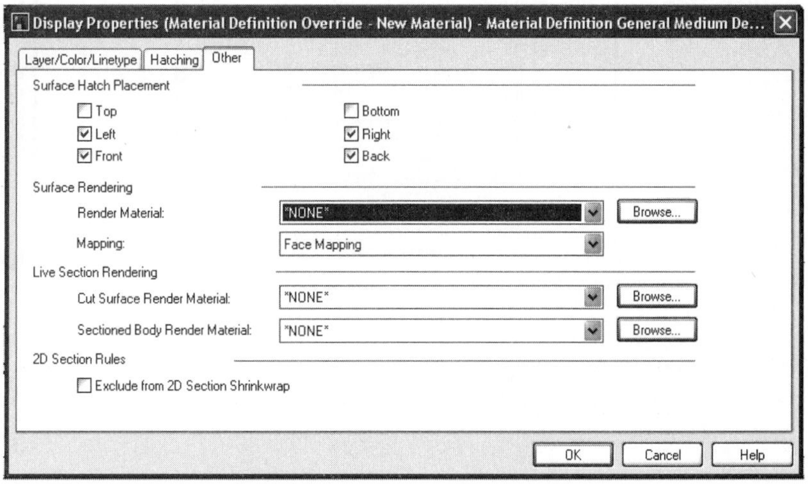

Figure 4-16

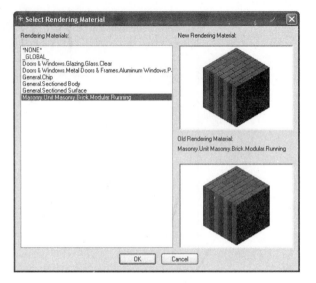

32.   Select the Prairie - 12 Lights from the **Pattern** drop-down list, check the **Clean Up Joints** and **Convert to body** check boxes, and then press the OK buttons to close the command and view the window (see Figures 4-17 and 4-18).

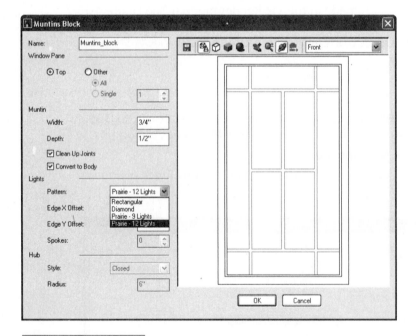

Figure 4-17

Figure 4-18

Doors

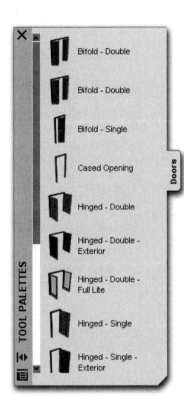

When you finish this section, you should understand the following:

- ✔ How to place a Door object using Reference.
- ✔ How to place a Door object using Offset/Center.
- ✔ How to change door size and swing location with Grips.
- ✔ How to control the door swing angle.
- ✔ How to add a Profile.
- ✔ How to add a door knob.
- ✔ How to move the door within the wall, and along the wall.
- ✔ How to edit Door Styles.
- ✔ How to use the Materials tab.

Wall objects can be dragged or inserted either from the Design tool palette, or by typing **dooradd** on the Command line.

Doors

In Autodesk Architectural Desktop 2004 Door objects are totally customizable. Whether it be the size and shape of the door, the size and shape of the jamb, whether it has side lights, or mullions, or whether it has a sill, all is possible in this program. As with other features of this program, a premade library of Door Styles greatly enhances productivity. Hopefully, manufacturers will jump on the ADT bandwagon and place their door styles on the Web. If they do this, you will be able to quickly "idrop" or update your catalogs with premade doors and door accessories. If this happens and the manufacturer makes changes, you will be able to update your catalogs and drawings automatically directly from the Internet.

Number	Name	Purpose
1	Layer	Change this to place the door on another layer
2	Style	Change this to change to another style such as double doors, etc.
3	Standard sizes	Sizes set in the door style dialog box
4	Width	Custom width
5	Height	Custom height
6	Measure to	Inside of frame or outside of frame
7	Swing angle	Door swing opening 0 to 90°
8	Position along	**Unconstrained** (any placement) **Offset/Center** (set offset from ends of wall or midpoint of wall)
9	Vertical alignment	Head height or threshold governs
10	Head height	Head height above wall baseline
11	Threshold height	Threshold height above wall baseline

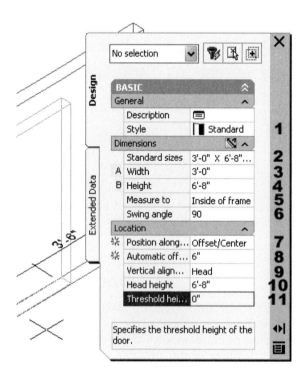

Doors can be placed directly into walls by right-clicking on the wall and selecting **Insert > Door** from the contextual menu, or by selecting from the **Doors** or **Design** tool palettes and pressing Enter.

Placing a Door Object Using Reference

1. Start a new drawing using the Architectural Building Model and View (Imperial - ctb) template.
2. Change to the Model Layout.
3. Change to the Top View.
4. Set the Object snap to End Point.
5. Place a standard 10'-long, 10'-high wall.
6. Select any door from the doors tool palette and drag your cursor over the Properties palette to open it.
7. Enter the following data:

   a. Style = **Standard**
   b. Width = **3'-0"**
   c. Height = **6'-8"**
   d. Measure to = **Outside of Frame**
   e. Swing angle = **90**
   f. Position along wall = **Unconstrained**
   g. Vertical alignment = **Head**
   h. Head height = **6'-8"**
   i. Threshold height = **0"**

8. Select the wall and enter **RE** (Reference point) in the command line.
9. Select the left corner of the wall, move the cursor to the right (0°), and enter **5'** on the keyboard. Press Enter to place the door 5'-0" from the left wall corner (see Figure 5-1).

Figure 5-1

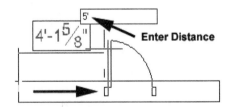

Placing a Door Object Using Offset/Center

1. Erase the door in the previous exercise.
2. Turn off all Object Snaps.
3. Select any door icon in the Doors tool palette and drag your cursor over the Properties palette to open it.

4. Enter the following data:

    a. Style = **Standard**
    b. Width = **3'-0"**
    c. Height = **6'-8"**
    d. Measure to = **Outside of Frame**
    e. Position along wall = **Offset/Center**
    f. Automatic Offset = **6"**
    g. Vertical alignment = **Head**
    h. Head height = **6'-8"**
    i. Threshold = **0**

5. Select the wall near the left end of the wall, click the mouse, and press Enter to complete the command and place the door.

The Door will be placed 6" from the left end of the wall (see Figure 5-2).

! **Note:** By pressing the tab key you can cycle the 6" dimension, and enter an overriding dimension.

Figure 5-2

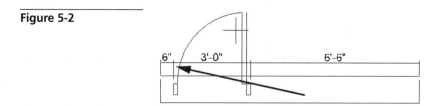

Hands-On

Changing Door Size and Swing Location with Grips

1. Select the door to activate its grips, and drag to the right (0°). If the door has sizes listed in its **Door Styles Properties > Standard Sizes**, it will snap at gray lines in plan.
2. To add doors to the Standard Sizes menu, RMB on the door and select Edit Door Style from the contextual menu that appears to bring up the **Door Style Properties** dialog box.
3. Select the **Standard Sizes tab**.
4. Press the Add button to bring up the Add Standard Size dialog box (see Figure 5-3).
5. Add the four doors shown in Figure 5-4 to the Standard Sizes tab, and close the Door Style Properties dialog box by pressing OK.
6. Again, select the door to activate its grips and drag to the right (0°). The door will now snap to the sizes you added in the Standard Sizes tab (see Figure 5-5).
7. Select the arrow grip shown in Figure 5-6 to flip the door swing in different directions. Save this file.

Figure 5-3

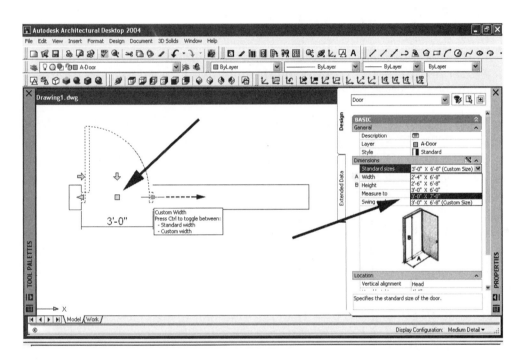

Figure 5-4

Figure 5-5

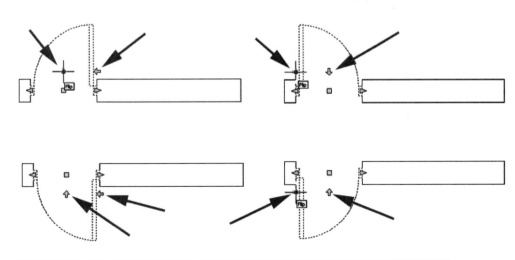

Figure 5-6

Hands-On

Controlling the Door Swing angle

1. Using the previous exercise, change to SW Isometric View.

Note that although the swing shows open in Top View (Plan), the door swing is closed in the SW Isometric (Model View). Architectural Desktop ships from the developer with the doors closed in Model View (see Figure 5-7).

2. Double-click the door to bring up its **Properties** palette.
3. Note that the swing angle is 90.
4. Change the swing angle to 45, and press Enter. Note that nothing happens.

This is because there is an override set at 0, which prevents the door's Properties palette from controlling the door swing angle. To allow control from the Properties palette do the following:

5. Select the door, RMB, and select Edit Door Style from the contextual menu that appears to bring up the **Door Style Properties** dialog box.
6. Select the **Display Properties** tab.
7. Double-click the **Model** field (don't check the style Override check box because that would control only the door selected, and not all the doors) to bring up the **Display Properties** dialog box.
8. Select the **Other** tab.
9. *Clear* the **Overide Open Percent** check box, and press the OK buttons until you return to the Drawing Editor (see Figure 5-8).

The Override Open Percent check box overrides the Properties palette. You can also change the door swing to a straight swing in the Other tab.

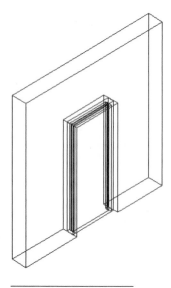

Figure 5-7

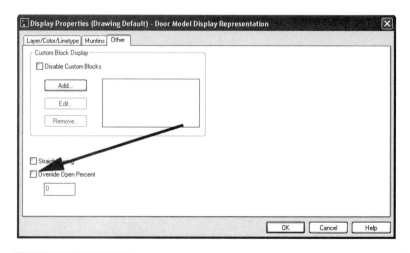

Figure 5-8

Figure 5-9

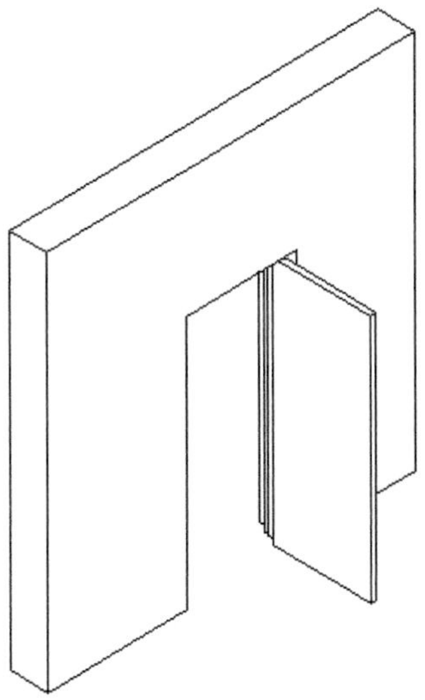

10. In the Drawing Editor, double-click the door again to bring up its Properties palette.
11. Change the swing angle to 90, and press Enter.

The door swing is open (see Figure 5-9).

Hands-On

Adding a Profile

1. Use the previous exercise.
2. Change to Front View.
3. Place the closed polylines shown in Figure 5-10 over the door.
4. Select the door, RMB, and select **Add Profile** from the contextual menu that appears to bring up the **Add Door Profile** dialog box.

Figure 5-10

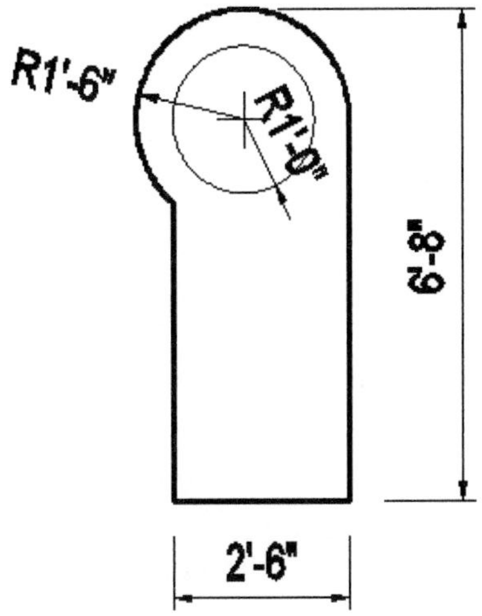

5. Select Start from scratch from the **Profile Definition** drop-down list, enter **TEST PIVOT DOOR** in the **New Profile Name** data field, and press Enter.

A blue hatch field will appear on the door (see Figure 5-11).

6. RMB on the blue hatch field and select **Replace ring** from the conceptual menu that appears.
7. Select the closed polyline that you created in Step 3 of this exercise.
8. Enter **Y** (Yes) in the command line, and press Enter.
9. RMB again on the blue hatch field and select **Add ring from** the contextual menu that appears.
10. Select the 1'-0" circle that you created with the polyline in Step 3 of this exercise.
11. Again enter **Y** (Yes) in the command line, and press Enter to complete the command.
12. Change to the NE Isometric View and select the **Hidden** icon from the Shading toolbar.
13. RMB on the blue hatch field and select Save Changes from the conceptual menu that appears (see Figure 5-12).

Save this exercise.

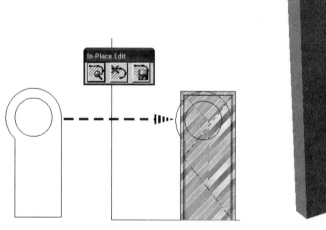

Figure 5-11

Figure 5-12

Hands-On

Adding a Door Knob

1. Use the previous exercise.
2. Draw the closed polyline shown in Figure 5-13.
3. Select **Door > Pulldowns > 3D Solids Pulldown** from the **Main** toolbar to place the **3D Solids** menu group on the Main toolbar.

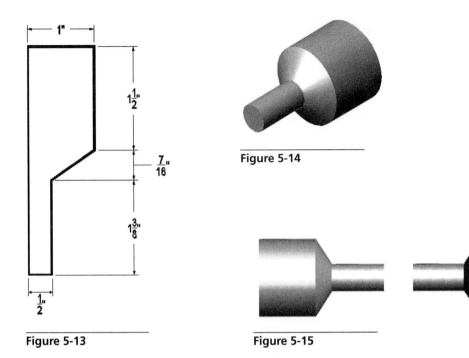

Figure 5-14

Figure 5-13

Figure 5-15

4. Now, select **3D Solids > Revolve** from the Main toolbar and revolve 360° (see Figure 5-14).

5. **Mirror** the Knob (see Figure 5-15).

6. Select **Format > Blocks > Block Definition** from the Main toolbar to bring up the block Definition dialog box.

7. Create two blocks named **KNOB1** and **KNOB2.**

8. Select the door you created in the previous exercise, RMB, and select Edit Door Style from the contextual menu that appears to bring up the **Door Style Properties** dialog box.

9. Select the **Display Properties** tab.

10. Double-click on the Elevation field to bring up the next **Display Properties** dialog box.

11. In this dialog box, select the **Other** tab.

12. Press the Add button to bring up the **Custom Block** dialog box (see Figure 5-16).

13. Select the **Select Block** button to bring up the **Select A Block** dialog box.

14. Select **KNOB1**, and press the OK button.

15. Use the settings shown in Figure 5-17 to move the KNOB1 into position in the Front view, and then press the OK button to return to the **Display Properties** dialog box > Other tab.

16. Select the **Add** button to again bring up the Custom Block dialog box.

17. Press the Select Block button, and this time select **KNOB2** and press OK to return to the Custom Block dialog box.

Figure 5-16

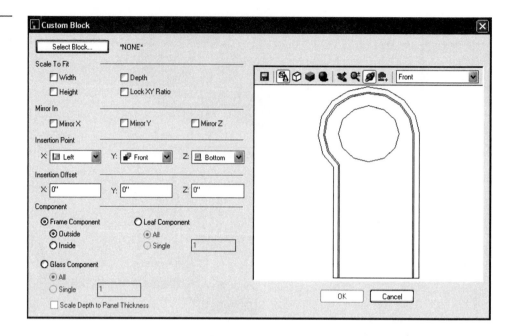

Figure 5-17

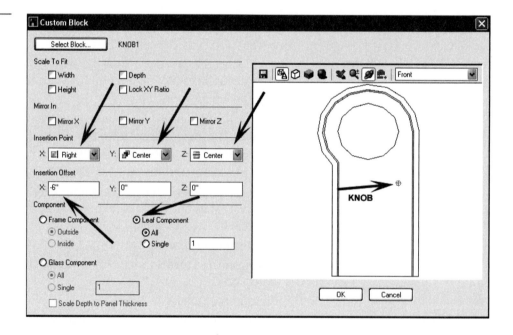

18. Use the same settings for KNOB2 that you set for KNOB 1, and press the OK buttons until you return to the Drawing Editor (see Figure 5-18).

Save this file.

Figure 5-18

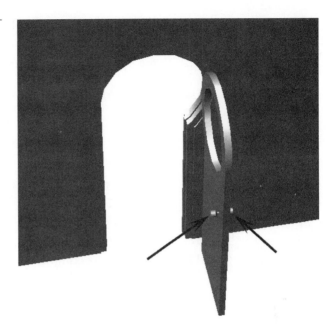

Hands-On

Moving a Door Vertically, Within the Wall, and Along the Wall

1. Use the previous exercise.
2. Change to the Front View.
3. Select the door to activate its grips.
4. Activate the square grip at the bottom of the door—a yellow dialog field appears (see Figure 5-19).

Figure 5-19

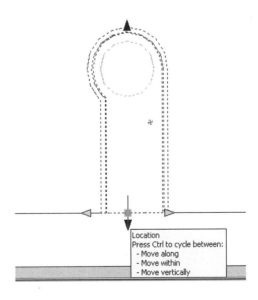

5. Activate the square grip at the bottom of the door.
6. Drag the grip to the right until the yellow dialog field appears.
7. Enter 3'-0" in the command line and press Enter.

The door will move horizontally 3'-0" in the direction that the grip was moved.

8. Enter 3'-0" in the command line and press Enter.
9. Change to the Top View.
10. Activate the square grip at the center of the door.
11. Press the **CTRL** key once until the dialog filed reads **Perpendicular move within width**.
12. Move the grip vertically.
13. Enter 2" in the command line and press Enter.

The door will move vertically within the wall 2" in the direction that the grip was moved.
Save this file.

Hands-On

Editing Door Styles

1. Use the previous exercise.
2. Change to the Front View.
3. Select the door, RMB, and select Edit Door Style from the contextual menu that appears to bring up the Door style properties dialog box.
4. Select the **Dimensions** tab.

This is where you set the Frame Width and Depth. Please note the Auto-Adjust check box; check this if you want the frame depth to match the wall in which it has been inserted.

The Stop Width and Depth plus the Door and Glass Thickness are also located in the Dimensions tab.

5. Select the **Floating Viewer** icon at the lower left corner of the Door Style Properties dialog box to bring up the Viewer.
6. Select the Hidden Shaded icon in the top Viewer toolbar (see Figure 5-20).
7. Enter the following data in the entry fields:

   a. Frame Width = **3"**
   b. Frame Depth = **6"**
   c. Stop Width = **1"**
   d. Stop Depth = **1"**

Press the enter key after entering the last data field, and note the change in door in the Viewer (see Figure 5-21).

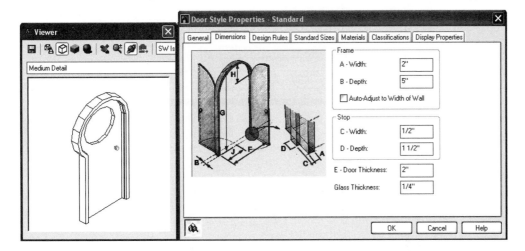

Figure 5-20

Figure 5-21

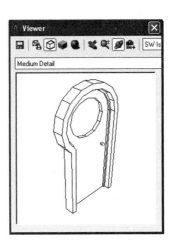

Hands-On

Using the Materials Tab

1. In the Materials tab, activate the **Frame** field, and click on the **Material Definition** drop-down list (see Figure 5-22).

There are four preset materials that are shipped with the program. If you need more materials, you need to add and edit a new material.

2. To add and edit a new material, press the **Add New Material** icon at the right side of the Materials tab.

3. Enter a new name for the new material in the **New Material** data field that appears, and press OK.

4. Activate the New Material field in the **Material Definition** column, and select the **Edit Material** icon above the Add Material icon to bring up the **Material Definition Properties** dialog box.

Figure 5-22

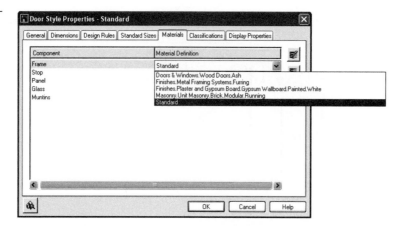

Figure 5-23

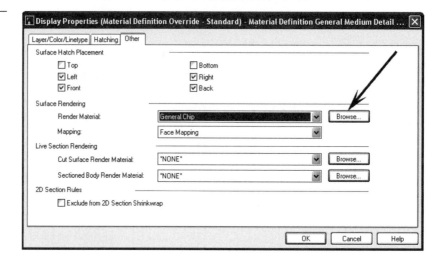

5. Check the **Style Override** check box for the **General Medium Detail** Display Representation to open the **Display Properties** dialog box.

6. Select the **Other** tab (see Figure 5-23).

In the Other tab you can control the placement of hatches on surfaces, and Browse for materials made in the VIZ Render module (see Figure 5-24).

7. Press the OK buttons until you return to the Door Style Properties dialog box.

8. Change to the **Display Properties** tab.

9. Select the **Elevation** field.

10. Press the **Edit Display** icon at the upper right side of the Display Properties tab to bring up the **Display Properties** dialog box.

11. Select the **Muntins** tab.

12. Press the **Add** button to bring up the **Muntins Block** dialog box.

13. Select the Prairie - 12 Lights from the **Pattern** drop-down list, check the **Clean Up Joints** and **Convert to body** check boxes, and then press the OK buttons to close the command and view the door (see Figures 5-25 and 5-26).

Figure 5-24

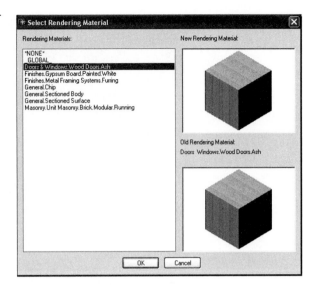

Figure 5-25

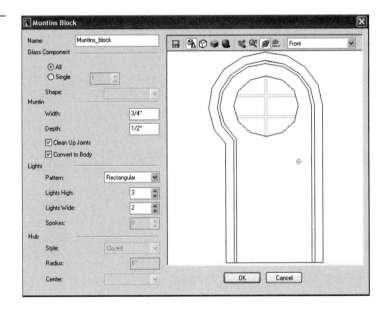

Figure 5-26

Curtain Walls

When you finish this section, you should understand the following:

✔ How to create a Curtain Wall tool palette.
✔ How to place a Curtain Wall.
✔ How to set Miter Angles.
✔ How to use the Roof Line/Floor Line command.
✔ How to Apply Tool Properties to a Layout Grid.
✔ How to Apply Tool Properties to an Elevation Sketch.
✔ How to Edit Grid-In Place.
✔ How to Edit Curtain Wall Styles.

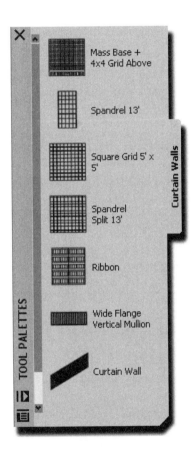

Wall objects can be dragged or inserted from the Design tool palette, or by typing **curtainwall add** on the Command line.

Curtain Wall objects can serve many purposes in Autodesk Architectural Desktop 2004. Originally created to represent storefront and nonbearing perimeter walls, Curtain Wall objects can easily be modified to represent many different kinds of walls. Their unique feature is their modifiable grid that can contain 3D solids, AEC Polygons, and door and window assemblies. Curtain Wall objects can even be modified to represent roof and floor trusses, with the Curtain Wall's parametrically changeable frames representing the truss members.

Besides being created from direct numerical input, **Curtain Wall objects** can be generated from **Layout Grids** and Elevation **Sketches.**

Once created, the resultant Curtain Wall styles can be applied to existing walls (the Curtain Wall object will replace the wall), or applied to a **Reference Base Curve** (the Curtain Wall will use a curve on the ground plane as a basis for its shape in Plan View).

Number	Name	Purpose
1	Style	Select from available Curtain Wall styles
2	Segment type	Line or Arc—choose for a linear or curved wall
3	Base height	Height of Curtain Wall
4	Length	Present length value of Curtain Wall object
5	Start Miter	Miter of Curtain Wall frame at corner, at start of wall (in degrees)
6	End Miter	Miter of Curtain Wall frame at corner, at start of wall (in degrees)
7	Roof line offset from base height	Any part of the Curtain Wall above the Base height such as parapet, gable end, etc.
8	Floor line offset from baseline	Any part of the Curtain Wall below the Floor line
9	Rotation	
10	Elevation	
11	Roof/floor line	

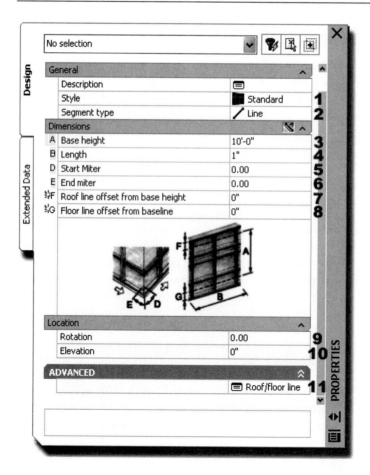

Hands-On

Creating a Curtain Wall Tool Palette

1. Select the Content Browser icon from the Navigation toolbar to bring up the Catalog Library in the Content Browser (see Figure 6-1).

2. In the Catalog Library, double-click the **Architectural Desktop Design Tool Catalog - Imperial** catalog to open it (see Figure 6-2).

3. Double-click on the area shown in Figure 6-3 to open the pages with all the Tool folders.

4. Change to Page 2, select the Curtain Wall folder, open it, and drag all the curtain walls to a new tool palette labeled **Curtain Walls.**

Figure 6-1

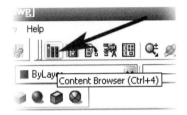

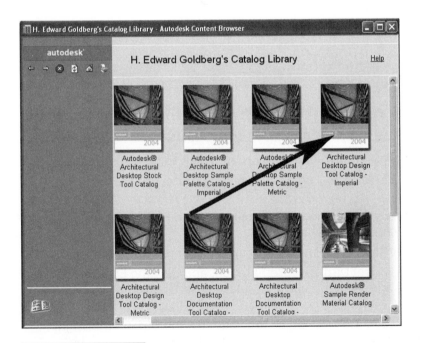

Figure 6-2

Figure 6-3

Hands-On

Placing a Curtain Wall

1. Start a new drawing using the Architectural Building Model and View (Imperial - ctb) template.
2. Change to the Model Layout.
3. Change to the Top View.
4. Turn the ORTHO button on.
5. Click on the Curtain Wall icon on the new Curtain Walls tool palette and move your cursor over the Properties tool palette to open it.
6. Set the following parameters:

   a. Style = **Standard**
   b. Segment type = **Line**
   c. Base height = **10′-0″**

7. Click to set the Curtain Wall start point, drag your cursor to the right, enter 10′-0″ in the command line, and press Enter.
8. Move your cursor vertically, and again enter 10′-0″ in the command line.
9. Press Enter twice to finish the command.

You have now created two joined sections of curtain wall.

Hands-On

Setting Miter Angles in the Contextual Menu and the Start and End Miters in the Curtain Wall Properties Toolbar

1. Press the SE Isometric View icon on the Views toolbar.
2. Press the Flat Shaded icon on the Shading toolbar to shade the curtain walls.
3. Select one of the segments of curtain wall and RMB to bring up the Curtain Wall contextual menu.
4. Select Edit Object Display to bring up the Object Display dialog box.
5. Select the Model Display representation, and click the Edit Display Properties icon to bring up the Display Properties dialog box (see Figure 6-4).
6. Open the Layer/Color/Linetype tab, and turn the Default Infill light off. Press all the OK buttons in the dialog boxes to return to the Drawing Editor.

Notice that your curtain walls now have no glass (infill) showing.

7. Zoom close to the top corner joint between the two sections of curtain wall (see Figure 6-5).

Figure 6-4

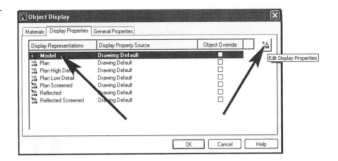

Figure 6-5   **Figure 6-6**

8. Select a section of curtain wall, RMB, and select Set Miter Angles
    from the curtain wall contextual menu (see Figure 6-6).

You have now mitered the corners of the curtain wall's frame.
    If you select one of the curtain wall sections and double-click to bring
up its Properties tool palette, you will see that its Start or End miter has
been set. The vertical part of the frame can also be mitered, as we will see
later.

9. Double-click each section of curtain wall separately to bring up its
    Properties tool palettes and check the End miter for the left section,
    and the Start miter for the right section.

The End miter for the left section should now read 45, and the right section of curtain wall should read 315.

10. Erase everything in the Drawing Editor.
11. Again, click on the Curtain Wall icon on the new Curtain Walls tool
    palette and move your cursor over the Properties tool palette to
    open it. This time, enter the Start and End miter values you got in
    the previous exercise.
12. Click to set the Curtain Wall start point, drag your cursor to the right,
    enter 10'-0" in the command line, and press Enter.
13. Move your cursor vertically, and again enter 10'-0" in the command
    line.

Figure 6-7

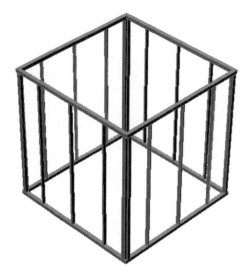

14. Enter OR (ORTHO) in the command line and press Enter.
15. Drag your cursor to the left and click in response to the Command line "Point on wall in direction of close."

You have now created a four-wall enclosure with mitered corners. Save this file (see Figure 6-7).

Hands-On

Using the Roof Line/Floor Line Selections in the Contextual Menu

1. Using the walls from the previous exercise, select a wall, RMB, and select **Roof Line/Floor Line > Edit In Place** from the contextual menu that appears (see Figure 6-8).

When Editing a Curtain Wall in place, an In-Place Edit toolbar will appear in the drawing editor, and blue shading will appear over the wall. This shading shape can be modified and saved back to the curtain wall (see Figure 6-9).

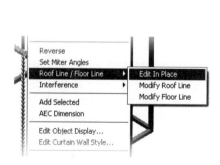

Figure 6-8

Figure 6-9

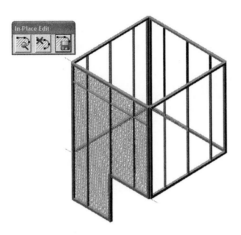

Figure 6-10

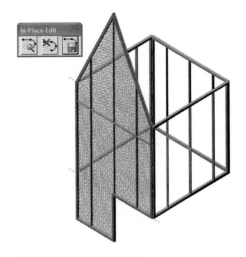

Figure 6-11

2. Select the blue shading, RMB, and select **Add Step** from the contextual menu that appears.

3. Select the floor line of the curtain wall. **The curtain wall steps** (see Figure 6-10). Repeat Step 2, this time picking **Add Gable** (see Figure 6-11).

4. Select the blue shading again, RMB, and select **Reverse** from the contextual menu that appears.

5. Select the floor line of the curtain wall.

The curtain wall step will reverse (see Figure 6-12).

6. Select the Left View icon from the Views toolbar to change to the left view.

7. Select the Polyline icon from the Shapes toolbar, and draw a polyline as shown in Figure 6-13. The polyline does not have to be in the same plane or touch the curtain wall.

8. Select the blue shading again, RMB, and select **Project to Polyline** from the contextual menu that appears.

Figure 6-12

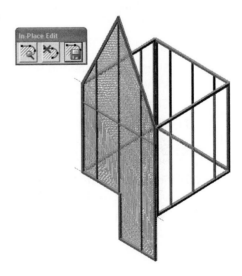

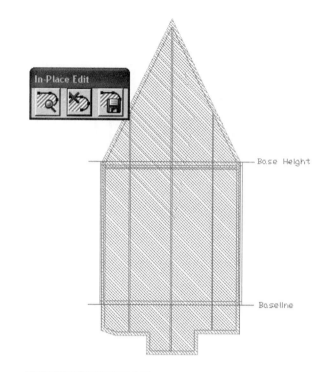

Figure 6-13

Figure 6-14

9. Select the Polyline that you just drew, enter **Y** for Yes in the command line, and press Enter.

The curtain wall changes shape to match the polyline (see Figure 6-14).

10. Press the Save All Changes icon in the In-Place Edit toolbar to save the changes.

Save this file.

Hands-On

Applying Tool Properties to a Layout Grid

1. Start a new drawing using the Architectural Building Model and View (Imperial - ctb) template.
2. Change to the Model Layout.
3. Change to the Front View.
4. Press the **Content Browser** icon in the **Main** toolbar or enter **CTRL 4** on the keyboard to bring up the **Content Browser**.
5. Select the **Autodesk Architectural Desktop Stock Tool Catalog** to open it.
6. Open the **General Purpose Tools > Parametric Layout & Anchoring** folder.

7. Drag the **Layout Grid 2D** icon into the Curtain Walls tool palette you created.

8. Select the **Layout Grid 2D** icon, RMB, and move your cursor over the Properties palette to open the palette.

9. Enter the following:

    a. Shape = **Rectangular**
    b. Boundary = ***NONE***
    c. Specify on screen = **No**
    d. X-Width = **30′-0″**
    e. Y-Depth = **15′-0″**
    f. (For X axis) Layout type = **Space evenly**
    g. Number of bays = **6**
    h. (For Y axis) Layout type = **Space evenly**
    i. Number of bays = **3**

10. Place a 30′-wide by 15′-high grid in the Top View Viewport. Set the grid to be divided by 6 in the X direction and 3 in the Y direction (see Figure 6-15).

11. Select the layout grid, RMB, and select **X-Axis > layout mode** from the contextual menu that appears.

12. Enter **M** (Manual) in the command line, and press Enter.

13. Select the layout grid again, and move some of the grips in the X direction to change the layout (see Figure 6-16).

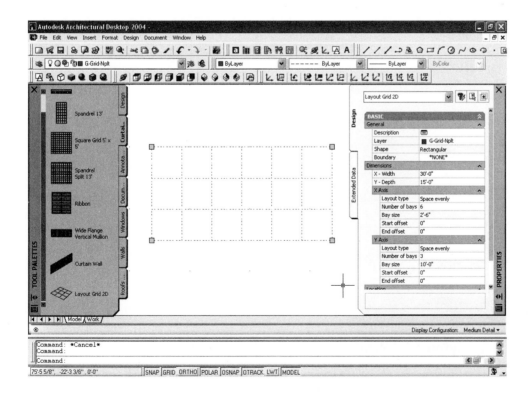

Figure 6-15

Figure 6-16

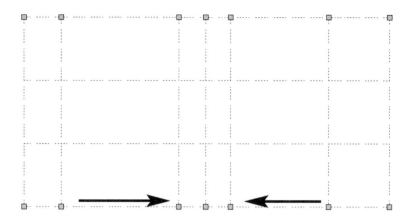

14. RMB on the **Layout Square Grid 5′x 5′** icon and select Apply Tool Properties to > Layout Grid from the contextual menu that appears.

15. Select the layout grid, enter **Y** (Yes) in the command line, and press Enter.

16. Enter **V** (vertical) in the Command line (to make the verticals one piece and the horizontals segments), and press Enter.

17. Give the curtain wall a new name in the Curtain Wall Style Name dialog box that appears and press Enter to create the new curtain wall (see Figure 6-17).

Save this exercise.

Figure 6-17

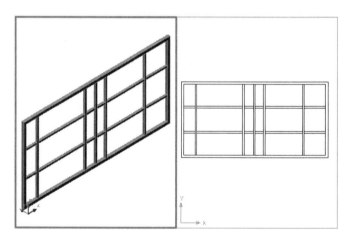

Hands-On

Applying Tool Properties to an Elevation Sketch

1. Start a new drawing using the Architectural Building Model and View (Imperial - ctb) template.

2. Change to the Work Layout.

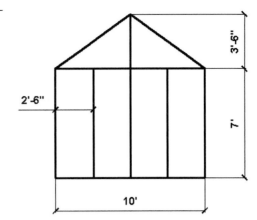

Figure 6-18

3. Select the Front View, and create the line drawing shown in Figure 6-18.
4. RMB on the **Square Grid 5′x 5′ Curtain Wall** Icon from the **Curtain walls** tool pallet you created to bring up its contextual menu.
5. Select **Apply Tool Properties to > Elevation Sketch** from the contextual menu.
6. Select the line drawing you made in Step 3 of this exercise, and press Enter twice.
7. Enter **Y** (Yes) in the command line when asked to Erase the Geometry, and press Enter to create the curtain wall.

Your line work will now create a curtain (see Figure 6-19).

8. Select the new curtain wall, RMB, and select **Infill > Show Markers** from the contextual menu that appears.

The Cell Markers will now become visible (see Figure 6-20).

9. Select the new curtain wall again, RMB, and select **Infill > Merge** from the contextual menu that appears.
10. When the command line reads, "Select cell A," select the leftmost cell marker, and press Enter.

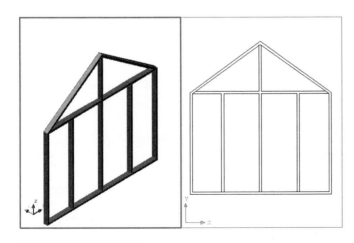

Figure 6-19

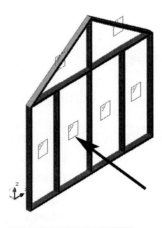

Figure 6-20

11. When the command line reads, "Select cell B," select the next cell marker, and press Enter.

The two curtain wall divisions merge into one cell.

12. Repeat Steps 8, 9, and 10 to merge the upper cell (see Figure 6-21).
13. Select the curtain wall again, RMB, and select **Infill > Override Assignment** from the contextual menu that appears.
14. Select the leftmost marker, and press Enter to bring up the **Infill Assignment Override** dialog box.
15. Check the Bottom check box and press OK to remove the bottom frame (see Figure 6-22).

! **Note:** For clarity, the author has removed the display of the window (infill) itself in these illustrations.

16. Select the curtain wall again, and select Hide Markers from the contextual menu that appears.

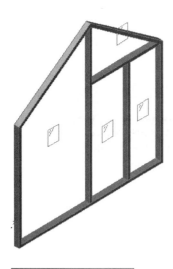

Figure 6-21

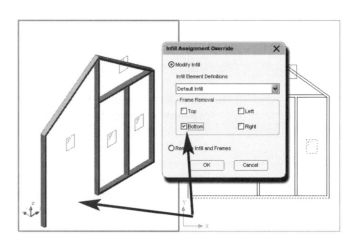

Figure 6-22

Hands-On

Editing Grid in Place

1. Start a new drawing using the Architectural Building Model and View (Imperial - ctb) template.
2. Change to the Model Layout.
3. Change to the Top View.
4. Place a Square Grid 5'x 5' curtain wall 10' high and 15' long.
5. Change to the Front View.
6. Click on the curtain wall to activate its grips.

Figure 6-23

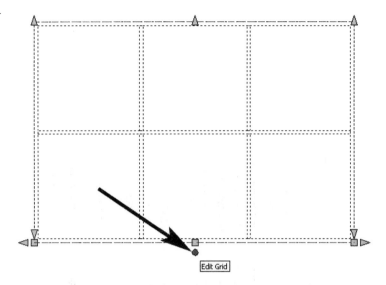

7. Click on the **Edit Grid** grip (see Figure 6-23).
8. Select the left edge of the grid to bring up the **In-Place Edit**.
9. RMB on the grid to bring up the contextual menu that appears, and select **Convert To Manual** (see Figure 6-24).

When you Convert To Manual, + and − icons appear.

10. Select the + icon to add and move a horizontal mullion (see Figure 6-25).
11. Select the **Exit Editing Grid** icon to bring up the Save Changes dialog box, press the **New** button to bring up the **New Division Override** dialog box, enter **New Horizontal Mullion** in the **New Name** data field, and press OK to complete the command (see Figure 6-26).
12. Repeat this process picking a vertical mullion and creating a **New Vertical Mullion** (see Figure 6-27).
13. Change the view to SW Isometric and press the Gouraud icon in the shading toolbar (see Figure 6-28). Save this file.

Figure 6-24

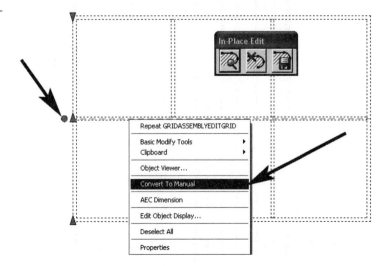

Figure 6-25

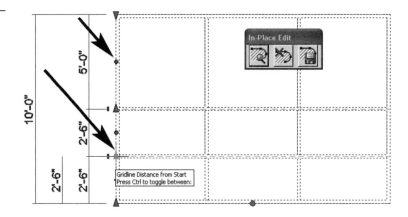

Figure 6-26

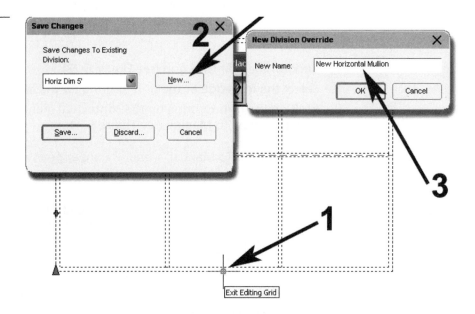

Figure 6-27

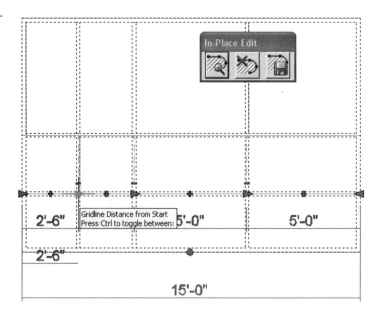

Figure 6-28

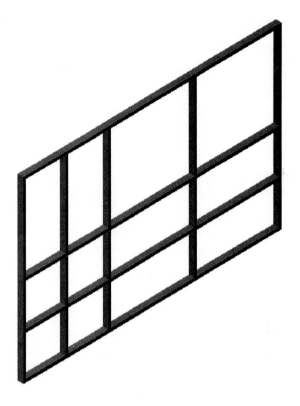

Hands-On

Editing Curtain Wall Styles

1. Use the previous exercise.
2. Select the curtain wall, RMB, and select Edit Curtain Wall Style from the contextual menu that appears to bring up the **Curtain Wall Style properties** dialog box.
3. Select the **Design Rules** tab.
4. Select the Floating Viewer icon at the bottom of the Curtain Wall Style Properties dialog box, and size it so that both the Viewer and the dialog box are open at the same time (see Figure 6-29).
5. Select the **Divisions** icon in the **Element Definitions** tree.

Note the divisions made and saved in the previous exercise, and the **New Division** icon for creating divisions in this dialog box (see Figure 6-30).

6. Select the **Horizontal Division** in the tree and select **New Horizontal Mullion** from the Division Assignment drop-down list shown in Figure 6-31.
7. Select **Vertical Division** from the tree and select **New Vertical Mullion** from its Division Assignment drop-down list.

We will need a Pivot Window for this next part of the exercise so use the Content Browser to drag a Pivot window style into your drawing.

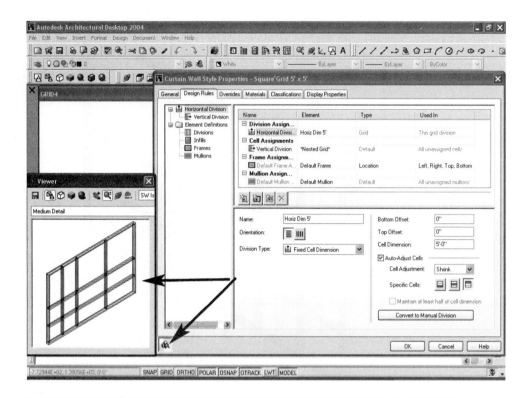

Figure 6-29

Figure 6-30

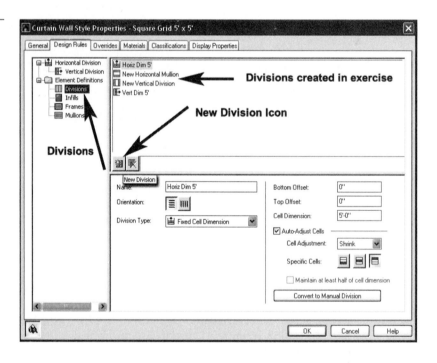

8. Select **Infills** from the tree, select the **New Infill** icon, name the new infill **Pivot Window**, select **Style** from the **Infill Type** drop-down list, and pick the **Pivot - Horizontal** style from the Style list (see Figure 6-32).

Figure 6-31

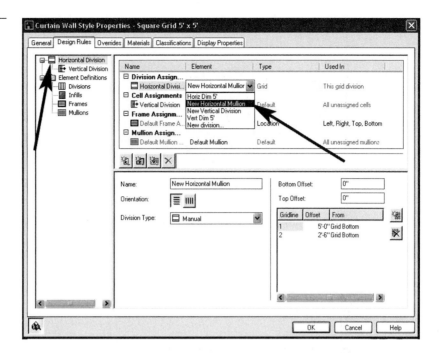

Figure 6-32

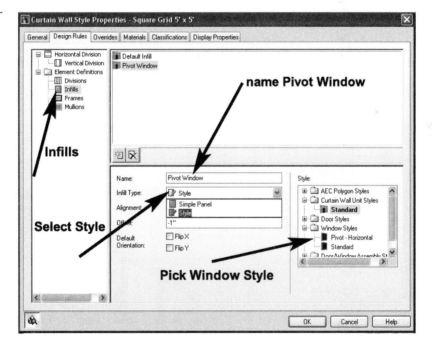

9. Select **Vertical Division** from the tree; select the **New Cell Assignment** icon to create a new cell assignment, select Pivot Window from the New Cell Assignment **Element** drop-down list, and select End from the **Used In** drop-down list (see Figure 6-33).

10. Press the OK buttons to complete the command and return to the Drawing Editor.

11. Select a pivot window that you just installed in the curtain wall, RMB, and select **Edit Object Display** from the contextual menu that appears to bring up the **Object Display** dialog box.

Figure 6-33

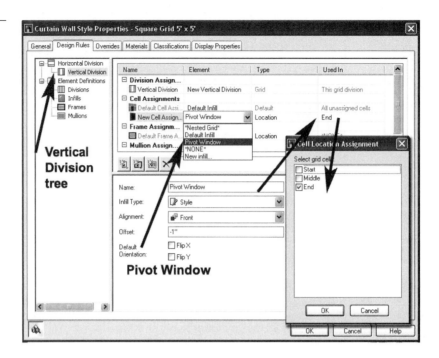

12. Make sure the Model field is selected, select the **Display Properties** tab, and press the **Edit Display Properties** icon at the upper right to bring up the **Display properties** dialog box.

13. Select the **Other** tab.

14. Set the Override Open Percent to 30, and press the OK buttons in all the dialog boxes to return to the Drawing Editor (see Figure 6-34).

Figure 6-34

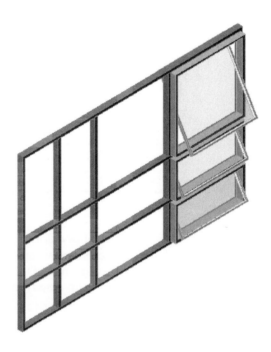

Section

7

Door and Window Assemblies

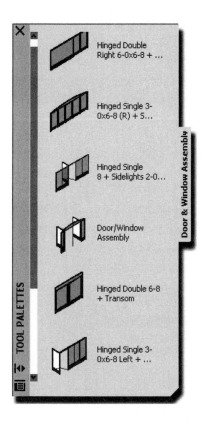

When you finish this section, you should understand the following:

✔ How to create a Primary Grid for a Door/Window Assembly.
✔ How to create a door style for double doors.
✔ How to assign doors to a Door/Window Assembly infill.
✔ How to test the partially complete Door/Window Assembly.
✔ How to add sidelites.
✔ How to size the frame of a Door/Window Assembly.
✔ How to remove the sill of a Door/Window Assembly.
✔ How to use a Door/Window Assembly.

Door/Window Assemblies provide a grid or framework for the insertion of windows or doors that are commonly used in the design of storefront Windows. With this framework, you can create complex window or door assemblies for insertion in a wall or as repetitive elements of the curtain wall.

Window Assemblies insert like doors and windows, and they are customized by using the same methods used to create Curtain Walls.

Hands-On

Creating a Primary Grid

1. Start a new drawing using the Architectural Building Model and View (Imperial - ctb) template.

2. Change to the **Model** Layout.

3. Select **Format > Style Manager** from the **Main** menu to bring up the **Style Manager.**

4. Select **Architectural Objects > Door/Window Assembly Styles.**

5. Select the Door/Window Assembly Styles icon, RMB, and select **New** from the contextual menu that appears.

6. Name the new style **TEST DRWIN ASSEM STYLE.**

7. Double click on the **TEST DRWIN ASSEM STYLE** icon to bring up the **Door/Window Assembly Style Properties** dialog box.

8. Select the **Floating Viewer** icon and place the viewer adjacent to the Door/Window Assembly Style Properties dialog box on the screen (see Figure 7-1).

9. Change to the **Design Rules** tab.

10. Select the Divisions icon and follow the directions in Figure 7-2.

11. Select the Primary Grid icon, and change its Element to the DOUBLE DOORS DIVISION that you just created (see Figure 7-3).

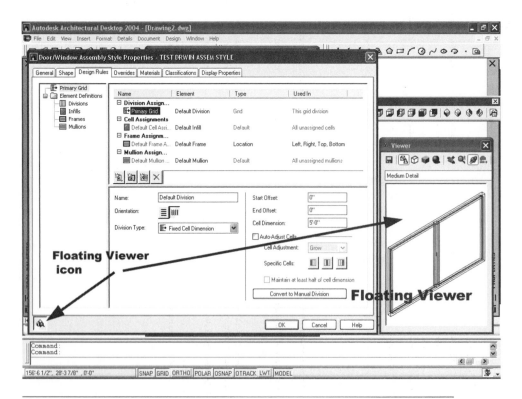

Figure 7-1

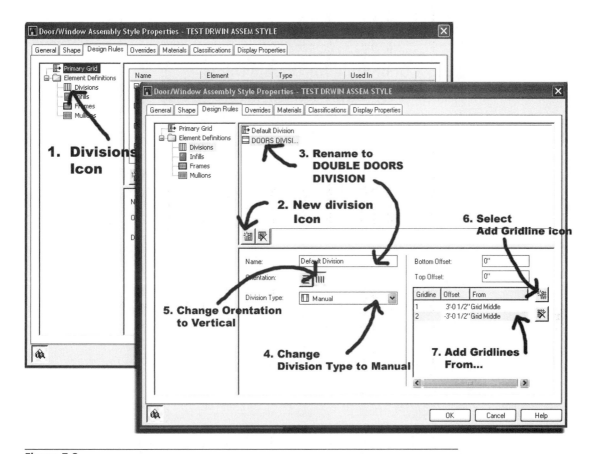

Figure 7-2

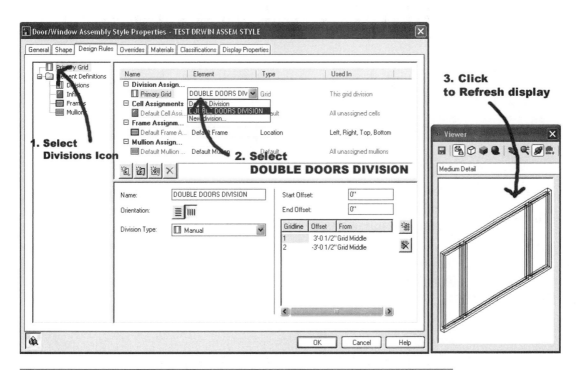

Figure 7-3

Hands-On

Creating a Door Style for Double Doors

1. Select the **Content Browser** icon to bring up the **Content Browser.**
2. Locate the **Architectural Desktop Design Tool Catalog – Imperial > Doors and Windows > Doors > Page 3 folder.**
3. In the Page 3 folder, locate the **Hinged-Single** door.
4. Drag the Hinged-Single door into your Design toolbar. (This makes the door available as a door style in your drawing).

Now you need a Double Door style using this door.

5. Select **Format > Style Manager** from the **Main** menu to bring up the **Style Manager.**
6. Locate the **Architectural Objects > Door Styles > Hinged-Single** icon.
7. Double-click on the Hinged-Single icon to bring up the **Door Styles Properties** dialog box.
8. Change to the **Dimensions** tab.
9. Set the **Frame A- Width** to 0″.

This makes the door frameless.

10. In the Door Styles Properties dialog box, change to the **Design Rules** tab.
11. Select **Double** from the **Door Type** list, and press **OK** to return to the **Style Manager.**
12. Rename the door to **DOUBLE HINGED SINGLE,** and then press the **Apply** and **OK** buttons to return to the Drawing Editor.

Hands-On

Assigning Doors to a Door/Window Assembly Infill

1. Select the **Infills** icon and follow the directions in Figure 7-4.
2. After Creating the DOUBLE DOORS infill, press the Primary Grid icon again, and follow the directions in Figure 7-5.
3. Click on the **New Nested Grid** icon below the **Primary Grid** icon and follow the directions in Figure 7-6.
4. Press OK to return to the Drawing Editor.

Figure 7-4

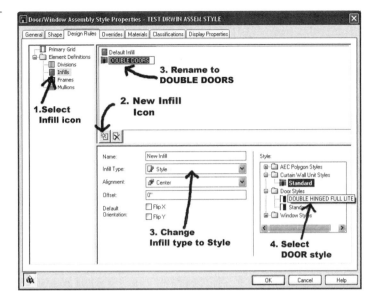

Figure 7-5

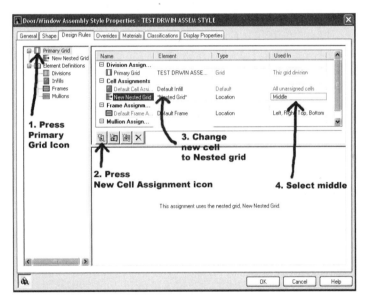

Figure 7-6

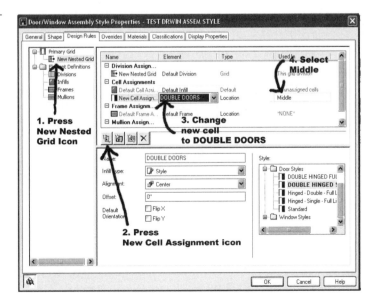

Hands-On

Testing the Partially Complete Door/Window Assembly

1. Select the **Door/Window Assembly** icon from the **Design** menu, and move your cursor over the Properties palette to open it.
2. Select **TEST DRWIN ASSEM STYLE** from the **Style** drop-down list.
3. In the Top View, press Enter, and place the door/window assembly.
4. Change to SW Isometric View (see Figure 7-7).

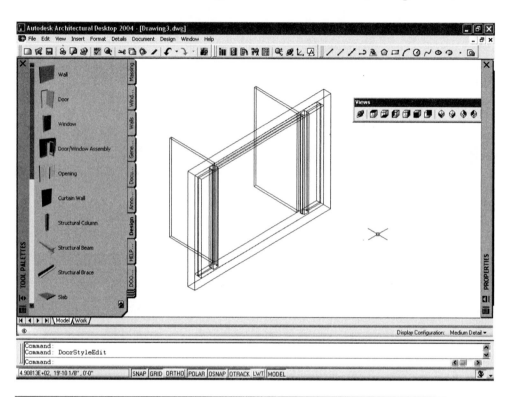

Figure 7-7

Hands-On

Adding Sidelites

1. Select the door/window assembly frame you just placed in the Drawing Editor, RMB, and select **Edit Door/Window Assembly Style** from the contextual menu that appears to bring up the **Door/Window Assembly Style Properties** dialog box.
2. Select the **Design Rules** tab again.
3. Select the **Primary Grid** icon and follow the directions in Figure 7-8.
4. Select the SIDELITE GRID icon below the **Primary Grid** icon and follow the directions in Figure 7-9.
5. Select the Infill icon and create another infill called **BASE** with a panel thickness of 1'-0" (see Figure 7-10).
6. Select the **SIDELITE GRID** icon below the Primary Grid and follow the directions in Figure 7-11.

Figure 7-8

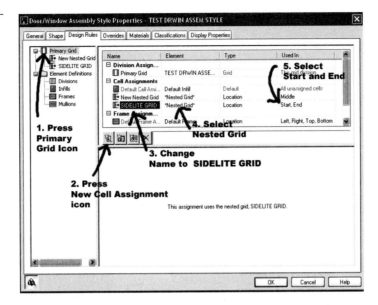

Figure 7-9

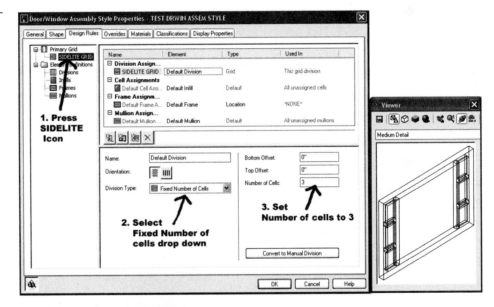

Figure 7-10

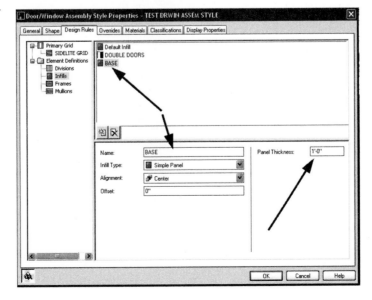

Figure 7-11

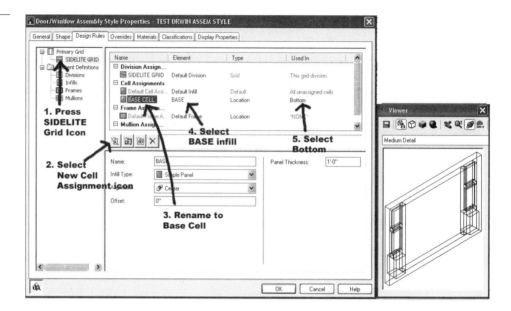

Hands-On

Sizing the Frame of a Door/Window Assembly

1. Click on the Frames icon, and change the **Width** to **2″**, the **Depth** to **6″**, and press OK to return to the Drawing Editor (see Figure 7-12).

Figure 7-12

Hands-On

Removing the Sill of a Door/Window Assembly and Changing the Sidelite

1. Select the Door/Window Assembly frame, RMB, and select **Infill > Show Markers** from the contextual menu that appears (see Figure 7-13).

2. Select the frame again, RMB, and select **Infill > Override Assignment** from the contextual menu that appears.

3. Select the cell marker in the center of the door opening, and press Enter to bring up the **Infill Assignment Override** dialog box.

4. Check the **Frame Removal - Bottom** check box (see Figure 7-14).

5. Press OK to remove the sill and return to the Drawing Editor.

6. Select the frame again, RMB, and select **Infill > Merge** from the contextual menu that appears.

7. Select the top two cells in each sidelite to merge the top cells.

8. Select the frame again, RMB, and select **Infill > Hide Markers** from the contextual menu that appears.

You have now created a new custom Door/Window Assembly. Save this file.

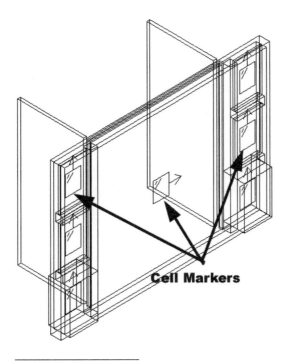

Cell Markers

Figure 7-13

Figure 7-14

Hands-On

Using the New Custom Door/Window Assembly

1. Use the previous file.
2. Change to the Top View.
3. Select the **Wall** icon from the **Design** tool palette, and place a **20'-0"** long standard wall **8"** thick and **10'-0"** high.
4. Select the Door/Window Assembly icon from the Design tool palette.
5. Move your cursor over the Properties palette to open it.
6. Select the following:

   a. **Style** = TEST DRWIN ASSEM STYLE
   b. **Position along the wall = Offset/Center**
   c. Vertical alignment = Sill
   d. Sill Height = 0"

7. Click on the wall to place the assembly (see Figure 7-15).

Figure 7-15

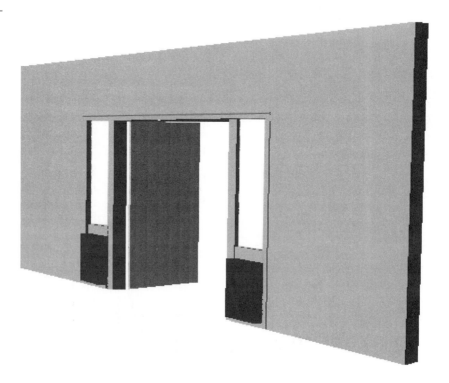

Section 8

Stairs

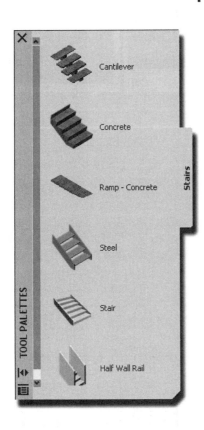

When you finish this section, you should understand the following:

- ✔ How to set AEC Object Settings.
- ✔ How to make a Stair tool palette.
- ✔ How to place a stair object.
- ✔ How to modify a stair with stair grips.
- ✔ How to change an AEC Stair object style.
- ✔ How add a Stair Rail object.
- ✔ How to Edit a stair style.
- ✔ How to place a Multi-landing Stair.
- ✔ Interference conditions for stairs.
- ✔ Anchoring a second stair to an existing landing.
- ✔ How to project a stair edge to a polyline.
- ✔ How to project a stair edge to a Wall or AEC object.
- ✔ How to generate a polyline from a stair object.

Stair objects can be dragged or inserted either from the Design tool palette, or by typing **stair add** on the Command line.

Stairs are an important part of almost every project, and it is here that designers often make mistakes. Autodesk Architectural Desktop 2004's Stair and Railing systems aid in the productivity and accuracy of these objects. Because of the complexity and variance of stairs, there is a multitude of settings. Once understood, and preset, placing and modifying stairs is quite easy.

In Autodesk Architectural Desktop 2004 much refinement has been done to the stair system. Stairs styles are controlled by three factors: style, shape, and turn type. The Content Browser contains eight different preset styles: standard, cantilever, concrete, steel, Half Wall Rail, Ramp Concrete, Ramp Concrete-Curb, and Ramp-Steel. As with the other styles in this program, there are many controls available for the styles in the Stair Styles dialog box. By creating your own styles, stairs can be quickly and efficiently placed into a project.

151

Properties Palette

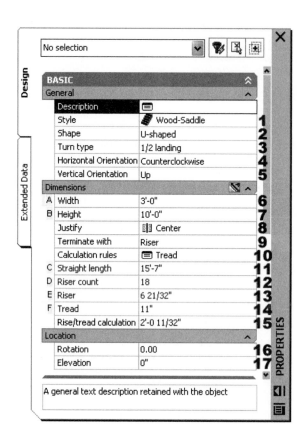
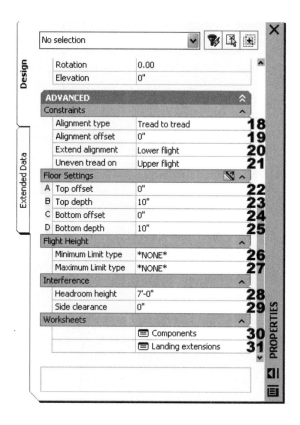

Number	Name	Purpose
1	Style	Select from available stair styles
2	Shape	U-shaped, Multi-landing, Spiral, Straight
3	Turn type	$1/2$ landing, $1/2$ turn, $1/4$ landing, $1/4$ turn
4	Horizontal Orientation	Balanced
5	Vertical Orientation	Stair direction—above or below main floor level
6	Width	Width of stair
7	Height	Height of stair vertically
8	Justify	Right, center, left insertion points
9	Terminate with	Terminate with Riser, Tread, or landing
10	Calculation rules	Brings up Calculation Rules dialog box
11	Straight length	Length of stair set by calculation rules dialog box

Number	Name	Purpose
12	Riser count	Amount of risers calculated by stair calculation rules
13	Riser	Riser height calculated by stair calculation rules
14	Tread	Length of tread set by calculation rules dialog box
15	Rise/tread calculation	Calculation formula used by stair calculation rules
16	Rotation	Rotation of stair
17	Elevation	Starting elevation of stair
18	Alignment type	Alignment between stairs at landings
19	Alignment offset	Offset at Alignment between stairs at landings
20	Extend alignment	Extend alignment on upper or lower stair flight
21	Uneven tread on	Uneven tread on upper or lower flight
22	Top offset	Floor surface depth above top riser or top treads depending on their setting
23	Top depth	Floor surface support depth above top riser or top treads depending on their setting
24	Bottom offset	Floor surface depth below first riser
25	Bottom depth	Floor surface support depth below first riser
26	Minimum Limit type	Riser or flight height minimums
27	Maximum Limit type	Riser or Flight height maximums
28	Headroom height	Used to control interference above the stair
29	Side clearance	Used to control interference at the sides of the stair
30	Components	Information on tread and riser thickness, nosing length, etc.
31	Landing extensions	Information on landings

Before beginning to use the stair object, the AEC Object Settings must be set for the stairs.

Hands-On

Setting the AEC Object Settings for Stairs

1. Select Format > Options from the Main toolbar to bring up the **Options** dialog box.

2. In the Options dialog box select the **AEC Object Settings** tab (see Figure 8-1).

3. In the Stair Settings area select **Flight & Landing Corners** from the Node Osnap drop-down list, and set Measure Stair Height to **Finished Floor to Floor** (see Figure 8-2).

Figure 8-1

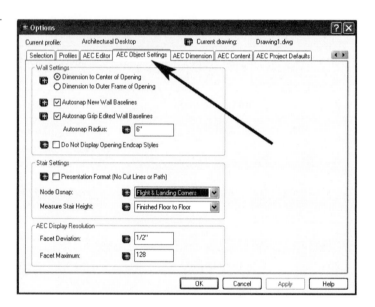

Figure 8-2

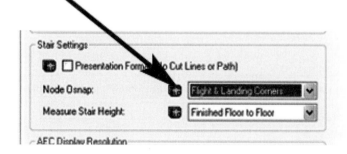

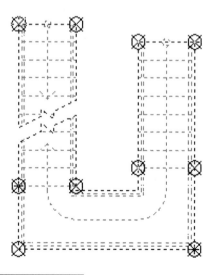

Hands-On

Making a New Stair Tool Palette.

1. Create a new Tool Palette, and name it **Stairs**.
2. Select the Content Browser icon from the Main toolbar to launch the Content Browser.
3. In the **Architectural Desktop Design Tool Catalog - Imperial,** locate the **Stairs** folder in the **Stairs and Railings** folder.
4. From the Stairs folder, drag all the stairs into the new tool palette you created.
5. Click and hold on the tab of your new tool palette and drag a copy to My Tool Catalog in the Content Browser.

Hands-On

Placing a Stair

1. Start a new drawing using the Architectural Building Model and View (Imperial - ctb) template.
2. Change to the Model Layout.
3. Change to Top View.
4. Select the Stair icon in the Stairs tool palette you created and drag your cursor over the Properties palette to open it.
5. Set the following in the Properties palette:

   a. Shape = **U-shaped**
   b. Turn type = **½ landing**
   c. Horizontal Orientation = **Clockwise**
   d. Vertical Orientation = **Up**
   e. Width = **3'-0"**
   f. Height = **10"**
   g. Top offset = **0"**
   h. Top depth = **10"**
   i. Bottom offset = **0"**
   j. Bottom depth = **10"**
   k. Headroom height = **7'-0"**
   l. Side clearance = **0**

6. Click in the viewport and drag the stair to the right, enter 10' in the command line and press Enter twice to complete the command and create the stair (see Figure 8-3).

Figure 8-3

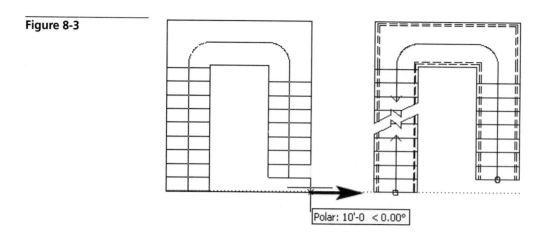

Polar: 10'-0 < 0.00°

Hands-On

Modifying the Stair with the Stair Grips

1. Select the stair object to activate the stair grips. Place and modify six stairs using Figures 8-4 through 8-9 as examples. After placing each stair, change to SW Isometric View to examine your stair. Save this DWG as **STAIR**.

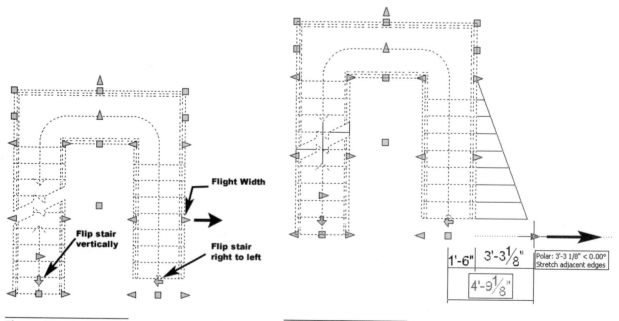

Flight Width

Flip stair vertically

Flip stair right to left

1'-6" 3'-3 1/8" Polar: 3'-3 1/8" < 0.00° Stretch adjacent edges

4'-9 1/8"

Figure 8-4   **Figure 8-5**

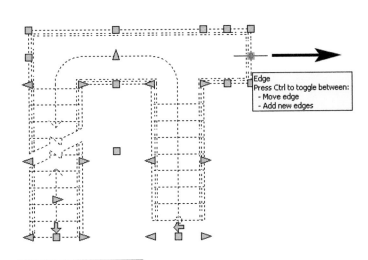

Figure 8-6

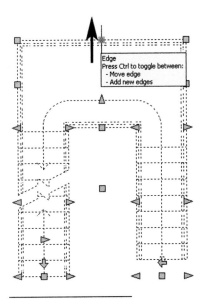

Figure 8-7

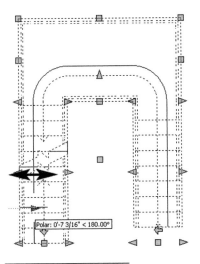

Figure 8-8

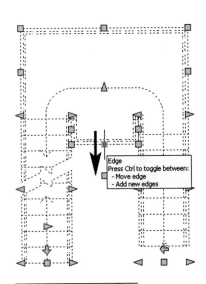

Figure 8-9

Hands-On

Changing Stair Styles

1. Change to SW Isometric View.

2. In your new Stairs tool palette, RMB on the **Half Wall Rail** icon and select **Apply Tool Properties to Stair** from the contextual menu that appears.

3. Select your stair, and press Enter to complete the command.

4. RMB in an empty space in the Drawing editor, and select Object Viewer from the contextual Menu that appears.

Figure 8-10

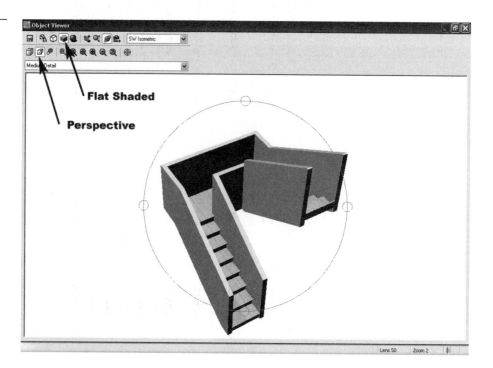

5. Select the stair, and press Enter to open the Object Viewer with the stair.
6. Expand the Object Viewer, and select the Perspective and Flat Shaded icons to display the stair in perspective and color (see Figure 8-10).
7. Close the Object Viewer to return to the drawing editor.
8. Repeat this process with all the other stair styles in your Stairs tool palette. Save the file.

Hands-On

Adding a Stair Rail (Modifying railings is explained in the next section, "Railings.")

1. Change your stair back to the **Stair** style by RMB and applying that style to your stair.
2. Select the stair, RMB, and select **Add Railing** from the contextual menu that appears.
3. Move your cursor over the closed Properties palette to open it.
4. Click on the * **Attached to** drop-down list, and select **Stair flight** (see Figure 8-11).
5. Select the lower corners of the lower stair flight to place a rail (see Figure 8-12).

! **Note:** If you have difficulty placing the rails in 3D or if the rails don't appear, change to Top View, and place the rails when in that view.

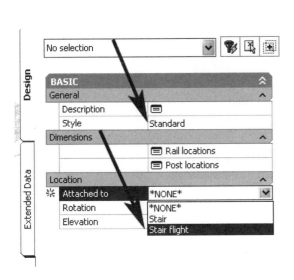

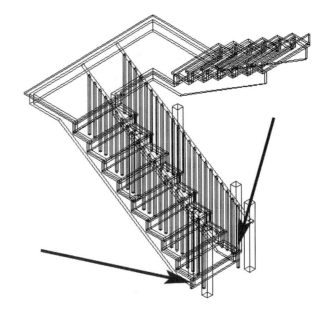

Figure 8-11

Figure 8-12

6. Remove the stair rails and repeat this using the **Stair** and **NONE** options in the Properties palette.

! **Note:** The NONE option is for custom placing of a rail. This railing option is explained in the "Railings" section.

Hands-On

Editing a Stair Style (This can also be done through the Style Manager.)

1. Select your stair, RMB, and select Edit Stair Style from the contextual menu that appears to bring up the Stair Styles dialog box.
2. Select the **Design Rules** tab. This is where the Riser Height, Tread Depth, as well as the stair calculator, are located (see Figure 8-13).
3. Change to the **Stringers** tab. This is where the stair stringers are added, removed, and modified.
4. Set the following for the Left Stringer:

   a. **Housed** option from the Type drop-down list
   b. D - Total = **12″**
   c. F - Total = **12″**

5. Press OK to return to the Drawing Editor and see the stair changes (see Figure 8-14).
6. Select the stair, RMB, and open the Stair Styles dialog box again.
7. Select the **Components** tab. This is where modifications to the tread, riser, and landing thicknesses are controlled. This is also where you con-

Figure 8-13

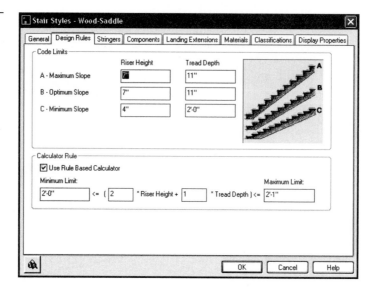

Figure 8-14

trol tread nosing length, and check the box for straight or sloping risers. (Sloping risers are typically used on steel and concrete stairs.)

8. Select the **Landing Extensions** tab. This is where modifications are made relating to the landings.

9. Select the **Materials** tab. This is where the materials for the stair are set.

10. Select the **Display Properties** tab. This is where modifications are made relating to the display of stair components in different views.

Hands-On

Placing a Multi-landing Stair

1. Erase the stair in the previous exercise.

2. Change to the Top View.

3. Select the **Stair** icon from your **Stairs** tool palette.

4. Select the Stair icon in the Stairs tool palette, and drag your cursor over the Properties palette to open it.

5. Set the following:

   a. Shape = **Multi-landing**

   b. Turn type = **¹/₂ landing**

   c. Horizontal Orientation = **Clockwise**

   d. Vertical Orientation = **Up**

   e. Width = **3'-0"**

   f. Height = **10"**

   g. Top offset = **0"**

   h. Top depth =**10"**

   i. Bottom offset = **0"**

   j. Bottom depth = **10"**

   k. Headroom height = **7'-0"**

   l. Side clearance = **0**

7. Click in the viewport and drag the stair vertically (90°) till 7/18 appears to the left of the stair, and click again.

8. Move the cursor in the direction of 90° and enter 5' in the command line and press Enter.

9. Drag the cursor to the right (0°) until 18/18 appears above the stair, and click the mouse to complete the stair.

10. Change to SW Isometric View and press the Flat shaded icon in the Shading toolbar (see Figure 8-15). Save this file.

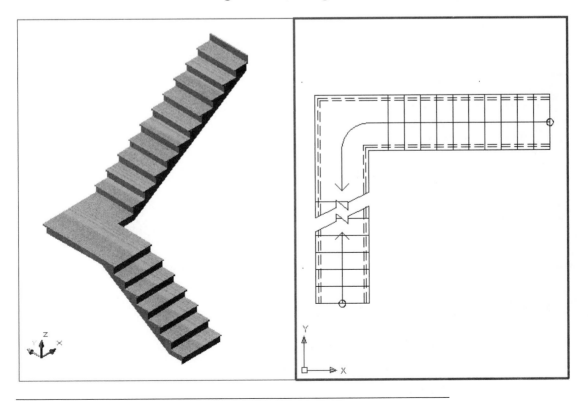

Figure 8-15

Hands-On

Interference Conditions

1.   Using the stair from the previous exercise, change to the Top View.
2.   Place a 20' high wall as shown in Figure 8-16.
3.   Select the wall, RMB, and select Interference Condition > Add from the Contextual menu that appears.
4.   Select the lower stair flight, and press Enter.
5.   Enter **S** (Subtractive) in the command line and press Enter to complete the command.

The wall is cut by the stair (Figure 8-17), and the Interference distance above the stair is set in the Stair properties under Interference Headroom height (Figure 8-18).

> **Note:** Stair Interference Conditions are also available for Slabs.

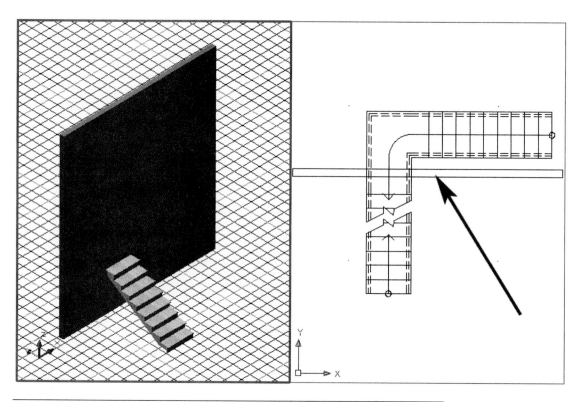

Figure 8-16

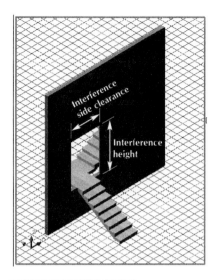

Figure 8-17

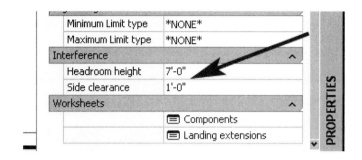

Figure 8-18

Hands-On

Anchoring a Second Stair to an Existing Landing

1. Use the stair created in "Placing a Multi-landing Stair" in this section.
2. Change to the Work Layout.
3. Change to the Top View.
4. Create a new straight **Standard** stair with **Vertical Orientation** set to **Up (see Figure 8-19).**
5. Select the new stair, RMB, and select Stair landing Anchor > Anchor to Landing from the contextual menu that appears.
6. Select the first stair's landing to attach the second stair to the landing.
7. Once attached, you can change to the top view and move the second stair into a desired location (see Figure 8-20).

Figure 8-19

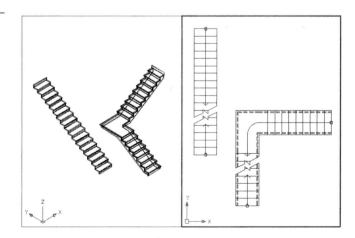

Figure 8-20

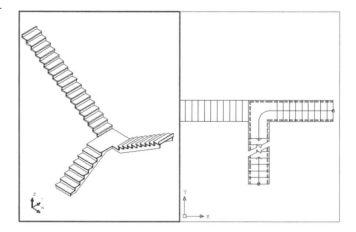

Hands-On

Projecting a Stair Edge to a Polyline

1. Start a new drawing using the Architectural Building Model and View (Imperial - ctb) template.

2. Change to the Model Layout.

3. Change to Top View.

4. Select the **Polyline** icon from the **Draw** toolbar and draw the shape shown in Figure 8-21.

5. Select the **Stair** icon from the **Stairs** tool palette and add a **U-shaped** stair 8′ high inside the polyline as shown in Figure 8-22.

6. Select the stair, RMB, and select **Customize Edge** > **Project** from the contextual menu that appears.

7. In the Top View select the front of the stair landing, then select the curved part of the polyline, and then press Enter to project the landing (see Figure 8-23).

Figure 8-21

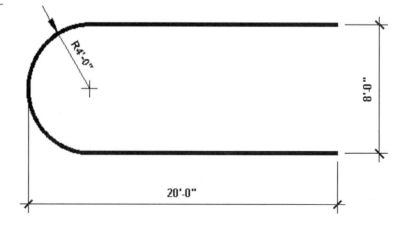

Figure 8-22

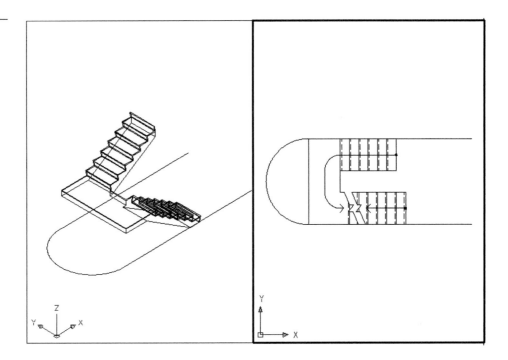

Figure 8-23

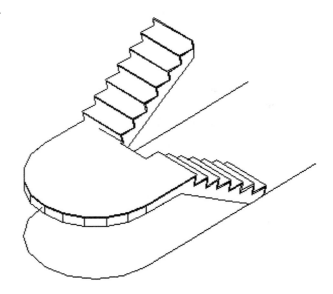

Hands-On

Projecting a Stair Edge to a Wall or AEC Object

1. Using the previous exercise, select the polyline to activate its grips.
2. Select an end grip, and modify the polyline as shown in Figure 8-24.
3. Select the **Wall** icon from the **Walls** tool palette, RMB, and select **Apply Tool properties to > Linework**.
4. Select the polyline and press Enter.
5. Enter **Y** (Yes) in the command line, and press Enter to create the wall.

Figure 8-24

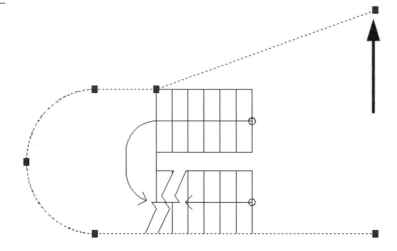

6. While the wall is still selected, move your cursor over the Properties palette to open it.

7. Set the following:

    a. Style = **CMU-8 Rigid-1.5 Air-2 Brick-4**

    b. Base height = **8′-0″**

    c. Justify = **Left**

Note: If you don't have the CMU-8 Rigid-1.5 Air-2 Brick-4 style in your Walls tool palette, you can find it in the Architectural Desktop Design Tool Catalog - Imperial > Walls > CMU > Page 4.

You now have a stair within a masonry enclosure (see Figure 8-25).

8. Select the stair, RMB, and select **Customize Edge** > Project from the contextual menu.

9. Select the right-hand edge of the stair run, then select the wall opposite it, and then press Enter to complete the command.

Figure 8-25

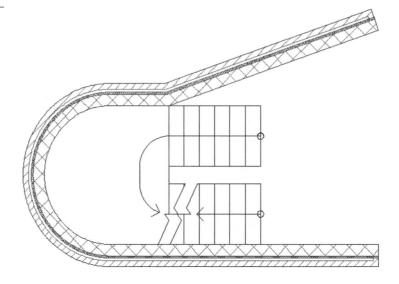

Figure 8-26

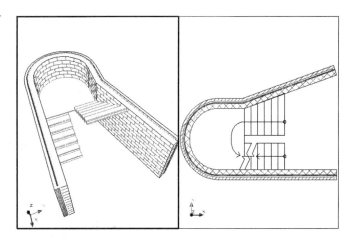

The stair run projects itself to the wall (see Figure 8-26).

Hands-On

Generating a Polyline from a Stair Object

The Generate Polyline command is very useful when you have created a stair, and need a polyline to create walls, or to create an opening in a slab.

1. Use the previous exercise.
2. Erase the walls leaving just the stair.
3. Select the **Slab** icon from the **Design** tool palette, and place a **Standard 6″, Direct Mode, Top Justified** slab underneath the stair as shown in Figure 8-27.
4. Select the stair, RMB, and select **Customize Edge > Generate Polyline** from the contextual menu that appears.
5. Select the outer edge of the stair, and then repeat Step 4, and touch the inside of the lower stair run. Press Enter to complete the com-

Figure 8-27

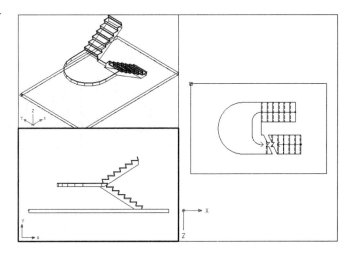

Figure 8-28

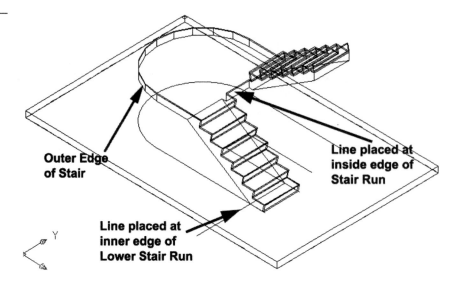

Outer Edge
of Stair

Line placed at
inside edge of
Stair Run

Line placed at
inner edge of
Lower Stair Run

mand, and then place a line at the inner edge of the stair run (see Figure 8-28).

6. Select the **Layers** icon from the Object Properties toolbar and **Freeze** the Stair layer (A-Flor-Strs) to hide the stair.

7. Using **Extend** and **Trim**, clean up the polylines created by the Generate polyline option of Customize Edges in Steps 4 and 5.

8. Type Pedit in the Command line and create two Polylines as shown in Figure 8-29.

9. Select the Slab object, RMB, and select Hole > Add from the contextual menu that appears.

10. Select the **Closed Polyline**, and press Enter.

11. Enter **Y** (Yes) in the command line, and press Enter to create the hole in the slab.

You have now made a hole in the slab exactly matching the stair through the use of the Generate poly option of the Customizing Edge command.

Figure 8-29

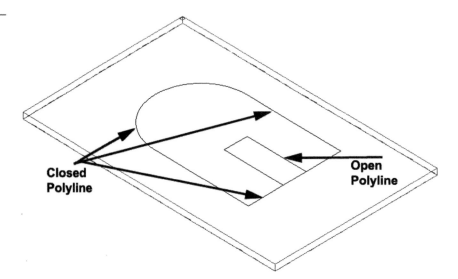

Closed
Polyline

Open
Polyline

Finishing the Stairway

12. Un-Freeze the stair layer to unhide the stair.

13. Select the **Wall** icon from the **Walls** tool palette, RMB, and select **Apply Tool Properties to > Linework** from the Contextual menu that appears.

14. Select the open polyline, enter **Y** (Yes) in the command line, and press Enter to create a wall.

15. While the wall is still selected, move your cursor over the Properties palette to open it.

16. Set the following parameters:

   a. Style = **Standard**
   b. Width = **6″**
   c. Base height = **8′-0″**
   d. Justify = **Left**

You have now created a stair, slab, and walls (see Figure 8-30).

17. Select the **Railing** icon from the Design tool palette, and move your cursor over the Properties palette to open it.

18. Select the following:

   a. Style = **Standard**
   b. Side offset = **2″**
   c. Automatic placement = **Yes**

19. Select the stair, and press Enter.

20. Array two more copies of the stairway in the Y direction to create the final stairway (see Figure 8-31).

Figure 8-30

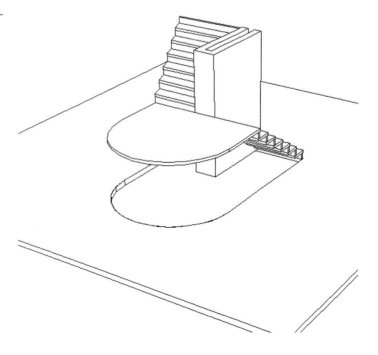

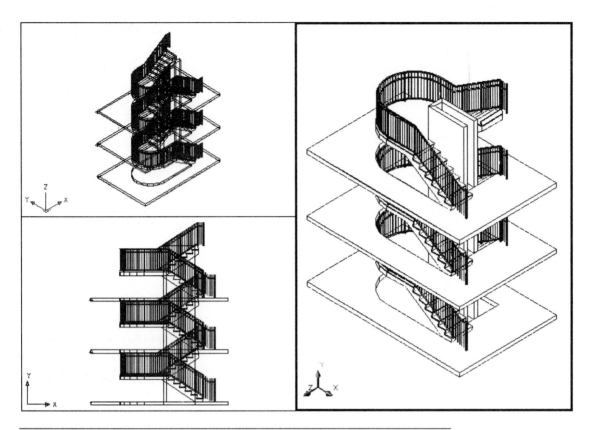

Figure 8-31

Section 9

Railings

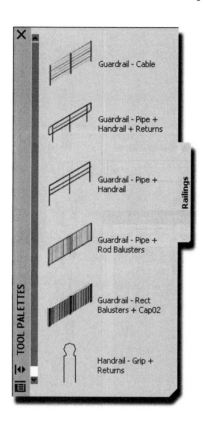

When you finish this section, you should understand the following:

- ✔ How to make a Railing tool palette.
- ✔ How to place a Railing.
- ✔ How to edit a Railing Style.
- ✔ How to modify Balusters.
- ✔ How to add a Railing to a stair and stair flight.
- ✔ How to add a Railing to a landing.
- ✔ How to add a railing and landing support—Anchor to Object.
- ✔ How to create a railing using a polyline.
- ✔ How to edit a railing profile in place.

Number	Name	Purpose
1	Style	Select from available Railing Styles
2	Rail locations	Locations of rails fixed by Style
3	Post locations	Locations of posts fixed by Style
4	Attached to	None, Stair, or stair flight
5	Rotation	Rotation of Railing
6	Elevation	Elevation of Railing

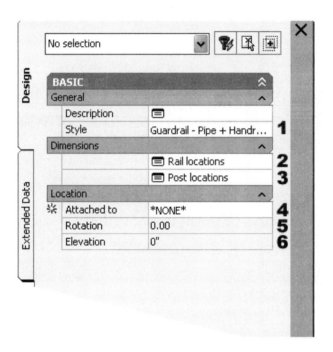

Hands-On

Making a New Railing Tool Palette

1. Create a new tool palette, and name it **Railings**.
2. Select the Content Browser icon from the Main toolbar to launch the Content Browser.
3. In the **Architectural Desktop Design Tool Catalog - Imperial,** locate the **Stairs** folder in the **Stairs and Railings** folder.
4. From the Railings folder, drag all the railings into the new tool palette you created.
5. Click and hold on the tab of your new tool palette and drag a copy to My Tool Catalog in the Content Browser.

Placing a Railing

1. Start a new drawing using the Architectural Building Model and View (Imperial - ctb) template.
2. Change to the Model Layout.
3. Change to Top View.
4. Select any Railing icon in the Railings tool palette you created and drag your cursor over the Properties palette to open it.
5. In the Properties palette select **Standard** from the Style drop-down list and *NONE* from the **Attached to** drop-down list.
6. Click in the Drawing Editor, drag your cursor to the right (0°), enter 10' in the command line, and press Enter three times to complete the command.

You have now placed a 10'-0" long Standard Railing.

Note: When you select *NONE*, you can use your railing as a fence, porch rail, and so on.

Editing a Railing Style

1. Select the railing you placed in the previous exercise, RMB, and select **Edit Railing Style** from the contextual menu that appears to bring up the **Railing Styles** dialog box.
2. Press the **Floating Viewer** icon to bring up the **Viewer**.
3. Resize the Viewer so that both Viewer and Railing Styles Dialog box are side by side, and open at the same time. In the Viewer, set the drop-down list to SW Isometric View, and press the Flat shading icon (see Figure 9-1).
4. In the Railing Styles dialog box, select the Rail Locations tab.
5. Check and uncheck **Guardrail**, **Handrail**, and **Bottomrail** check boxes and view the changes in the Viewer.
6. Change the **Side for Offset** by clicking on the Side for Offset drop-down lists and view the changes in the Viewer.
7. Enter **8** in the **Number of Rails** value entry field, and **4"** in the **Spacing of Rails** value entry field. Press Enter, and view the changes in the Viewer (see Figure 9-2).
8. Reset to all the original settings.
9. Change to the Post Locations tab.
10. Check and uncheck **Guardrail**, **Handrail**, and **Bottomrail** check boxes and view the changes in the Viewer.
11. Check and uncheck **Fixed Posts**, **Dynamic Posts**, and **Balusters** check boxes and value entry fields. View the changes in the Viewer.

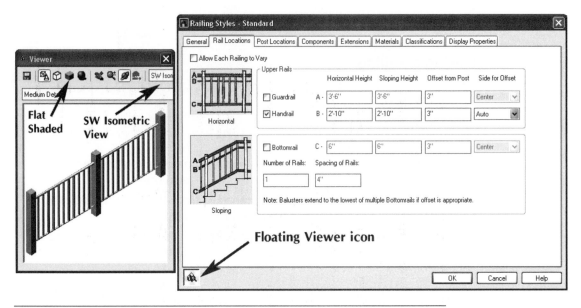

Figure 9-1

Figure 9-2

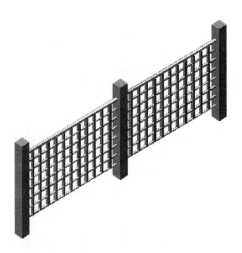

12. Change to the Post Locations tab.

13. Check the **Fixed Posts** check box, and change the value in the **Extension of ALL Posts from Top Railing** value entry field to 18″.

14. Check the **Dynamic Posts** check box, and change the value in the **Maximum Center to Center Spacing** value entry field to 2′-0″. View the changes in the Viewer (see Figure 9-3).

15. Reset to all the original settings.

16. Change to the Components tab.

17. Select the D - Fixed Post field.

18. Select ***circular*** from the drop-down list under **Profile Name**, and press Enter. Set its width to 1′-0″, and again press Enter.

19. View the changes in the viewer (see Figure 9-4).

20. Reset to all the original settings.

21. Change to the **Extensions** tab.

Figure 9-3

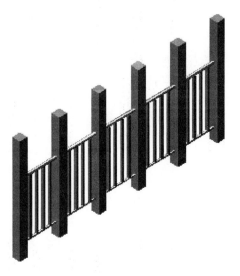

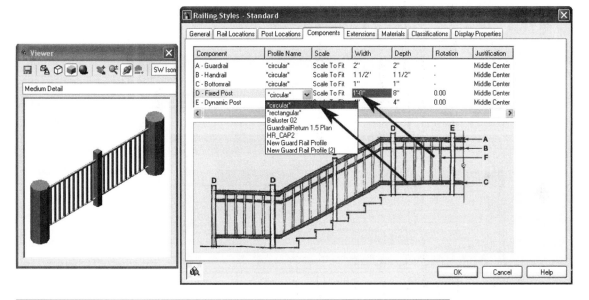

Figure 9-4

The settings in this tab are used to set the extensions to the railings when the rails are connected to stairs. These extension dimensions are usually governed by the building codes (see Figure 9-5).

22. Change to the **Materials** tab.

23. Select the **Fixed Post** field and press the **Edit Material** icon to bring up the **Material Definition Properties** dialog box. Press the Edit Display Properties icon to bring up the **Display Properties** dialog box (see Figure 9-6).

24. Select the **Other** tab. In the Other tab select **Woods & Plastics. Architectural Woodwork. Wood Stairs and Railings. Ash** from the **Surface Rendering - Rendering Material** drop-down list (see Figure 9-7).

Figure 9-5

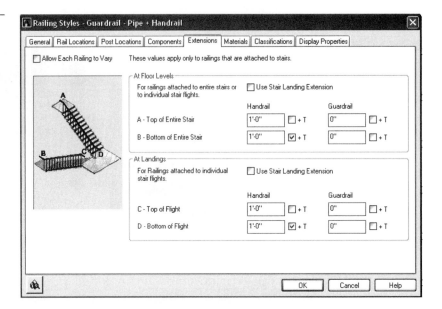

Figure 9-6

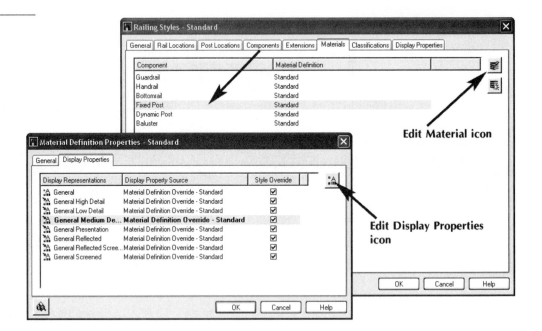

Edit Material icon

Edit Display Properties
icon

Figure 9-7

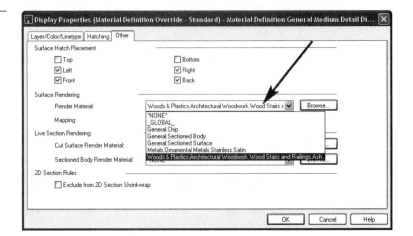

Figure 9-8

25. Press the OK buttons in the Display Properties and Material Definition Properties dialog boxes to return to the Railing Styles dialog box. View the material changes in the Viewer (see Figure 9-8).

Hands-On

Modifying Balusters

1. Return to the Drawing Editor.
2. RMB on the Guardrail - Wood Balusters 02 icon in the Railings tool palette you created, and select Apply Tool Properties to > Railing from the contextual menu that appears. (If this Railing style is not available in the tool palette, get it from the **Architectural Desktop Design Tool Catalog - Imperial**).
3. Select the railing that you placed in "Placing a Railing" in this section, and press Enter.

The Railing changes to the new railing style.

4. Select the railing again, RMB, and select **Edit Railing Style** from the contextual menu that appears to bring up the **Railing Styles** dialog box.
5. In the Railing Styles dialog box, press the **Floating Viewer** icon to bring up the **Viewer**.
6. Again resize the Viewer so that both Viewer and Railing Styles dialog box are side by side, and open at the same time. In the Viewer set the drop-down list to SW Isometric View, and press the Flat shading icon.
7. View the Railing (see Figure 9-9).
8. In the Railing Styles dialog box select the **Display Properties** tab and press the **Edit Display Properties** icon to bring up **Display properties** dialog box. Select the **Other** tab (see Figure 9-10).
9. Press the **Remove** button to remove the Baluster 02 block.

Figure 9-9

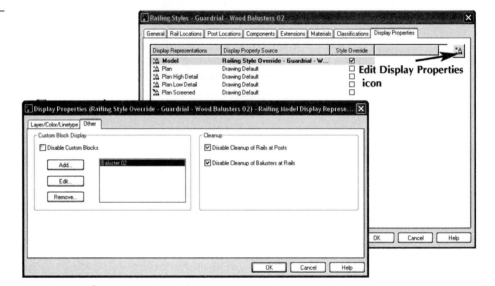

Figure 9-10

Figure 9-11

10. Press OK and view the railing in the Viewer again. This time the balusters are the default balusters (see Figure 9-11).

If you Press the Edit button in the Display Properties dialog box, you can add your own balusters made from 3D solid model or surface model blocks.

Hands-On

Adding a Railing to a Stair and Stair Flight

1. Start a new drawing using the Architectural Building Model and View (Imperial - ctb) template.
2. Change to the Work Layout.
3. Change to Top View.
4. Place a **Standard** Style U-shaped stair with 3'-0"-wide stair flights, a total of 9'-0" overall in width, and 10' height.
5. Select the Guardrail icon in the Railings tool palette you created and move your cursor over the properties palette to open it.
6. Select **Stair** from the **Attached to** drop-down list.
7. Select the Outside side of the stair and inside side of the stair to place the rail (see Figure 9-12).

Note: You can add a Railing to a stair in the 3D View, but it is easier in the Top View.

8. Erase the railing, and repeat this process using the **Stair flight** option from the Properties palette (see Figure 9-13).

Figure 9-12

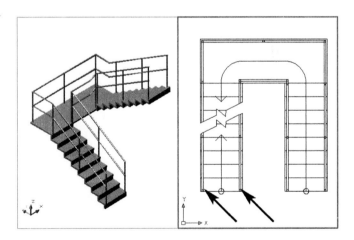

Figure 9-13

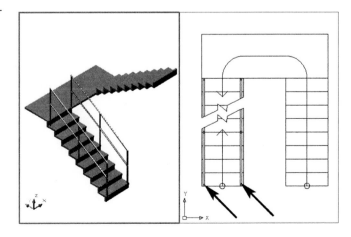

Hands-On

Adding a Railing to a Landing

1. Erase the previous railing.

2. Activate the SW Isometric View.

3. Type **UCS** in the command line and press Enter twice to make sure the SW Isometric View is in the **World** UCS.

4. Measure the railing landing. Type ID in the command line, press Enter, and snap to any top corner of the landing. Read the **Z** dimension (5'-0" for my landing). See Figure 9-14.

5. Activate the Top View.

6. Turn the End Point Osnap on.

7. Select the Guardrail icon in the Railings tool palette you created and move your cursor over the properties palette to open it.

8. Select **NONE** from the **Attached to** drop-down list.

9. Start at the corner, and place a rail as shown in Figure 9-15.

10. Double-click on the Railing to bring up the Properties palette for the railing.

11. Enter 5' in the **Elevation** data entry field—the Railing will move to the top of the landing (see Figure 9-16). Save the file.

Figure 9-14

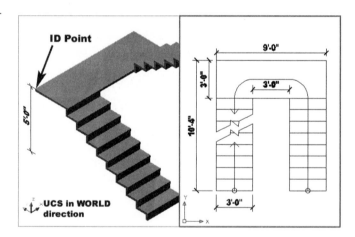

Figure 9-15

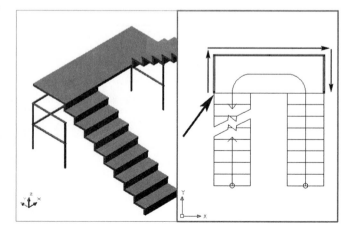

Figure 9-16

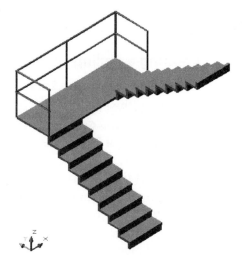

You can return to the Top View and use the Stretch command to adjust the railing lengths.

Hands-On

Adding a Railing and Landing Support—Anchor to Object

1. Undo to Step 9 of the previous exercise.
2. Select the railing, RMB, and select Railing Anchor > Anchor to Object from the contextual menu that appears.
3. Select the landing and press Enter.
4. Enter **Y** (Yes) in the command line and press Enter.
5. Enter **F** (Follow surface) in the command line and press Enter.

The Railing moves to the top of the landing, but the posts extend to the ground (see Figure 9-17).
  Save the file.

Figure 9-17

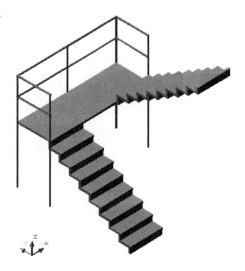

Creating a Railing Using a Polyline

1. Clear the Drawing Editor.
2. Using the Polyline tool, create the shape shown in Figure 9-18.
3. RMB on the **Guardrail - Cable** icon in your railings palette and select **Apply Tool Properties to > Polyline** from the contextual menu that appears.
4. Select the Polyline and press Enter.
5. Enter **Y** (Yes) in the command line to erase the layout geometry and press Enter to create the railing (see Figure 9-19).
6. Select the railing, RMB, and select **Edit Railing Style** from the contextual menu that appears to bring up the **Railing Styles** dialog box.
7. Select the Post Locations tab.
8. Check the **Dynamic Posts** check box and enter 1'-0" in the **Maximum Center to Center Spacing** data entry field.

Your Railing changes to include more posts (see Figure 9-20).

Figure 9-18

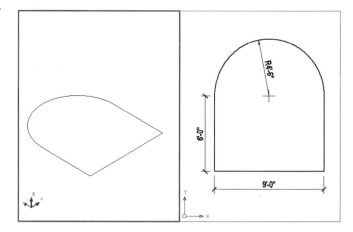

Figure 9-19

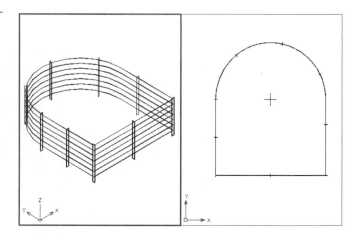

Figure 9-20

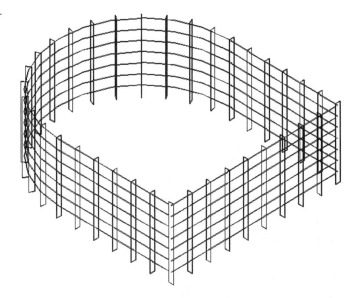

Hands-On

Editing a Railing Profile in Place

1. Clear the Drawing editor.
2. Change to the Model Layout.
3. Change to Top View.
4. Select the **Guardrail - Wood balusters 02** Railing icon in the Railings tool palette you created and drag your cursor over the Properties palette to open it.
5. Select **Standard** from the Style drop down-list and ***NONE*** from the **Attached to** drop-down list.
6. Click in the Drawing Editor, drag your cursor to the right (0°), enter 12′ in the command line, press Enter three times to complete the command.
7. Change to the Work Layout, Zoom Extents in the SW Isometric View, and Zoom Window the Top Rail in the Right View.
8. In the Right View, select the railing, RMB, and select Edit Profile in Place from the contextual menu that appears.
9. Select the top rail of the railing. The top rail end will turn light blue with magenta grips (see Figure 9-21).

You can drag on the grips to edit the profile, or do the following:

10. Draw a circle and a rectangle similar to that shown in Figure 9-22.
11. Select the blue shaded top rail, RMB, and select **Add Ring** from the contextual menu that appears.
12. Select the circle you drew in Step 10, enter **Y** (Yes) in the command line, and press Enter.
13. Enter **J** (Join) in the command line and press Enter.

Figure 9-21

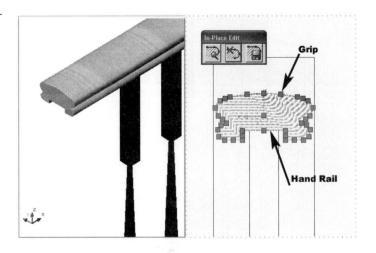

Figure 9-22

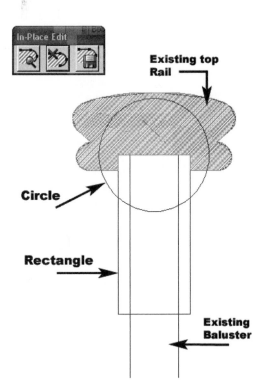

14. Repeat Steps 11 through 13 of this exercise for the rectangle.
15. Select the blue shaded top rail again, RMB, and select **Save As New Profile** from the contextual menu that appears to bring up the **New Profile** dialog box.
16. Type the name TEST PROFILE, and press OK.

The profile will probably change shape (see Figure 9-23). To fix this you must adjust its size in the Railing Styles dialog box.

17. Select the railing, RMB, and select **Edit Railing Style** from the contextual menu that appears to bring up the **Railing Styles** dialog box.
18. Select the **Components** tab.

Figure 9-23

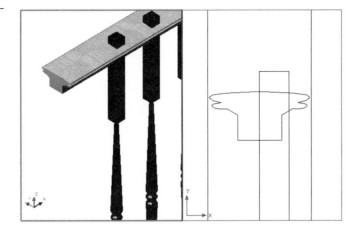

19. Select the **A- Guardrail** field.
20. Make sure that the **Profile Name** reads **TEST PROFILE**.
21. Select **Scale to Fit** from the **Scale** drop-down list.
22. Set The **Width** to **3"** and the **Depth** to **5"**.
23. Press OK to complete the command.

You have now edited the top rail in place (see Figure 9-24).

Figure 9-24

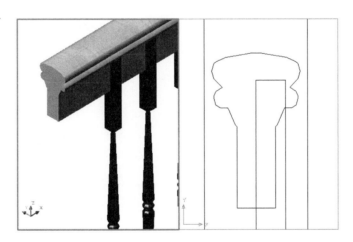

10

Roofs and Roof Slab Objects

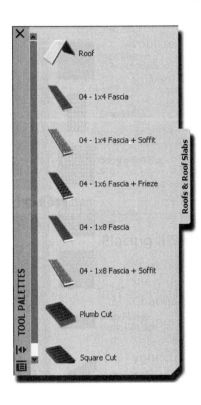

When you finish this section, you should understand the following:

- ✔ How to make a Roof and Roof Slabs tool palette.
- ✔ How to place a Roof object.
- ✔ How to modify a Roof object.
- ✔ How to edit a Roof Edge.
- ✔ How to convert to Roof and surfu.
- ✔ How to use convert to roof slabs.
- ✔ Using the roofslabmodifyedges command.
- ✔ How to use Apply Tool Properties.
- ✔ How to cut a hole in a roof slab.
- ✔ Adding Edge Profiles in place.
- ✔ How to create a Roof dormer.

Roofs

Number	Name	Purpose
1	Thickness	Thickness of the roof structure
2	Edge cut	Square (perpendicular to the roof) or Plumb (parallel to the walls)
3	Shape	Single slope, Double slope, or Gable
4	Overhang	Distance beyond roof edge
5	Lower Slope—Plate height	Height above elevation
6	Lower Slope—Rise	Vertical rise per foot dimension
7	Lower Slope—Run	Horizontal dimension
8	Slope	Angle in degrees of slope
9	Rotation	Rotation of roof
10	Elevation	Elevation

Roof Slabs

Number	Name	Purpose
1	Style	Style created in the Style Manager
2	Mode	Projected (elevated) or direct (at 0 elevation)
3	Thickness	Thickness of the roof structure
4	Vertical offset	Offset from wall top
5	Horizontal offset	Offset from wall edge
6	Justify	Top, Center, Bottom, Slopeline
7	Base height	Height above 0 elevation
8	Direction	Direction of slope
9	Overhang	Distance beyond wall edge
10	Baseline edge	Edge type at baseline
11	Perimeter edge	Edge type at perimeter
12	Slope—Rise	Vertical height per foot dimension
13	Slope—Run	Horizontal run per foot dimension
14	Slope	Slope angle in degrees
15	Rotation	Rotation of roof slab
16	Elevation	Elevation of roof slab

Roofs

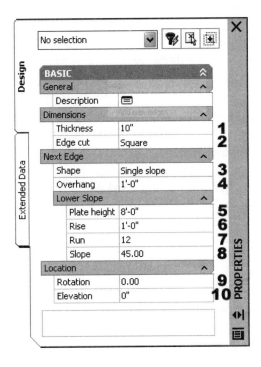

Roof Slabs

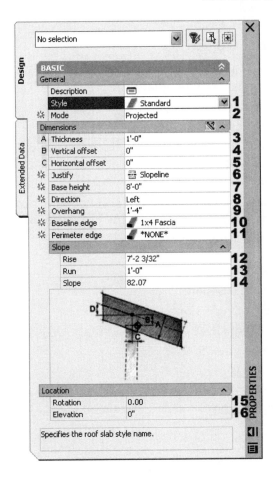

Hands-On

Making a New Roof and Roof Slabs Tool Palette

1. Create a new tool palette, and name it **Roof & Roof Slabs.**
2. Select the Content Browser icon from the Main toolbar to launch the Content Browser.
3. In the **Autodesk Architectural Desktop Stock Tool Catalog** locate the **Roof object** in the **Architectural Object Tools** folder.
4. Drag all the Roof objects into the new tool palette you created.
5. In the **Architectural Desktop Design Tool Catalog - Imperial,** locate the **Roof Slabs** folder in the **Roof and Roof Slabs** folder.
6. Drag all the Roof Slabs into the new tool palette you created.
7. Click and hold on the tab of your new tool palette and drag a copy to My Tool Catalog in the Content Browser.

Roofs are intelligent AEC Objects. There are several ways to place them, and many controls to modify them. It is probably easiest to place a roof, then modify it rather than set the Roof controls before placement.

Do the following lesson to experience how to Add, Convert, and Modify Roof objects.

Hands-On

Placing a Roof Object

1. Start a new drawing using the Architectural Building Model and View (Imperial - ctb) template.
2. Change to the Model Layout.
3. Change to Top View.
4. Using the Wall object, place the floor plan shown in Figure 10-1. Make the walls 6″ wide and 9′-0″ high.
5. Set Object Snap to **End Point**.
6. Select the Roof icon in the Roof and Roof Slabs tool palette you created and drag your cursor over the Properties palette to open it.
7. Set the following:

   a. Thickness = **10″**
   b. Edge cut = **Square**
   c. Shape = **Single slope**
   d. Overhang = **1′-0″**
   e. Plate height = **9′-0″**
   f. Rise = **1′-0″**
   g. Run = **12**
   h. Slope = **45.00**

Figure 10-1

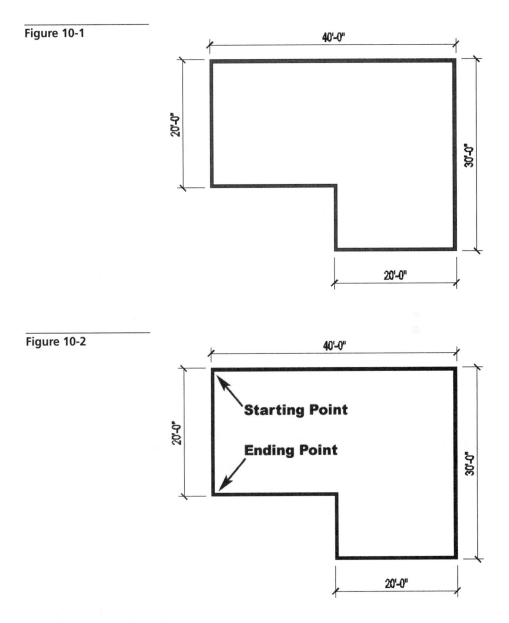

Figure 10-2

8. Starting at the top left outside corner shown in Figure 10-2, move clockwise until you get back to the last point shown in the figure, then press Enter or the space bar on your keyboard. You have now placed a roof object.

Hands-On

Modifying a Roof Object

1. Change to the **Work** Layout, and zoom extents in both viewports.
2. In the **SW Isometric View**, select the **Flat Shaded, Edges On** icon from the Shade menu to shade the SW Isometric View.

Figure 10-3

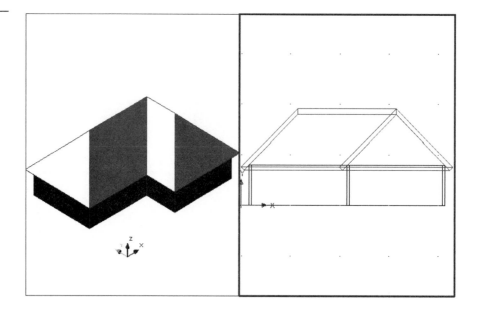

3. Change the other viewport to Front View (see Figure 10-3).
4. Double-click on the roof to bring up its Properties palette.
5. In the Properties palette, change the **Shape** to **Double,** and the **Upper slope's Upper height** to **12'**, and **Slope** to **55.00.** Notice the change to the roof (see Figure 10-4).
6. In the Front View viewport, zoom close to the edge of the Roof.
7. Again, double-click on the roof to bring up its Properties palette.
8. Change the **Edge cut** to **Plumb**, and notice the change (see Figure 10-5).

Figure 10-4

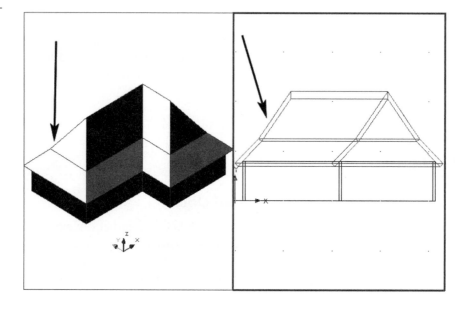

Figure 10-5

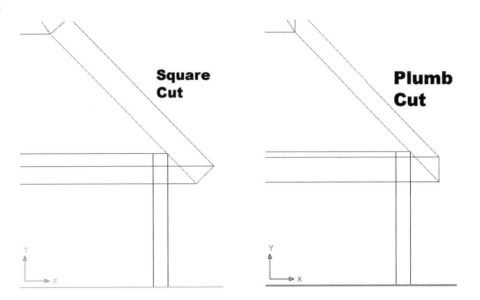

Hands-On

Editing a Roof Edge

1. Double-click and reset the Roof Object to single slope in the Properties palette.
2. Select the roof, RMB, and select **Edit Edges/Faces** from the menu that appears.
3. Select a roof edge and press Enter to bring up the Roof Edges and Faces dialog box (see Figure 10-6).
4. Set **Slope** to **90**, and press OK to return to the Drawing Editor.

The roof now has a gable end, but there is no infill between the top of the lower end wall and the underside of the roof (see Figure 10-7).

Figure 10-6

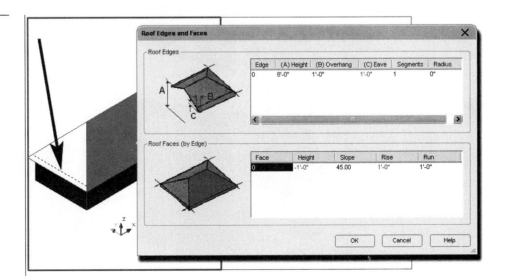

Figure 10-7

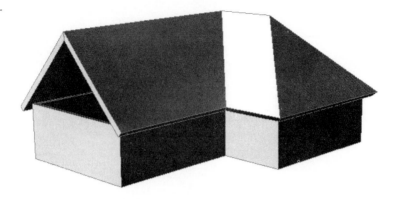

5. Select the end wall, RMB, and select Modify Roof line from the con-textual menu that appears.
6. Enter **A** (Auto project) in the command line, and press Enter.
7. Select the wall again, and press Enter.
8. Select the Roof object and press Enter twice to end the command.

The wall now meets and closes the gable end (see Figure 10-8).
  This same process can be done with a curtain wall (see Figure 10-9).

9. Change to the Work Layout.
10. In the Top View viewport, select the roof and pull on the vertex shown in Figure 10-10.

You have now created a simple roof and roof overhang. Save this file.

Figure 10-8

Figure 10-9

Figure 10-10

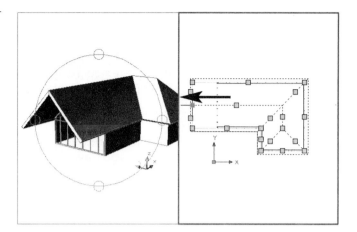

Hands-On

Using Apply Tool Properties to Roof and Surfu

Another way to create a roof is to use **Apply Tool Properties to.** In the following exercise **Apply Tool Properties to** was used because of the curved walls.

1. Using the AEC Arch Imperial template, select the **Work** viewport tab.
2. Activate the **Top View** viewport.
3. Create the floor plan with 6″-wide walls 9′ high as shown in Figure 10-11.
4. Type **surfu_** on the command line, and press Enter.
5. Set the new value to **4** on the command line and press the space bar or Enter key.

Surfu is the variable that controls the smoothness of the roof curves. This variable must be set before the roofs are placed or reapplied.

6. Select the **Roof** icon from the **Roof and Roof Slabs** tool palette you created previously, RMB, and select **Apply Tool Properties to** from the contextual menu that appears.

Figure 10-11

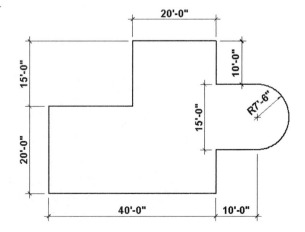

7.   Select all the walls.

8.   At the command line question "Erase layout geometry?" type **N** (No) and press Enter to create a roof.

9.   While the new roof is still lit (grips showing), move your cursor over the Properties palette to open it.

10. Change the **Edge cut** to **Plumb**, and Elevation to 9'-0".

You have now created a roof with one command. This technique is very useful when you have rounded roofs (see Figure 10-12).

11. Erase the roof.

12. Type **surfu_** on the command line, and press Enter.

13. Set the new value to **24** on the command line and press Enter.

14. Again use **Apply Tool Properties to** in order to make a roof, and save this file.

Figure 10-13 shows the effects of increasing the surfu variable to 24 (more facets).

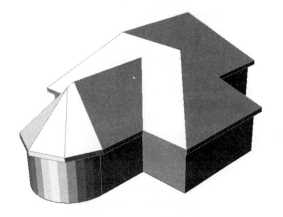

Figure 10-12

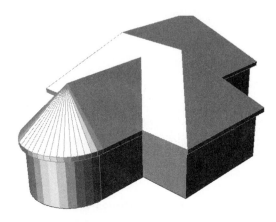

Figure 10-13

Hands-On

Converting to Roof Slabs

Note: Roofs can also be created by adding roof slab objects. This system is identical to that for creating slabs (see the next section, "Slabs and Slab Objects," for exercises on creating, modifying and editing slabs).

Converting roofs to slabs allows you the flexibility to adjust one slab or cut holes inherent in slabs. For pitched roofs it is often best to start with a standard Roof object, and then convert it to Roof Slabs.

1.   Use the previous exercise.

2.   Select the roof, RMB, and select **Convert to Roof Slabs** from the contextual menu that appears.

3. Type **Y** (Yes) at the command line question **"Erase layout geometry"** and press Enter. Accept the Standard roof, and again press Enter to complete the command.

The Roof color should now change because the roof will now be made of Roof Slab objects, and is now on the A-Roof-Slab layer.

Hands-On

roofslabmodifyedges

Although not documented in the manual, **roofslabmodifyedges** allows you to adjust all the roof slab edges at one time.

1. Using the previous exercise.
2. Type **Slabmodifyedges** in the command line and press Enter.
3. Type **All** at the command line request to select slabs to modify, and press Enter.
4. Select the **Baseline** option at the command line, and press Enter.
5. Enter **OV** (Overhang) in the command line, and press Enter.
6. Enter 3′-0″ at the command line, and press Enter.

You have now adjusted the overhang for all the Roof Slab objects (see Figure 10-14).

Figure 10-14

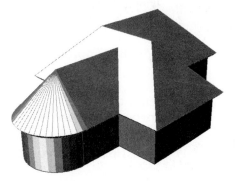

Hands-On

Applying Tool Properties to a Roof Slab

1. Select the Roof Slabs (this can be done by selecting the **Quick Select** icon at the top of the Properties palette to bring up the Quick select dialog box and selecting **Roof Slab** from the **Object type** drop-down list).
2. RMB on any Roof Slab icon in the Roof and Roof Slabs toolbar that you created.

Figure 10-15

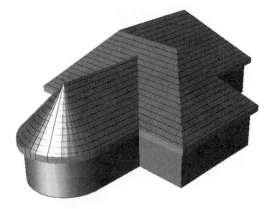

3. Select Apply Tool properties to > Roof Slab from the contextual menu that appears and press Enter. Press the Gouraud icon in the Shading toolbar. Save this file.

The roof slabs change to the new applied roof slabs style, and the roof slab material is displayed (see Figure 10-15).

Hands-On

Cutting a Hole in a Roof Slab

1. Zoom close to a roof slab in which you wish to place a hole.
2. Select the **Object UCS** icon from the **UCS** toolbar.
3. Select the roof slab in which you wish to place a hole.

The UCS (User Coordinate System) now matches the surface of the roof slab.

4. Select the Rectangle icon in the Draw toolbar and place a rectangle on, over, or under the roof slab (see Figure 10-16).
5. Select the roof slab in which you wish to place a hole, RMB, and select **Hole > Add** from the contextual menu that appears.

Figure 10-16

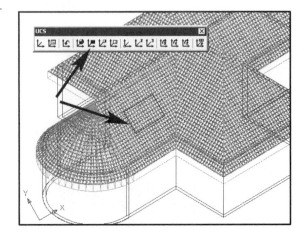

6. Select the Rectangle created in Step 4 of this exercise, and press Enter.
7. Enter **Y** (Yes) in the command line and press Enter to complete the command.

You have now created a hole in the roof slab (see Figure 10-17).

Figure 10-17

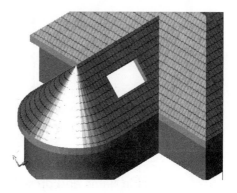

Hands-On

Adding Edge Profiles in Place

1. Select **Format** > **Style Manager** from the **Main** toolbar to bring up the **Style Manager** dialog box.
2. Expand the **Architectural Objects** tree, select Slab edge Styles, RMB, and select New from the contextual menu that appears.
3. Rename the New Style to **TEST** style, and press OK to return to the Drawing Editor.
4. Select a roof slab and select Add edge profiles from the contextual menu that appears.
5. Select an edge of the roof slab, and a dialog box will appear (see Figure 10-18).
6. Press the **Yes** button to bring up the **Edit Roof Slab Edges** dialog box.
7. In the Edit Roof Slab Edges dialog box select **Standard** for the Edge Style and press OK (see Figure 10-19).
8. The **Add Fascia/Soffit Profiles** dialog appears.
9. Check the **Fascia Profile** check box, select **Start from scratch** from the drop-down list, and enter the name **FASCIA PROFILE TEST** as the New

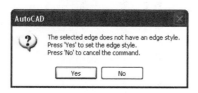

Figure 10-18

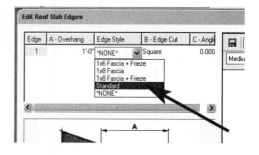

Figure 10-19

Figure 10-20

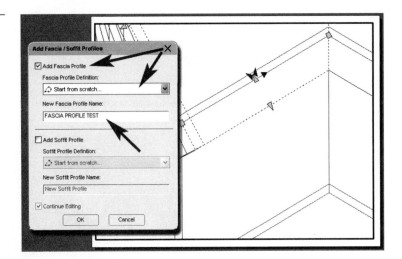

Profile Name and press OK to enter the **In-Place Edit** mode (see Figure 10-20).

10. Change to the Right View, and zoom close to the blue shading that signifies the In-Place Edit area.

11. Create a gutter from a closed polyline as shown in Figure 10-21.

12. Select the blue area and grips will appear.

13. RMB on the blue area and select Replace ring from the contextual menu that appears.

14. Select the gutter drawn in Step 11 of this exercise, enter **Y** (Yes) in the command line, and press Enter.

The blue hatch will be replaced by the gutter in blue hatch.

15. Select the blue gutter, RMB, and select **Save Profile** from the contextual menu that appears.

The FASCIA PROFILE TEST is now the gutter.

Figure 10-21

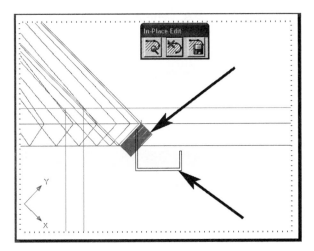

Hands-On

Creating a Roof Dormer

Dormers are in vogue today, and ADT 2004 has a command that aids in the creation of these objects.

1. Start a new drawing using the Architectural Building Model and View (Imperial - ctb) template.
2. Change to the Model Layout.
3. Change to the Top View.
4. Select the **Wall** icon from the **Design** tool palette, and create a 43' × 31'-wide structure 8'-0" high with 6"-wide Standard walls.
5. Add a **15'** × **8'** enclosure **14'-0"** high with **6"**-wide Standard walls.
6. Add a Gable roof to the 43' × 31' enclosure with a **30°** slope (see Figure 10-22).
7. Select the **Roof Slab** icon from the **Design** menu, RMB, and select **Apply Tool Properties to > Linework, Walls, and Roof** from the contextual menu.
8. Select the left wall of the 15' × 8' enclosure, and press Enter.
9. Enter **N** (No) in the command line and press Enter.
10. Enter **B** (Bottom) in the command line and press Enter.
11. Enter **R** (Right) in the command line and press Enter.
12. Enter **L** (Left) in the command line and press Enter to create the first roof slab of the dormer (see Figure 10-23).
13. Again, select the **Roof Slab** icon from the **Design** menu, RMB, and select **Apply Tool Properties to > Linework, Walls, and Roof** from the contextual menu.
14. Select the right wall of the 15' × 8' enclosure, and press Enter.
15. Enter **N** (No) in the command line and press Enter.
16. Enter **B** (Bottom) in the command line and press Enter.
17. Enter **L** (Left) in the command line and press Enter.

Figure 10-22

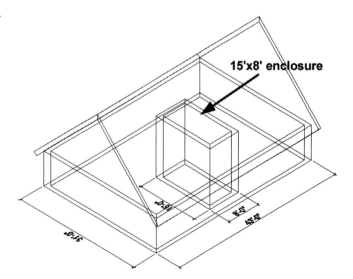

15'x8' enclosure

Figure 10-23

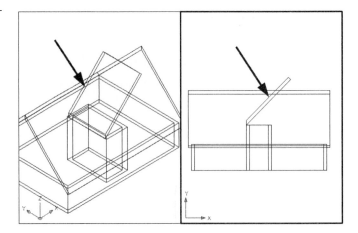

18. Enter **R** (Right) in the command line and press Enter to create the first roof slab of the dormer.

! **Note:** If your roof slab doesn't follow the above rules, reverse the wall direction and repeat (see Figure 10-24).

19. Select both new roof slabs, and move your cursor over the **Properties** palette to open it.

20. Change the **Slope** to **25** (25°).

21. Select one of the roof slabs, RMB, and select **Miter** from the contextual menu.

22. Accept the default **<Intersection>** in the command line and press Enter.

23. Select the lower part of the slab at the intersection of the two slabs, and then select the lower part of the other slab.

The two roof slabs will now miter, forming the roof of the Dormer. This could also have been done with the Roof object, and making it a gable roof.

24. Change to the Top View and drag each roof slab 2'-0" (see Figure 10-25).

Figure 10-24

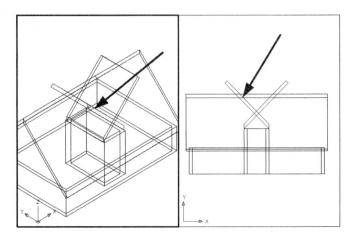

Figure 10-25

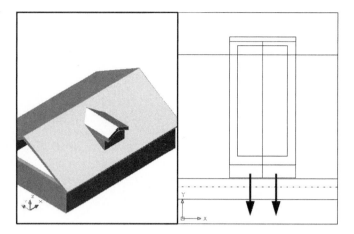

25. Select the main gable roof over the 43′ × 31′ enclosure, RMB, and select Convert to Roof Slabs from the contextual menu.

26. Enter **N** (No) in the command line, and press Enter twice to change the Roof object into Roof Slabs.

27. Press the ESC key to deselect the slabs.

28. Select the Roof Slab shown in Figure 10-26, RMB, and select **Roof Dormer** from the contextual menu.

29. Select the 15′ × 8′ enclosure and its roof slabs, and then press Enter.

30. Enter **Y** (Yes) in the command line, and press Enter to form the dormer.

31. Erase any unneeded walls (see Figure 10-27).

Figure 10-26

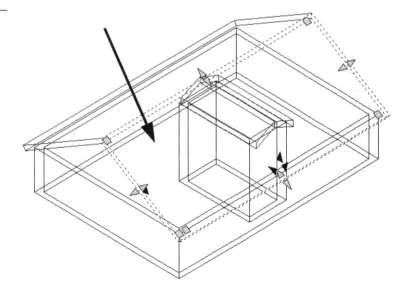

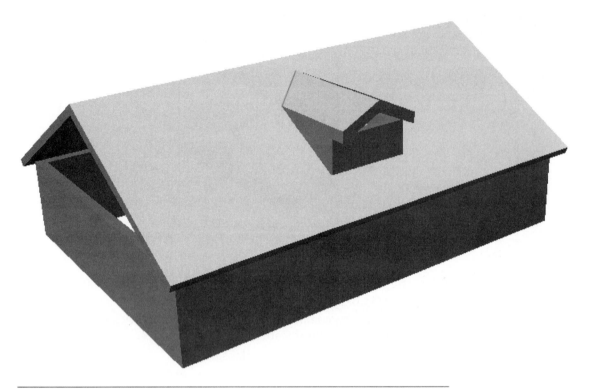

Figure 10-27

11

Slabs and Slab Objects

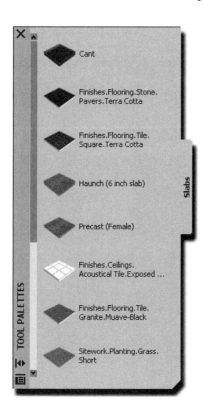

When you finish this section, you should understand the following:

✔ How to make a Slabs tool palette.
✔ Direct Mode and Direction.
✔ Projected Mode.
✔ Applying Tool Properties to slabs.
✔ How to cut slabs.
✔ How to Modify a Slab Object.
✔ How to make a new edge from a Profile.

Number	Name	Purpose
1	Style	Select from available slab styles
2	Mode	U-shaped, Multi-landing, Spiral, Straight
3	Thickness	$1/2$ landing, $1/2$ turn, $1/4$ landing, $1/4$ turn
4	Vertical offset	Slopeline offset
5	Horizontal offset	Offset from wall edge
6	Justify	Top, Center, Bottom, Slopeline
7	Direction	Right/left slope
8	Overhang	Distance of overhang
9	Perimeter edge	Profile type for edge
10	Rotation	Rotation of slab horizontally
11	Elevation	Elevation of slab

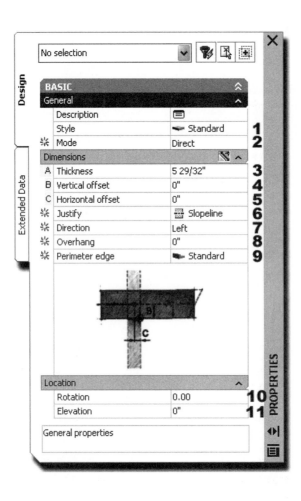

Hands-On

Creating a New Slabs Tool Palette

1. Create a new tool palette, and name it **Slab**.
2. Select the Content Browser icon from the Main toolbar to launch the Content Browser.
3. In the **Architectural Desktop Design Tool Catalog - Imperial,** locate the **Slabs** folder in the **Roof Slabs and Slabs** folder.
4. From the **Slabs** folder, drag all the slabs into the new tool palette you created.
5. Click and hold on the tab of your new tool palette and drag a copy to My Tool Catalog in the Content Browser.

Hands-On

Direct Mode and Direction

Slabs can be either Direct or Projected modes. Direct Mode allows you to place a Flat slab; Direct Projected Mode allows you to place a slab at a location in space with a given slope. **Direction** is used when using **"Ortho Close."**

    The first point establishes slab origin and pivot point. The first line establishes the baseline.

1. Start a new drawing using the Architectural Building Model and View (Imperial - ctb) template.
2. Change to the Model Layout.
3. Change to Top View.
4. Select the **Slab** icon from the **Slabs** toolbar you created.
5. Move your cursor over the Properties palette to open it.
6. Set the following parameters:

    a. Style = **Standard**
    b. Mode = **Direct**
    c. Thickness = to **12″**
    d. Overhang = **0″**
    e. Mode = **Direct**
    f. Justify = **Bottom**
    g. Direction = **Left**

7. Set the first point of your slab.
8. Moving clockwise set the second point at 10′ to the right.
9. Enter **O** (Ortho close) in the command line, and press Enter.
10. Repeat Steps 5, 6, and 7 slightly below the first slab in the top viewport, but *change* the direction arrow to the **Right** direction arrow.

11.   Select each slab, and change the slope of each slab to 45 (45°).

Ortho Close works differently for Slabs than for Walls. For Slabs only one line is drawn so the direction arrow dictates which direction the slab is cast (see Figures 11-1 and 11-2).

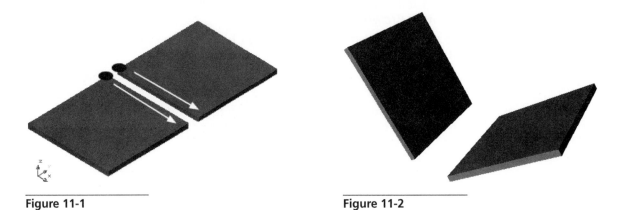

Figure 11-1   **Figure 11-2**

Hands-On

Projected Mode

1.   Erase everything.
2.   Again select the **Slab** icon from the **Slabs** tool palette.
3.   Move your cursor over the Properties palette to open it.
4.   Set the following parameters:

    a.   Style = **Standard**
    b.   Mode = **Projected**
    c.   Thickness = to **12″**
    d.   Justify = **Bottom**
    e.   Base height = **0**
    f.   Direction = **Right**
    g.   Overhang = **0″**

Note that selecting the projected mode causes the Slope option to now be available in the Properties palette.

5.   In the Properties palette under **Slope**, set **Rise** to **6**, and **Run** to **12**.
6.   Set a point, and moving clockwise set the second point at 10′ to the right.

Note that the Pivot symbol is at your starting point. Note that selecting the projected mode causes the slope option to be available.

7.   Enter **O** (Ortho close) in the command line, and press Enter.
8.   Repeat Steps 5, 6, and 7 but change the direction to **Left** (see Figure 11-3).

Figure 11-3

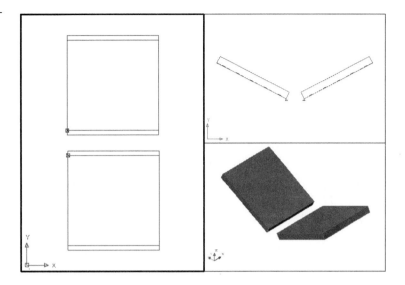

You change only the **Rise** numbers. Leave **Run** at 12.000, and the **Angle** will automatically calculate.

Hands-On

Applying Tool Properties to: for Slabs

Convert to Slabs uses closed polylines or walls as a basis for creating Slabs. You don't need closed walls to Convert to Slabs; one wall will work just fine. The default location for Slabs created by Convert to Slabs using walls is at the top of the wall.

1. Start a new drawing using the Architectural Building Model and View (Imperial - ctb) template.
2. Change to the Model Layout.
3. Change to Top View.
4. Select the **Wall** icon from the **Walls** tool palette.
5. Starting at the bottom left and moving clockwise, place a 8′ × 8′ enclosure (see Figure 11-4).
6. Convert the **Slab** icon from the **Slabs** tool palette, RMB, and select **Apply Tool properties to > Linework and Walls** from the contextual menu that appears.
7. In the Top View, select all the walls of the 8′ × 8′ enclosure starting at the bottom wall and moving *counterclockwise*.

! **Note:** The first wall you pick becomes the pivot wall.

8. At the command line accept **N** to leave the Walls in place.
9. For slab justification, select **Bottom**, for **Wall justification** select **Right**; for **Slope direction,** either **Right** or **Left** is OK, and accept the **Standard** Slab Style.

Figure 11-4

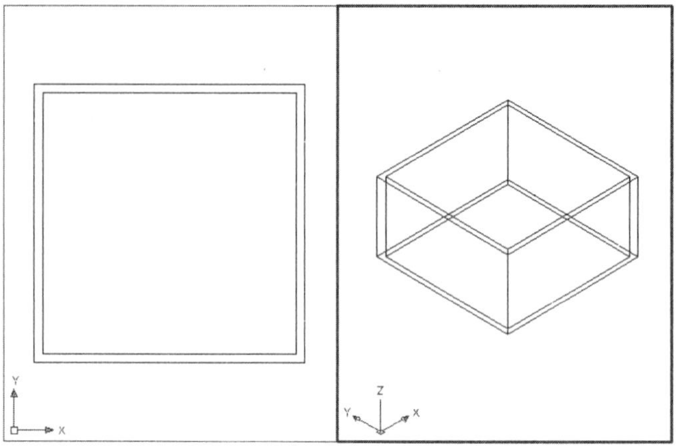

Figure 11-5

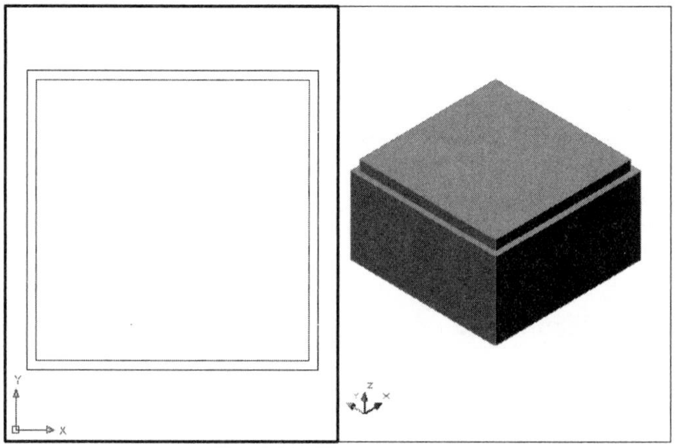

You have now placed a Standard Slab Object at the top of the wall enclosure (see Figure 11-5).

10. Repeat the above exercises changing the Wall justification, Slab justification, and Slope direction until you feel comfortable with the controls.

11. Save your exercise.

Hands-On

Cutting Slabs

1. Use the previous exercise.

2. In the Top View, place and **Offset** several Polylines as shown in Figure 11-6.

We are going to cut the slab with the polylines even though the polylines are at 0″ elevation, and the slab is at 8′-0″ elevation.

3. Select the slab, RMB, and select **Cut** from the contextual menu that appears.

Figure 11-6

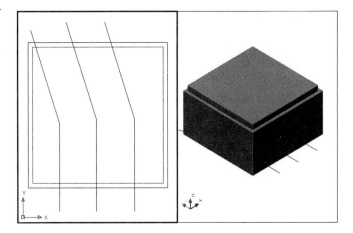

4. Select one of the polylines, and press Enter.
5. Enter **Y** (Yes) in the command line, and press Enter.
6. Repeat Steps 3 through 5 for the other polylines.

You should now have three slab sections.

7. Select each slab section, and move your cursor over the Properties palette to open it.
8. Set the elevation for each section 8″ lower than the previous one (see Figure 11-7). Save this file

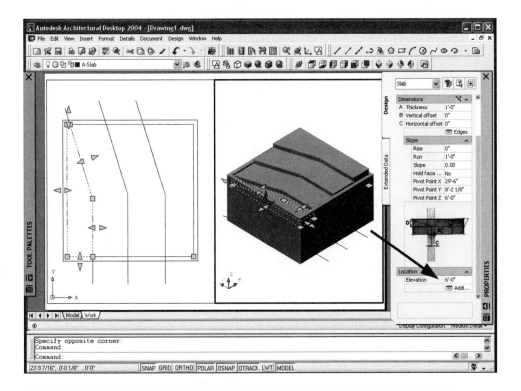

Figure 11-7

Hands-On

Modifying a Slab Object

Once you have placed a Slab object, there are many controls to manipulate the object.

1. Erase the slabs created in the previous exercise, and place a new slab 12″ slab starting at the upper left corner moving clockwise.

2. Set **Wall Justification - Left.** Making the justification left moves the edges of the slab to the outside of the enclosure.

3. Double-click the slab to open the Properties palette.

4. Set the Slope **Rise** to **12** (12″) (see Figure 11-8).

5. Select Edges from the Properties palette to bring up the **Slab Edges** dialog box.

6. Change the **Edge Cut** to **Plumb** (see Figures 11-9 and 11-10).

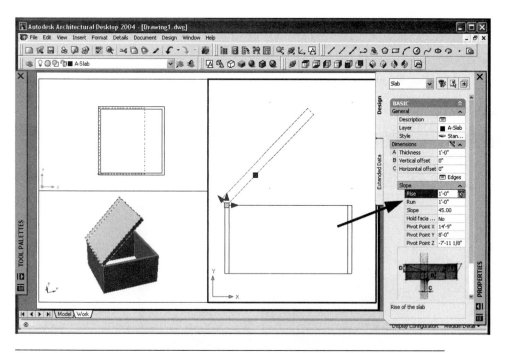

Figure 11-8

Figure 11-9

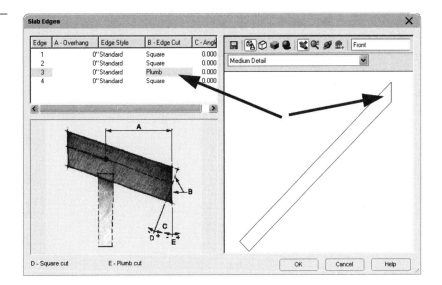

Figure 11-10

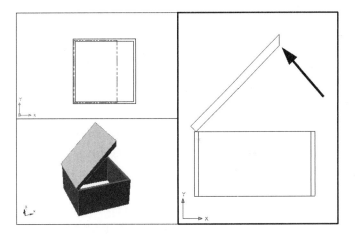

Making a New Edge from a Profile

7. Return the Slab object to its original position by changing the **Rise** to 0.00, and change the Edge Cut back to **Square**.

8. In the Top View drag select the slab's grips and move each edge 1'-0" as shown in Figure 11-11.

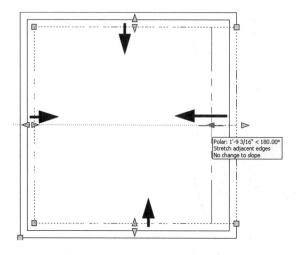

Figure 11-11

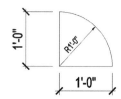

Figure 11-12

9. Create a profile polyline shape by drawing the polyline shown in Figure 11-12.

10. Select the polyline, RMB, and select **Convert to > Profile Definition** from the contextual menu that appears.

11. Select the upper left corner of the polyline you just created, and press Enter.

12. Press Enter again to bring up the new **Profile Definition** dialog box.

13. Enter **CURVED EDGE PROFILE**, and press OK.

14. Select **Format > Style Manager** to bring up the **Style Manager**.

15. Select Architectural > Slab Edge Styles, RMB, and select **New** from the contextual menu that appears.

16. Rename the new style to **CURVED EDGE STYLE**.

17. Double-click on the CURVED EDGE STYLE icon you just created to bring up the **Slab Edge Styles** dialog box.

18. Check the **Fascia** check box, and select CURVED EDGE PROFILE from the Fascia **Profile** drop-down list, and press the OK and Apply buttons to return to the Drawing editor (see Figure 11-13).

19. Double-click the slab to bring up the Properties palette.

20. Select Edges to bring up the **Slab Edges** dialog box.

21. Select all the edges, and select **CURVED EDGE STYLE** from the **Edge Style** drop-down list, and then press OK.

You have now placed a new curved edge on all the slab edges (see Figure 11-14).

Figure 11-13

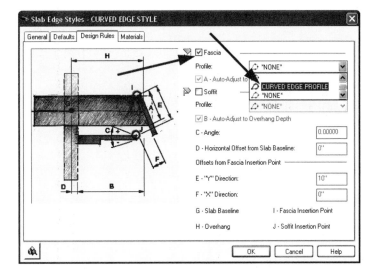

Figure 11-14

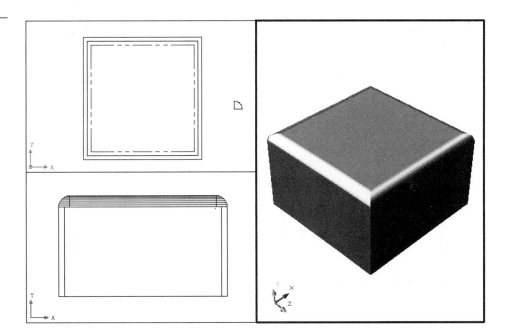

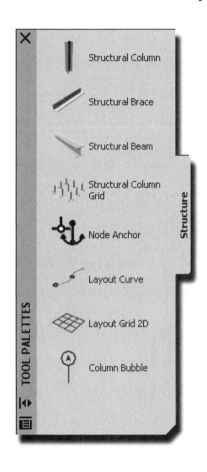

When you finish this section, you should understand the following:

- ✔ How to make a Structure palette.
- ✔ How to place a column and column grid.
- ✔ How to modify structural members.
- ✔ How to create a round composite concrete and steel column.
- ✔ How to add bar joists.
- ✔ How to label a grid.
- ✔ How to add and label a layout grid 2D.
- ✔ How to create and use a layout curve.
- ✔ How to use a wall as a layout curve.

All buildings have a structural system. In the design of commercial buildings, the understanding and documentation of the structural system is of utmost importance. In Autodesk Architectural Desktop 2004, structural members give control over this phase of construction.

Structural members, column grids, grids and anchors often work in concert.

Structural members can be used as columns, beams, and braces, and can be configured in many ways not originally intended by the developers of the program. In reality, columns, beams, and braces are the same AEC object used in different work planes. When understood, structural members can be one of the most important AEC objects in your portfolio of tools.

Column grids are a variant on grids; they can be planar (flat) or volumetric (three-dimensional). Columns can be attached to any grid, but column grids can have columns attached upon input of the grid.

Number	Name	Purpose
1	Style	Select from available Structural Member Styles.
2	Member type	Column, Beam, or Brace.
3	Start offset	Distance offset from the start end of member.
4	End offset	Distance offset from the end of member
5	Logical length	Actual length of structural member.
6	Specify roll on screen	Specify roll angle around the main axis through member.
7	Roll	Roll angle around the main axis through member.
8	Justify	Insertion node location.
9	Justify using overall extents	
10	Rotation	Rotation of the structural member.
11	Elevation	Elevation of the structural member.
12	Trim planes	Planes used to modify end conditions of the structural member.

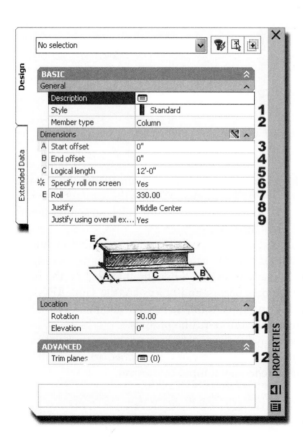

Hands-On

Making a New Structure Tool Palette

1. Create a new tool palette named **Structure**.

2. Select the Content Browser icon from the Main toolbar to launch the Content Browser.

3. In the **Autodesk Architectural Desktop Stock Tool Catalog** locate the **Structural Beam, Structural Brace, Structural Column, and Structural Grid Object** in the **Architectural Object Tools** folder.

4. From the Architectural Object Tools folder, drag the objects into the new tool palette you created.

5. In the **Autodesk Architectural Desktop Design Stock Tool Catalog** locate the **Cell anchor, Node anchor, and Layout Grid 2D** tools in the **General Purpose Tools** > **Parametric Layout & Anchoring** folder, and drag these tools to the **Structure** palette you created.

6. Click and hold on the tab of your new tool palette and drag a copy to My Tool Catalog in the Content Browser.

7. In the **Autodesk Architectural Desktop Sample Palette Catalog - Imperial** locate the **Column Bubble** tool in the **Annotation** folder, and drag these tools to the **Structure** palette you created.

8. Click and hold on the tab of your new tool palette and drag a copy to My Tool Catalog in the Content Browser.

Hands-On

Placing a Column and Grid

1. Start a new drawing using the Architectural Building Model and View (Imperial - ctb) template.

2. Change to the Work Layout.

3. Erase the existing viewports.

4. Select **View > Viewports > 3 Viewports** from the Main menu.

5. Enter **L** (Left) on the command line, and press Enter.

6. Enter **F** (Fit) on the command line, and press Enter.

7. Activate the Top View.

8. Set the Object Snap to NODE.

9. Place a standard 10'-long, 10'-high wall.

10. Select Structural Column Grid from the Structure tool palette you created and drag your cursor over the Properties palette to open it.

11. Enter the following data:

    a. Shape = **Rectangular**

    b. Boundary = ***NONE***

    c. Specify on screen = **No**

    d. X - Width = **60'**

e.   Y - Depth = **40'**

f.   XAXIS Layout type = **Repeat**

g.   Bay size = **20'-0"**

h.   YAXIS

i.   Bay size = **20'-0"**

j.   Column Style = **Standard**

k.   Column Logical Length = **10'-0"**

l.   Justify = **Middle Center**

12. Click in the Drawing Editor to place the grid and columns, and press Enter twice to complete the command (see Figure 12-1).

Figure 12-1

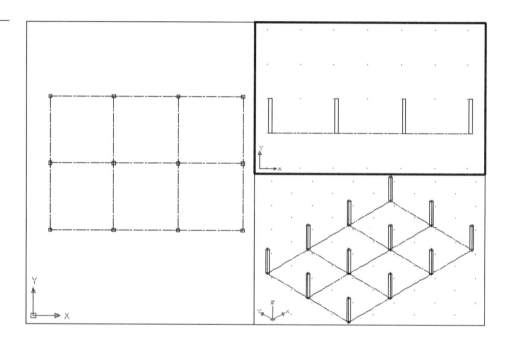

Hands-On

Modifying Structural Members

1.   Select the middle row of columns, and move your cursor over the Properties palette to open it.

2.   Set the **Logical length** to **14'-0"**, and press Enter.

3.   Select the **Structural Beam** icon from the **Structure** toolbar, set the Style to **Standard**, and Justify to **Bottom Center**.

Note: Bottom Center is the location of the grips now set for the beam.

4.   Click at the top of the first center column, then at the top of the second center column.

5.   Repeat the above process with the top center nodes of the columns (see Figure 12-2).

Figure 12-2

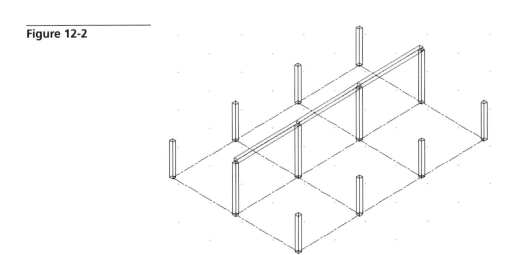

6. Repeat the process for the other columns to create the frame illustrated in Figure 12-3.
7. Select the end beams on the left side and right sides, and move your cursor over the Properties palette to open it.
8. Set the Start Offset to –2′-0″ (see Figure 12-4).
9. Repeat this process on the beams at the opposite end.

Figure 12-3

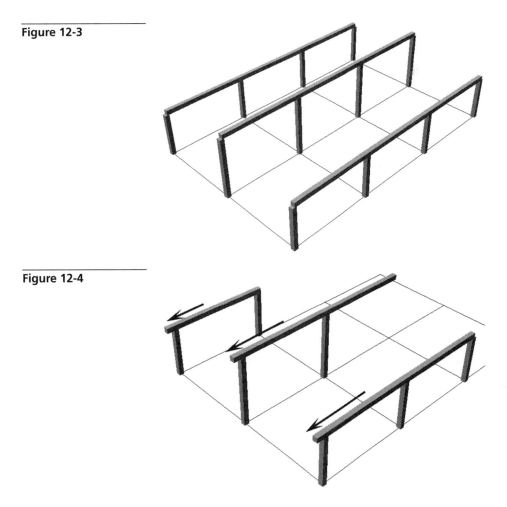

Figure 12-4

10. Select **Format** > **Structural Member Catalog** from the Main toolbar.

11. Select **Imperial | Steel | AISC | Channels | MC, Miscellaneous Channels.**

12. Double-click the **MC12x10.6** channel.

13. When the **Structural Member Style** dialog box appears, accept the default **MC12x10.6** name (see Figure 12-5).

14. Select all the outer beams, RMB, and select Member Properties from the contextual menu. At the structural Member Properties dialog box, select the Style tab, and change the style to **MC12x10.6** (see Figure 12-6).

15. Repeat the above process for the beams on the other side. This time also change **Roll** to **180**, and Justification to **Top Center**. This will cause the other channels to rotate 180° with the grip on the bottom.

Figure 12-5

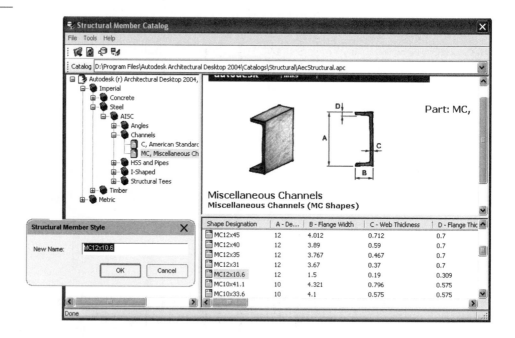

Figure 12-6

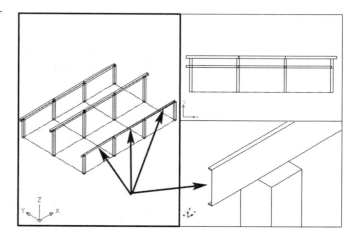

Hands-On

Creating a Round Composite Concrete and Steel Column

1. Select **Format > Structural Member Catalog** from the Main toolbar.
2. Select **Imperial > Concrete > Cast - in place > Circular Columns**.
3. Double-click the 14″ diameter.
4. When the **Structural member style** dialog box appears, enter **14″ DIA. CONC. COL** and then press OK.
5. Select **Imperial | Steel | AISC | Channels | I Shaped, Wn Wide-Flange Shapes**.
6. Double-click **W6x25**.
7. When the **Structural member style** dialog box appears, accept **W6x25** and then press OK.
8. Close the Structural Member Catalog.
9. **Select Format > Style Manager** to bring up the **Style Manager** dialog box.
10. RMB on the **Structural Member Styles** icon in the **Architectural Objects** folder in the display tree and select New from the contextual menu that appears.
11. Rename the new style **COMPOSITE COL,** and press OK.
12. Double-click on the icon adjacent to the new COMPOSITE COL style to bring up the **Structural Members Style Properties** dialog box.
13. Select the **Design Rules** tab.
14. Rename the Unnamed Component to **CONC**.
15. Under **Start Shape Name**, select 14″-diameter from the drop-down list.
16. Press the Add button, and rename the next component **W6x25**.
17. Select W6x25 under **Start Shape Name**, and press OK (see Figure 12-7).

You have now created the composite round concrete column with steel shape inside.

18. Select all the columns in the Drawing Editor, and move your cursor over the Properties palette to open it.

Figure 12-7

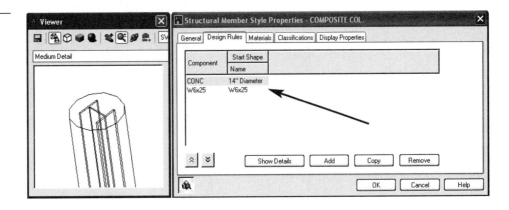

Figure 12-8

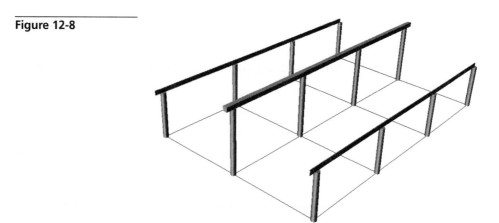

19. Select **COMPOSITE COL Structural Beam** from the **Style** drop-down list. All the columns change to composite columns (see Figure 12-8).

Hands-On

Adding Bar Joists

1. Select the **Content Browser** icon from the Main toolbar to launch the Content Browser.

2. In the **Autodesk Architectural Desktop Design Tool Catalog - Imperial** locate the **Bar Joists** in the **structural** folder.

3. From the Bar Joists folder, drag the **Steel Joist 24** into the **Structure** tool palette you created, and close the Content Browser.

4. Select **Line** from the **Draw** toolbar, and place a line from the middle beam to the channel (see Figure 12-9).

5. Select the **Steel Joist 24** icon from the Structure menu you created, RMB, and select **Apply Tool Properties to > Linework** from the contextual menu that appears.

6. Select the line you placed in Step 4 of this exercise, and press Enter.

Figure 12-9

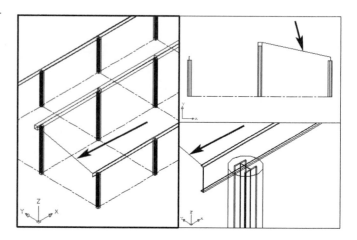

7. Enter **Y** (Yes) in the command line, and press Enter.

The line changes to a 24″ steel bar joist. If it is on its side, change the Roll to 0 in the Properties palette while it is still selected (see Figure 12-10).

8. Change to the **Model** Layout.

9. Change to the Left View, and zoom window around the location of the joist seat and the channel (see Figure 12-11).

10. Select the bar joist, RMB, and select **Edit Member Style** from the contextual menu that appears to bring up the **Structural Member Style** dialog box.

11. Select the **Design Rules** tab. This is where you control the components of the bar joist.

12. Set the settings shown for the **TopChord** and **JoistSeat-End** and press OK (see Figure 12-12). The bar joist top chord and joist seat changes (see Figure 12-13).

13. RMB in an empty space in the Drawing Editor and select **Basic Modify Tools** > **Array** from the contextual menu that appears to bring up the **Array** dialog box.

14. Set the following:

Figure 12-10

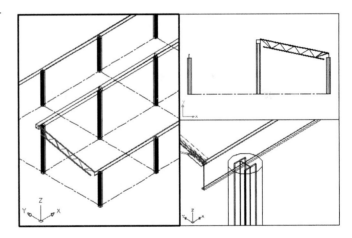

Figure 12-11

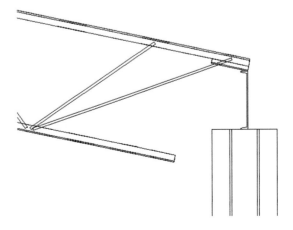

Figure 12-12

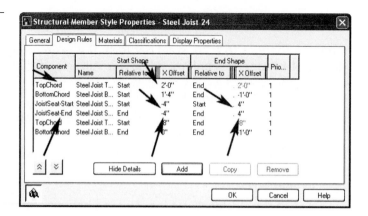

Figure 12-13

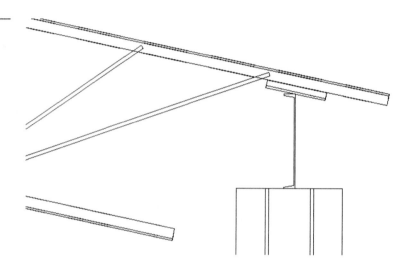

    a. Rectangular array = **selected**

    b. Columns = **33**

    c. Row offset = **1″**

    d. Column offset = **2′-0″**

15. Select the bar joist that you created, and press OK.

16. Mirror the bar joists to the other side of the structure, and you are finished (see Figure 12-14). Save this exercise.

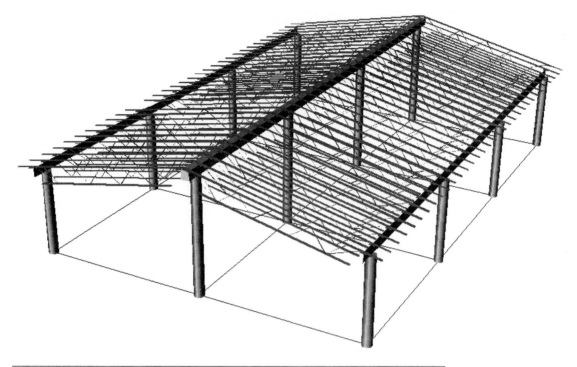

Figure 12-14

Hands-On

Labeling a Column Grid

1. Use the previous exercise.
2. Change to the Top View.
3. Select the **Layer Manager** icon from the **Layer Properties** toolbar to bring up the **Layer Manager**.
4. Turn the **S-Beam** and the **S-Cols** layers off, and press OK to return to the Drawing Editor.

The column grid will now be exposed.

5. Select the column grid, RMB, and select **Label** from the contextual menu that appears to bring up the **Column Grid Labeling** dialog box.
6. Select the **X - Labeling** tab.
7. In the X - Labeling tab, in the Number list enter the letter **A** and press Enter to fill the other letters automatically.
8. In the X - Labeling tab enter the following:

   a. Check the **Automatically Calculate Values for Labels** check box.

b. Select the **Ascending** radio button.

c. Check the **Bottom** check box for Bubble Parameters.

d. Enter **4'-0″** in the Bubble Parameters **Extension**.

e. Check the **Generate New Bubbles On Exit** check box.

9. Change to the **Y - Labeling** tab.

10. In the Y - Labeling tab, in the Number list enter the Number **1** and press Enter to fill the other numbers automatically.

11. In the X - Labeling tab enter the following:

a. Check the **Automatically Calculate Values for Labels** check box.

b. Select the **Ascending** radio button.

c. Check the **Right** check box for Bubble Parameters.

d. Enter **4'-0″** in the Bubble Parameters **Extension**.

e. Check the **Generate New Bubbles On Exit** check box.

12. Press OK to return to the Drawing Editor (see Figure 12-15).

13. Select the bubble containing the letter A to activate its grips.

14. Drag the grip above the bubble to the right; the leader will follow (see Figure 12-16).

Figure 12-15

Figure 12-16

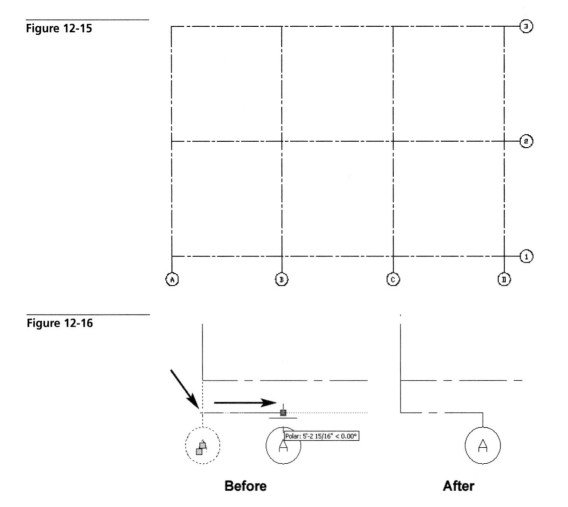

Before   **After**

Hands-On

Adding and Labeling a Layout Grid 2D

1. Start a new drawing using the **Architectural Building Model and View (Imperial - ctb)** template.
2. Change to the **Work** Layout.
3. Activate the Top View.
4. With various tools from the Draw menu, create the plan shown in Figure 12-17.
5. Select the **Layout Grid 2D** icon from the Structure palette that you created, RMB, and select **Apply Tool Properties > Linework** from the contextual menu that appears.
6. Select the plan you created in Step 4 of this exercise and press Enter.
7. Enter **Y** (Yes) in the command line, and press Enter.
8. Select the **Column Bubble** from the Structure tool palette, and click the bottom left node of the plan to bring up the **Create Grid Bubble** dialog box.
9. In the Create Grid Bubble dialog box enter **A1** in the **Label** data field, **4'-0"** in the **Extension** data field; uncheck the **Apply at both ends of gridline** check box, and press OK.
10. Repeat for the following right-hand nodes (see Figure 12-18).

Figure 12-17

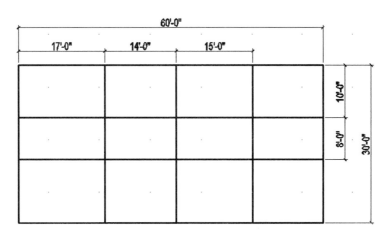

Figure 12-18

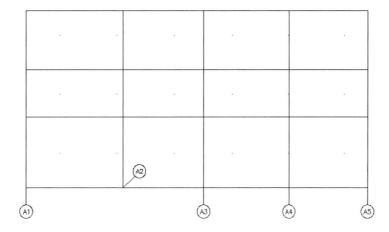

If a Column Bubble is misplaced or at an angle, do the following:

11.   Select the column bubble, RMB, and select **Leader Anchor** > **Set Direction** from the contextual menu that appears.

12.   For this example, enter 270° and press Enter (see Figure 12-19).

Figure 12-19

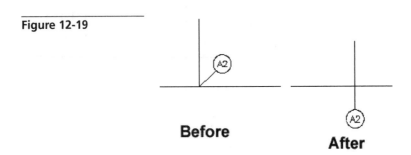

Layout Curves

Layout curves are not necessarily curves. Straight lines and many AEC objects such as walls, stairs, and doors can also be used as layout curves. If a line was placed on a wall and changed to a layout curve, and the line then moved vertically 24″ up the wall, attached content would move with the layout curve. If the wall had been used as a layout curve, the nodes would have been at its base.

Use a layout curve to anchor objects along a path. You can define the following objects as layout curves:

- Walls
- Curtain walls
- Window assemblies
- Spaces
- Mass elements
- Roofs
- Lines
- Arcs
- Circles
- Ellipses
- Polygons
- Polylines
- Splines

Hands-On

Creating and Using a Layout Curve

1. Erase the previous exercise.
2. Select **Spline** from the **Draw** menu, and place a spline.
3. Select the **Layout Curve** icon from the **Structure** palette.
4. Select the spline, enter **S** (Space evenly) in the command line, and press Enter.
5. Enter **5** in the command line for the **Number of nodes**, and press Enter.
6. Change to the SW Isometric View.
7. Turn on the Node object snap.
8. Select Structural Column from the Structure tool palette, select one of the nodes on the spline, and click the mouse to place it.
9. Select **Node Anchor** from the Structure tool palette.
10. Enter **C** (Copy to each node) in the command, and press Enter.
11. Select the column you placed, and press Enter.
12. Select any other node on the spline, and press Enter.
13. Enter **Y** (Yes) in the command line, and press Enter.

All the nodes on the spline now have columns (see Figure 12-20).

_____

Figure 12-20

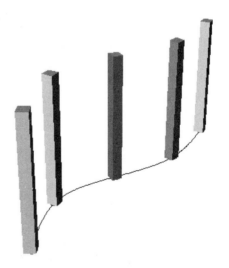

Hands-On

Using a Wall as a Layout Curve

1. Select the **Wall** icon from the **Design** menu and place a **Standard 15'-0"** long **10'**-high, 6"-wide wall.
2. Select the **Layout Curve** icon from the **Structure** palette, and select the wall you just created.
3. Enter **S** (Space evenly) in the command line, and press Enter.
4. Enter 24" for the **Start offset**, and press Enter.
5. Enter 24" for the **End offset**, and press Enter.

6. Accept 3 as the **Number of nodes**, and press Enter to place the nodes.

7. Select the **Content Bowser** icon from the Main toolbar and select and drag into the drawing the **Regular** drinking fountain from the **Autodesk Architectural Desktop Design Tool Catalog - Imperial** > **Mechanical** > **Plumbing Fixtures** > **Fountain** folder (see Figure 12-21).

8. Select the **Node Anchor** icon from the Main toolbar.

9. Enter **C** (Copy to each node) and press Enter.

10. Select the drinking fountain, and then select one of the nodes anchored to the wall. The fountains are now anchored to the wall.

11. Select all the fountains and move your cursor over the **Properties** palette to open it.

12. Select the **Anchor** field to bring up the **Anchor** dialog box.

13. Change the **Insertion Offset Z** to **3′-0″**, the **Rotation Z** to **270**, and press OK to return to the Drawing Editor. All the Fountains move vertically up the wall 3′-0″ (see Figure 12-22).

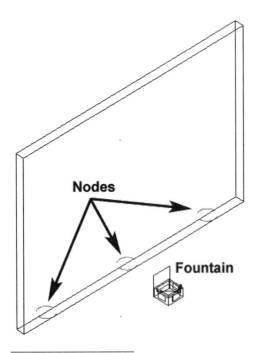

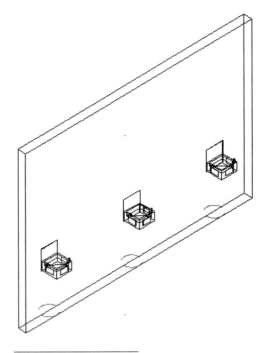

Figure 12-21

Figure 12-22

Hands-On

Layout Grid (2D)

1. Start a new drawing using the Architectural Building Model and View (Imperial - ctb) template.

2. Change to the Model Layout.

3. Change to the Top View.

4. Create a 40′-long × 30′-wide building with a 6″-rise roof.

5. Select the **Roof Slab** icon from the **Design** tool palette, RMB, and select **Apply Tool Properties to > Linework, Walls, and Roof** from the contextual menu that appears.

6. Select the Roof object, Enter **N** (No) in the command line, and press Enter to change the Roof object to Roof Slabs.

7. Select the **Object UCS** from the **UCS** toolbar, and select the front roof slab. Make sure the **ucsicon OR** option is on (see Figure 12-23).

8. Select the **Layout Grid (2D)** icon from the Structure tool palette.

9. Center a 15' × 10' grid on the front roof slab with three divisions in the X direction, and two divisions in the Y direction. The grid will lie parallel to the roof because the UCS was set parallel to the roof in Step 7 (see Figure 12-24).

10. Place a 5'-0"-high × 1'-0"-radius **Mass Element Cylinder** in a convenient place in your drawing.

11. Select the **Cell Anchor** icon from the **Structure** tool palette.

12. Type **C** at the command line to copy to each cell, and press Enter.

13. Select the Mass object, and then select the Layout grid on the Roof slab (see Figures 12-25 and 12-26).

Note in Figures 12-25 and 12-26 that the Mass Elements in the cells of the Layout grid match the size of the grid.

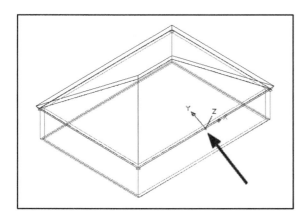

Figure 12-23

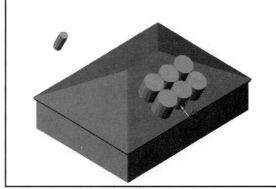

Figure 12-24

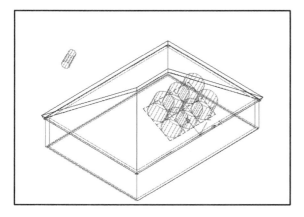

Figure 12-25

Figure 12-26

14. Select the grid, and move your cursor over the **Properties** palette to open it.

15. Change the grid size to 5'-0" in the X-Width and 5'-0" in the Y-Depth.

Note that the Mass Elements in the cells automatically change size (see Figures 12-27 and 12-28).

16. UNDO back to Step 9 (after the Layout grid was placed).

17. Select the **Node Anchor** icon from the Structure tool palette.

18. Enter **C** (Copy to each node) in the command line, and press Enter.

19. Select the Mass Element, and then select the Layout grid (see Figure 12-29).

Note that the Mass Elements attached to the nodes of the Layout grid. Moving or modifying the grid will then move the anchored objects.

The Layout Volume Grid (3D) works and is modified in a similar manner to the 2D Layout grid.

Experiment with all the different settings, and try anchoring and rotating different kinds of content to AEC objects and AutoCAD entities. Don't forget that you can use the Layout grid to put a series of skylights or windows on a roof or wall.

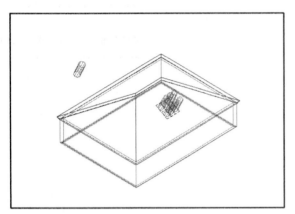

Figure 12-27

Figure 12-28

Figure 12-29

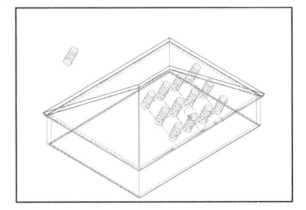

Section 13

AEC Dimensions

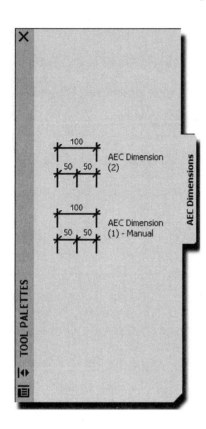

When you finish this section, you should understand the following:

- ✔ How to set the Text style.
- ✔ How to create a Dimension style.
- ✔ How to create an AEC Dimension style.
- ✔ How to use and modify an AEC Dimension style.
- ✔ How to dimension doors and windows with AEC Dimension styles.
- ✔ How to add a manual AEC Dimension.
- ✔ How to detach objects from AEC Dimensions.
- ✔ AEC Dimension Chains.
- ✔ The Dimension Wizard.

AEC Dimensions

AEC Dimensions are automatic dimensions based on Styles. Because there are so many variables in the dimension system, there are many dialog boxes. To make it easier, the developers have also added a Wizard to aid in variable setup.

Standard AutoCAD dimensions can be converted into AEC Dimensions, and AEC Dimensions can be mixed with the manual AEC and standard AutoCAD dimensioning systems.

AEC Dimensions can dimension only AEC objects such as walls, windows, stairs, structural members, and so on. If you add non-AEC objects to AEC objects, you have to add manual dimension points to the automatic AEC dimension, or create manual AEC or standard AutoCAD dimensions.

The following table from the Autodesk Architectural Desktop 2004 on-line help describes the difference between the three available dimensioning systems.

Automatic AEC DImensions	Manual AEC Dimensions	AutoCAD Dimensions
Logical dimension points taken from object	Manual dimension points taken from drawing	Manual dimension points taken from drawing
Dimension AEC objects	Dimension picked points in drawing	Dimension picked points in drawing
Associative towards building elements	Associative or nonassociative towards points, depending on user settings	Associative towards points
Dimension groups	Dimension groups	Single dimensions
Support superscripting, variable extension line length	Support superscripting, variable extension line length	Supports no superscripting, variable extension line length
Dimension texts cannot be edited	Dimension texts cannot be edited	Dimension texts can be edited
Defined by AEC dimension style and AutoCAD dimension style	Defined by AEC dimension style and AutoCAD dimension style	Defined by AutoCAD dimension style

 Tip Since the AEC Dimensions are based on AutoCAD's standard dimensioning variables, it is imperative that you have a good understanding of that system and its operation. This includes an understanding of the relationship between dimensioning and Model - Paperspace. This book assumes that understanding.

Hands-On

Setting the Text Style

Before setting the Dimension Styles, change the Standard text style; I prefer Stylus BT, which comes with Architectural Desktop.

1. Start a new drawing using the Architectural Building Model and View (Imperial - ctb) template.
2. Select **Format > Text Style** from the Main toolbar to bring up the **Text Style** dialog box.
3. Select the **New** button and create a new style name called **NEW Text**.
4. Set the NEW Text font to **Stylus BT** in the **Font Name** drop-down list and apply and close (see Figure 13-1).

You have now created a Text style that you can use with AutoCAD Dimensions and Architectural Desktop AEC Dimensions. Save this file.

Figure 13-1

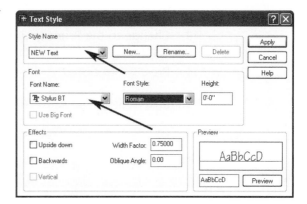

Hands-On

Creating a Dimension Style

1. **Select Format > Dimension Style** from the **Main** toolbar to bring up the **Dimension Style Manager** dialog box.
2. Press the **New** button to bring up the **Create New Dimension Style** dialog box.
3. Set the following:

    a. New Style Name = **HEGRA** (author's business name)
    b. Start With = **Standard**
    c. Use for = **All dimensions**

4. Press the **Continue** button to bring up the **New Dimension Style** dialog box.
5. Select the **Text** tab.
6. Set the following:

    a. Text style = **NEW Text**
    b. Text height = **1/8″**
    c. Text Placement Vertical = **Above**
    d. Text Placement Horizontal = **Centered**
    e. Text Alignment = **Aligned with dimension line**

7. Change to the **Lines and Arrows** tab.
8. Set the following:

    a. Extend beyond dim lines = **1/16″**
    b. Offset from origin = **1/16″**
    c. Arrowheads 1st = **Architectural tick**
    d. Arrowheads 2nd = **Architectural tick**
    e. Leader = **Closed filled**
    f. Arrow size = **1/16″**

9. Change to the **Fit** tab, and set **Use overall scale of:** to **48.0.**
10. Change to the **Primary Units** tab, and set the **Unit format** to **Architectural.**
11. Press OK to close the dialog boxes and return to the Drawing Editor.

You have now set the AutoCAD dimension style for HEGRA Dimensions.

Hands-On

Creating an AEC Dimension Style

1. Select **Format > AEC Dimension Styles** from the **Main** toolbar.
2. At the **Style Manager** dialog box, select the **New Style** icon in the top toolbar, and rename the new style to **HEGRA AEC DIM** (see Figure 13-2).
3. Select **HEGRA AEC DIM, RMB,** and select **Edit** from the contextual menu that appears to bring up the **AEC Dimension Style Properties** dialog box.
4. Select the **Display Properties** tab.
5. Double-click on **Plan** in the **Display Representations** column to bring up the **Display Properties** dialog box.
6. Select the **Contents** tab.
7. Select **Wall** from **Apply to**, check the **Length of Wall** check box, check the **Chain 1** check box, and select **Wall Length** from the **Length of Wall** drop-down list (see Figure 13-3).

Select the **Other** tab, and select **HEGRA** at the **Dimension Style** drop-down list. Make sure the check boxes are unchecked, and then press the OK buttons to return to the Drawing Editor.

You have now created modified an AEC Dimension Style called **HEGRA AEC DIM**. Save this file.

Figure 13-2

Figure 13-3

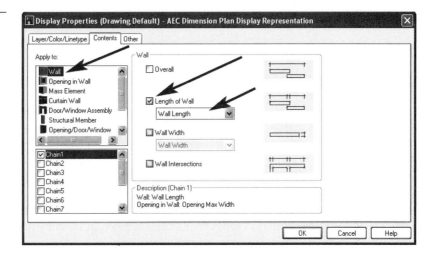

Hands-On

Using and Modifying an AEC Dimension Style

1. Use the previous exercise.
2. Change to the Work Layout.
3. Clear the viewports and create one viewport.
4. Change to the Top View.
5. Change to **Paper** space, select the viewport frame, and move your cursor over the Properties palette to open it.
6. Set the following settings:

    a. Standard scale = **1/4″ = 1′-0″**

7. Change to **Model** space.
8. Select the **Wall** icon from the Design tool palette, and move your cursor over the Properties palette to open it.
9. Set the following settings:

    a. Style = **Standard**
    b. Width = **6″**
    c. Justify = **Left**

10. Create the walls shown in Figure 13-4. *Don't include dimensions shown.*
11. Select all wall segments, RMB, and select **AEC Dimension** from the contextual menu that appears.
12. Move your cursor over the Properties palette to open it.
13. Set the **Style** to **HEGRA AEC DIM** from the Style drop-down list.
14. Drag your cursor above the walls, and click to place dimensions for the walls.

Figure 13-4

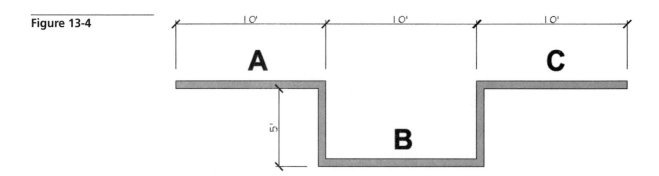

15. Select the dimension string you just placed, RMB, and select **Remove Dimension Points** from the contextual menu that appears.
16. Select the dimension extension lines that you want removed, and they will turn red (see Figure 13-5).
17. Press Enter, the extension lines will disappear, and the dimension string will show the total width between walls (see Figure 13-6).
18. Select the dimension string again, RMB, and select **Add Dimension Points** from the contextual menu that appears.
19. Using an object snap, snap on a point you wish to add, press Enter, and then select the Dimension chain to complete the command (see Figure 13-7).
20. Select the dimension string again, RMB, and select **Edit AEC Dimension Style** from the contextual menu that appears to bring up the **AEC Dimension Style Properties** dialog box.
21. Select the **Display Properties** tab.

Figure 13-5

Figure 13-6

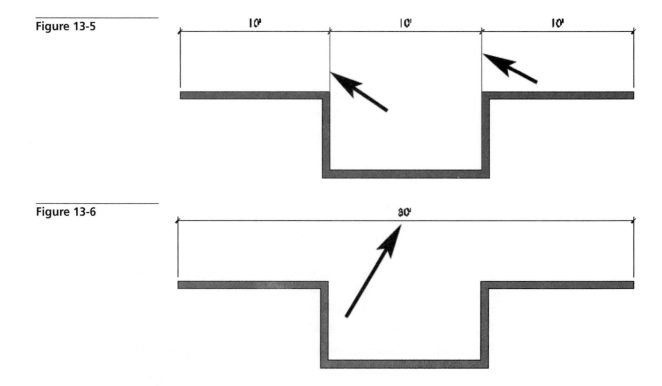

Figure 13-7

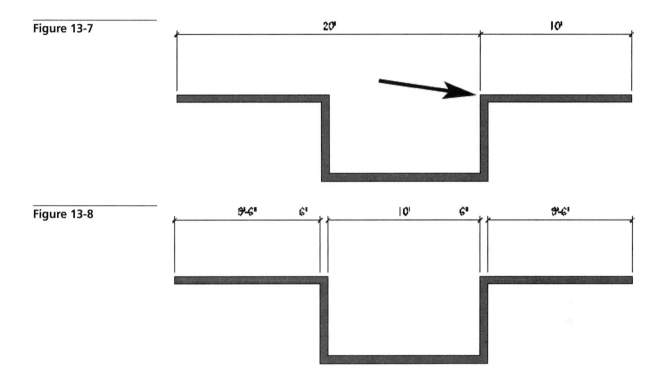

Figure 13-8

22. Double-click on **Plan** in the **Display Representations** column to bring up the **Display Properties** dialog box.
23. Check the **Wall Intersections** check box, and press the OK buttons to close the dialog boxes and return to the Drawing Editor.

The AEC Dimension string now shows the wall intersections (see Figure 13-8). Save this file.

Hands-On

Dimensioning Doors and Windows with AEC Dimension Styles

1. Use the previous exercise.
2. Erase the dimension strings you placed in the previous exercise.
3. Select **Format > AEC Dimension Styles** from the **Main** toolbar again to bring up the **Style Manager**.
4. Double-click on **HEGRA AEC DIM** to bring up the **AEC Dimension Style Properties** dialog box.
5. Select the **Display Properties** tab.
6. Double-click on **Plan** in the **Display Representations** column to bring up the **Display Properties** dialog box.
7. Select the **Contents** tab, and select **Opening/Door/Window** from the **Apply to** list.
8. Check the **Center** checkbox, and clear the other check boxes (see Figure 13-9).

Figure 13-9

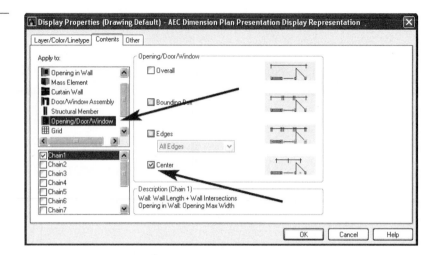

9. Select **Opening in Wall**, from the **Apply to** list.

10. Check the **Center** checkbox, and clear the other check boxes.

11. Select wall (Figure 13-4), RMB, and select Insert > Window from the contextual menu.

12. Make sure to check the Automatic Offset/Center checkbox, and insert a Standard 3'-wide, 5'-high window in the center of the wall.

13. Select all the walls, RMB, and select **AEC Dimension** from the contextual menu that appears.

14. Drag your cursor vertically above the horizontal walls, and click the mouse to place the dimension string.

The window will now be dimensioned by its center (see Figure 13-10).

15. Select the dimension string again, RMB, and select **Edit AEC Dimension Style** from the contextual menu that appears to bring up the AEC Dimensional Style properties dialog box.

16. Select the **Display Properties** tab.

17. Double-click on **Plan** in the **Display Representations** column to bring up the **Display Properties** dialog box.

18. Select the **Contents** tab, and select **Opening/Door/Window** from the **Apply to** list

19. Check the **Center** checkbox, and clear the other check boxes (see Figure 13-11).

Figure 13-10

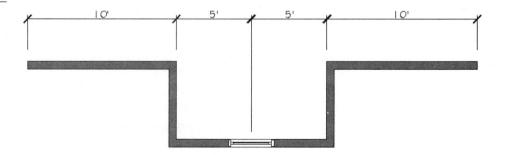

Figure 13-11

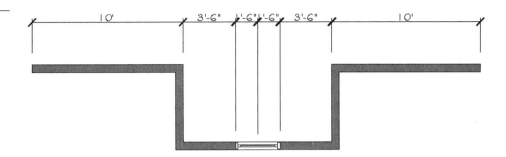

If there is some problem where dimension text overlaps, or if you want to modify the *location* of the text, you must do the following:

You can only display and move the **Edit in Place** grips of an AEC dimension text if the underlying AutoCAD dimension style has the correct text placement settings. To do this, select the AEC dimension string, RMB, and select **Edit AEC Dimension Style** from the contextual menu that appears. Then, select the display representation where you want the changes to appear, and check the **Style Override** checkbox to bring up the **Display Properties** dialog box. Click **Edit,** and in the **Dimension Style Manager** click Modify. Click the **Fit** tab, and select **Over the dimension line, without a leader** for **Text Placement** (see Figure 13-12).

Now when you select the Edit in Place button for the AEC Dimensions, a grip will appear on the dimension itself. You can grab that grip and move the dimension text anywhere you wish.

20. Move the window 24″ to the left. (Use the move command, or activate the window's grips.)

Note that the AEC Dimensions move with the window.

21. Select wall **B**, RMB, and again select **Insert > Window** from the contextual menu that appears.
22. Move your cursor over the Properties palette to open it.
23. Set the **Automatic Offset/Center** to **18**″, and pick a spot near the right side of wall B.

You should now have two windows centered in wall B, and the AEC Dimensions should show the dimensions for the new window (see Figure 13-13).

Explore the other Display Props for Dimension Styles. Save this exercise. Sometimes you will want to create an AEC dimension manually. Per-

Figure 13-12

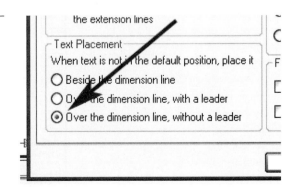

Figure 13-13

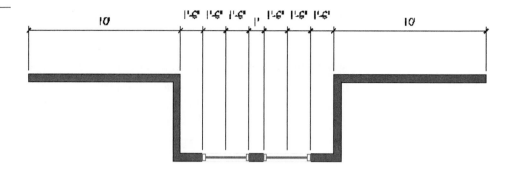

haps you want to dimension somewhere else than the built-in logical points.

Save this file.

Hands-On

Adding a Manual AEC Dimension

1. Use the previous exercise.
2. Lock your viewport.
3. Be sure the **MODEL** space button is activated.
4. Zoom in close to the two windows inserted in the B wall.
5. Select **Format > Point Style** from the **Main** menu.
6. At the **Point Style** dialog box select the × (see Figure 13-14).
7. Type **dimpointmode** at the command line, and press the space bar or Enter.
8. Type **T** at the command line, and press the space bar or Enter.

This sets the dimension points to transformable. Transformable dimension points move and are updated with the object; static points stay in place and don't move.

9. Set the **Intersection** Object Snap.
10. Select the **AEC Dimension (1) - Manual** icon from the Annotation tool palette.

Figure 13-14

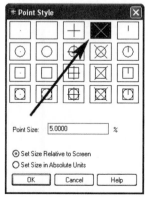

11. Pick the two corners of the two window jambs, and press the space bar or Enter.

12. Pick a point to place the dimension string, and then pick a second point to complete the command (see Figure 13-15).

13. Select the Move icon from the Modify toolbar, and select the left window with a window marquee (see Figure 13-16), and move it to the left 1'-0". Repeat with the right window (see Figure 13-17).

You must move the points with the window to maintain the associative dimensions. Repeat steps 7 through 12, but select S (Static) when prompted for dimpointmode points. Note that the dimensions don't move.

14. The point style you set in Step 6 will cause the points to show as × when you plot. To stop this, bring up the Point Style dialog box again, and change the point style to NONE (see Figure 13-18). Save this file.

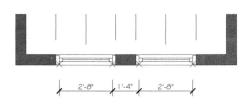

Figure 13-15

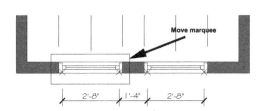

Figure 13-16

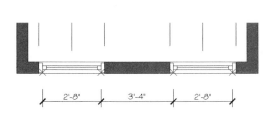

Figure 13-17

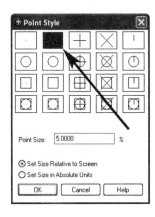

Figure 13-18

Hands-On

Detaching Objects from AEC Dimensions

1. Use the previous exercise.

2. Zoom Extents (since the viewport is locked the paperspace view will zoom extents).

3. Select the AEC dimension string, RMB, and select **Detach Objects** icon from the contextual menu that appears.

4. Select the top AEC Dimension Group (dimension string), and press the space bar or Enter.

5. Select the left window object, and press the space bar or Enter (see Figure 13-19).

You have now detached the left window from the top AEC Dimension Group. Save this file.

Figure 13-19

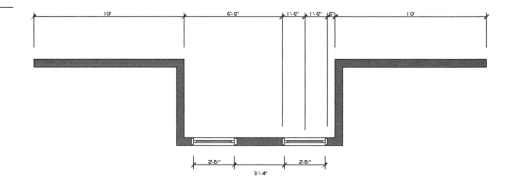

Hands-On

AEC Dimension Chains

In order to clarify dimension strings, architects and architectural drafts-people often add additional dimension strings. Architectural Desktop 2004 calls these *chains*. The chain nearest the AEC Object is called "Chain1," the next is "Chain2," and so forth up to ten chains.

1. Use the previous exercise, and adjust the windows and AEC dimension settings to match Figure 13-20.

2. **Select the AEC dimension string, RMB, and select Edit AEC Dimension Style** from the contextual menu that appears to bring up the **AEC Dimensional Style** properties dialog box.

3. Select the **Chains** tab.

4. Change the Number of Chains to **2**.

5. Change to the **Display Properties** tab.

Figure 13-20

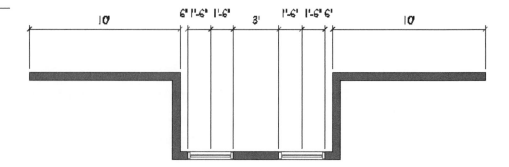

6. Double-click on **Plan** in the **Display Representations** column to bring up the **Display Properties** dialog box.
7. Select the **Contents** tab.

Notice that two Chain check boxes now appear at the lower right of the Contents tab (see Figure 13-21).

8. Activate the **Chain1 field**; select the **Wall** icon in the **Apply to** field, and clear all the Wall check boxes.
9. Change to the **Opening/Door/Window** icon in the **Apply to** field, and check the Opening/Door/Window **Center** check box.
10. Activate the **Chain2 Field**; select the **Wall** icon in the **Apply to** field, and check the **Length of Wall** check box.
11. Press the OK buttons to return to the Drawing Editor (see Figure 13-22).
12. Select the AEC Dimension string, RMB, and select **Add Dimension Points** and add a point to locate the windows.
13. Repeat Step 12, selecting Remove Dimension points, and remove the two Chain2 dimension extension lines to create Figure 13-23.

Figure 13-21

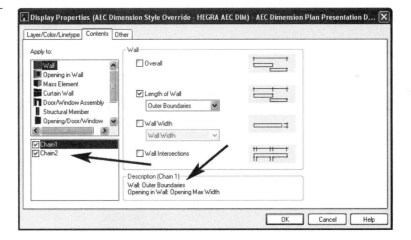

Figure 13-22

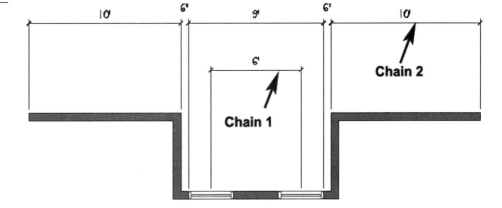

Figure 13-23

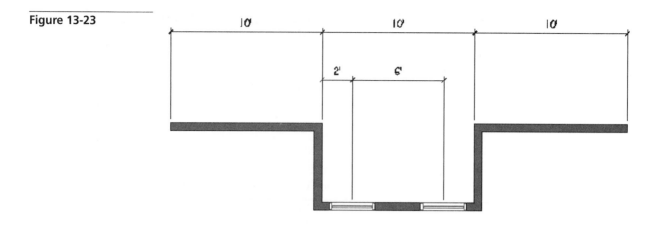

Hands-On

The AEC Dimension Wizard

Although you can set the AEC Dimension display manually as shown at the beginning of this section, Autodesk Architectural Desktop 2004 has provided a Wizard to aid you in setting the display.

Selecting the Format > AEC Dimension Style Wizard from the Main toolbar activates the dialog boxes shown in Figures 13-24, 13-25, 13-26, and 13-27.

Figure 13-24

Figure 13-25

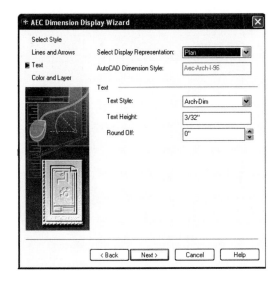

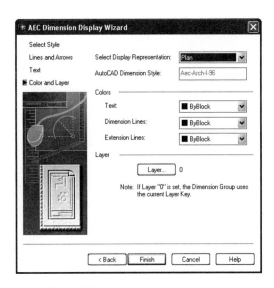

Figure 13-26

Figure 13-27

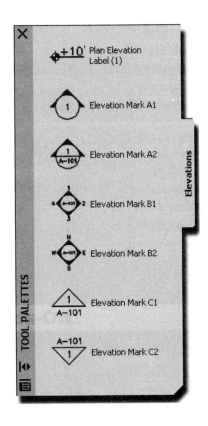

When you finish this section, you should understand the following:

✓ How to make a new Elevation tool palette.
✓ How to create a simple building.
✓ How to make an Elevation.
✓ How to modify and update the 2D Elevation.
✓ How to understand Elevation subdivisions.

Hands-On

Making a New Elevation Tool Palette

1. Create a new tool palette, and name it **Elevations**.
2. Select the **Content Browser** icon from the Main toolbar to launch the **Content Browser**.
3. In the Content Browser locate the **Architectural Desktop Documentation Tool Catalog - Imperial.**
4. Locate the **Elevation Marks** folder.
5. Drag all the Elevation Marks into the new tool palette you created.
6. Click and hold on the tab of your new tool palette and drag a copy to **My Tool Catalog** in the Content Browser.

For the following exploration of elevations, first create a simple three-story building.

Hands-On

Creating a Sample Building for the Elevation Exercises

1. Start a new drawing using the Architectural Building Model and View (Imperial - ctb) template.
2. Change to the Work Layout.
3. Change to Top View, and create the outline shown in Figure 14-1.
4. Select the **Wall** icon from the Walls tool palette, RMB, and select **Apply Tool properties to > Linework** from the contextual menu that appears.
5. Select the outline you created.
6. Enter **Y** (Yes) in the command line to erase the geometry, and press Enter to create walls from the outline.
7. While the walls are still selected, move your cursor over the Properties palette to open it.
8. Set the following:

   a. Style = **Standard**
   b. Wall Width = **8″**
   c. Base Height = **10′-0″**
   d. Justify = **Baseline**

9. Save the drawing as **Floor 1**.
10. Save the drawing two more times as **Floor 2** and **Floor 3**.

Figure 14-1

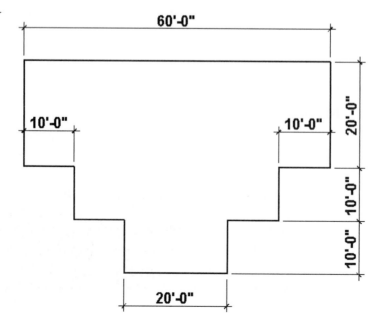

11. Open **Floor 3**, select the **Roof** icon from the **Design** tool palette, RMB, and select **Apply Tool Properties to > Linework and Walls** from the contextual menu that appears.

12. Select all the walls in the **Floor 3** drawing.

13. Enter **N** (No) in the command line, and press Enter to create the roof.

14. While the roof is still selected, move your cursor over the Properties palette to open it.

15. Set the roof to the following:

    a. Thickness = **10″**

    b. Edge cut = **Square**

    c. Shape = **SingleSlope**

    d. Plate height = **10′-0″**

    e. Rise = **6″**

16. Save **Floor 3**.

17. Start a new drawing and save it as **Composite**.

18. Using **Insert > Xref Manager** from the Main toolbar, **Attach** the three floors at Z elevation of 0′ for Floor 1, 10′ for Floor 2, and 20′ for Floor 3 in the **Composite** drawing.

You have now created the building in Figure 14-2.

19. Select Floor 1 in the Composite drawing, RMB, and select **Edit Xref in place** from the contextual menu that appears to bring up the **Reference Edit** dialog box.

20. Press OK to return to the Drawing Editor.

21. Select different walls in the floor, RMB, and insert windows and a door.

22. Press the **Save back changes to reference** icon in the **Refedit** dialog box, and press the OK button that appears.

23. Repeat for each floor until you have a building similar to that shown in Figure 14-3. Save this exercise.

Figure 14-2

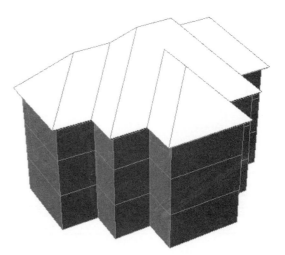

Figure 14-3

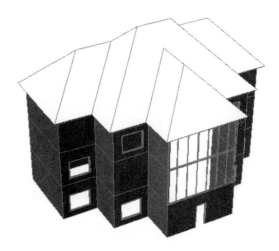

Hands-On

Making an Elevation

Using the previous exercise, select the **Composite** drawing.

1. Select the **Model Layout,** and activate the **Top View**, and then pan the building to the left until it take up a little less than half the page and looks like Figure 14-4.

2. Select the **Elevation Mark A1** from the Elevations tool palette, and place an elevation line starting at the lower center, in front of the building. Drag your cursor as shown in Figure 14-5.

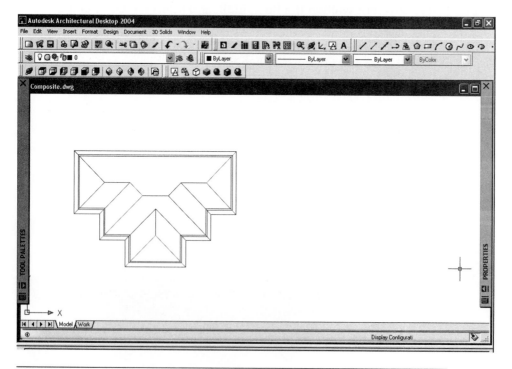

Figure 14-4

Figure 14-5

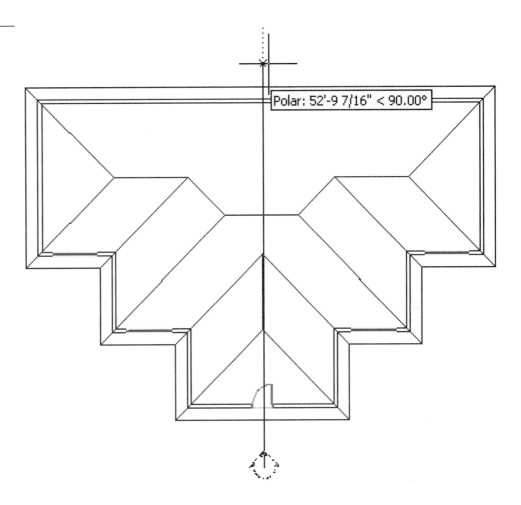

Polar: 52'-9 7/16" < 90.00°

3. Click your mouse to bring up the Edit Attributes dialog box.

4. Enter **1** for the elevation number, and press Enter.

5. Enter **Y** (Yes) in the command line, and press Enter.

6. Enter **80'** in the command line, and press Enter to place the Elevation Line object (see Figure 14-6).

7. Select the Elevation Line object, and move your cursor over the Properties palette to open it.

8. Set the **Use model extents for height** to Yes.

9. RMB and select **Generate Elevation** from the contextual menu that appears.

10. At the **Generate Section/Elevation** dialog box, select the **2D Section/Elevation Object with Hidden Line Removal** radio button, and select the **Pick Point** button.

11. Pick a point to the right of the building floor plan.

12. When the Generate Section/Elevation dialog box reappears, select the **Select Objects** button, and marquee the floor plan with a window, or type **All** at the command line; and press Enter.

13. When the Generate Section/Elevation dialog box reappears again, press OK.

The Elevation of the building will now appear (see Figure 14-7). Save this exercise, and all its files.

Figure 14-6

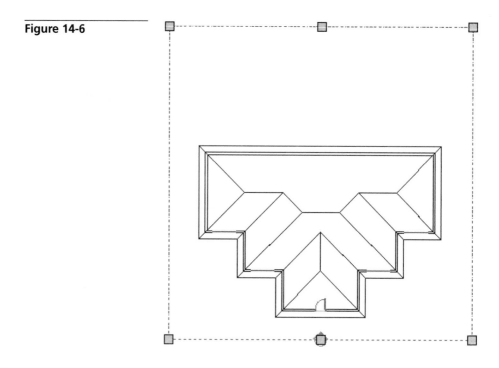

Figure 14-7

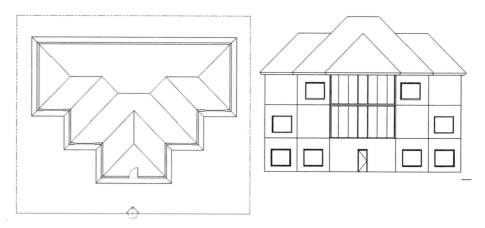

Hands-On

Modifying and Updating the 2D Elevation

1. Open the **Composite** drawing.
2. Change to the SW Isometric View.
3. Select the first floor in the Composite drawing, RMB, and select **Edit Xref in place** from the contextual menu that appears to bring up the **Reference Edit** dialog box.
4. Press OK to return to the Drawing Editor.
5. Select the front wall of the first floor, RMB, and insert windows on either side of the front door.

6. At the Refedit dialog box, press the **Save back changes to reference** icon button, and press OK at the AutoCAD message.
7. Change back to the Top View, and select the 2D elevation that you created.
8. RMB the 2D elevation, and select **Refresh** from the contextual menu that appears.

The 2D Elevation now reflects the changes made in the 3D model (see Figure 14-8). Save this exercise.

Figure 14-8

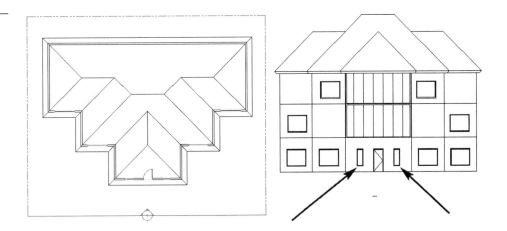

Hands-On

Subdivisions

1. Using the previous exercise, select the elevation line object, and move your cursor over the Properties palette to open it.
2. Click in the **Subdivisions** field to open the **Subdivisions** dialog box.
3. Press the **Add** button, add a 10'-0" subdivision, and press OK to return to the Drawing Editor.

You have now created Subdivision 1 (see Figure 14-9).

Note: Once you have a subdivision, you can select the elevation, and move the subdivision with grips.

4. Move the Subdivision 1 line so that the front extension of the building is within the first subdivision (see Figure 14-10).
5. Select the 2D elevation, RMB, and select **Edit 2D Section/Elevation Style** from the contextual menu that appears to bring up the **2D section/Elevation style** dialog box.
6. Select the **Display Props tab,** and check the Override check box to bring up the Display Properties dialog box.
7. Select the **Layer/Color/Linetype** tab.
8. Change the **Subdivision 1** color to **blue**, select OK, and close all the dialog boxes.

Figure 14-9

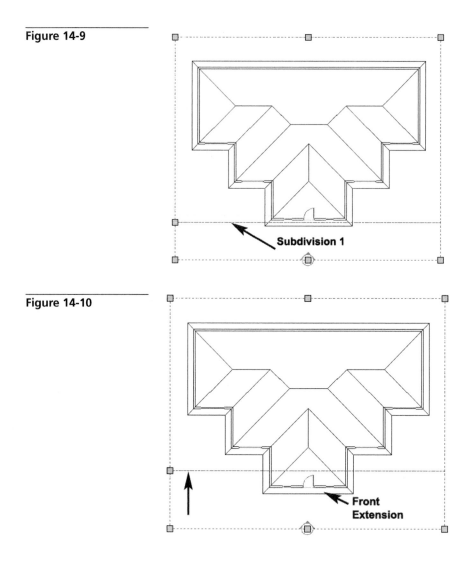

Subdivision 1

Figure 14-10

Front
Extension

9. Select the elevation, RMB, and select **Refresh** from the contextual menu.

You have now changed Subdivision 1 to blue color. Anything between the Defining line and Subdivision 1 will be blue in the elevation. You can also set the line width to be different in a subdivision (see Figure 14-11).

10. Select the elevation line object, RMB, and add two more subdivisions.

11. Select the elevation, RMB, and again select **Edit 2D Section/Elevation Style** from the contextual menu that appears.

12. Change the **Subdivision 2** color to **green**, and **Subdivision 3** to **black**. Change the **lineweight** of Subdivision 3 to 1.40 mm, then select OK and close all the dialog boxes to return to the Drawing Editor.

13. Select the elevation line to activate it, and using the grips (be sure your Object Snap is turned off) move the subdivisions to look like Figure 14-12.

14. Select the elevation, RMB, and select **Refresh** from the contextual menu that appears. Make sure the **LTW** button at the bottom of the screen is active (it visually shows lineweights in the drawing).

Figure 14-11

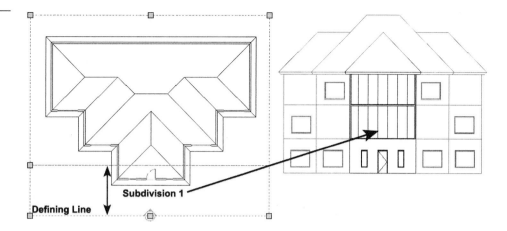

Figure 14-12

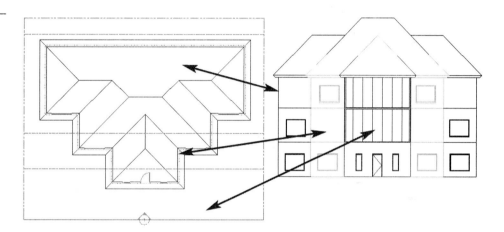

Note that the back outline of the building is black with a 2.00-mm outline. This is because everything between Subdivision 2 and 3 will have the attributes of Subdivision 3. Notice that there is a problem at the roof. Since the roof is pitched, it crosses both Subdivisions 2 and 3. You might also want the base to be all one color (see Figure 14-13).

To fix these problems, you will use the Linework > Edit command.

1. Select the 2D elevation, RMB, and select **Linework > Edit** from the contextual menu that appears.
2. Select the segment of line that you wish to edit, RMB, and select Modify Component from the contextual menu that appears (see Figure 14-14).
3. The **Select Linework Component** dialog box will appear.
4. Select **Erased Vectors** from the **Linework Component** drop-down list (see Figure 14-15).

The lines will now disappear (see Figure 14-16).

5. Select Line from the draw menu, and place lines from the top of the top roof pitch to the ridge of the lower roof (see Figure 14-17).

Figure 14-13

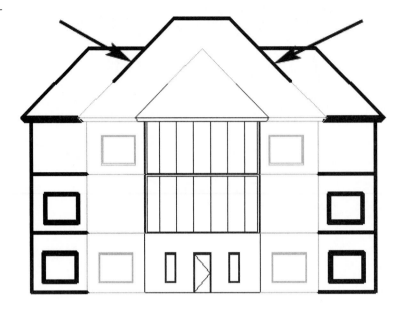

Figure 14-14

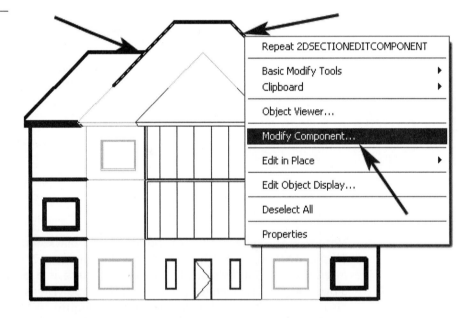

6. Select any line in the 2D elevation (except the new lines you placed), RMB, and select **Edit in Place > Save Changes** from the contextual menu that appears.

7. Select the 2D elevation again, RMB, and select **Linework Merge** from the contextual menu that appears.

8. Select the two lines you just placed in Step 5 of this exercise, press Enter to bring up the **Select Linework Component**, and select **Subdivision 3** (Black division) from the **Linework Component** drop-down list, and press OK to return to the Drawing Editor.

The new lines are now part of the 2D Elevation (see Figure 14-18). Using this exercise, fix the other lines.

Figure 14-15

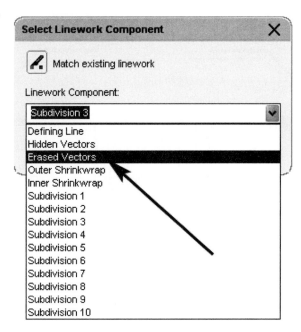

Figure 14-16

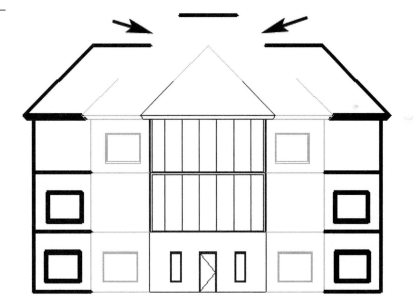

Figure 14-17

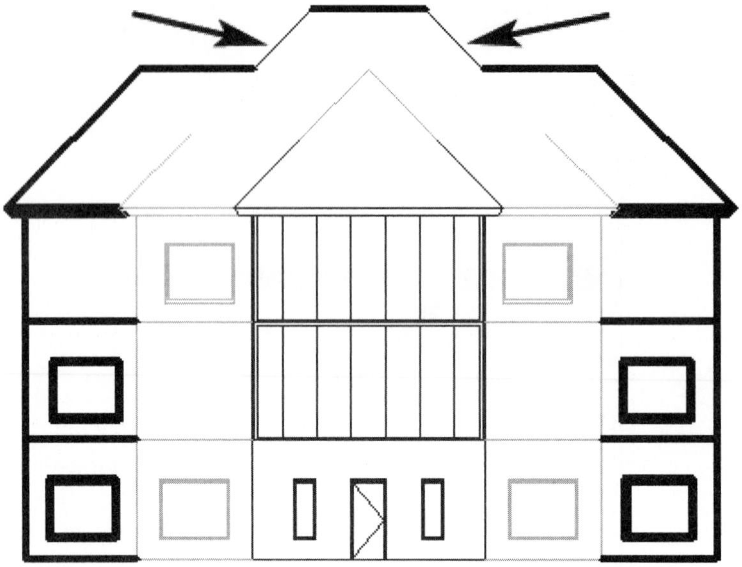

Figure 14-18

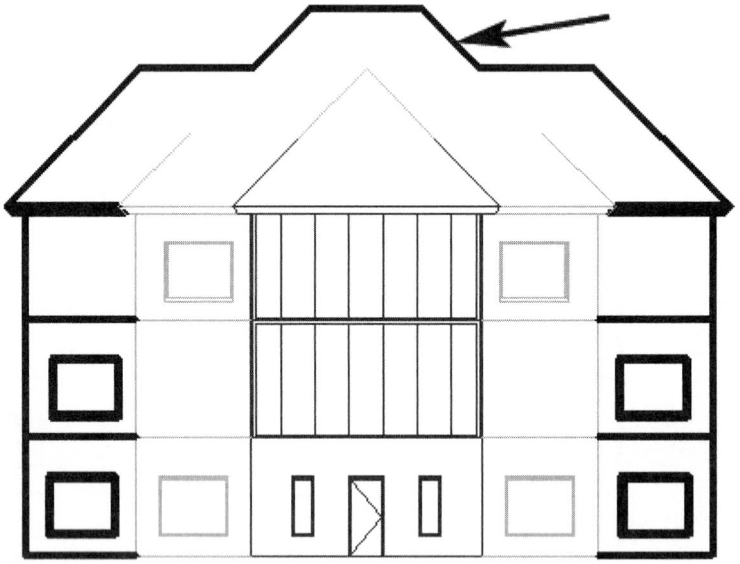

When you finish this section, you should understand the following:

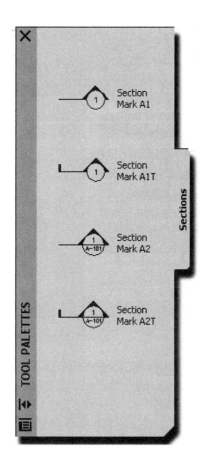

- ✔ How to make a new Section tool palette.
- ✔ How to create a simple building.
- ✔ How to place a Standard Section object.
- ✔ How to generate a Section.
- ✔ How to change the Section Arrow appearance.
- ✔ Live Section definitions.
- ✔ How to create a sample building for a Live Section.
- ✔ How to create and modify a Live Section.

Sections

There are two different types of sections you can create in Architectural Desktop: **Standard Sections** and **Live Sections**.

Live Sections cut only in Model Views, and are limited to the following AEC Objects only:

- ■ Walls
- ■ Doors, windows, and window assemblies
- ■ Mass elements and mass groups
- ■ Stairs and railings
- ■ Roofs and roof slabs

- Spaces and space boundaries
- Curtain wall layouts and units
- Structural members

Hands-On

Making a New Section Tool Palette

1. Create a new tool palette, and name it **Sections**.
2. Select the **Content Browser** icon from the Main toolbar to launch the **Content Browser**.
3. Locate the **Architectural Desktop Documentation Tool Catalog - Imperial.**
4. Locate the **Section Marks** folder.
5. Drag all the section marks into the new tool palette you created.
6. Click and hold on the tab of your new tool palette and drag a copy to **My Tool Catalog** in the Content Browser.

For the following exercise create a sample residence.

Hands-On

Creating the Sample Building

1. Start a new drawing using the Architectural Building Model and View (Imperial - ctb) template.
2. Change to the Model Layout.
3. Change to Top View, select the **Wall** icon from the **Design** tool palette, and move your cursor over the Properties palette to open it.
4. Set the following:

   a. Style = **Standard**
   b. Wall Width = **8**″
   c. Base Height = **8′-0**″
   d. Justify = **Baseline**

5. Place the walls as shown in Figure 15-1.
6. Select the **Roof** icon from the **Design** tool palette, RMB, and select **Apply Tool Properties to > Linework and Walls** from the contextual menu that appears.
7. Select all the walls in your drawing.
8. Enter **N** (No) in the command line, and press Enter to create the roof.
9. While the roof is still selected, move your cursor over the Properties palette to open it.

Figure 15-1

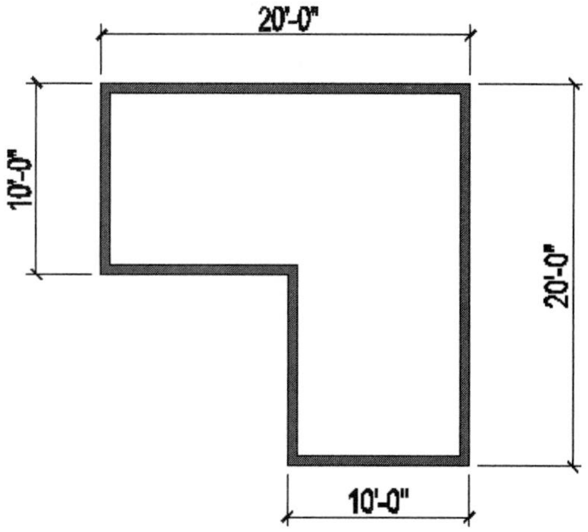

10.   Set the roof to the following:

a.   Thickness = **10″**
b.   Edge cut = **Square**
c.   Shape = **SingleSlope**
d.   Plate height = **8′-0″**
e.   Rise = **12″**

11.   Select the **Slab** icon from the **Design** tool palette, RMB, and select **Apply Tool Properties to > Linework and Walls** from the contextual menu that appears.

12.   Again, select all the walls in your drawing, and press Enter.

13.   Enter **N** (No) in the command line, and press Enter.

14.   Enter **T** (Top) in the command line, and press Enter.

15.   Enter **R** (Right) in the command line, and press Enter twice to place the slab.

16.   While the slab is still selected, move your cursor over the Properties palette to open it.

17.   Set the following:

a.   Style = **Standard**
b.   Thickness = **4″**
c.   Elevation = **0″**

18.   Select the **Quick Select** icon in the Properties palette, select all the walls, and press OK.

19.   With the walls selected, RMB anywhere in the Drawing Editor, and select **Insert > Window** from the contextual menu that appears.

20.   Place 2′ × 4′-high standard windows on each wall.

21.   With the walls still selected, RMB anywhere in the Drawing Editor, and select **Insert > door** from the contextual menu that appears.

22.   Place a 3′-0″ × 6′-8″-high standard door as shown in Figure 15-2.

Figure 15-2

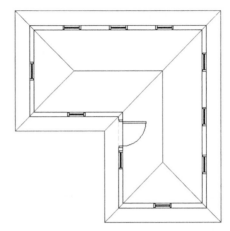

Hands-On

Placing the Standard Section Object

1. Select the **Section Mark A1** from the **Sections** tool palette, click and drag through a window, and then click again through another window similar to that shown in Figure 15-3.

2. The Edit Attributes dialog box will now appear, enter **1** in the Section Mark Number field, and press OK.

3. Move your cursor in the view direction you wish to cut the section, and press Enter.

4. Enter **Y** (Yes) in the command line to **Add building Section Line Object**, and press Enter.

5. Select the Section Line object, and move your cursor over the Properties palette to open it.

6. Set the Use model extents for height to Yes.

You have now placed the Section object.

Figure 15-3

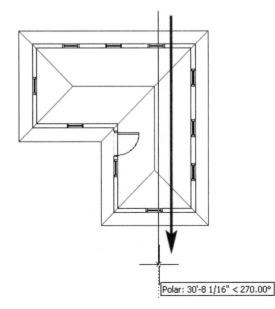

Polar: 30'-8 1/16" < 270.00°

Hands-On

Generating the Section

1. Select the section object, RMB, and select **Generate Section** from the contextual menu that appears.
2. At the **Generate Section/Elevation** dialog box, select the **2D Section/Elevation_Object with Hidden Line Removal** radio button, and select the **Pick Point** button.
3. Pick a point to the right of the building floor plan.
4. When the Generate Section/Elevation dialog box reappears, select the **Select Objects** button, and marquee the floor plan with a window, or type All at the command line; and press Enter.
5. When the Generate Section/Elevation dialog box reappears again, press **OK**.

The 2D Section of the building will now appear (see Figure 15-4).

6. Select the Section object line again, RMB, and select **Reverse** from the contextual menu that appears.
7. Select the 2D section, RMB, and select **Refresh** from the contextual menu that appears (see Figure 15-5).
8. Double-click the window next to the door in the plan view, and change it to a 4'-wide window.
9. Again, select the 2D section, RMB, and select **Refresh** from the contextual menu that appears.

Anything you change in the building model will change in the 2D section when you Refresh it (see Figure 15-6).

Figure 15-4

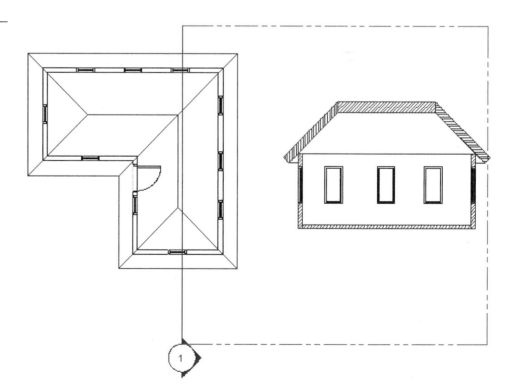

Figure 15-5

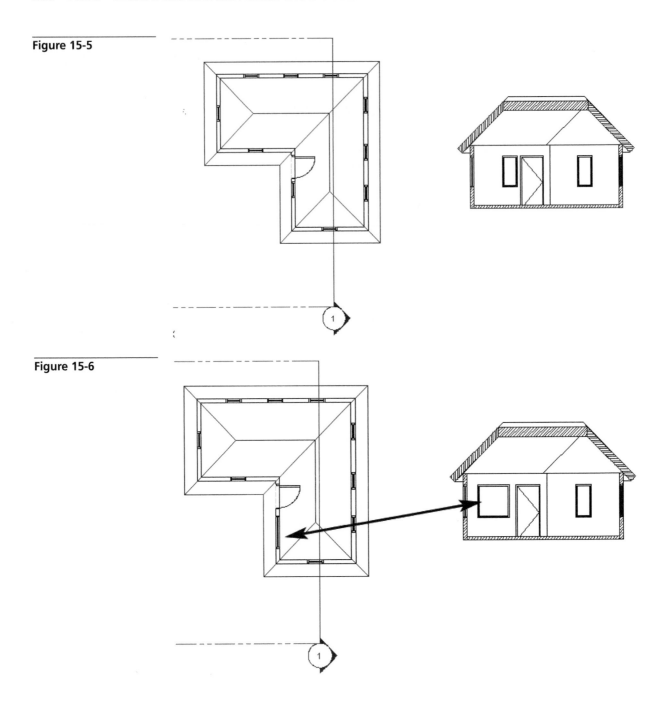

Figure 15-6

Hands-On

Changing the Section Arrow Appearance

1. Select the direction arrow, RMB, and select **Edit Attributes** from the contextual menu that appears to bring up the **Enhanced Attribute Editor** dialog box.

2. Change to the Attribute tab.

3. Change the Value from **1** to **AA**.

4. Change to the **Text Options** and **Properties** tabs to see more controls for the Section Line object arrow, and press the OK button to return to the Drawing Editor.

The Section Line object arrow now reads AA.

5. Change to the **Text Options** and **Properties** tabs to see more controls for the Section Line object arrow, and press the OK button to return to the Drawing Editor.
6. Select the direction arrow again, RMB and select **Edit Block in place** from the contextual menu that appears to bring up the **Reference Edit** dialog box.
7. In the **Reference Edit** dialog box, select the Identity Reference tab, and press OK to return to the Drawing Editor.
8. Zoom close to the arrow (see Figure 15-7).
9. While in **Refedit**, erase the existing **arrow**, and using standard lines, create a new custom arrow.
10. Solid-hatch the new arrow, and press the **Add objects to working set** icon in the **Refedit** toolbar.
11. Select the new arrow, press Enter.
12. Press the **Save back changes to reference** icon, and press the OK button that appears to return to the drawing editor.

You now have a custom Section Line object arrow (see Figure 15-8).

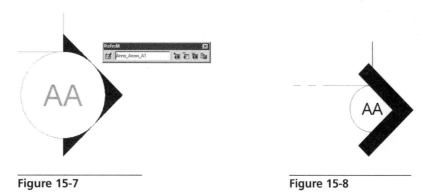

Figure 15-7   Figure 15-8

Live Section Definitions

Unlike standard sections, live sections retain the original objects after sectioning, can set display properties for all objects in section, and can set hatching for section boundaries.

Note: Each new Live Section is displayed in a separate display configuration created specifically for that section. See the explication of Display Configurations in this book.

Figure 15-9

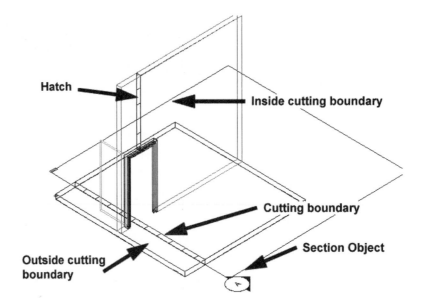

Hatch

Inside cutting boundary

Cutting boundary

Section Object

Outside cutting boundary

Live Sectioned AEC Objects consist of six components (see Figure 15-9).

- **The Cutting boundary**—outside limit of the section (section line)
- **The Hatch**—graphic indication of area inside the cutting boundary
- **Inside cutting boundary**—remaining object cut by cutting boundary *inside* cutting boundary
- **Outside cutting boundary**—remaining object cut by cutting boundary *outside* boundary
- **Inside full body**—object completely *inside* section
- **Outside full body**—object completely *outside* section

Before a Live Section or any section can be created, a Section Mark or Section line must be placed in your drawing to identify where the section is to take place.

Hands-On

Creating a Sample Building for a Live Section

1. Start a new drawing using the Architectural Building Model and View (Imperial - ctb) template.
2. Change to the Model Layout.
3. Change to Top View.
4. Select the **CMU-8 Rigid-1.5 Air-2 Brick-4 Furring Wall** icon from the **Walls** tool palette in the **Autodesk Architectural desktop Sample Palette Catalog - Imperial**, and create a 10'-0" × 10'-0" enclosure.
5. Select the left wall, RMB, and select **Insert Door** from the contextual menu
6. Place a 3'-0" standard door, centered in the left wall, swinging inward (see Figure 15-10).
7. Select **Format > Drawing Setup** from the Main toolbar to bring up the **Drawing Setup** dialog box.

Figure 15-10

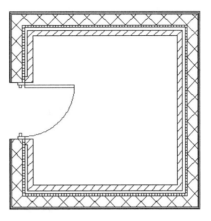

8. In the Drawing Setup dialog box, select the **Scale** tab, and set the **Drawing Scale** to **1/4″ = 1′-0″**, change the **Annotation Plot Size** to 1/8″, and press OK.

9. Select the **Sections Mark A1** from the **SECTIONS** tool palette.

10. Place the start point at the left of the door, and place the second point to the right of the right wall, and press Enter.

11. The Edit Attributes dialog box appears; enter **1** in the Section Mark Number field, and press OK.

12. Move your cursor in the view direction you wish to cut the section, and press Enter.

13. Enter **Y** (Yes) in the command line to **Add building Section Line Object**, and press Enter.

14. Select the Section Line object, and move your cursor over the Properties palette to open it.

15. Set the Use model extents for height to Yes.

You have now created a selection object (see Figure 15-11).

Figure 15-11

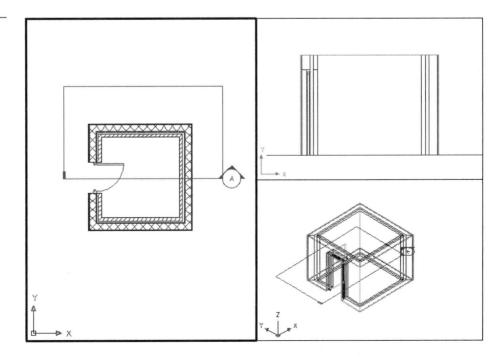

Creating a Live Section

1. Use the previous exercise.
2. Select the section object, RMB, and select **Enable Live Section** from the contextual menu that appears. A 3D sectioned model of the enclosure appears (see Figure 15-12).
3. Change to the Work Layout.
4. Place one viewport of the enclosure in Top View and the other in Front View.
5. Change to the **Front View.**
6. Select the **Hidden** icon in the Shading toolbar to display the live section in hidden display.
7. Note that all the sectioned views display symbols of all the materials set for the wall components (see Figure 15-13).
8. Select Front wall, and move your cursor over the Properties palette to open it.
9. Change the Style to Standard.

Figure 15-12

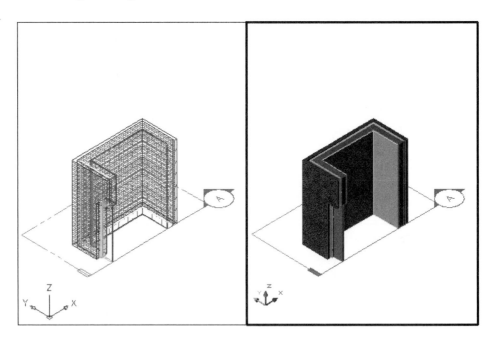

Figure 15-13

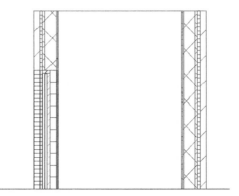

10. Return to the Drawing Editor; notice that the front wall in the Top View (Plan View) has changed.

All the AEC components in the section such as door size, hatching, and so on can be changed in the section, and the changes will reflect in the 2D plan drawing (see Figure 15-14).

Modifying a Live Section

11. Select the Section Line object and move it so that it does not pass through the door, and see that the Live Section changes (see Figure 15-15).

12. Select the Section Line object and rotate it, and see that the Live Section changes (see Figure 15-16).

Figure 15-14

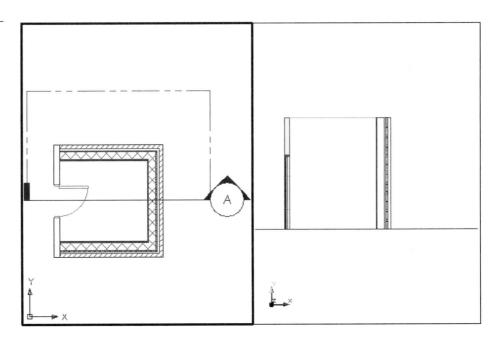

Figure 15-15

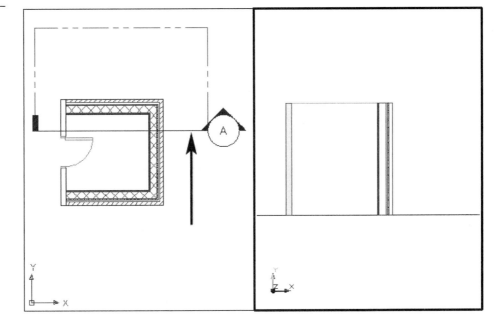

Using the Live Section, you can automatically adjust your sections, even in another drawing, by changing the plan, and vice versa.

If you need to hide the Section Line object itself, do the following:

1. Select the **Section Line Object**, RMB, and select **Edit Object Display** from the contextual menu that appears.
2. Select the **Plan** field, and check the **Object Override** check box to open the **Display Properties** dialog box.
3. Turn off the visibility for the **Boundary,** and press the OK buttons to return to the Drawing Editor (see Figure 15-17).

Figure 15-16

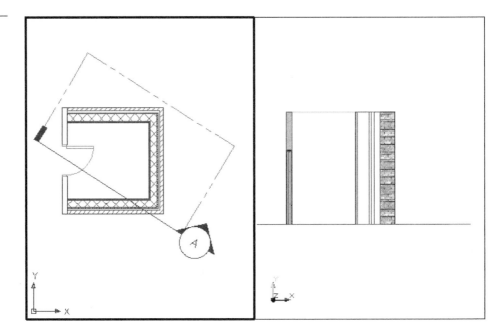

Figure 15-17

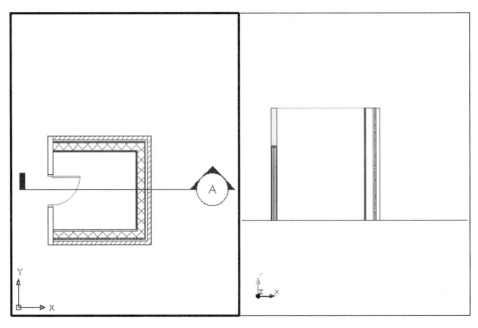

16

Mask Blocks

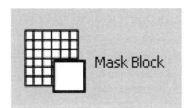

Mask Block

When you finish this section, you should be able to do the following:

✔ Understand the purpose of Mask Blocks.
✔ Understand how to create, modify, and use Mask Blocks.

Mask Blocks are two-dimensional blocks that mask the graphic display of AEC Objects in Plan View.

Mask Blocks are often combined with AutoCAD objects such as lay-in fluorescent fixtures to mask the AEC ceiling grid. With a thorough understanding of Mask Blocks, you will probably find a myriad of uses for these objects.

Hands-On

Creating a Custom Fluorescent Fixture Called New Fixture

1. Start a new drawing using the Architectural Building Model and View (Imperial - ctb) template.
2. Change to the Model Layout.
3. Change to the Top View.
4. Using the standard AutoCAD drawing commands, draw the ceiling fixture shown in Figure 16-1.

Figure 16-1

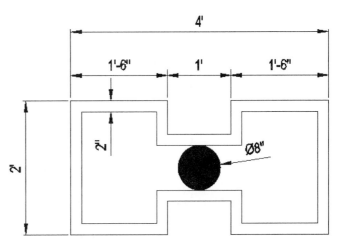

5. Enter **Pedit** in the command line, select the outline, and **Join** the outline into a closed polyline.

> **Note:** If you don't know how to convert and join a line into a polyline, consult the AutoCAD 2004 help for **Polyline Edit (Pedit).**

6. RMB anywhere in the Drawing Editor and select basic modify Tools > Offset from the contextual menu that appears.
7. Enter 2″ in the command line, and press Enter to create the 2″ outline shown in Figure 16-1.
8. Select **Format > Style Manager** from the **Main** toolbar to bring up the **Style Manager** dialog box.
9. Open the **Multi-Purpose** folder and double-click on the **Mask Block Definitions** icon.
10. Select the New Style icon in the Main Style Manager toolbar.
11. Rename the New Style to **NEW LIGHT FIXTURE**.
12. Select the **NEW LIGHT FIXTURE** icon, and select the **Set From** icon from the Main Style Manager toolbar.
13. Select the outline when asked to **"Select a close polyline"** at the command line.
14. Accept **N** when asked to **"Add another ring?"** at the command line.
15. Make the insertion point for the Mask the center point of the outline.
16. When asked to **"Select additional graphics"** at the command line select everything except the outline.
17. At the **Style Manager** dialog box, press the **Apply** button, then press OK.

The outline will become the Mask Block, and the interior objects of the drawing will become the fixture graphics.

Hands-On

Testing the New Light Fixture Mask Block

1. Erase everything.
2. Create a 30′ × 30′ standard wall enclosure 10′ high.

For this exercise you will need to add the Mask Block tool to your Design tool palette, so do the following:

a. Select the **Content Browser** icon from the **Main** toolbar to launch the **Content Browser.**
b. Locate the **Autodesk Architectural Desktop Stock Tool Catalog - Imperial.**
c. Locate the **General Purpose Tools** folder.
d. In the General Purpose Tools folder locate the **Helper Tools** folder.
e. From the Helper Tools folder, drag the Mask Block tool into your Design tool palette.

Figure 16-2

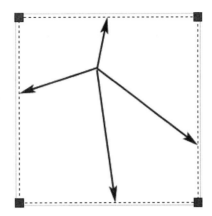

3. Select the Rectangle icon from the Draw toolbar, and place a rectangle inside the 30′ × 30′ enclosure you created (see Figure 16-2).
4. Change the **Display Configuration** to **Reflected**.
5. Select the **Ceiling Grid** icon from the Design tool palette, and enter **S** (Set boundary) in the command line, and press Enter.
6. Pick the Rectangle you placed in Step 13 of this exercise.
7. Move your cursor over the Properties palette to open it.
8. Set the following:

   a. Specify on screen = **no**
   b. X-Width = **40′**
   c. Y-Depth = **40′**
   d. XAxis Layout type = **Repeat**
   e. XAxis Bay size = **2′-0″**
   f. YAxis Layout type = **Repeat**
   g. YAxis Bay size = **4′-0″**

9. Enter SN (Snap to center), press Enter twice, and then press the Esc key to complete the command.

You have now placed a centered ceiling grid, but it is located at elevation 0″.

10. Select the ceiling grid again, and move your cursor over the Properties palette to open it.
11. Set the Elevation to 8′-0″ (see Figure 16-3).
12. Select the Mask Block tool icon that you placed in the Design palette.
13. Move your cursor over the Properties palette to open it.
14. Enter **R** (Rotation) in the command line, enter **90,** and press Enter.
15. Insert 12 copies of the Mask Block vertically.
16. Insert two more copies horizontally (see Figure 16-4).

Notice that the horizontal Mask Blocks cross over a grid (see Figure 16-5). To correct this do the following:

17. Select the horizontal Mass Blocks you placed, RMB, and select **Attach Object** from the contextual menu that appears.

Figure 16-3

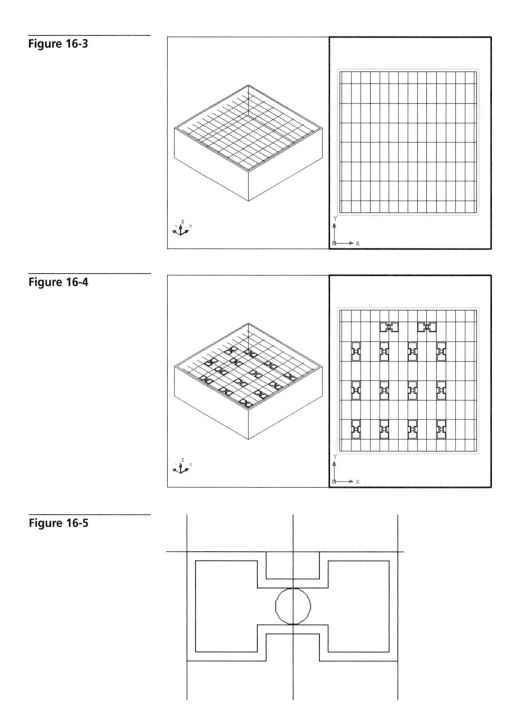

Figure 16-4

Figure 16-5

18. Select the ceiling grid to bring up the **Select Display Representation** dialog box.
19. Press OK to return to the Drawing Editor.

The grid is now masked by the NEW LIGHT FIXTURE mask block (see Figure 16-6). Save this file.

Figure 16-6

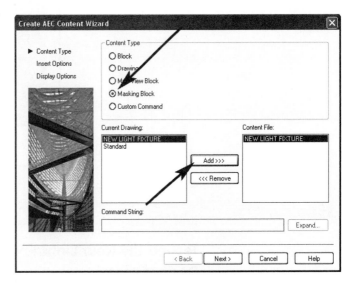

masked
ceiling
grid

Hands-On

Using Create AEC Content to Place the New Light Fixture in the DesignCenter

1.   Erase everything but one **NEW LIGHT FIXTURE** in the Top View.

The icon that will be used in the DesignCenter will be taken from the current view.

2.   Select the **Format > AEC Content Wizard** from the **Main** toolbar to bring up the **Create AEC Content Wizard** dialog box.

3.   Select the Masking Block radio button, press the **Add** button to add the **NEW LIGHT FIXTURE** mask bock to the **Content File,** and press the **Next** button (see Figure 16-7).

4.   At the next Create AEC Content Wizard dialog box (**Insert Options**), press the **Select Layer Key** button to bring up the **Select Layer Key** dialog box.

5.   Select the **LIGHTCLG** layer key, and press OK (see Figure 16-8).

Selecting the **LIGHTCLG** layer key assures you that when you insert the content it will be placed on that layer.

Figure 16-7

Figure 16-8

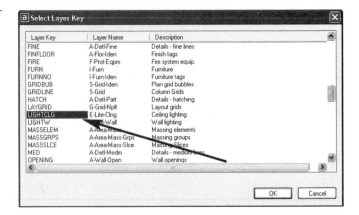

6. Select the **Next** button in the Create AEC Content Wizard dialog box.

7. In Display Options press the **Browse** button.

8. At the Save Content File, locate the Program Files\Autodesk Architectural Desktop 2004\Sample\Design Center folder, name the file **CEILING FIXTURES**, and press the **Save** button to return to the Create AEC Content Wizard dialog box.

9. Type in a description for the Masking Block in the **Detailed Description** space, and press the **Finish** button (see Figure 16-9).

Note that the current viewport drawing is shown as an icon.

Figure 16-9

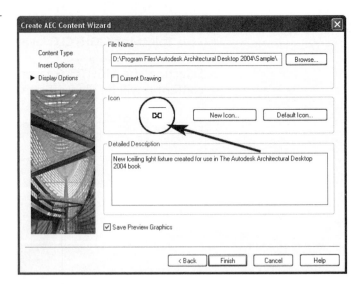

Hands-On

Testing the New Light Fixture Mask Block from the DesignCenter

1. Erase everything in the previous drawing.

2. Select the DesignCenter icon from the Main toolbar or enter **CTRL + 2** to bring up the **DesignCenter** palette.

3. Click on the **CEILING FIXTURES** drawing that you saved.

4. Select and drag the **NEW LIGHT FIXTURE** icon into a new drawing, and zoom extents (see Figure 16-10).

The Create AEC Content Wizard will place Blocks, Drawings, Mask Blocks, and custom command strings in the DesignCenter. The process is essentially the same for all these different forms of content.

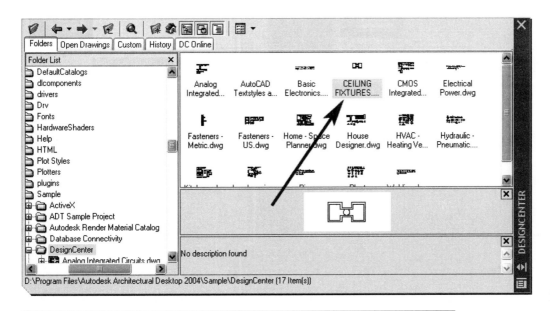

Figure 16-10

Multi-View Blocks

When you finish this section, you should be able to do the following:

- ✔ Understand the purpose of Multi-View blocks.
- ✔ Understand how to create and use Multi-View blocks.
- ✔ Create the Autodesk Website icon.
- ✔ Create the content from the 3D mesh.
- ✔ Create the Multi-View block.

In combination with Autodesk Architectural Desktop's display system, the program uses a multiview block system. This system allows you to place content in one view, and have the appropriate view appear in the other viewports. Although the program comes with a great deal of content, it includes controls that enable you to create your own custom content.

The following exercise illustrates the creation of a custom Multi-View block.

The Chair

For this exercise you will need to use the Web to get content. You can go directly to the Web from inside Autodesk Architectural Desktop 2004 by activating the Autodesk Website icon from the Main toolbar icon.

Hands-On

Creating the Autodesk Website Icon

If you do not have this icon on any toolbar do the following:

1. RMB on any toolbar icon, and pick **Customize** from the contextual menu that appears to bring up the **Customize** dialog box.
2. In the Customize dialog box Change to the **Commands** tab.
3. In the Commands tab, select **Tools** in the **Categories** list.
4. Drag the **Autodesk Website** icon to the drawing editor.

Hands-On

Going to the Chair at the Nsight3D Website

1. Go to http://www.nsight3d.com/nsfree1.htm; the owner of the site has given us permission to use one of his free objects for this exercise (see Figures 17-1 and 17-2).

   ! **Note:** From time to time the owner of the Website makes changes so the following picture may change slightly.

2. Download the Nsight Onsite Chair 3DS file, unzip it, and place it in a folder on your computer.

Figure 17-1

Figure 17-2

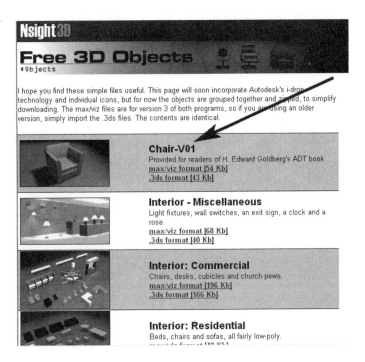

Hands-On

Creating Content from a 3D Mesh

1. Start a new drawing using the Architectural Building Model and View (Imperial - ctb) template.

2. Change to the **Model** Layout.

3. Change to the **SW Isometric** View.

4. Select **Insert > 3D Studio** from the Main toolbar, and import the Onsit3ds file that was downloaded and unzipped from the Web.

5. At the 3D Studio File Import dialog box select the **Chair-V01** mesh from the Available Objects, select the Don't Assign a Material radio button, press the Add button, and add it to the Selected Objects (see Figure 17-3).

Figure 17-3

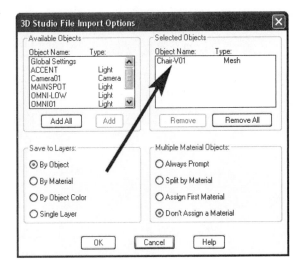

6. Change to the **Work** Layout.

7. Erase all the viewports.

8. Select **View > 4 Viewports** from the Main menu, and press Enter.

9. Change all the views in each viewport to **Top, Front, Left,** and **SW Isometric,** respectively.

You have now imported a 3D mesh model of a chair (see Figure 17-4).

10. Select the **Content Bowser** icon from the **Main** toolbar to open the **Contact Browser**.

11. Select the **Autodesk Architectural Desktop Stock Tool Catalog**.

12. Select the **Helper Tools** folder.

13. Change to the Model Layout, and change to the Left View.

14. From the Helper Tools folder drag the **Hidden Line Projection** to the Design tool palette.

15. Select the Hidden Line Projection icon, select the chair, and press Enter.

16. Select any Block insertion point, and type **Y** at the command line to insert in plan view.

17. Return to a SW Isometric View to see the chair and its new 2D hidden line projection.

You have now created a 2D hidden line projection of the left view of your model (see Figure 17-5).

18. Repeat this process for the top and front views (see Figure 17-6).

19. Select an empty place in the viewport, RMB, and select Basic Modify Tools > #D Operations > 3D Rotate from the contextual menu that appears. Rotate the front and side views, and place them as shown in Figure 17-7. Create insertion points that align all the views and the model.

20. Select Format > Blocks > Block Definition and save each view as a **block,** naming them **CHAIR FRONT, CHAIR SIDE, CHAIR TOP,** and **CHAIR MODEL,** respectively, using the insertion points also shown in Figure 17-7.

Figure 17-4

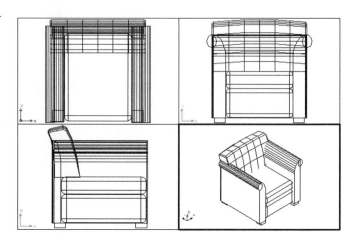

Figure 17-5

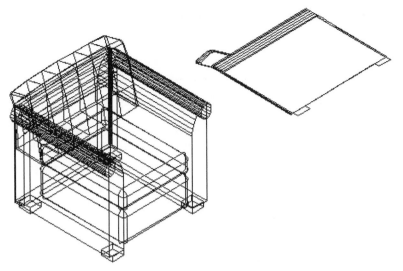

Figure 17-6

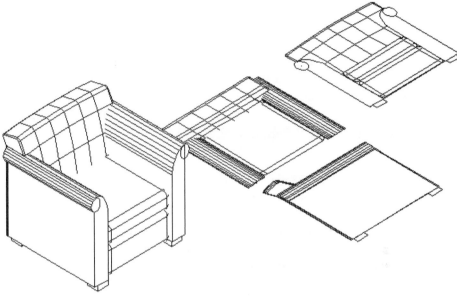

Figure 17-7

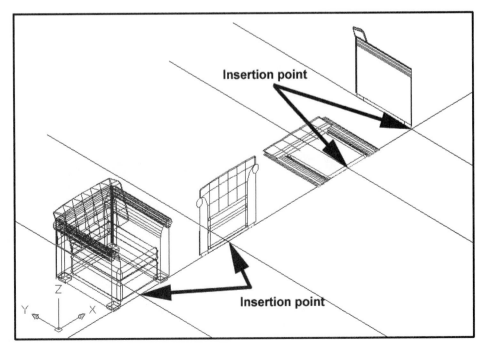

Insertion point

Insertion point

Hands-On

Creating the Multi-View Block

1. Select **Format** > **Multi-View Block** > **Multi-View Block Definitions** from the **Main** toolbar to bring up the Style Manager dialog box.
2. Select the **New Style** icon and create a new style; name it **CHAIR**.
3. Select Chair Style, RMB, and select **Edit** from the contextual menu that appears to bring up the **Multi-View Block Definition Properties** dialog box.
4. Select the **View Blocks** tab.
5. In the View Blocks tab, select **General**, then press the add button and select the **CHAIR FRONT** block.
6. After adding the **CHAIR FRONT** block, check the **Front** and **Back** check boxes under View Directions (see Figure 17-8).
7. Repeat this process for the CHAIR SIDE, and CHAIR TOP blocks selecting the check boxes as shown (see Figures 17-9 and 17-10).

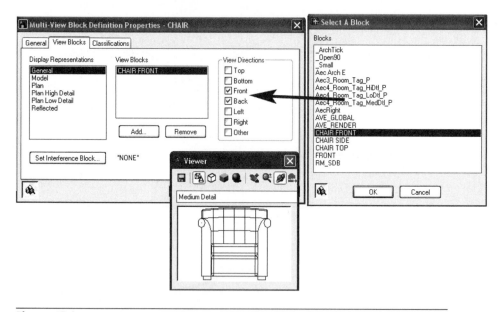

Figure 17-8

Figure 17-9

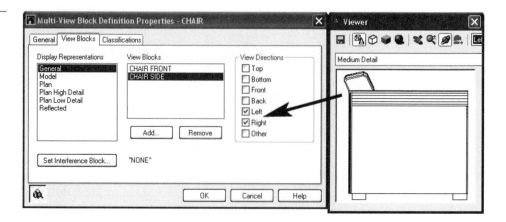

Figure 17-10

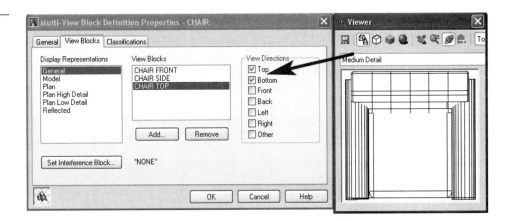

Figure 17-11

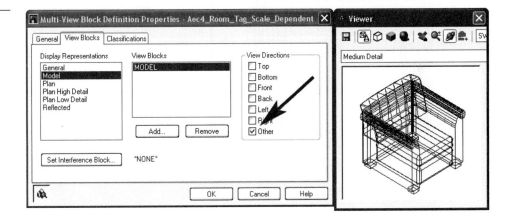

8. Select **Model** from the Display Representations, then add the Model block, and check the **Other** check box (see Figure 17-11).

You have now created the Multi-View Block.

Hands-On

Testing the Multi-View Block

1. Erase everything in the drawing.
2. Change to the Work Layout.
3. Activate the Top View viewport.
4. Select the **Content Bowser** icon from the **Main** toolbar to open the **Contact Browser**.
5. Select the **Autodesk Architectural Desktop Stock Tool Catalog.**
6. Select the **Helper Tools** folder.
7. From the Helper Tools folder drag the **Multi-View Block Reference** icon to the **Design** tool palette.
8. Select **Multi-View Block Reference** icon from the Design tool palette.
9. Move your cursor over the Properties palette to open it.

10.   Select **CHAIR** from the **Definition** drop-down list.

11.   Click in the Top viewport, and press Enter to complete the command.

The correct view of the chair appears in all the different viewports. Zoom extents in each viewport (see Figure 17-12). Save this exercise.

There are many ways to make 3D content. You can use AutoCAD's 3D modeling capability, 3D Studio Viz, or search the Web for free content. With Multi-View Blocks, the sky is the limit.

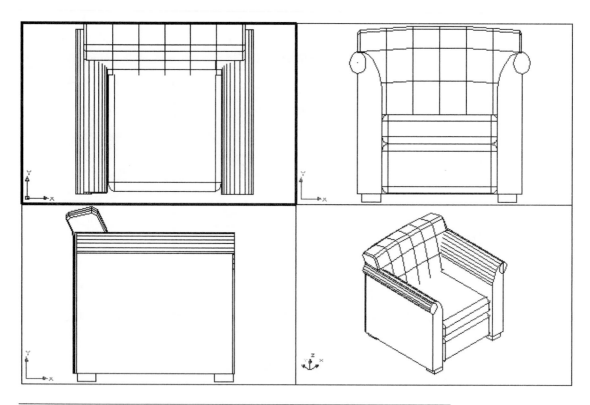

Figure 17-12

Schedules and
Schedule Tags

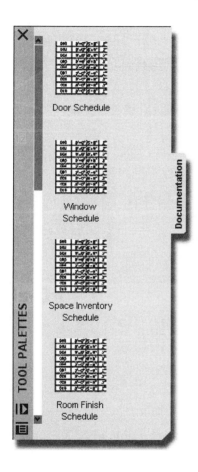

Door Schedule

Window
Schedule

Space Inventory
Schedule

Room Finish
Schedule

Documentation

TOOL PALETTES

When you finish this section, you should understand the following:

- ✔ How to create Schedule Tags and Schedules Tool Palette.
- ✔ How to place Door and Window tags.
- ✔ How to place schedules.
- ✔ How to use schedules to locate objects.
- ✔ How to create and use custom schedules.

Hands-On

Making a New Schedule Tag and Schedule Tool Palette

1. Create a new tool palette named **SCHEDULES**.
2. Select the **Content Browser** icon from the Main toolbar to launch the **Content Browser**.
3. In the **Autodesk Architectural Desktop Documentation Tool Catalog - Imperial**, locate the **Schedule Tables** folder.
4. Drag the **Door** and **Window** schedules and tags into the new tool palette you created.

5. In the **Autodesk Architectural Desktop Documentation Tool Catalog - Imperial**, locate the **Schedule Tags** folders.

6. Drag the **Door Tag** and **Window Tag** tags into the new tool palette you created.

7. Click and hold on the tab of your new tool palette and drag a copy to **My Tool Catalog** in the Content Browser.

Schedule Tags

In order to compile data into a schedule, objects must be tagged. Autodesk Architectural Desktop 2004 contains tags for the following objects:

- Doors
- Windows
- Room number
- Room Finish
- Space
- Beams, Braces, and Columns
- Equipment
- Furniture
- Walls

Hands-On

Placing Door and Window Tags

1. Start a new drawing using the Architectural Building Model and View (Imperial - ctb) template.

2. Change to the Model Layout.

3. Change to the Top View.

4. **Select Format > Drawing Setup** from the **Main** menu.

5. Select the **Scale** tab, and set the **Drawing Scale** to **1/4″ = 1′-0″**, and the **Annotation Plot Size** to **1/8″**.

6. Select the Wall icon in the Design tool palette, and create a 30′-0″ × 20′-0″-wide enclosure. Make the walls **Standard 6″** wide, **8′** high.

7. Select a wall, RMB, and select Insert > Door from the contextual menu.

8. Place a **3′-0″** wide **Standard** door in each wall.

9. Repeat Steps 7 and 8 placing 3′ × 5′ windows along side the doors (see Figure 18-1).

Figure 18-1

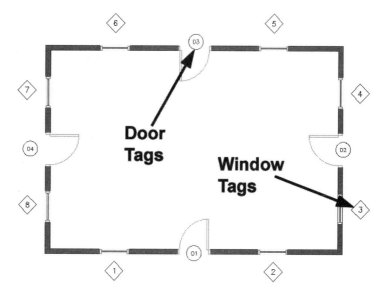

10. Select the **Door Tag** icon from the SCHEDULES tool palette you cre-
     ated and select the bottommost door, and place the tag in the mid-
     dle of the door opening.

The Edit Property Set Data dialog box will now appear. You can now
change data such as Fire Rating, etc. (see Figure 18-2).

11. When you are finished, press OK in the dialog box to place the
     schedule tag.

Figure 18-2

If you do not want to see this dialog box every time you place a tag, do the following:

    a.   Select **Format > Options** to bring up the Options dialog box.

    b.   In the Options dialog box, select the **AEC Content** tab.

    c.   In the AEC Content tab, uncheck the **Display Edit Property Data Dialog During Insertion** check box. See Figure 18-3.

12.   Repeat for the other doors.

13.   Zoom close to the doors.

Notice that they are automatically numbered incrementally. To change the settings of the tag, do the following:

14.   Select **Format > Style Manager** to bring up the Style Manager dialog box from the Main toolbar.

15.   Select **Documentation Objects > Property Set Definitions > Door Objects**.

Property Set Definitions are groups of properties for particular objects that you want to manage in schedules. They can be automatic, deriving their values from the properties of objects, or user-defined.

16.   Select Door Objects, RMB, and select Edit from the contextual menu to bring up the **Property Set Definitions** dialog box.

17.   Select the **Definition** tab.

If you want to automatically increment the objects number system, select **Auto Increment,** and set the start number as the **Default.** The tags can also be created or modified to display the information defined in the property Definition.

Figure 18-3

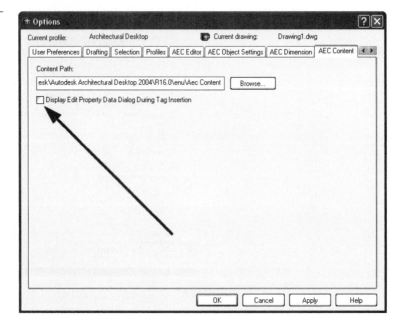

18. Place window tags for the windows. If the tags don't increment automatically, change their setting in the Property Definition Set for window objects. Save this exercise.

Placing Schedules

1. Using the Previous exercise, select the **Door Schedule** icon from the Schedules tool palette you created.
2. Move your cursor over the Properties palette to open it.
3. Set the following:

   a. Update automatically = **Yes**
   b. Add new Objects = **Yes**
   c. Scan xrefs = **Yes**
   d. Scan block references = **Yes**

4. Select all the doors (this can be done with a marquee).
5. Click in a spot on the page to start the upper left corner of the schedule.
6. Press the space bar or Enter key when requested for the lower right corner.

Pressing Enter (Architectural Desktop calls it **Return** in the command line) causes the schedule to automatically be scaled at the size set by the drawing scale you set earlier.

7. Select all the Doors and their tags, and press Enter.
8. Repeat Steps 1 through 5 for the Window Schedule (see Figure 18-4).

DOOR AND FRAME SCHEDULE

MARK	SIZE WD	SIZE HGT	SIZE THK	MATL	GLAZING	LOUVER WD	LOUVER HGT	MATL	EL	HEAD	JAMB	SILL	FIRE RATING LABEL	SET NO	KEYSIDE RM NO	NOTES
1	3'-0"	6'-8"	2"	--	--	0"	0"	--	--	--	--	--	--	--	--	--
2	3'-0"	6'-8"	2"	--	--	0"	0"	--	--	--	--	--	--	--	--	--
3	3'-0"	6'-8"	2"	--	--	0"	0"	--	--	--	--	--	--	--	--	--
4	3'-0"	6'-8"	2"	--	--	0"	0"	--	--	--	--	--	--	--	--	--

WINDOW SCHEDULE

MARK	WIDTH	HEIGHT	TYPE	MATERIAL	NOTES
1	3'-0"	5'-0"	--	--	--
2	3'-0"	5'-0"	--	--	--
3	3'-0"	5'-0"	--	--	--
4	3'-0"	5'-0"	--	--	--
5	3'-0"	5'-0"	--	--	--
6	3'-0"	5'-0"	--	--	--
7	3'-0"	5'-0"	--	--	--
8	3'-0"	5'-0"	--	--	--

Figure 18-4

Hands-On

Updating Schedules

1. Remove two of the doors.
2. Notice that the schedule has a line going across it.

This indicates that some object in the schedule has been removed or changed.

3. Select the Door schedule, RMB, and select **Update Schedule Table** from the contextual menu.

The schedule will update, removing or changing object data.

4. Add more windows and window tags.

The schedule does not indicate the additions.

5. Select the Window schedule, RMB, and select **Selection > Add** from the contextual menu.
6. Select all the windows and tags.

The Window schedule updates, showing the new windows.

Hands-On

Using Schedules to Locate Objects

If you need to quickly locate an object listed in the schedule, do the following:

1. Select the Door schedule, RMB, and select **Selection > Show** from the contextual menu.
2. Hold down the **Ctrl** key on the keyboard, and pick any number in a field.

The screen will zoom to the object in that field.

Hands-On

Exporting Schedules to Databases

If you have Microsoft Excel, or a text Editor such as Word or even Windows Notepad software, you can export your schedules to these formats.

1. Select the Door schedule, RMB, and select **Export** the contextual menu to bring up the **Export Schedule Table** dialog box.

2. Select **Microsoft [Tab delimited] [*.xls]** from the **Output - Save As Type** drop-down list.

3. Browse to a convenient folder, and press OK.

You will now be able to open the file in Microsoft Excel 95 and later.

4. If you set the **Output - Save As Type** to **Text [Tab delimited] [*.txt]**, you will be able to open the file in any text Editor (see Figures 18-5 and 18-6).

Figure 18-5

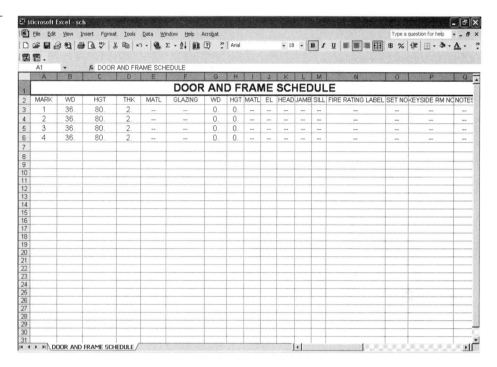

Figure 18-6

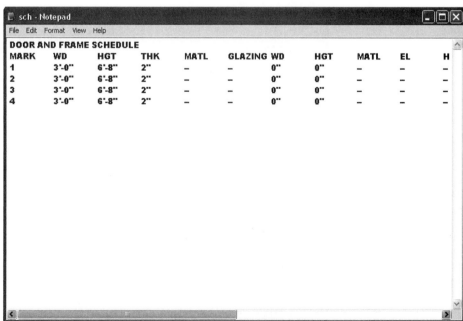

Creating and Using Custom Schedules

The Drawing

1. Erase everything from the previous exercise
2. Place three circles in the drawing with radii of 2', 4', and 6', respectively.

You are going to create a schedule that records information about the circles in your drawing. In order to make a schedule you will need to create a **Property Set Definition.**

The Property Set Definition

3. Select **Format > Style Manager** to bring up the Style Manager dialog box from the main toolbar.
4. Select **Documentation Objects > Property Set Definitions**, RMB, and select new from the contextual menu to create a new **Property Set Definition.**
5. Rename the new Property Set Definition **CIRCLE SCHEDULE.**
6. Double-click on CIRCLE SCHEDULE to bring up the **Property Set Definition Properties** dialog box.
7. Select the **Applies To** tab.

This dialog box contains all the objects from which schedules can be made; after this exercise be sure to explore it.

8. Select the **Objects** radio button, and then select the **Clear All** button at the lower left of the dialog box. After this is done check the **Circle** check box (see Figure 18-7).

Figure 18-7

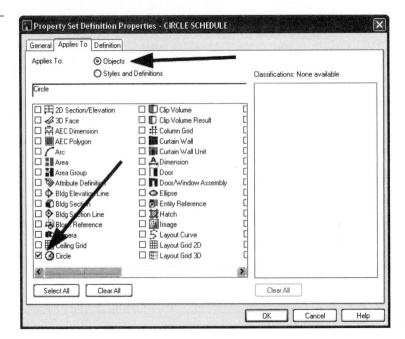

9. In the same dialog box, select the **Definition** tab.

10. In the Definition tab, press the **Add Manual Property Definition** icon button at the top right side of the dialog box, to bring up the **New Property** dialog box.

11. Enter the word **NUMBER** in the **Name** section, and press OK.

This brings up the Property Set Definition Properties dialog box. In "Placing Door and Window Tags" you found that this dialog box is where you control the automatic increments. In this exercise you are creating a new Property Set Definition, and you want the schedule to automatically number each circle (see Figure 18-8).

12. Set the Type to **Auto Increment - Integer** and Default to **1**, and **Format** to **Number - Object**.

13. In the Definition tab, again press the **Add Automatic Property Definition** icon button at the top right side of the dialog box to bring up the **Automatic Property Source** dialog box.

The Automatic Property Source dialog box shows all the properties of a circle (see Figure 18-9).

14. In the Automatic Property Source dialog box, check the **Area** check box, and press OK to return to the **Property Set Definition Properties** dialog box.

15. Add two more **Automatic Property Definitions** called **radius** and **circumference**, and check their **Automatic Property Sources** check boxes for **radius** and **circumference,** respectively.

16. Press the **Apply** button to apply all this to the **CIRCLE SCHEDULE Property Set Definition**.

You have now defined all the properties of circles that you wish to be recorded in a schedule (see Figure 18-10).

Figure 18-8

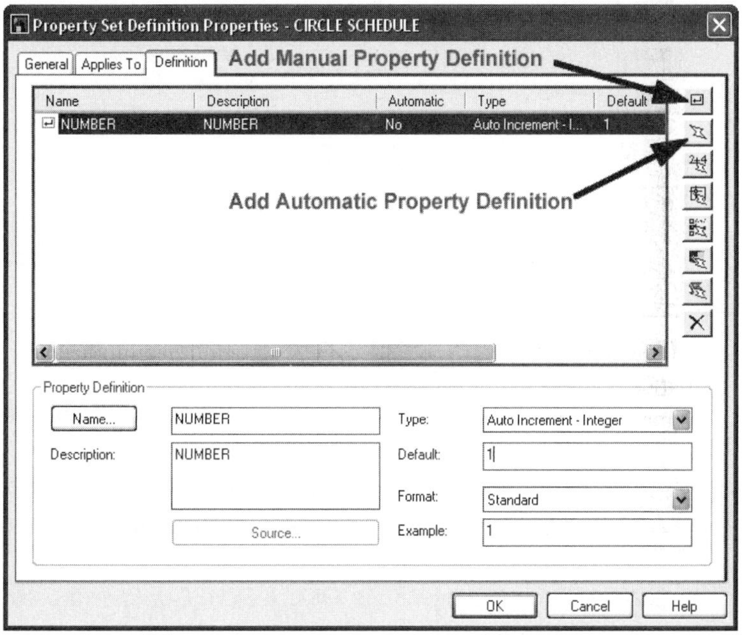

Figure 18-9

Figure 18-10

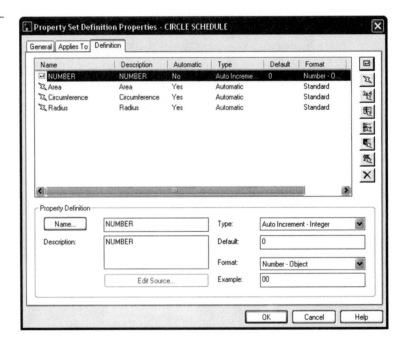

The Table Style

17. Select **Format > Style Manager** from the **Main** menu to bring up the **Style Manager** dialog box.

18. Select **Document Objects > Schedule Table Styles**.

19. RMB on Schedule table Styles, and select **New** from the contextual menu.

20. Name the new style **CIRCLE SCHEDULE**, and press the **Apply** and **OK** buttons.

21. Select **Format > Style Manager** from the **Main** menu to bring up the **Style Manager** dialog box again.

22. Select the **CIRCLE SCHEDULE** style you just created, RMB, and select **Edit** from the contextual menu to bring up the **Schedule Table Style Properties** dialog box.

23. Select the **Applies To** tab.

24. In the Applies To tab, press the **Select All** button to clear the list, and then check the **Circle** check box.

This tells the program that the schedule applies to circles and their properties (see Figure 18-11).

25. Change to the **Columns** tab and press the **Add Column** button at the lower left.

You should now see the Property Definition Set you created in Steps 3 through 27 (see Figure 18-12).

Figure 18-11

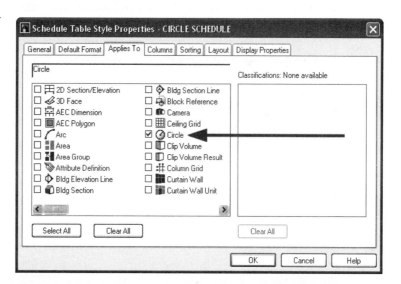

Figure 18-12

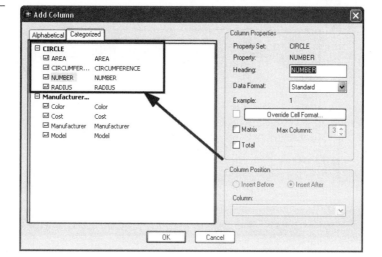

26. At the Add Column dialog box, select the **NUMBER** property, then press OK to return to the **Schedule Table Style Properties** dialog box.

27. Again press the **Add Column** button.

28. Repeat the steps adding **RADIUS, CIRCUMFERENCE,** and **AREA** columns (see Figure 18-13).

29. At the **Schedule Table Style Properties** dialog box, hold down the CTRL key and select the **Radius** and **Circumference** headers.

30. Press the Add Header button at the bottom of the Schedule Table Style Properties dialog box.

31. Enter a header name of **CIRCLE DATA** (see Figure 18-14).

32. Change to the **Sorting** tab in the **Schedule Table Style Properties** dialog box.

33. In the Sorting tab, press the **Add** button at the top left to bring up the **Select Property** dialog box.

Figure 18-13

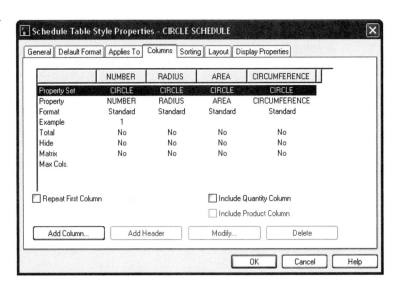

Figure 18-14

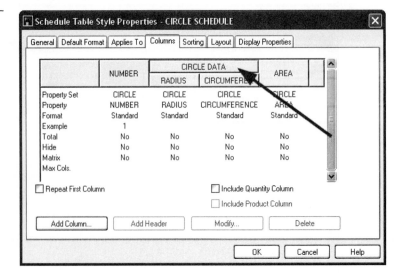

Figure 18-15

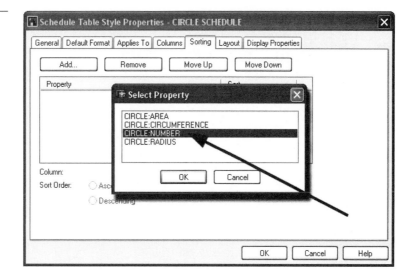

34. At the Select Property dialog box select **Circle: Number**, and press OK (see Figure 18-15).
35. Repeat for all the other properties.
36. Select the **Layout** tab in the Schedule Table Style Properties dialog box.
37. Enter a **Table Title** of **CIRCLE TABLE**, and press OK until you are out of all dialogs (see Figure 18-16).

The Table Style has now been created, and the columns and title have been named.

Using the Custom Schedule

38. Return to your drawing of the 3 circles (see Figure 18-17).
39. Select the **Door Schedule** icon from the Schedule tool palette you created.
40. Move your cursor over the Properties palette to open it.

Figure 18-16

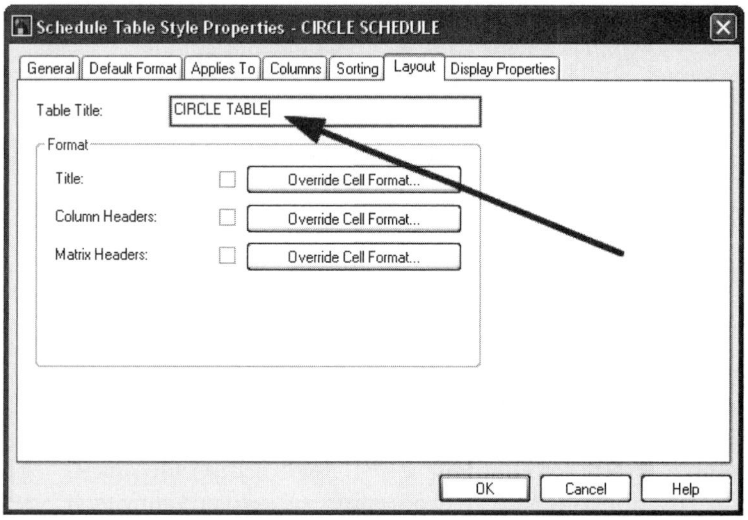

Figure 18-17

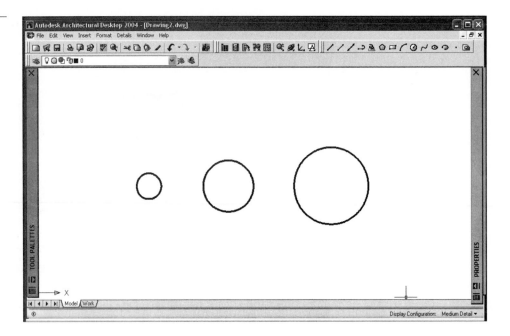

41. Select the following:

   a. Style = **CIRCLE SCHEDULE**
   b. Add new objects automatically = **Yes**
   c. Scan xrefs = **Yes**
   d. Scan block references = **Yes**

42. Select all the circles in your drawing, and press Enter.

43. Place the upper left corner of the table, and press Enter.

! **Note:** Remember, pressing Enter after placing the upper left corner of a schedule table automatically places the table according to your annotation scale settings (see Figure 18-18).

Figure 18-18

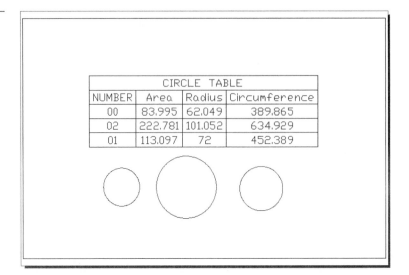

CIRCLE TABLE			
NUMBER	Area	Radius	Circumference
00	83.995	62.049	389.865
02	222.781	101.052	634.929
01	113.097	72	452.389

44.   Select one of the circles, and use grips to change its size.

Note that the schedule automatically updates to reflect the change in circle size.

45.   Add some more circles.

Note that they automatically show up in the table, but their sizes are question marks.

46.   Select the schedule, RMB, and select **Add All Property Sets** from the contextual menu.

47.   The new circle is now listed in the schedule.

As mentioned at the beginning of this section, you can create tables to record many things in your drawing. You can even record XREF data from several drawings.

19

The Detailer

When you finish this section, you should understand the following:

✔ Creating a 2D Building Section with the Detailer.
✔ Labeling a 2D Building Section with the Detailer.

The Detailer has been around since the beginnings of Autodesk Architectural Desktop. It contains routines that are meant to aid in the creation of 2D details. The Detailer is not installed in a "Typical" install of the program, but must be designated separately, or installed with the "Full" install.

After installation, **Details** appears as one of the menus on the Main menu toolbar (see Figure 19-1).

Figure 19-1

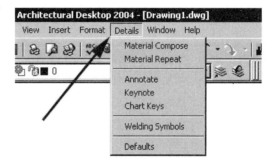

Hands-On

Creating a 2D Building Section with the Detailer

1. Start a new drawing using the Architectural Building Model and View (Imperial - ctb) template.
2. Change to the Model Layout.
3. Change to the Top View.
4. Select **Details > Material Compose** from the **Main** menu to bring up the **Select Material** dialog box (see Figure 19-2).
5. In the Select Material dialog box, select **03 - Concrete > Cast-In –Place > Slabs with Optional Haunch** (see Figure 19-3).

Figure 19-2

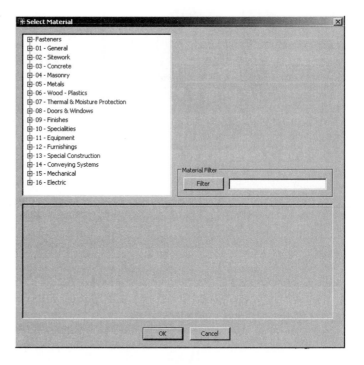

Figure 19-3

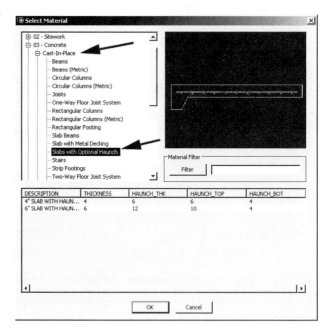

6. In the Slabs with Optional Haunch, select the 6″ **SLAB WITH HAUNCH** option, and press OK to return to the Drawing Editor.

7. Press Enter to accept the Command line Default.

8. Click a point in the Drawing Editor, and with POLAR on, drag to the right 4′, and press Enter.

The basic slab and haunch will now appear.

9. Accept the 1-1/2″ Edge 1 clear distance, and press Enter to bring up the **Select Material - Lateral bar size** dialog box.

10. Select the **# 4** Size bar, and press OK.

11. Accept the **Longitudinal bar spacing**, and press Enter.

12. Accept the **Longitudinal bar on outside**, and press Enter.

13. Enter **S** (Skip) in the command line, and press Enter to complete the commands.

The slab is now complete with reinforcing. If the hatching is wrong, do the following:

a. Select the hatch in the slab, and move your cursor over the **Properties** palette to open it.

b. In the Properties palette change the **Pattern Scale** to **12**.

The slab is now totally complete (see Figure 19-4).

14. Again select **Details > Material Compose** from the **Main** menu to bring up the **Select Material** dialog box.

15. Select **04 - Concrete Masonry > 3 Core CMU**.

16. In the 3 Core CMU, select the 12″ × 8″ × 16″ CMU option, and press OK to bring up the **Block Specifications** dialog box.

17. Select the **View - Section**, and **End Conditions - Regular** radio buttons, plus the **Hatch Block** check box. Leave the **Mortar Joints** as **Rodded** (see Figure 19-5).

18. Press OK to return to the Drawing Editor.

19. With the **End Point** Osnap on, click on the top left corner of the slab to place a block, and bring up the **Select Material - Mortar** dialog box.

20. In the Select Material - Mortar dialog box, select **TYPE "S" MORTAR**, and press OK to return to the Drawing Editor.

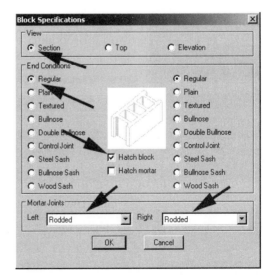

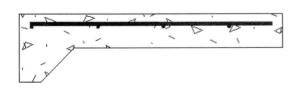

Figure 19-4   **Figure 19-5**

21. Press Enter to accept **Quit** in the command line.

22. Move your cursor in the direction of **90°**, enter **10′-0″** in the command line, and press Enter.

You have now placed all the CMUs on the concrete slab (see Figure 19-6).

23. Again select **Details > Material Compose** from the **Main** menu to bring up the **Select Material** dialog box.

24. Select **06 - Wood - Plastics > Nominal Cut Lumber**.

25. In the Nominal Cut Lumber, select the **2x12** option, and press OK to return to the Drawing Editor.

26. In the Drawing Editor, press Enter to Draw material by default.

27. Enter **S** (Section) in the command line, and press Enter.

28. Enter **L** (Lumber) in the command line, and press Enter.

29. With the End Point Osnap on, move the 2x12 to the top of the CMU wall, click and then press Enter to place it and quit (see Figure 19-7).

30. Again select **Details > Material Compose** from the **Main** menu to bring up the **Select Material** dialog box.

31. Select **Fasteners > Bolts > Anchor Bolts**.

32. In the Anchor Bolts, select the **3/8″ ANCHOR BOLT** option (see Figure 19-8).

33. Press OK to return to the Drawing Editor.

34. Enter **S** (Side) in the command line, and press Enter.

35. Pick the top midpoint of the 2x12.

36. Accept the Rotation angle of 270°, and press Enter.

37. Enter **1″** in the command line for **Bolt Projection**, and press Enter.

38. Enter **8″** in the command line for **Overall bolt length,** and press Enter.

39. Enter **3″** for **Length of threads,** and press Enter.

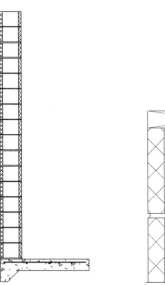

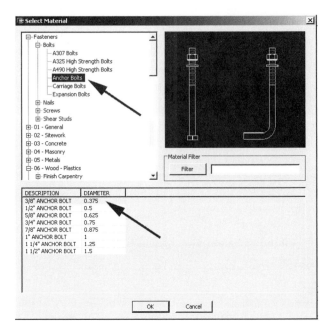

Figure 19-6   **Figure 19-7**   **Figure 19-8**

40. Accept the J type bolt, and press Enter.
41. Drag to the left for the end of the hook.
42. Enter **W** (washer) in the command line, and press Enter.
43. Place the washer at the top of the 2x12 centered on the J bolt.
44. Enter **N** (nut) in the command line, and press Enter.
45. Place the nut on top of the washer.
46. Press Enter to complete the command.

You have now placed the J bolt, washer, and nut (see Figure 19-9).

47. Again select **Details > Material Compose** from the **Main** menu to bring up the **Select Material** dialog box.
48. Select **05 - Metals > Joists > H-Series Open Web Joists**.
49. In the **> H-Series Open Web Joists**, select the **16H4 STEEL JOIST** option, and press OK to return to the Drawing Editor.
50. Enter **E** (Elevation) in the command line, and press OK.
51. Select the top right corner of the 2x12 lumber you placed, drag your cursor to the right, enter 5'-0" in the command line, and press Enter.
52. Accept 4" as Bearing length, and press Enter.

You have now placed the Bar joist on the 2x12 (see Figure 19-10).

Note: Steel bar joists are not normally placed on wood, but the author did this to show how to place wood planks.

53. Again select **Details > Material Compose** from the **Main** menu to bring up the **Select Material** dialog box.
54. Select **05 - Metals > Decking**.

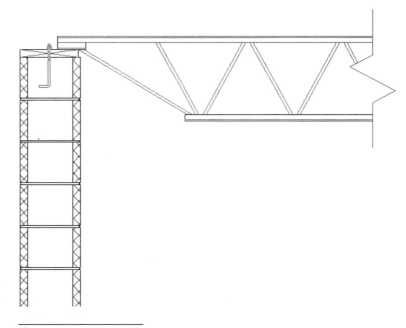

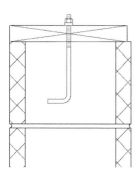

Figure 19-9   **Figure 19-10**

55. In the Decking, select the **3DR 16** option, and press OK to return to the Drawing Editor.

56. Enter **E** (End) in the command line, and press OK.

57. Select the top left corner of the bar joist as the start point, and drag your cursor to the right, enter 4'-0" in the command line, and press Enter.

58. Move your cursor in the direction of 90°, and click to create the roof decking (see Figure 19-11).

Figure 19-11

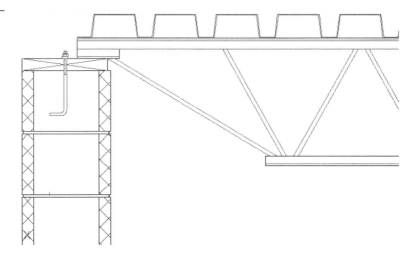

Hands-On

Labeling a 2D Building Section with the Detailer

1. Use the previous exercise.

2. Change to the **Work** Layout.

3. Select **Format > Drawing Setup** from the **Main** menu to bring up the **Drawing Setup** dialog box.

4. Select the **Scale** tab.

5. Set the **Drawing Scale** to **1-1/2" = 1'-0"**, and the **Annotation Plot Size** to **3/32"**.

6. Press the **Apply** and **OK** buttons to return to the Drawing Editor.

7. In Paper Space, clear the existing viewports, and create one single viewport.

8. In Paper Space, select the viewport frame, and move your cursor over the **Properties** palette to open it.

9. Set the set the **Standard scale** to **1-1/2" = 1'-0"**, and set **Display Locked** to **Yes**.

10. Select **Details > Keynote** from the **Main** menu.

11. In Model Space, click on the CMU wall you placed earlier.

12. Enter **Y** (Yes) in the command line to select the CMU wall, and press Enter.

13. Drag your cursor to the left and click again to bring up the **Select Keynote** dialog box.
14. Press OK to place the keynote, and complete the command.
15. Return to Paperspace, and using the Distance command, measure the Keynote height; it should measure 3/32″, which you set as the Annotation Plot size.

Continue to place keynotes. See Figure 19-12.

Figure 19-12

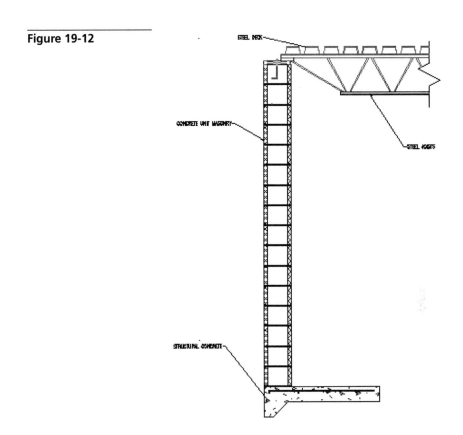

The DesignCenter

When you finish this section, you should understand the following:

✔ What Design Content is in Architectural Desktop.
✔ Where to find Design Content.

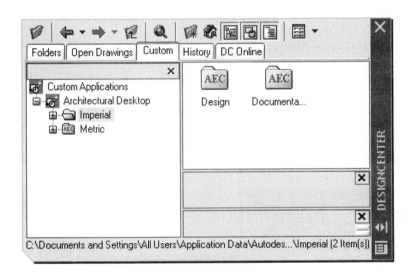

Note: Everything shown in this section can also be gotten from the Content Browser Catalogs; the DesignCenter is another method.

In order to understand architectural construction documents, designers include symbols of equipment such as bathroom fixtures, beds, chair, and kitchen cabinets. Autodesk Architectural Desktop 2004 includes a very comprehensive set of generic content symbols in both 2D and 3D. Much of the content is created utilizing Architectural Desktop's Multi-View block representation system. (See Section 16, page 279, "Using Create AEC Content to Place the New Light Fixture in the DesignCenter," and Section 17, "Multi-View Blocks," in this book). Multi-View blocks allow the Display System to place the representation of the object in the appropriate view (for example, 3D in Model View, plan representation in Plan View, etc.)

Content

All the symbols and as well as schedules, documentation symbols, and styles are contained in a folder called **Aec Content** in **C:\Documents and Settings\All Users\Application Data\Autodesk\Autodesk Architectural Desktop 2004\ R16\enu\Aec Content**. This content is placed in this location by default. Be sure you have sufficient space on your C drive regardless if you assign the Architectural Desktop 2004 program to a different drive than the C drive.

All content is held in standard AutoCAD drawings (dwg), and can be modified using standard AutoCAD commands.

Hands-on

Using the DesignCenter to Create a Kitchen

Creating the Kitchen

1. Start a new drawing using the Architectural Building Model and View (Imperial - ctb) template.
2. Change to the **Model** Layout.
3. Change to the **Top** View.
4. Place a 15' × 10'-0" rectangle.
5. Select the **Walls** icon from the **Design** tool palette, RMB, and select **Apply Tool Properties to > Linework** from the contextual menu that appears.
6. Select the rectangle.
7. Type **Y** (Yes) to erase the geometry (rectangle), and press Enter to create walls.
8. With the walls still selected, move your cursor over the Properties palette to open it.
9. Set the following parameters:

    a. Wall width = **4"**
    b. Base height = **8'-0"**
    c. Justify = **Right**

10. Modify the walls to create the enclosure shown in Figure 20-1.

Adding the Appliances

11. Select the **DesignCenter** icon from the Main toolbar (or Ctrl + 2 from the keyboard) to bring up the **DesignCenter**.
12. In the DesignCenter, select **Architectural Desktop > Imperial > Design > Equipment > Food Service > Refrigerator**
13. Double-click the **Refrigerator** folder to open it.
14. Select the Side-Side refrigerator, RMB, and drag it into the Drawing Editor.

Figure 20-1

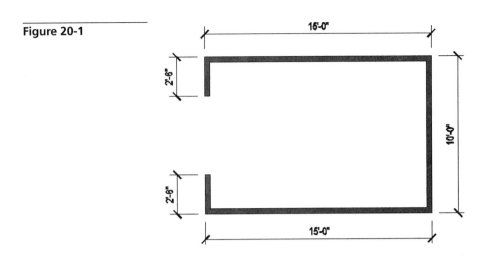

The refrigerator will come into the drawing with the insertion point at its rear center.

15.   At the command line, enter **270**, and press Enter.

16.   Select the refrigerator again, at the command line Enter **B** for Base point, and press the space bar or Enter.

This will allow you to relocate the insertion point of the refrigerator. Select the upper left corner of the refrigerator in plan.

17.   With the **End point** Object Snap set, place the refrigerator as shown in Figure 20-2.

18.   Return to the Design Center and select **Architectural Desktop > Imperial > Design > Furnishing > Casework.**

19.   At the **Casework** folder, double-click the **Base with Drawers** folder to open it.

20.   Continue to place base cabinets, a stove, and a tall cabinet until you create a kitchen layout similar to Figure 20-3. Save this drawing as **Kitchen.**

Figure 20-2

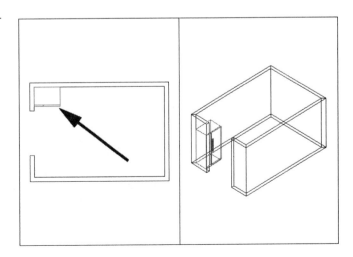

Figure 20-3

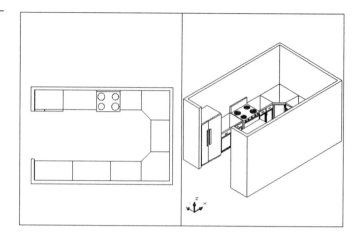

The Counter: The Splash Edge Style

1. Continue to place base cabinets, a stove, and a tall cabinet until you create a kitchen layout similar to Figure 20-3. Save this drawing as **Kitchen.**

2. Start a new drawing and save it as **COUNTER DRAWING**.

3. Select the **Rectangle** icon from the **Draw** toolbar, and create a **1"** × **4"**-high rectangle.

4. Select the rectangle, RMB, and select **Convert To > Profile Definition** from the contextual menu that appears.

5. Pick the lower right corner of the rectangle to bring up the **New Profile Definition** dialog box.

6. Enter **SPLASH PROFILE** in the **New Name** field, and press OK to create the profile.

7. Select **Format > Style Manager** to bring up the **Style Manager**.

8. In the Style Manager, select **Architectural Objects > Slab Edge Styles**.

9. Select the **Slab Edge Styles** icon, RMB, and select **New** from the contextual menu that appears.

10. Rename the new Slab Edge Style to **SPLASH EDGE**.

11. Select SPLASH EDGE, RMB, and select **Edit** from the contextual menu to bring up the **Slab edge styles-SPLASH EDGE** dialog box.

12. Select the **Design Rules** tab.

13. Check the Fascia check box, and pick Splash profile from the drop-down list (see Figure 20-4).

14. Press OK, and close all the dialog boxes.

You have now created the splash edge style. You can keep this style for any future use.

Now it's time to place the counter.

1. In the Top View, place polylines where you want counters (make sure the polylines are on the 0 layer).

2. Using the layer manager, turn off visibility for everything but the 0 layer (see Figure 20-5).

Figure 20-4

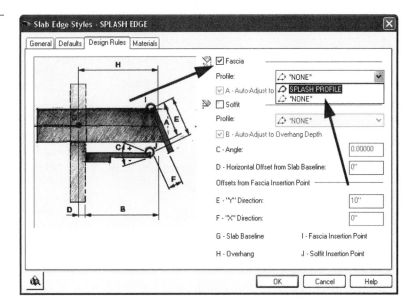

Figure 20-5

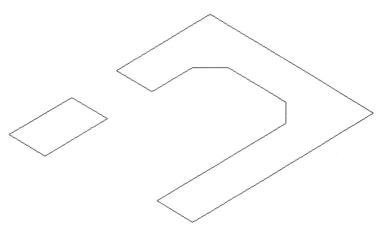

3. Select the **Slab** icon from the **Design** tool palette, RMB, and select **Apply Tool Properties to > Linework and Walls** from the contextual menu that appears.

4. Select the two polylines you just created.

5. Enter **Y** (Yes) in the command line, and press Enter.

6. Enter **P** (Projected) in the command line, and press Enter.

7. Enter **36″** in the command line, and press Enter.

8. Enter **T** (Top) in the command line, and press Enter to create the counter.

9. Turn the visibility of everything back on in the Layer Manager, and regenerate the drawing.

You have now created the counter over the appliances (see Figure 20-6).

10. Select a counter you created, and move your cursor over the Properties palette to open it.

11. Set the **Thickness** to **2″**, and press the **Edges** icon to bring up the **Slab Edges** dialog box.

Figure 20-6

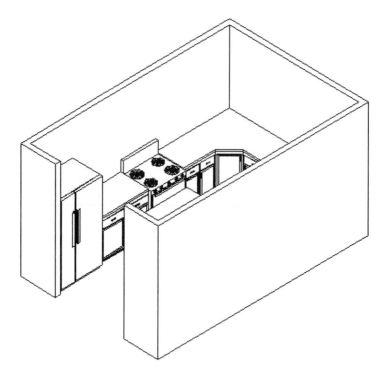

12. Select all the **Edges**, and then change the **Edge Style** drop-down list to **SPLASH EDGE**, and then press OK.
13. Repeat Steps 11 and 12 for the other counter.

You have now added a splash edge to all the edges of the counter. You need to remove the splash from the front edges. To do this, do the following:

    a. Select a counter, RMB, and select **Edit Slab Edges** from the contextual menu that appears.
    b. Select the slab edge you wish to remove, and press Enter to bring up the **Edit Slab Edges** dialog box.
    c. In the Edit Slab Edges dialog box, change the **Edge Style** drop-down list to **Standard**, and press OK.
    d. Repeat Steps b and c for the other counter.

You have now completed the counters (see Figure 20-7).

Placing the Sink

1. Change the **UCS** (User Coordinate System) to a **Z** height of 3'-2".

This will allow the sink to be brought in at counter height.

2. Select the **Architectural Desktop > Imperial > Design > Mechanical > Plumbing Fixtures > Sink** from the **DesignCenter**.
3. Double-click the **Sink** folder to open it.
4. Select the Kitchen-Double B sink, RMB, and drag it into your drawing.
5. Place the sink in the center of the counter.

Figure 20-7

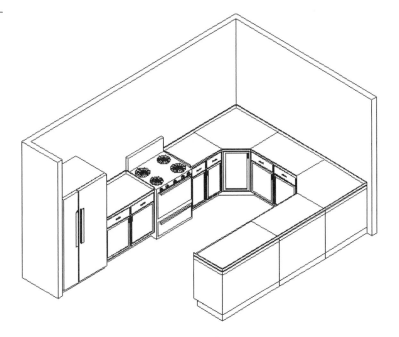

Turning on Gouraud shading shows that the counter cuts through the sink (see Figure 20-8).

Real counters need cutouts for sinks.

6. Select the **Rectangle** icon from the Draw menu and place a rectangle as shown in Figure 20-9.
7. Select the **Slab**, RMB, and select **Hole Add** icon from the contextual menu that appears.

Figure 20-8

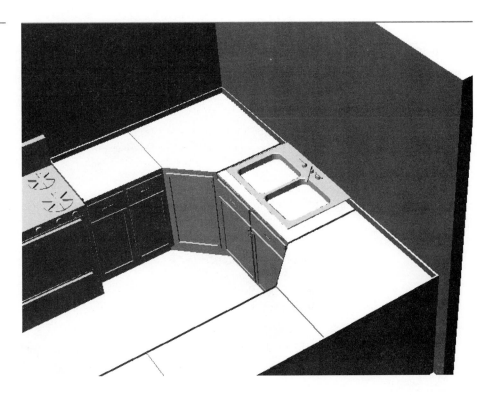

Figure 20-9

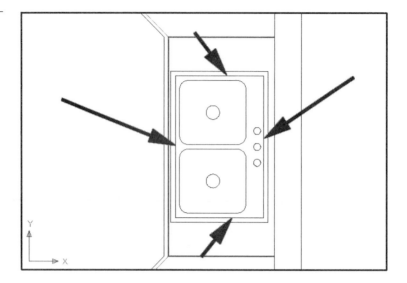

8. Select the rectangle, and press Enter.
9. Enter **Y** (Yes) in the command line, and press Enter.

The Sink and counter shade correctly (see Figure 20-10).

10. Place the upper cabinets, a window, and complete the kitchen (see Figure 20-11).

Figure 20-10

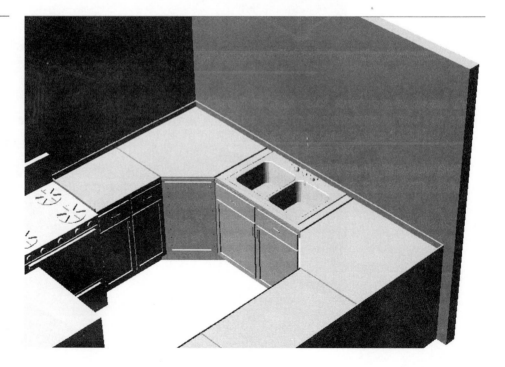

Figure 20-11

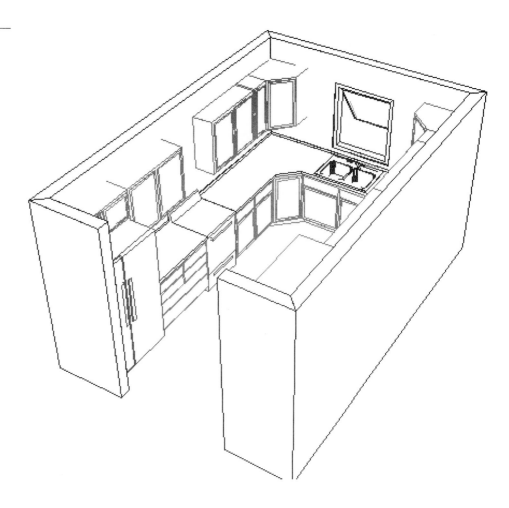

Kitchen Section/Elevation

11.   Select the **Elevation Line** icon from the **Design** tool palette.

12.   Place an Elevation line through the kitchen as shown in Figure 20-12.

Figure 20-12

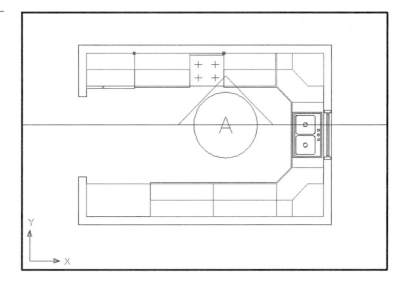

13. Select the elevation line, RMB, and select **Generate Elevation** from the contextual menu, and generate an elevation of your finished kitchen (see Figure 20-13).

Figure 20-13

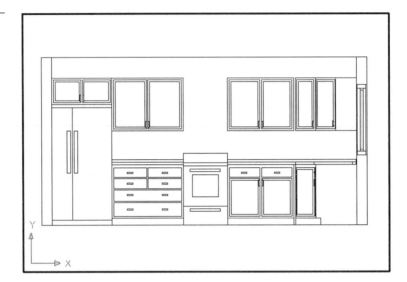

Drawing Management

When you finish this section, you should understand the following:

- ✔ The Drawing Management Concept.
- ✔ How to use the Project Browser.
- ✔ Creating Constructs and Elements in the Project Navigator.
- ✔ Working with Constructs and Elements in the Project Navigator.
- ✔ Assigning Constructs and Elements in the Project Navigator.
- ✔ Creating Views in the Project Navigator.
- ✔ Creating Plotting Sheets in the Project Navigator.

Autodesk Architectural Desktop 2004's Drawing Management feature automates the building design and document process. With this feature all your project document files are codified in a central location from which you can call up and modify any drawing. This feature allows you to manage projects, automatically control levels, and create views and sheets. See Figure 21-1.

Figure 21-1

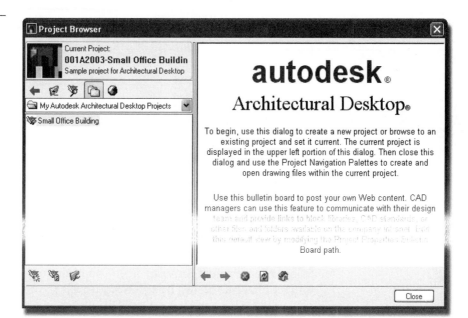

In reality, the new Drawing Management feature is an advanced form of external referencing (XREF), which has been a feature of AutoCAD and Architectural Desktop for many releases. Using XML programming in conjunction with external referencing, the programmers have created a very comprehensive system for automating this process.

Because the Drawing Management system is so closely related to the XREF system, those who understand how to use the conventional XREF will find the learning curve for this advanced feature easily comprehendible. For those who are totally new to AutoCAD or Architectural Desktop, this author suggests that you first read the on-line help on XREF before going on to the Drawing Management system.

The Drawing Management Concept

The Drawing Management system is based on a hierarchy starting with the **Project,** which is made of Constructs, Elements, Views, and Plot sheets. Through sophisticated automated XREF commands, **Elements** are XREFed into **Constructs,** which are XREFed into **Views** and then XREFed into **Plot sheets**. See Figure 21-2.

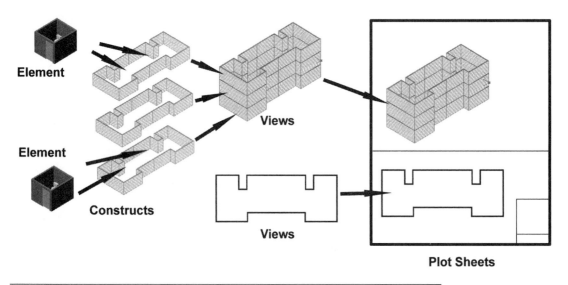

Figure 21-2

Hands-On

Using the Project Browser

1. In **Windows Explorer**, create a Microsoft Windows file directory and name it **ADT 2004 Projects**.

2. Start **Autodesk Architectural Desktop 2004**.

3. Start a new drawing using the Architectural Building Model and View (Imperial - ctb) template.

4. Select **File > Project Browser** from the **Main** menu to bring up the **Project Browser** dialog box (see Figure 21-3).

5. Locate the ADT 2004 projects directory from the drop-down list.

Figure 21-3

6. Press the **Add Project** icon to bring up the **Add Project** dialog box.
7. Enter the following information (see Figure 21-4):

   a. Number = **100**

   b. Name = **TEST PROJECT**

   c. Description: **3 Story Building**

   d. Bulletin Board = (Any Intranet or leave Default directory)

   e. Project Image = (Any small GIF image or leave Default directory)

   f. Prefix Filenames with project Number = **Yes** (from drop-down list)

   g. Default Construction Template = (accept default - Architectural Building Model and View (Imperial - stb).dwt)

   h. Default Element Template = (accept default - Architectural Building Model and View (Imperial - stb).dwt)

   i. Default View Template = (accept default - Architectural Building Model and View (Imperial - stb).dwt)

   j. Default Sheet Template = (accept default - Architectural Sheet (Imperial - stb).dwt)

Figure 21-4

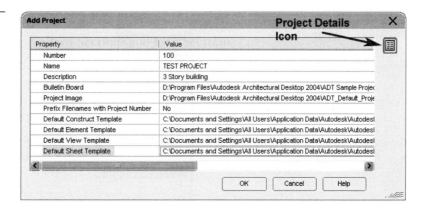

8. After entering the above information, press the project details icon to bring up the Project Details dialog box. Here you can add information such as telephone numbers, billing addresses, and owner's representative (see Figure 21-5).

9. Press the OK buttons to return to the Project Browser.

10. In the Project Browser, press the Project History icon to open the past created projects.

11. Select the drop-down list shown in Figure 21-6 to locate past projects by the **Most Recently Used, By Date, By Project**, or **By Location** options.

12. RMB on **TEST PROJECT** in the list and select **Set Project Current** from the contextual menu that appears.

The project will now appear in the Project Browser's header (see Figure 21-7).

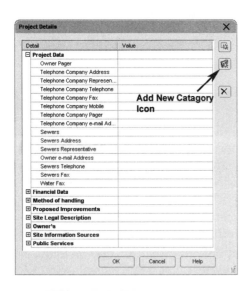

Figure 21-5

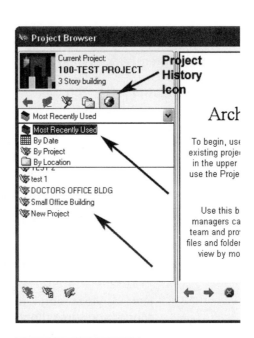

Figure 21-6

Figure 21-7

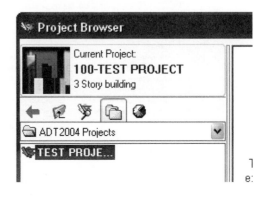

Figure 21-8

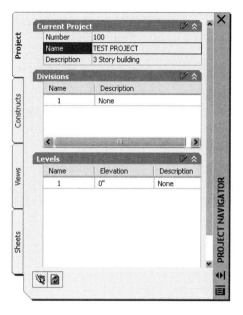

13. Press the **Close** button to return to the Drawing Editor, and automatically open the **Project Navigator** palette (see Figure 21-8).

Hands-On

Creating Constructs and Elements in the Project Navigator

This project will have three floors with a basement. The second and third floors will each have two apartments, and the apartments will have bathrooms.

1. In the Project tab, select the **Edit Levels** icon in the top right corner of the Levels information to bring up the **Levels** dialog box.
2. In the levels dialog box, press the **Add Level**, create four levels, and enter the information as shown in Figure 21-9. Be sure to check the Auto-Adjust check box so that the Floor Elevation adjusts when you enter the Floor to Floor Height.
3. Press OK to return to the **Project Navigator** palette.
4. Select the Constructs tab.

Figure 21-9

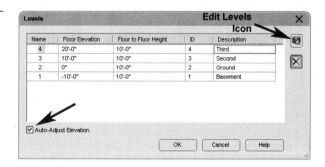

Figure 21-10

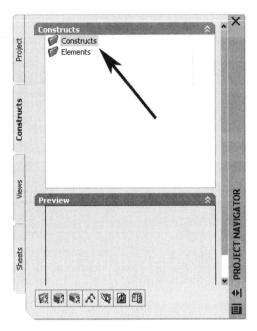

The Constructs tab contains the Constructs and Elements folders, plus a preview screen to view their contents (see Figure 21-10).

5. In the Constructs tab, select the Constructs folder, RMB, and select **New > Construct** from the contextual menu that appears to bring up the **Add Construct** dialog box (see Figure 21-11).

6. Create new Constructs, and name them **Apartment Walls**, **Exterior Walls**, and **Column Grid.**

7. Repeat this process with the **Elements** folder, and create two Elements called **Bath Room** (see Figure 21-12).

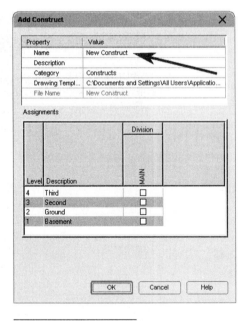

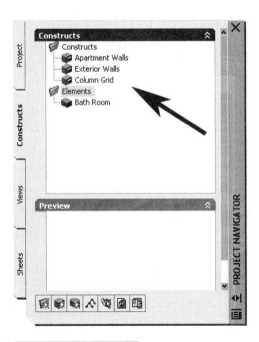

Figure 21-11

Figure 21-12

Hands-On

Working with Constructs and Elements in the Project Navigator

1. After the Constructs and Elements have been labeled, double-click on the **Column Grid** icon to bring up the **Column Grid.dwg.**

2. Allow the Project Navigator palette to close in order to provide more room to work in the Drawing Editor.

3. In the Column Grid.dwg, change to the **Model Layout, Top View,** and place a **Column Grid** 100′ wide by 60′ deep with 10′-0″ bays in both directions.

4. Select the column grid, RMB, and select **Label** from the contextual menu that appears.

5. Label the Bottom and Right of the grid with letters and numbers, respectively (see Figure 21-13).

6. Select **File > Save** from the **Main** toolbar, and save **Column Grid.dwg.**

7. Move your cursor over the **Project Navigator** palette and double-click on the **Exterior Walls** icon to open the **Exterior Walls.dwg.**

8. In the Exterior Walls.dwg, change to the **Model** Layout, and **Top** View.

9. Open the **Project Navigator** again, select the **Column Grid** icon, RMB, and select **Xref Overlay** from the contextual menu that appears.

The Grid you made previously will now be XREFed into the Exterior Walls.dwg.

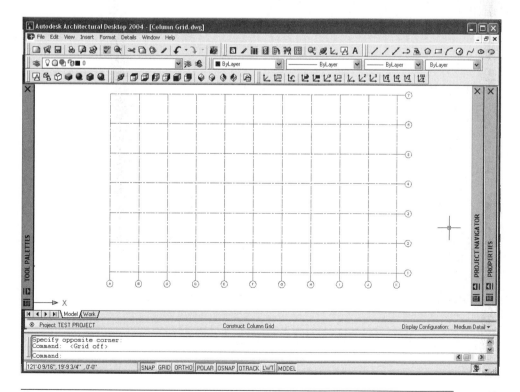

Figure 21-13

10. Turn the **Node** object snap on.

11. Using the Node snap, place standard 12"-wide walls as shown in Figure 21-14.

12. Erase the Grid, and save the Exterior Walls.dwg.

13. Move your cursor over the **Project Navigator** palette and double-click on the **Apartment Walls** icon to open the **Apartment Walls.dwg.**

14. Change to the **Model** Layout, and **Top** View.

15. Open the **Project Navigator** again, select the **Column Grid** icon, RMB, and select **Xref Overlay** from the contextual menu that appears.

16. Repeat the same process and Xref Overlay the Exterior Walls.

17. Place standard walls 4" wide and 8'-0" high and erase the column grid as shown in Figure 21-15.

18. While still in the **Apartment Walls.dwg**, erase the Exterior Walls so that only the apartment walls remain.

19. Select **File > Save** from the Main toolbar to save the **Apartment Walls.dwg.**

Figure 21-14

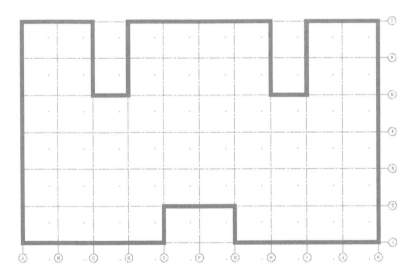

Figure 21-15

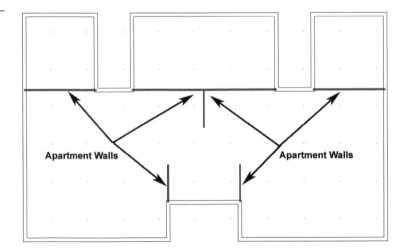

20. Open the Project Navigator again, and double-click on the **Bath Room** icon under the Elements folder to bring up the **Bath Room.dwg.**

21. With the **Bath Room.dwg** open, create a 10'-0" square enclosure using standard 4"-wide by 8'-0"-high walls.

22. Select one wall, RMB, and insert a standard door 2'-6" wide by 6'-8" high.

23. Place a vanity, toilet, and spa tub from the **Architectural Desktop Design Tool Catalog – Imperial > Mechanical > Plumbing Fixtures** catalog.

24. Select the **Ceiling Grid** icon from the **Design** tool palette, and center a 2'-0" × 2'-0" ceiling grid at 7'-6" elevation.

25. Erase the column grid, and save the **Bath Room.dwg** (see Figure 21-16).

Figure 21-16

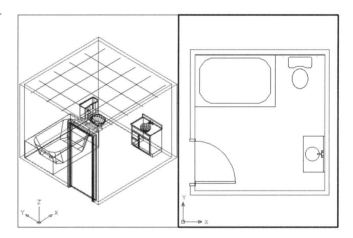

Hands-On

Assigning Constructs and Elements in the Project Navigator

1. While still in the **Constructs** tab...

2. Select the **Exterior Walls** icon, RMB, and select **Copy Constructs to Levels** from the contextual menu that appears to bring up the **Copy Construct to Levels** dialog box.

3. Check all the **Copy to Levels** check boxes, and press OK.

This will copy the Exterior walls to all four levels (see Figures 21-17 and 21-18).

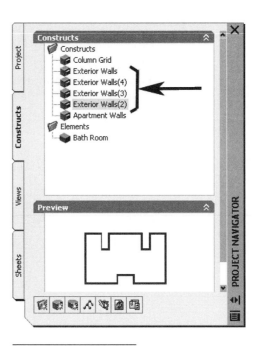

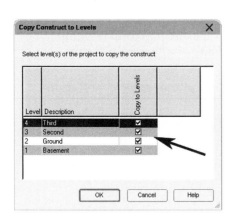

Figure 21-17

Figure 21-18

> *!* **Note:** The Apartment walls are to be used only on the third and fourth floors, but were created as Constructs. They should have been created as Elements. This is easy to fix by doing the following:
>
> In the Constructs tab, drag the **Apartment Walls** icon to the **Elements** folder.
>
> An Add Element dialog box will appear; press the OK button, and Apartment Walls will move to the Elements folder, and will now be an element (see Figure 21-19).

Figure 21-19

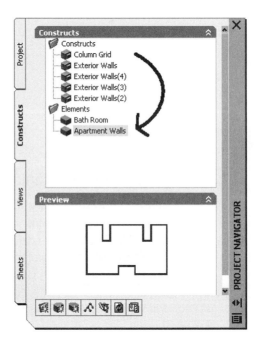

4. Double-click on the **Exterior Walls(4)** icon in the **Constructs** tab to bring up the **Exterior Walls(4).dwg.**

5. Select the **Apartment Walls** Element, RMB, and select **Attach Element To Constraints** from the contextual menu that appears to bring up the **Attach Element to Construct** dialog box.

6. Check the Exterior Walls(3) and Exterior Walls(4) check boxes, and press OK.

The apartment walls are now shown in the Exterior walls(4).dwg (see Figure 21-20).

7. Repeat Step 5 of this exercise with the **Bath Room** Element, and attach to the **Exterior Walls**, **Exterior Walls(3)**, and **Exterior Walls(4)** Constraints, which are the Basement and third and fourth floors, respectively.

8. Save the **Exterior Walls**, **Exterior Walls(3)**, and **Exterior Walls(4)** drawings.

We will need two bathrooms on the fourth floor. Since we might decide to change both bathrooms at the last moment, we will make AEC Entity References of the second bathrooms. To do that, do the following:

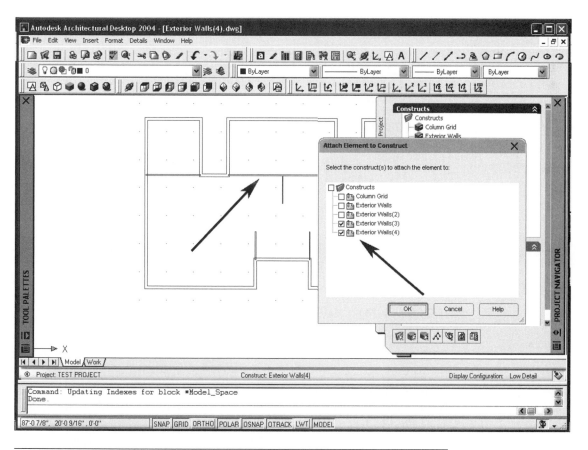

Figure 21-20

9. Double-click on the **Exterior Walls(4)** icon in the **Constructs** tab to bring up the **Exterior Walls(4).dwg.**

10. Drag the **AEC Entity Reference** icon from the **Autodesk Architectural Desktop stock Tool Catalog > General Purpose Tools > Helper Tools** to your **Design** tool palette.

11. Select the **AEC Entity Reference** icon in the Design tool palette, and Enter **AD** (Add) in the command line, and press Enter.

12. Select the bathroom, then any point near the bathroom, and then drag the bathroom to the right.

13. Press Enter twice to complete the command.

You have now created an AEC Reference of the Bath Room. This will allow you to change one bathroom, and have the copy change too (see Figure 21-21).

You have now created all the Constructs, Elements, and AEC References you need for your project. Now you need to place them together to create views of your building. Be sure to save all the .dwgs (just double-click to open them, and press Ctrl + S on the keyboard, or File > Save from the Main toolbar.

Figure 21-21

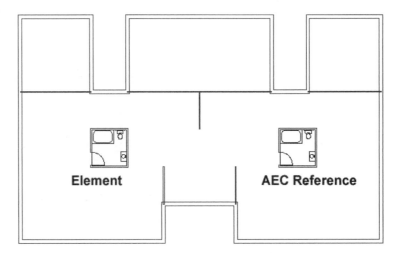

Hands-On

Creating Views in the Project Navigator

1. Open the **Project Navigator**, and make sure you are in **TEST PROJECT**.

2. Change to the Views tab.

3. **RMB** on the **Views** icon and select **New > View** from the contextual menu that appears to bring up the **Add View** Wizard dialog box.

4. In the Add View dialog box, enter **TEST PROJECT PERSPECTIVE** in the **Name** field, and click in the **File Name** field to make the file name **TEST PROJECT PERSPECTIVE** also (see Figure 21-22).

5. Press the **Next** button to move to the **Context** screen, and check the check boxes for all the levels.

Figure 21-22

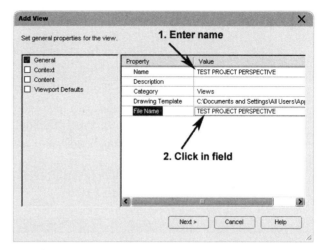

Figure 21-23

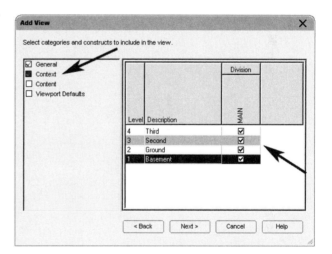

This tells the Drawing Manager that the view will include Constructs on these floors (see Figure 21-23).

6. Press the **Next** button again to move to the **Content** screen.
7. Since this is a perspective view, check all the check boxes *except* the Column Grid (see Figure 21-24).

Figure 21-24

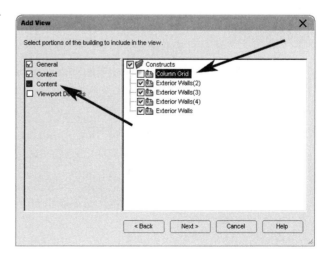

8. Select the **Next** button to move to the **Viewport Defaults** screen.

9. Select **SW Isometric** from the **View Direction** drop-down list, **Standard** from the **Display Configuration** list, and set the **Viewport Scale** to **1/8″ = 1′-0″**.

10. Press the **Finish** button to complete creating the view.

11. In the Views tab, double-click on the TEST PROJECT PERSPECTIVE icon to bring up the TEST PROJECT PERSPECTIVE.dwg.

12. Select View > 3D Views > SW Isometric from the Main toolbar.

You have now created your first view, which *does not* include the Column Grid (see Figure 21-25).

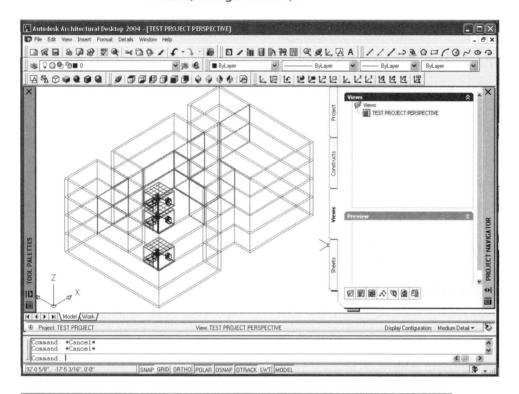

Figure 21-25

Hands-On

Creating Plotting Sheets in the Project Navigator

1. Change to the Sheets tab.

2. Select the Sheet icon, RMB, and select **New > Sheet** from the contextual menu that appears to bring up the **Add Sheet** dialog box.

3. Enter **TEST PROJECT SHEET** in the Name field.

! **Note:** If you had a special template sheet with your own title block, you would locate that in the Drawing Template field. For this exercise, accept the default template.

4. Double-click the **TEST PROJECT SHEET** icon in the Sheets tab to bring up the **TEST PROJECT SHEET.dwg.**

5. Return to the Views tab.

6. Drag the **TEST PROJECT PERSPECTIVE** icon into the **TEST PROJECT SHEET.dwg.**

The TEST PROJECT PERSPECTIVE appears in the sheet (see Figure 21-26).
    Let's now go back and add a roof to the building and add two more views.

7. Return to **Constructs** tab.

8. RMB on the **Constructs** icon, and select **New Construct** from the contextual menu that appears to bring up the **Add Construct** dialog box.

9. Enter **ROOF** in the Name field.

10. Check the **Level 4** check box, and press OK.

11. Double click on the **ROOF** icon to bring up the **ROOF.dwg** in the Drawing Editor.

12. Change to **Model** Layout, **Top** View.

13. Drag the Exterior Walls(4) icon from the Constructs tab into the Drawing Editor.

The Exterior Walls have now been XREFed into the ROOF.dwg.

14. Set the **Osnap** to **Intersection**.

15. Select the **Roof** icon from the **Design** toolbar.

16. In the Properties palette set the following:

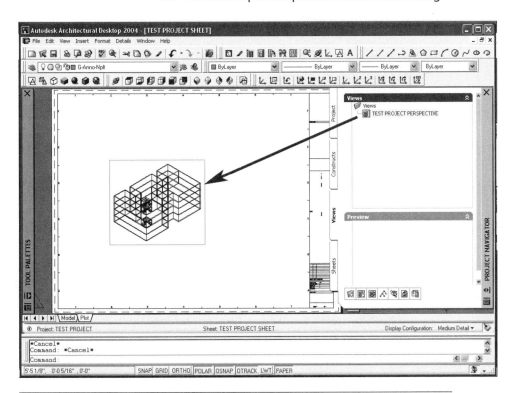

Figure 21-26

    a.   Thickness = **10″**

    b.   Overhang = **18″**

    c.   Plate height = **10′-0″** (to match the height of the exterior walls)

    d.   Rise = **1′-0″**

    e.   Run = **12**

17. Place a roof following the perimeter of the exterior walls, and press Enter.

18. Erase the Exterior Walls(4) XREF that you added in Step 7, and press **Ctrl + S** on the keyboard to save **ROOF.dwg.**

19. Return to the **Views** tab, **RMB** on the **Views** icon, and select **New > View** from the contextual menu to bring up the **Add View** Wizard.

20. In the **General** screen Enter **TEST PROJECT ROOF PERSPECTIVE** in the **Name Field.**

21. Press the **Next** button to go to the **Context** screen.

22. Check all the **Level** check boxes.

23. Press the **Next** button to go to the **Content** screen.

24. Check all the **Constructs** check boxes except the Column Grid.

25. Press the **Next** button to go to the Viewports Defaults screen.

26. Set the following:

    a.   View Direction = **NE Isometric**

    b.   Display Configuration = **Standard**

    c.   Layer Snapshot = **None**

    d.   Viewport scale = **3/16″ = 1′-0″**

27. Press OK, and press **Ctrl + S** on the keyboard to save **TEST PROJECT ROOFPERSPECTIVE.dwg.**

28. Change to the Sheets tab.

29. Double-click the **TEST PROJECT SHEET** icon in the Sheets tab to bring up the **TEST PROJECT SHEET.dwg.**

30. Drag the **TEST PROJECT ROOF PERSPECTIVE** icon into the **TEST PRO-JECT SHEET.dwg.**

The TEST PROJECT ROOF PERSPECTIVE appears in the sheet (see Figure 21-27).

31. Return to the **Views** tab, **RMB** on the **Views** icon, and select **New > View** from the contextual menu to bring up the **Add View** Wizard.

32. In the **General** screen enter **TEST PROJECT PLAN** in the **Name Field.**

33. Press the **Next** button to go to the **Context** screen.

34. Check all the **Level** check boxes.

35. Press the **Next** button to go to the **Content** screen.

36. Check the **Column Grid and Exterior Walls** check boxes.

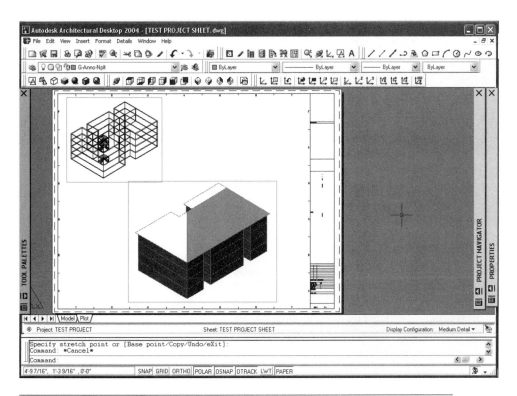

Figure 21-27

37. Press the **Next** button to go to the Viewports Defaults screen.
38. Set the following:

    a. View Direction = **Top**
    b. Display Configuration = **Standard**
    c. Layer Snapshot = **None**
    d. Viewport scale = **1/8″ = 1′-0″**

39. Press OK, and press **Ctrl + S** on the keyboard to save **TEST PROJECT PLAN.dwg.**
40. Change to the Sheets tab.
41. Double-click the **TEST PROJECT SHEET** icon in the Sheets tab to bring up the **TEST PROJECT SHEET.dwg.**
42. Drag the **TEST PROJECT PLAN** icon into the **TEST PROJECT SHEET.dwg.**

The TEST PROJECT PLAN now appears in the sheet. Notice that the Column Grid and Exterior wall show, but the Roof doesn't appear (see Figure 21-28).

43. Enter **Ctrl + S** on the keyboard to save the **TEST PROJECT SHEET.dwg.**

!   **Note:** You have now set up your building in the **Project Navigator.** You can return to the Constructs and Elements and modify the parts of your building. You must remember, though, to press **Ctrl +S** on the keyboard or **File > Save** from the Main

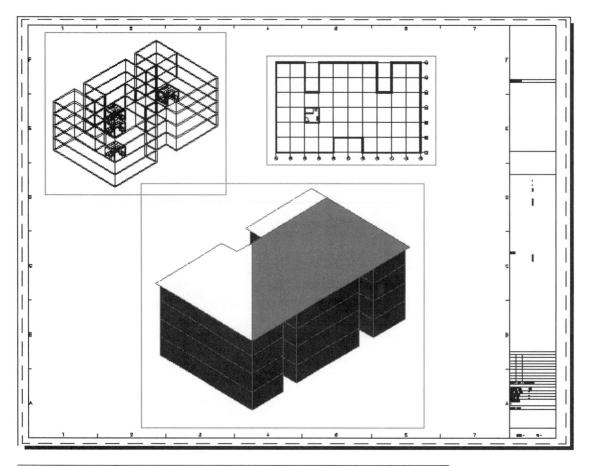

Figure 21-28

toolbar after you have made changes to the file. You can also have the program set to automatically save, but this author discourages that because it removes the control from the operator.

To test the ability of the Project Navigator to control all the XREFs, as changes are made, do the following:

1. After saving all the project drawings, close and restart the program.
2. After the program restarts, select **File > Project Browser** from the **Main** toolbar to bring up the **Project Browser**.
3. Select **Set Project Curren**t from the contextual menu that appears, and press the **Close** button to bring up the **Project Navigator** palette.
4. Select the Constructs tab.
5. In the Constructs tab, select the Exterior Walls(4) icon to bring the Exterior Walls(4).dwg into the Drawing Editor.
6. Select the rear walls and insert nine 3'-wide by 8'-high standard windows with a head height of 9'-0".
7. Press Ctrl + S from the keyboard to save the drawing (see Figure 21-29).

8. Repeat this for **Exterior Walls(2)**, and **Exterior Walls(3),** adding nine windows on each level.

9. Change to the Views tab, and double-click on the **TEST PROJECT ROOF PERSPECTIVE** icon to bring the **TEST PROJECT ROOF PERSPEC-TIVE.dwg** into the Drawing Editor.

Notice that a large yellow warning message appears reminding you that an **External Reference File Has Changed** (see Figure 21-30).

10. Either click on the blue underlined words in the message, or on the adjacent tag with a yellow warning exclamation mark (see Figure 21-31).

11. This will bring up the **Xref Manager** dialog box with a **red** exclamation mark next the file that need to be reloaded.

12. Select the file, and press the **Reload** button to reload the changed Xref (see Figure 21-32).

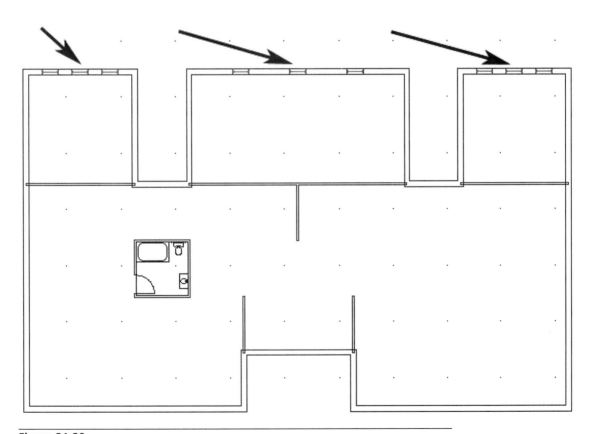

Figure 21-29

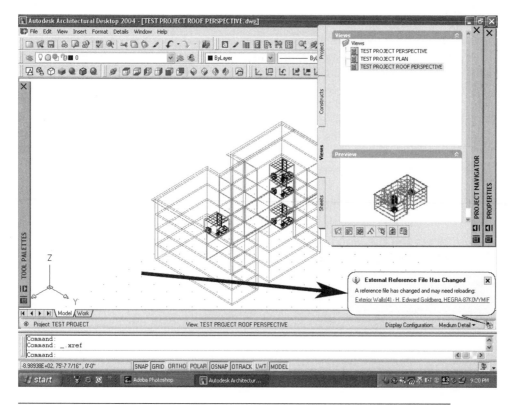

Figure 21-30

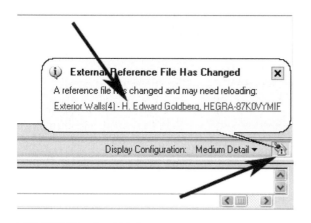

Figure 21-31

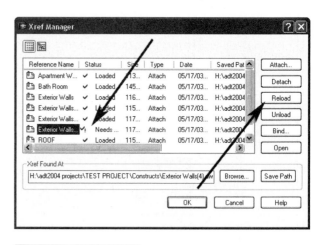

Figure 21-32

22

VIZ Render

When you finish this section, you should understand the following:

- ✔ How best to learn to operate VIZ Render.
- ✔ Making a simple scene.
- ✔ Using VIZ Render.
- ✔ Separating Surfaces.
- ✔ Applying Materials.
- ✔ Creating and Modifying Materials.
- ✔ People and Trees.
- ✔ Using ArchVIsion RPC content plug-in.
- ✔ Using the Bionatics EASYnat plug-in.

VIZ Render is new to Autodesk Architectural Desktop 2004, and brings much of the power of Autodesk VIZ 4 to the program. Although the render engine is a separate module, it should be activated from within ADT 2004 directly. Selecting VIZ Render from within ADT links the two programs together. While the original ADT dwg has to be saved, once saved, any changes to the ADT dwg can be updated within VIZ Render.

Besides the ability to create and place materials, and to render (color wireframe models), VIZ Render brings Radiosity and animation to ADT. Radiosity is a system that accurately and easily represents lighting. In this system, one places a sun, light-bulbs, light fixtures, and so on and the render engine calculates the effects of these light sources on the scene. Rendered output can be as a bitmap (JPG, TIF, TGA, GIF), as a movie file (MOV, AVI, FLI), or other formats for the Web (PGN), and for $2^1/_2$ D programs such as Piranesi (RLA). Professional high-resolution movies can be made from numbered TGA files, AVIs, or MOVs, but can best be played back from the hard drive when used in conjunction with hardware compression devices such as Pinnacle's $800 Pro-One video board. The movies can also be compressed as MP2s and burned to CDs or DVDs giving excellent results.

Besides VIZ Render, ADT 2004 also comes with plug-ins from ArchVision and Bionatics. Using its RPC concept, ArchVision has become the de facto standard for Architectural 3D digital content. Bionatics provides an excellent 3D vegetation solution, which can be modified by season. Its trees, flowers, bushes, and so on can be animated to show wind.

How Best to Learn to Operate VIZ Render

The best way to learn the VIZ render techniques is to start out with a very simple structure. Once you have learned the techniques, you can easily apply those techniques to more complex structures. Keep your experimentation simple, make one change at a time, and observe the changes.

Hands-On

Making a Simple Scene

1. Start a new drawing using the Architectural Building Model and View (Imperial - ctb) template.
2. Change to the Model Layout.
3. Change to the Top View.
4. Using **Standard** 6″ × 8′-high walls, create a 20′-long by 10′-wide enclosure.
5. Place a roof on the structure with the following parameters:

   a. Thickness = **10″**
   b. Edge cut = **Plumb**
   c. Overhang = **1′-0″**
   d. Plate height = **8′-0″**
   e. Slope = **45.00**

Figure 22-1

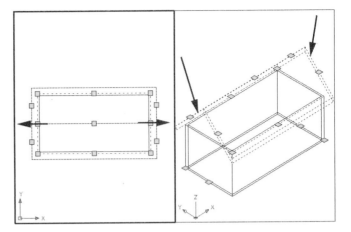

6. Select the roof to activate its grips, and pull the center end grips to create gable ends (see Figure 22-1).

7. Enter **roofline** in the command line, and press Enter.

8. Enter **A** (Auto project) in the command line, and press Enter.

9. Select the two end walls, and press Enter.

10. Select the roof and press Enter twice to make the walls meet the roof peak, and finish the command (see Figure 22-2).

11. Add windows and doors as shown in Figure 22-3. The glass in the windows has been turned off; the doors have been opened to 90°.

12. Change to the Front View.

13. Place a rectangle as shown in Figure 22-4.

14. Select the rectangle, RMB, and select Polyline Edit from the contextual menu that appears.

15. Enter **E** (Edit vertex) in the command line and press Enter.

16. Enter **I** (Insert) in the command line and press Enter.

17. Repeat this process and place new vertices where shown in Figure 22-5.

Figure 22-2   **Figure 22-3**

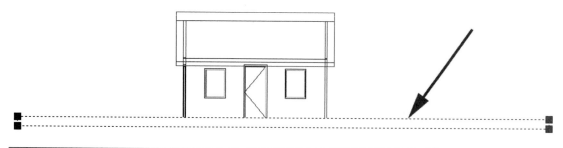

Figure 22-4

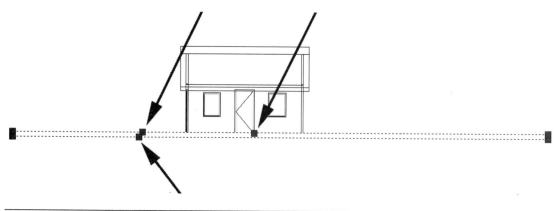

Figure 22-5

Figure 22-6

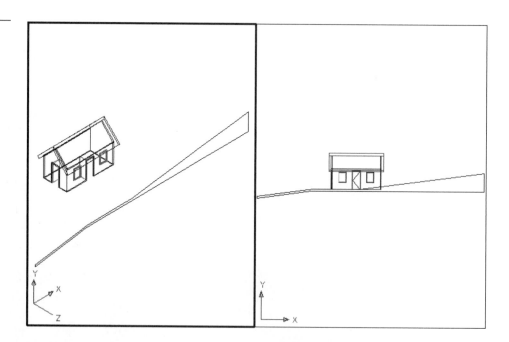

18. Move the vertices until you achieve a result similar to that in Figure 22-6.

19. Enter **extrude** in the command line and press Enter.

20. Select the modified rectangle that you just created and press Enter.

Figure 22-7

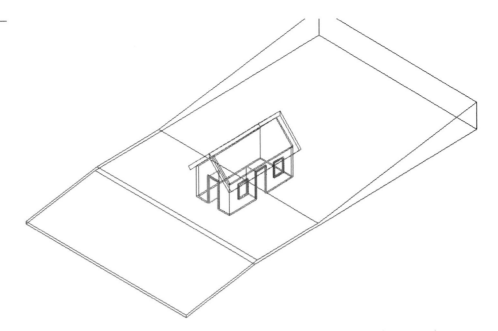

21. Enter **50′-0″** in the command line and press Enter twice to finish the command. (I rotated the UCS 180° on the X axis before entering the extrude command. If you did not do this, just move the finished extrusion into position.) See Figure 22-7.

22. Create a new **Layer**, and name it **BASE**.

23. Select the extrusion you created, and assign it the new layer **BASE**.

24. Save the File as **ADTVIZ RENDER PROJECT**.

You have now created a scene with a simple building and a Base.

Hands-On

Using VIZ Render

1. Select the **Open drawing menu** icon as shown in Figure 22-8 to bring up its contextual menu.

After about 15 seconds, the VIZ Render interface will appear with your scene, and the File link Settings dialog box (see Figure 22-9).

2. In the File link Settings dialog box, press OK to accept the defaults.

3. Press the VIZ **Minimize Viewport** icon to change the interface into four viewports (see Figure 22-10).

4. Press the **Zoom Extents All** icon to fill each viewport view (see Figure 22-11).

5. Select **Create > Daylight System** from the **Main** toolbar to bring up the **Daylight Object Creation** dialog box.

6. Press **Yes**.

7. Click in the Top viewport in the middle of the structure.

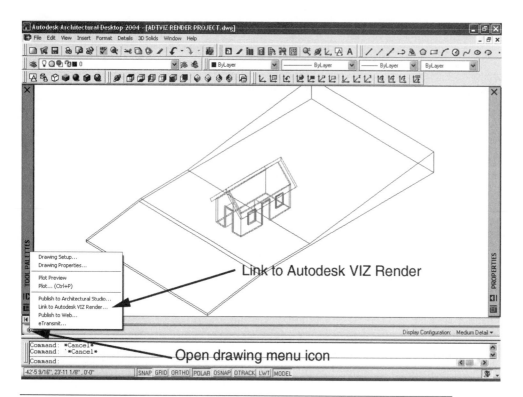

Figure 22-8

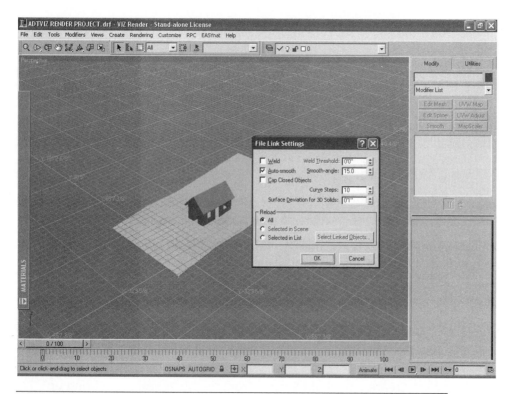

Figure 22-9

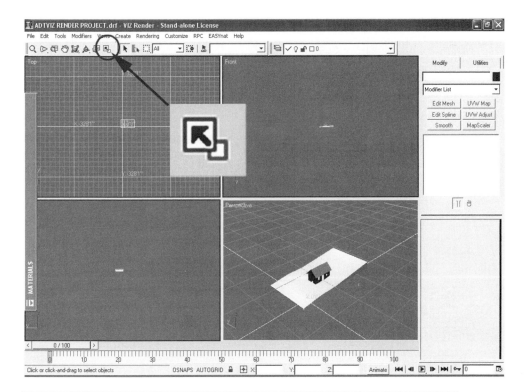

Figure 22-10

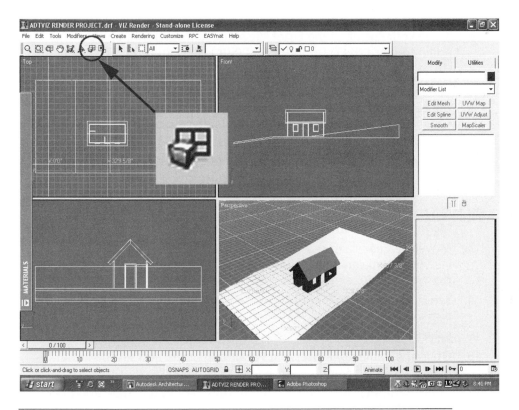

Figure 22-11

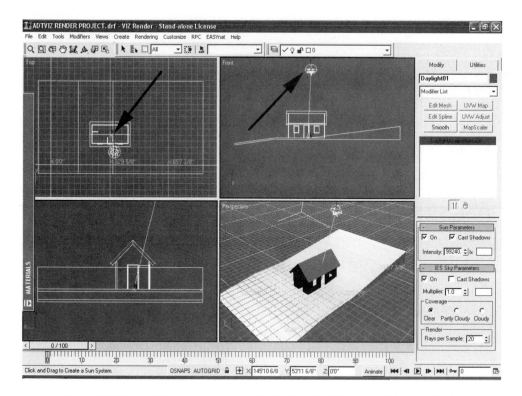

Figure 22-12

8. Move your cursor to the Front View, move it vertically, and click again to place the Daylight Object (Sun) (see Figure 22-12).

9. Select **Create > Cameras > Target Camera** from the Main toolbar.

10. Click to the left of the enclosure in the **Top** viewport, click again in the center of the enclosure, and move your cursor over the **Front** viewport; move it vertically and click again to set the camera (see Figure 22-13).

11. Click in the **Perspective** viewport, and press the letter **C** on the keyboard to change the Perspective viewport into a Camera viewport. (The Camera viewport shows what the camera sees.)

12. Change to the **Top** viewport, select the Camera, RMB, and select **Move** from the contextual menu that appears.

13. Move the Camera in the Top viewport while watching the camera viewport. You can adjust the height of the Camera by moving it in the **Front** view (see Figure 22-14).

14. Select **Rendering > Render** from the **Main** menu to bring up the **Render Scene** dialog box.

15. Select the **Radiosity** tab.

16. Open the **Radiosity Processing Parameters** tree, and set the Initial quality to 85%.

17. In the Radiosity tab, open the **Rendering Parameters** tree, and press the **Render Direct Illumination** radio button.

18. Press the Start button at the top of the Radiosity Processing Parameters tree to change to the **Render** tab.

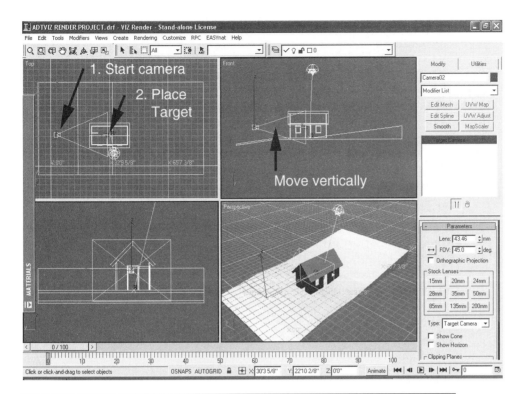

Figure 22-13

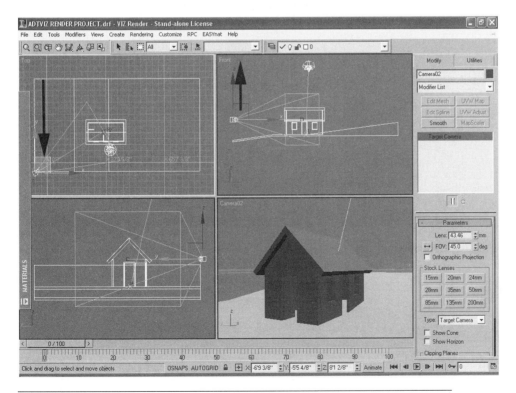

Figure 22-14

The top bar above the Process will indicate the progress in running the Radiosity solution.

What is the Radiosity solution?

In order for the VIZ Render engine to create realistic lighting, a Radiosity solution is generated as a mesh throughout your scene. Each part of the mesh tells the render engine what shade of color and shadow to use for each area. If you move an object or change the number of light fixtures, you must reset the solution and start it again before rendering.

19.   In the Render tab, open the **Common Parameters** tree.

20.   Select the **Single** radio button, and press the **640x480** button for the **Output** size.

21.   Select Production with Radiosity from the drop-down list, **Camera** from the Viewport drop-down list, and press the Render button (see Figure 22-15).

The render engine will now create a 640 × 480 image with shading and shadows (see Figure 22-16).

22.   Select **file > Save Copy As** from the VIZ Render Main menu, and save the file as **ADTVIZ RENDER PROJECT.drf**.

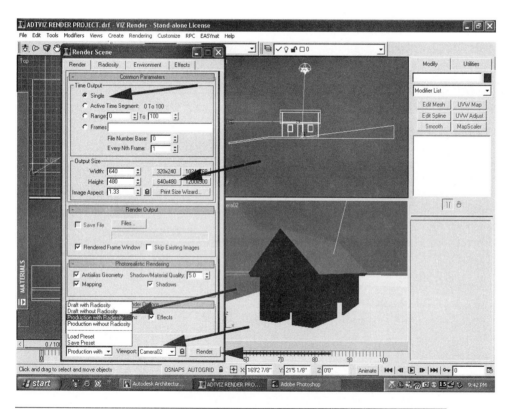

Figure 22-15

Figure 22-16

Hands-On

Creating and Using Materials

1. Using the previous saved file.

2. Activate the Camera viewport, and press the letter **P** (Perspective) on the keyboard to change the viewport to the Perspective View.

3. Press the letter **W** on the keyboard to maximize the perspective viewport. (This is an easier way to toggle viewports from minimize to maximize that was done with an icon in Step 3 of the previous exercise).

4. Select the Roof of the building.

5. Select the **Edit Mesh** button in the **Modify** tab (a warning message will appear, read it, then press **OK**) (see Figure 22-17).

6. The **Edit Mesh** tool controls will now appear.

7. Press the **Polygon** icon (the Polygon icon will select full faces of a mesh), and select the right roof face; it will turn red when selected (see Figure 22-18).

8. In the Edit Mesh tools, press the **Detach** button to bring up the Detach dialog box.

9. Enter **RIGHT ROOF SURFACE** in the **Detach as:** data field, and press OK. This will create the right roof surface as a separate element called **RIGHT ROOF SURFACE** (see Figure 22-19).

10. Select the **Arc Rotate** icon from the VIZ Render **Viewport Navigation Tools** toolbar, and rotate the view so that you can see the left side of the roof. Repeat Steps 5 thru 9 of this exercise, and detach the left roof as **LEFT ROOF SURFACE** (see Figure 22-20).

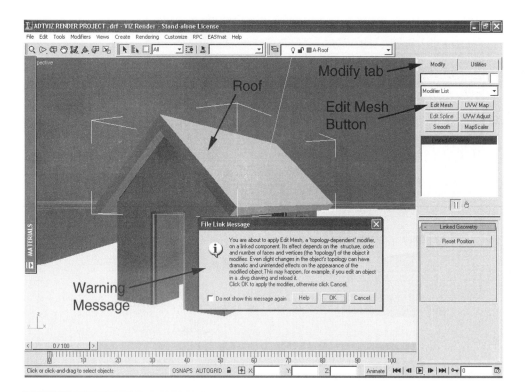

Figure 22-17

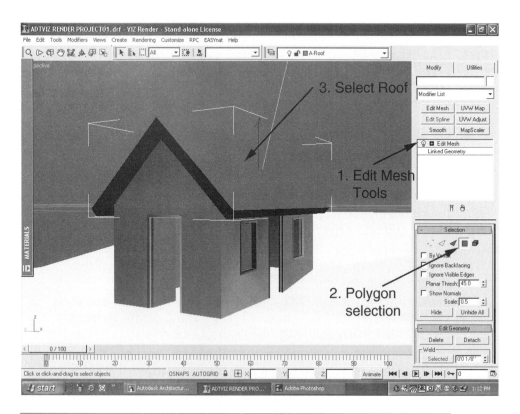

Figure 22-18

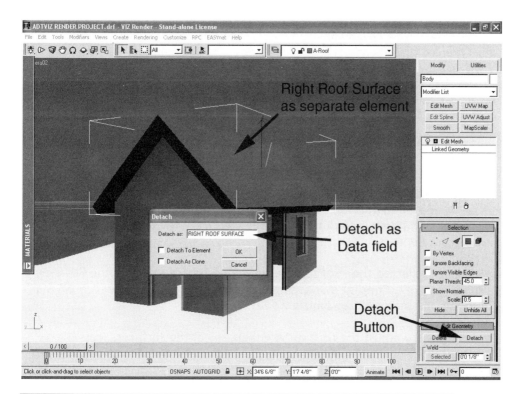

Figure 22-19

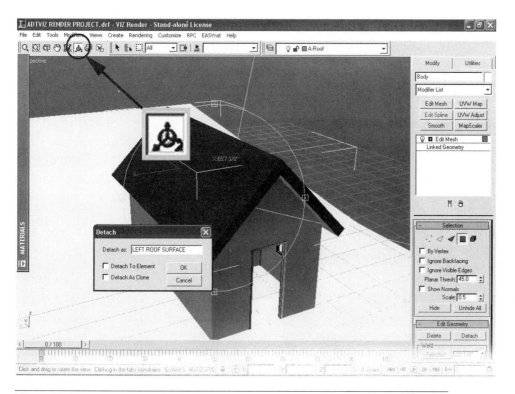

Figure 22-20

Hands-On

Applying Materials

1. Open the **Materials** palette.

2. In the Materials palette, select the **Tiling** tab.

3. Press **H** on the keyboard to bring up the **Select Objects** dialog box.

4. In the Select Objects dialog box highlight **LEFT ROOF SURFACE** and **RIGHT ROOF SURFACE**, and press the Select button to select these elements that you previously created (see Figure 22-21).

5. In the Tiling palette, select the **Finishes, Tiling. Ceramic. Checker** icon, RMB, and select **Apply To Selected** from the contextual menu that appears.

Since you selected the roof surfaces in Step 4 of this exercise, the Finishes, Tiling. Ceramic. Checker map is applied to those surfaces. *Note:* A MAP is a bitmap of a material (see Figure 22-22).

6. To easily adjust the roof surface map, select the surfaces, press the **MapScaler** button, and change the scale in the MapScaler parameters (see Figure 22-23).

7. Repeat the exercises "Creating and Using Materials" and "Applying Materials," and add materials to the walls of the enclosure.

If you don't separate the faces of the walls, and just apply a material directly to a wall, all the walls will become that material. You can also add a material to the Roof edges by separating them.

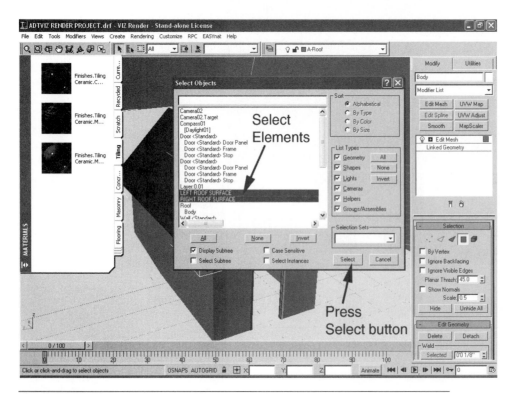

Figure 22-21

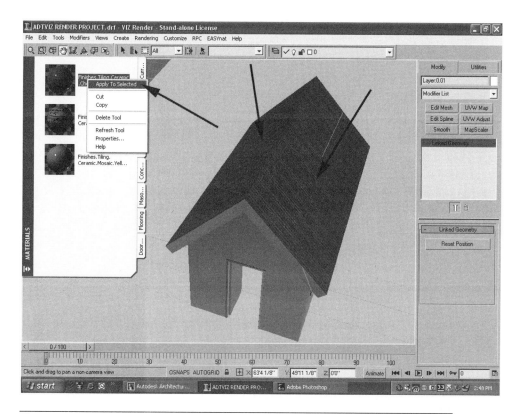

Figure 22-22

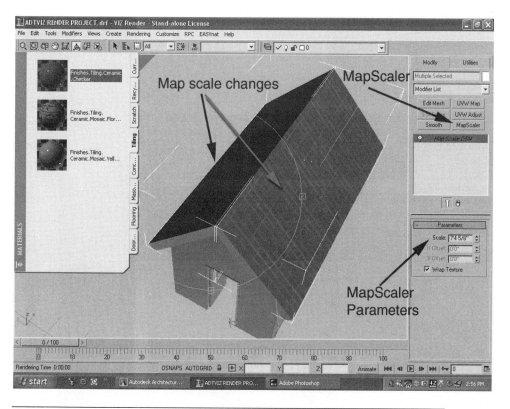

Figure 22-23

Figure 22-24

8. Press **C** from the keyboard to change the view back to the **Camera** view, and select **Rendering > Render** from the Main menu to bring up the Render Scene dialog box.

9. Press the **Render** button to render the scene (see Figure 22-24).

The Sky

10. Go to http://www.3dcafe.com/asp/texturesky1.asp or hunt for a site with sky texture maps on the Internet.

11. Download and save one of the sky maps as a JPG, TIF, or BMP and place it in a folder labeled **Maps** on your computer (see Figure 22-25).

12. Name the bitmap **SKY**.

13. Select **Rendering > Environment** from the **Main** menu to bring up the **Environment** tab in the **Render Scene** dialog box.

14. In the Environment tab, select the **None** bar to bring up the browse Images for Input dialog box and browse to the folder where you downloaded your SKY bitmap.

Figure 22-25

15. If you do not see your bitmap listed in the folder, change the Files of type to **All Files** in the drop-down list.

16. Select the Sky you downloaded, and press the **Open** button to return to the Environment tab.

17. Under **Exposure Control** press the **Render Preview** button to see a preview of your scene with the sky (see Figure 22-26).

18. Press the **Render** button to render the scene (see Figure 22-27).

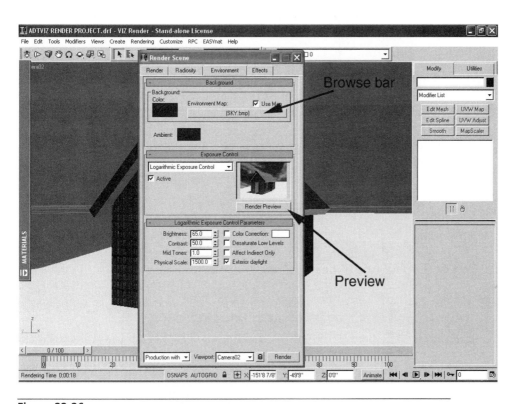

Figure 22-26

Figure 22-27

Hands-On

Creating and Modifying Materials

VIZ Render comes with a series of preconfigured materials, but you can make your own. Materials can be made from bitmaps, or directly from color. The bitmaps can be scanned or photographed images, or can be created in software programs such as Adobe PhotoShop or Illustrator. These bitmaps and colored materials can then be modified to have various levels of opacity and shininess. By using "bump map" versions of the images, which utilize the gray scale, additional three-dimensional characteristics can be incorporated. Bump maps are often used to enhance materials such as brick.

People often ask if the materials can look "real"; in fact, they can look more than real. In VIZ Render you can even make transparent steel.

1. Open the **Materials** palette, and select the **Scratch** tab.

2. Select the **Create New** icon, RMB, and select **User Defined** from the contextual menu that appears to create a new **User Defined** material (see Figure 22-28).

3. Select the new User Defined material, RMB, and select Properties from the contextual menu that appears to bring up the **Material Editor** dialog box (see Figure 22-29).

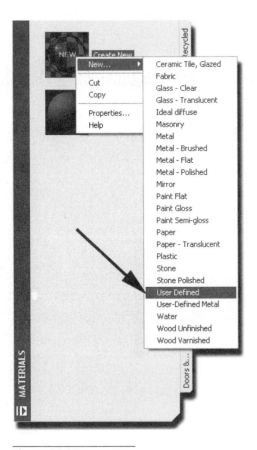

Figure 22-28

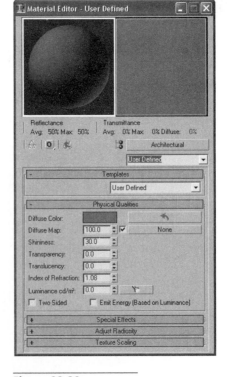

Figure 22-29

4. In the Material Editor, select the **Diffuse Color** area, to bring up the Color Selector.

5. Set the following (see Figure 22-30):

    a. Red = **210**
    b. Green = **217**
    c. Blue = **32**

6. In the Material Editor, set **Shininess** to 87.0.

Notice the small highlight that gets smaller as the shininess is increased (see Figure 22-31).

To see if a material is transparent, you need a background behind the sample globe.

7. Set **Transparency** to 75.0, RMB on the globe sample, and select Background to place a checkered background behind the sample (see Figure 22-32).

8. Return to Architectural Desktop 2004.

9. Enter **isolines** in the command line and press Enter.

10. Enter **16** in the command line and press Enter.

11. Enter **sphere** in the command line and press Enter.

12. Create a new layer and name it **SPHERE**.

13. Place a 3'-0" sphere in the scene near the enclosure, and assign it to the SPHERE layer (see Figure 22-33).

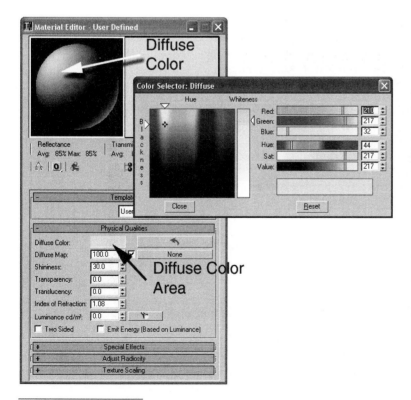

Figure 22-30

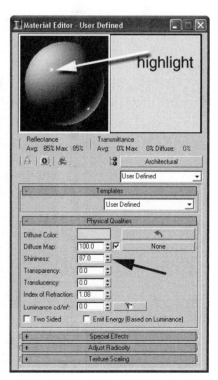

Figure 22-31

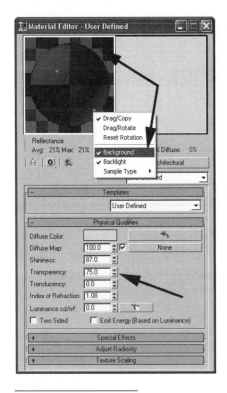

Figure 22-32

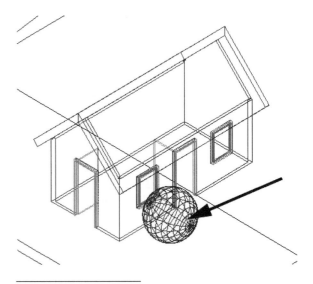

Figure 22-33

14. Return to VIZ Render.

15. Select the **File Link Manager** button under the Utilities tab to bring up the **File Link Manager** dialog box.

16. Press the **Reload** button to bring up the **File Link Settings** dialog box.

17. Press OK.

The VIZ Render scene will now be reloaded from ADT 2004, and will include the sphere you created in ADT 2004.

18. Press **H** on the keyboard to bring up the **Selection Floater**.

19. Select **Layer: SPHERE.01**, press the **Select** button, and close the Selection Floater.

20. Open the **Materials** palette and select the **Scratch** tab.

21. **RMB** on the new transparent yellow material you created, and select Apply to Selected from the contextual menu that appears.

With a normal video card, the sphere in the scene should be filled with small dots indicating that a transparent material has been applied to that object.

22. Press the **Render** button in the Render Scene dialog to render the scene (see Figure 22-34).

Figure 22-34

Create Grass

23. Open the **Materials** palette, and again select the **Scratch** tab.

24. Select the **Create New** icon, RMB, and select **User Defined** from the contextual menu that appears to create a new **User Defined** material.

25. **RMB** on the new material and select Properties to bring up the **Material Editor**.

26. Select the **None** button to the right of the Diffuse Map data field to bring up the Material/Map Browser (see Figure 22-35).

27. In the Material/Map Browser, click on the **Noise** icon, and press OK to bring up the **Material Editor** for the new Grass material with the Noise options.

Figure 22-35

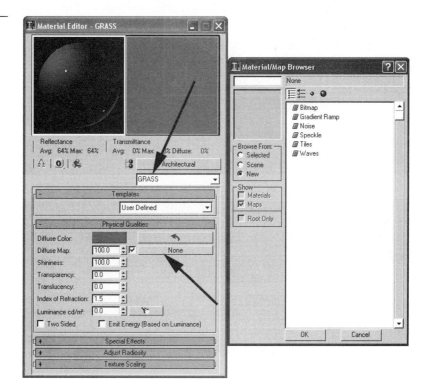

28. Set the following:

Noise Type = **Turbulence**
Size = **0.1**

Color #1
a. Red = **0**
b. Green = **109**
c. Blue = **13**

Color #2
a. Red = **79**
b. Green = **84**
c. Blue = **80**

29. Return to the **Materials** palette and drag the **GRASS** icon to the **BASE** in your scene.

30. Render the scene (see Figure 22-36).

Figure 22-36

Hands-On

People and Trees

VIZ Render comes with content from two developers, Archvision and Bionatics.

Archvision is the developer of the RPC people, foliage, and automobiles that have become the industry standard and are available in most of the leading visualization and CAAD packages. A sample demo person is included with VIZ Render, and more libraries are available by download at http://www.archvision.com.

Bionatics's EASYnat software brings highly customizable trees and plants to VIZ Render. Three trees and a plant are included, and more libraries are available online at http://www.bionatics.com. EASYnat trees can be made to wave in the wind, and can be automatically modified according to season.

To load the Archvision RPC plug-in do the following:

1. Return to Architectural Desktop 2004.
2. Select the **Content Browser** icon in the **Main** menu to bring up the **Content Browser**.
3. Select the **Architectural Desktop/VIZ Render Plug-ins** catalog.
4. Double-click on the catalog to open it. Inside the Catalog are two folders—one labeled **RPC**, the other **EasyNat**.
5. Double-click the RPC folder and follow the directions to go to the RPC website and download the RPC plug-in and Tina, the sample person. (You can also browse the dozens of RPC content libraries that include people, trees, cars, and even furniture.)

RPC content is unusual in that it is absolutely photorealistic, but renders very quickly. This is because it uses a unique system of compiled photographs of actual objects that appear correctly in relation to camera position. Content is constantly being upgraded and improved. RPC's Moving People content creates the most realistic architectural visualization animations available.

Once installed, the RPC content will become available as a menu choice on the Main menu bar.

To use Archvision RPC content do the following:

1. Return to **VIZ Render**.
2. In VIZ Render, press **W** on the keyboard to change to four viewports.
3. Activate the Top viewport and press **W** on the keyboard again to maximize the Top viewport.
4. Select **RPC > RPC** from the Main menu to bring up the RPC tools.

I have more content than you will have if you use only the demo content, but the process will be the same. The demo person (Tina) is not the highest resolution available.

5. Select the name of the person (Tina if only demo content) in the **RPC Selection** tree (see Figure 22-37).

Figure 22-37

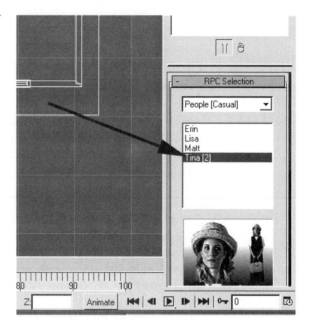

6. Push the RPC Selection tools upward to expose the **RPC Parameters** tools.

7. In the Parameters set the following:

   a. **Height = 5.6666**

If this is preset in meters, select **Customize > Units Setup** from the main menu, and set the units to feet and inches.

   b. **Check** the **Cast Reflections** check box if you intend to reflect your RPC content in windows or mirrors.

   c. **Uncheck** the **Jitter check box**. Jitter is used when animating, and makes smoother animated content.

   d. **Uncheck Billboard**. Billboard is used when you want to concentrate several pieces of content into one quick rendering object, such as trees into a tree line.

   e. **Check** the **Cast Shadows** check box.

   f. **Uncheck** the **Apply Filter Effect** check box. This allows you to use Photoshop filter effects on the content. The effects must be loaded into the RPC directory.

8. Move your cursor into your scene.

9. Click and hold the left mouse button to place and rotate Tina into position (see Figure 22-38).

10. Press **W** on the keyboard to change to four viewports, and adjust Tina in relation to the Base.

11. Add more people if you have them, or just add more copies of Tina.

12. Since you have placed new content, it is a good idea to **Reset** and **Start** a new Radiosity solution.

13. After finishing the Radiosity solution, render the Camera view (see Figure 22-39).

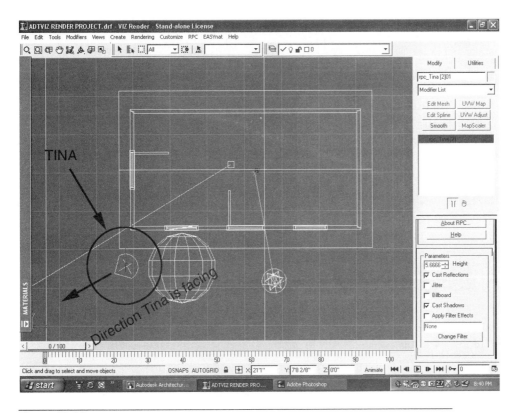

Figure 22-38

Figure 22-39

Note that several of the figures are "washed out." To fix this do the following:

14. Press the **Mass Edit** button in the **RPC Edit Tools** tree above the RPC Parameters that you set in Step 12 to bring up the **RPC Mass Edit** dialog box.

15. In the RPC Mass Edit dialog box select all the people you used to populate the scene and set their Self Illumination to 100.0 (see Figure 22-40).

16. If you have more **RPC** content such as trees or cars, add it, adjust the **Self Illumination**, and **Render** the scene (see Figure 22-41).

Figure 22-40

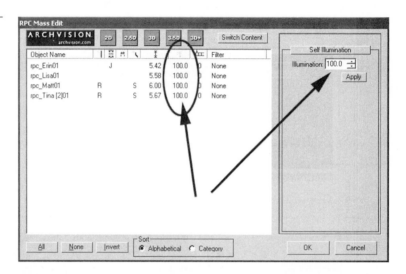

Figure 22-41

To load the Bionatics EASYnat plug-in do the following:

1. Return to Architectural Desktop 2004.
2. Select the **Content Browser** icon in the **Main** menu to bring up the **Content Browser**.
3. Select the **Architectural Desktop/VIZ Render Plug-ins** catalog.
4. Double-click on the catalog to open it.
5. Double-click the EASYnat folder and follow the directions to go to the EASYnat website and download the plug-in.

EASYnat content is a high-quality plant modeler featuring virtual plants that can be modified for age and season. Once installed, the EASYnat content will become available as a menu choice on the Main menu bar.
    To use Bionatics EASYnat content do the following:

1. Return to **VIZ Render**.
2. Delete the Archvision content you placed in the previous exercise.
3. Select **EASYnat > Create** from the Main menu to bring up the **Create EASYnat Plant** dialog box (see Figure 22-42).
4. Select the tree desired from the main screen or press the **Nursery** button to open the **EASYnat Nursery** dialog box.
5. Double-click on Horsechestnut, and return to the Create EASYnat Plant dialog box.
6. Select the Plant Tuning **Hybrid** radio button, and set the age of the tree to **12**.
7. Set the Season to **Summer**, and press the **Generate tree** button to generate the tree.

The Tree Generation timer will appear. After it closes, your tree will be in the scene.

Figure 22-42

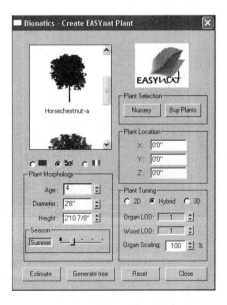

8. Move your tree into position, and repeat the generation and placement of another tree, but set the **Age** to **9** for this tree.

9. Reset and start a new radiosity solution, and then render the scene (see Figure 22-43).

Select the different radio buttons for 2D and 3D trees, and then press the Estimate button to see the difference in triangles. The more the triangles, the more realistic, the more time it takes to render. The above scene with two hybrid trees took 6 minutes to render on a 2-GHz, 1/2-GHz RAM computer.

Figure 22-43

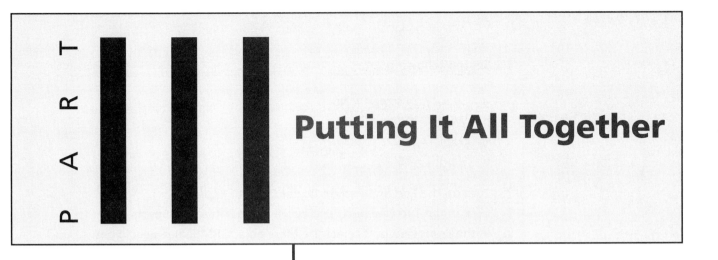

Putting It All Together

PART III

Tutorial Project

For the tutorial project you will work with a seven-story office building. The project starts with a Massing model and progresses through the design process to the construction documentation stage.

The building will have six floors, four stairways, and two elevators. The floor-to-floor height for the first floor will be 15'-0", and for the other floors 9'-4". The main structure will be 175' deep and 100' wide with concrete columns and slabs. Steel bar joists and corrugated steel pan with exterior rigid insulation will be used for the roof structure. A Massing model will be made to show the client, and when approved, construction documents will be created.

Hands-On

The Massing Model

1. Start a new drawing using the Architectural Building Model and View (Imperial - ctb) template.
2. Change to the **Work** Layout.
3. In **Paperspace**, erase all the viewports, and using **View > Viewports** from the **Main** menu create **3** viewports.
4. Assign **Top, Front,** and **SW Isometric** to the viewports, and set them all to **Medium Detail Display Configuration.**
5. From the **Massing** toolbar select the **Box** icon, and move over the Properties palette to open it.

6. Set the following:

    a. Specify on screen = **No**
    b. Width = **175′**
    c. Depth = **100′**
    d. Height = **75′**

7. Turn on the **End** and **Perpendicular** Object Snaps.
8. Click in the **Top** viewport, and zoom extents in all viewports.
9. In the **Front** viewport select the Mass object, RMB, and select **Split** from the contextual menu.
10. Enter **fro** in the command line, and press Enter.
11. Pick the lower left corner, lift the cursor vertically above the mass object, enter **15′-0″** in the command line and press Enter.
12. Move to the right side of the Mass object, and Perpendicular snap to that side.

You have now split the Mass object into two parts (see the figure below).

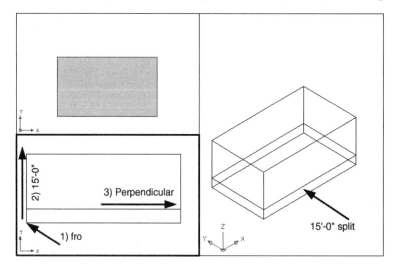

13. Select the floor you just created (First Floor) drag it to the right enter **25′**, and press Enter.
14. Repeat this at the other side entering **−25′** (see the figures below and in Step 15).

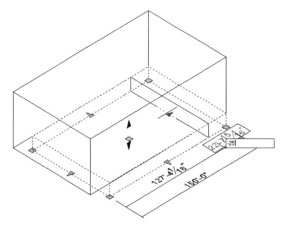

15. RMB anywhere in the drawing editor, select Object viewer from the contextual menu, select the mass objects, and select the Perspective icon (see the figure below).

16. Change to the **Top** View and create another mass object with the following dimensions:

    a. Width = **25′**
    b. Depth = **25′**
    c. Height = **50′-8″**

17. Make three more copies of this Mass object.

18. Place one Mass object at each corner of the upper main Mass object. This may be easier in SW Isometric View (see the figure below).

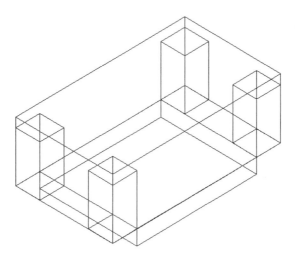

19. Select the upper main Mass object, RMB, and select **Boolean > Subtract** from the contextual menu. Select the four Mass objects you placed at the corners, and press Enter.

20. Enter **Y** (Yes) in the command line, and press Enter.

You have now removed the corners from the upper Massing object (see the figure below).

21. For the stairways, create another Mass object with the following dimensions:

    a. Width = **25′**
    b. Depth = **10′**
    c. Height = **65′-8″**

22. Make three more copies of this Mass object.

23. **Rotate** the stairway object **45°**, and place it in one of the Booleaned corners. Mirror to the other corners, as shown in the figure below.

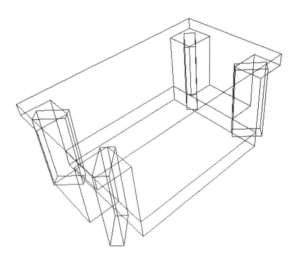

24. Select **Polyline** from the **Draw** menu and create the closed polyline form shown in the figure below.

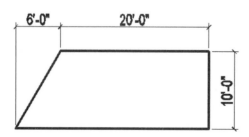

25. Select the closed polyline, RMB, and select **Convert To > Mass Element** from the contextual menu.

26. Enter **Y** (Yes) in the command line and press Enter.

27. Specify the extrusion height as **65′-8″**, and press Enter to create the **Side** Mass element.

28. Make a copy of the new **Side** element you just made, and place both on the side of the main mass element. Mirror both elements to the other side.

29. Select the first floor and **Boolean > Union** it to the Main Mass object.

30. **Boolean > Subtract** the Side elements from the Main mass.

31. Add two 1′-6″ radius cylinder mass objects as concrete columns at both ends (see the figure below).

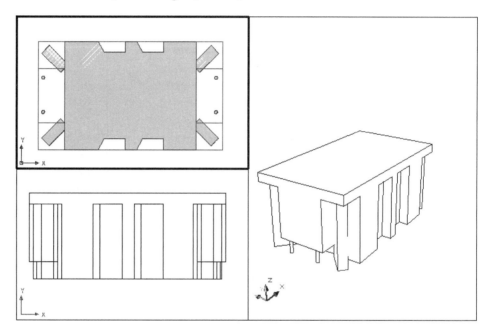

32. Place a 210′ × 185′ rectangle around the Mass elements at 0 elevation.

33. Offset the rectangle 30′-0″.

34. Set the elevation of the offset rectangle to −4'-0" (see the figure below).

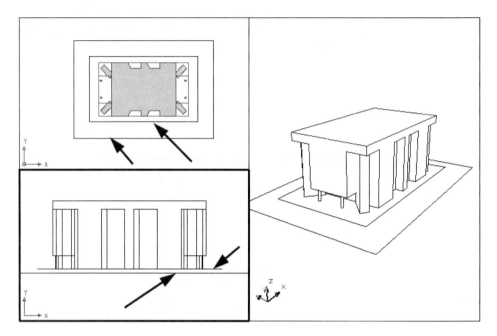

35. Select **Drape** from the Massing tool palette, and select the two rectangles you made in Steps 32 and 33, and press Enter.

36. Select the upper left corner of the larger rectangle, and select the other corner diagonal to the first.

37. Accept 30 as the mesh size in the command line, and press Enter.

38. Enter 10' as the Base thickness, and press Enter to create the base.

39. Save the file as **TUTORIAL MASSING PROJECT.**

Hands-On

Rendering the Massing Model

1. Press the Open menu icon at the lower left part of the screen and select **Link to Autodesk VIZ Render.**

The model will appear in VIZ Render.

2. In VIZ Render Select **Create > Cameras > Target Camera** from the **Main** menu and place a camera.

3. Select **Create > Daylight System** from the **Main** menu place a Daylight System.

4. Select **Rendering > Radiosity** from the **Main** menu, and Start a Radiosity solution with initial Quality of 85.0%.

5. Select **Rendering > Environment** from the **Main** menu, and browse to select a **sky** map.

6. Select **RPC** from the **Main** menu, and place some RPC people.

7. Select **Rendering > Render from** the **Main** menu, and **Render** a **JPG** of your model (see the figure below).

If you have Architectural Studio, Photoshop, Alias Sketch Book Pro, or a similar software program, you can mark up your JPG and send it to the client. If you have a strong understanding of VIZ, you can add Maps to illustrate fenestration, etc. You can even run the JPG through a filter for presentation (see the figure below).

8. Select **File > Save Copy As** from the Main menu and save the as **MASS MODEL RENDERING.**

9. Close VIZ Render.

Hands-On

Creating Slice Plates from the Massing Model

1. Return to ADT 2004.
2. Place the base layer on a new layer called BASE.
3. Turn the visibility of the BASE layer off.
4. Activate the SW Isometric viewport.
5. Select the **Slice** icon from the Massing tool palette.
6. Enter **7** for the number of slices and press Enter.
7. Click two places to create a rectangle (size doesn't matter).
8. Press Enter again to accept the **Rotation.**
9. Press Enter again to accept the **Starting height at 0".**
10. Enter **9'-4"** for the **Distance between slices,** and press Enter.

Seven rectangular objects with an X across their axis will appear. Each of these objects will have a small number next to them representing the elevation of each rectangle.

11. Change to the **Front** View.
12. Enter **M** (Move) in command line, and press Enter.
13. Select the top six rectangle objects and move them vertically **5'-8"** (see the figure below).

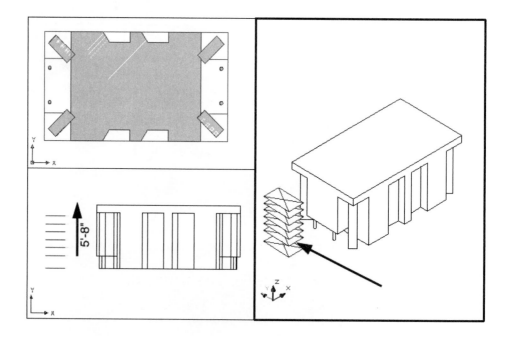

14. Select all the rectangular objects, RMB, and select **Attach Objects** from the contextual menu.

15. Select all the parts of your mass model, and press Enter.

The model will now be sliced into seven polyline slices.

16. Select the mass model, and turn off its visibility in the layer properties toolbar (see the figure below).

! **Note:** Selecting an object brings up its layer in the Properties toolbar. Just click on the layer to open it, and then click on its adjacent lightbulb to turn off its visibility.

The Polylines can now be used to begin the creation of the Construction documents.

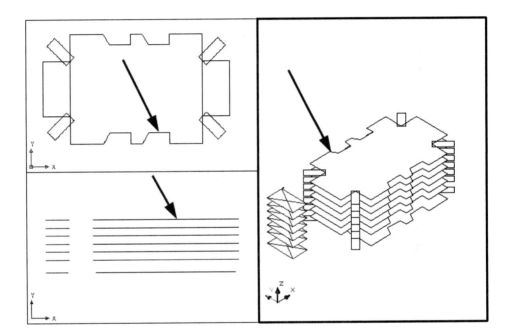

17. Delete the top six polylines.

You will now have only the first-floor polyline. (Don't save the drawing because you will UNDO and bring it back later.)

18. Enter **WBLOCK** in the command line, and press Enter to bring up the **Write Block** dialog box.

19. Set the following:

   a. Select the **Objects** radio button under **Source**.

   b. Select the **Retain** radio button under **Objects**.

   c. Browse and place the **Destination** in a new folder called **FLOOR POLYS.**

   d. Call the file **FIRST FLOOR POLY.**

   e. Select the polyline slice.

20. Press OK to write the file to the FLOOR POLYS directory (see the figure below).

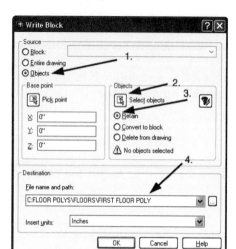

21. Repeat this process for the second-level slice, naming it.

Now that you have made a massing model and created slices from it, it is now time to set up the project.

Hands-On

Setting Up the Project

1. Select **File > Project Browser** from the **Main** menu to bring up the **Project Browser** dialog box.
2. Press the **New Project** icon to bring up the **Add Project** dialog box.
3. Enter **TUTORIAL PROJECT** in the **Name** field, and press OK to return to the Project Browser.
4. Select the TUTORIAL PROJECT, RMB, and select **Set Project Current** from the contextual menu.
5. Press the **Close** button to bring up the **Project Navigator** palette.
6. Select the **Project** tab.
7. Select the **Edit Levels** icon to bring up the Levels dialog box.
8. Press the **Add Level** icon and create seven levels.

9. Make the first floor 15'-0" high, and the other floors 9'4" high (see the figure below).

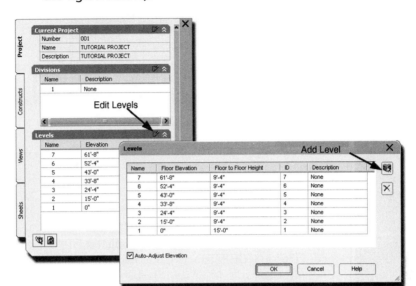

10. Press OK to return to the Project Navigator.

Hands-On

Using Slice Plates from the Massing Model

1. In the Project Navigator, change to the **Constructs** tab.
2. Select the Constructs icon, RMB, and select **New > Construct** from the contextual menu.
3. Name the New Construct **FIRST FLOOR MAIN WALLS,** check the **Level 1** check box, and press OK to return to the Drawing Editor.
4. In the Construct tab, double-click the **FIRST FLOOR MAIN WALLS** icon to bring up the **FIRST FLOOR MAIN WALLS.dwg.**
5. Select **Insert > Xref manager** from the **Main** menu to bring up the **Xref Manager** dialog box.
6. Press the **Attach** button to bring up the **Select Reference file** dialog box.
7. Select **FIRST FLOOR POLY.dwg** that you **WBLOCKED** from the mass model in Steps 18 through 20 of the exercise "Creating Slice Plates from the Massing Model" in this section.
8. Press the **Open** button to bring up the **External Reference** dialog box.

9. Set the settings shown in the figure below, and press OK to return to the Drawing Editor.

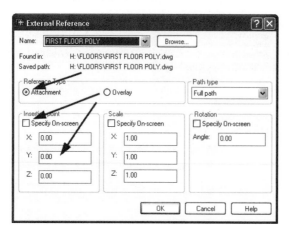

You have now placed an Xref copy of the First Floor Polylines in your project's FIRST FLOOR MAIN WALLS.dwg.

10. Press the **Manage Xrefs** icon to bring up the **Xref Manager** dialog box (see the figure below).

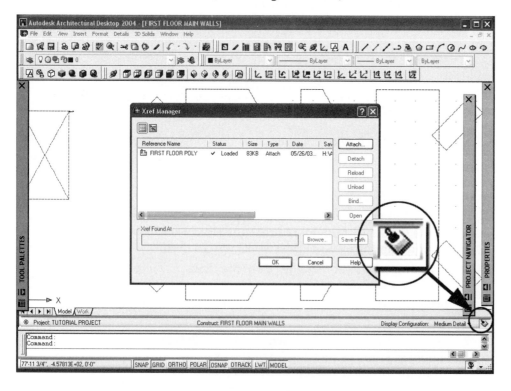

11. Select **FIRST FLOOR POLY** and press the **Bind** button to bring up the **Bind Xrefs** dialog box.

12. Press the OK buttons until you return to the Drawing Editor.

13. Select the bound Xref, type **EXPLODE** in the command line, and press Enter.

14. Select the bound Xref again, press the space bar on the keyboard to repeat the Explode command, and press Enter again.

15. Select the bound Xref for a third time, press the space bar on the keyboard to repeat the Explode command, and press Enter again to complete the commands.

16. Erase the Rectangle object with the X in it, and the elevation text.

17. Using **EXTEND** and **TRIM,** clean up the building outline to look like the following figure.

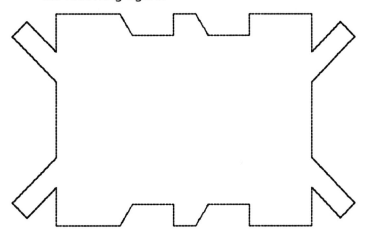

18. Select the Wall icon in the Design menu, RMB, and select **Apply Tool Properties to > Linework** from the contextual menu.

19. Select all the lines of the building outline and press Enter.

20. Enter **Y** (Yes) in the command line, and press Enter to create the walls.

21. While the walls are still selected, move your cursor over the **Properties** palette to open it.

22. Set the following:

   a. Style = **Standard**

   b. Width = **12″**

   c. Base Height = **15′-0″**

   d. Justify = **Right**

23. Press the Esc key on the keyboard to deselect the walls, change to the SW Isometric View, and select **File > Save** from the **Main** menu to save the drawing. See the figure below.

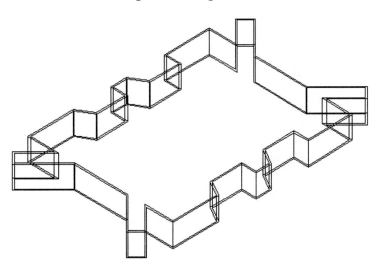

Hands-On

Adding Stairs

1. In the **Project Navigator,** in the **Constructs** tab, select the **Constructs** icon, RMB, and select **New > Construct** from the contextual menu.

2. Name the New Construct **FIRST FLOOR STAIRS,** check the **Level 1** check box, and press OK to return to the Drawing Editor.

3. Double-click **FIRST FLOOR STAIRS** to bring up the drawing in the Drawing Editor.

4. From the Project navigator, drag **FIRST FLOOR MAIN WALLS** into the FIRST FLOOR STAIRS drawing that is in the Drawing Editor. (This will automatically Xref the FIRST FLOOR MAIN WALLS into the new FIRST FLOOR STAIRS drawing.)

5. Select the **Stair** icon from the **Design** menu, move your cursor over the **Properties** Palette to open it, and place a stair in one stairwell with the following parameters:

   a. Style = **Standard**
   b. Shape = **U Shaped**
   c. Turn Type = **1/2 Landing**
   d. Horizontal Orientation = **Clockwise**
   e. Vertical Orientation = **Up**
   f. Width =**3'-8"**
   g. Base Height = **15'-0"**
   h. Justify = **Left**
   i. Terminate with = **Landing**

6. Select the **Railing** icon from the **Design** menu, move your cursor over the **Properties** Palette to open it, and place a railing with the following parameters:

   a. Style = **Standard**
   b. Attached to = **Stair Flight**
   c. Side Offset = **2"**

7. Using the **MIRROR** command, mirror the stair and rails to the other three stairways.

8. Press the **Manage Xrefs** icon to bring up the **Xref Manager** dialog box, and **Detach** the **FIRST FLOOR MAIN WALLS** drawing from the **FIRST FLOOR STAIRS drawing.**

9. Save the **FIRST FLOOR STAIRS drawing.**

Hands-On

The First-Floor Slab

1. In the **Project Navigator,** in the **Constructs** tab, select the **Constructs** icon, RMB, and select **New > Construct** from the contextual menu.

2. Name the New Construct **FIRST FLOOR SLAB,** check the **Level 1** check box, and press the OK button to return to the Drawing Editor.

3. Double-click **FIRST FLOOR SLAB** to bring up the drawing in the Drawing Editor.

4. From the Project navigator, drag **FIRST FLOOR MAIN WALLS** into the FIRST FLOOR STAIRS drawing that is in the Drawing Editor. (This will automatically Xref the FIRST FLOOR MAIN WALLS into the new FIRST FLOOR SLAB drawing.)

5. Enter **BPOLY** in the Command line and press Enter to bring up the **Boundary Creation** dialog box.

6. Select the **Pick Points** button, pick a point inside the Main Walls, and press Enter.

7. Press the **Manage Xrefs** icon to bring up the **Xref Manager** dialog box, and **Detach** the **FIRST FLOOR MAIN WALLS drawing** from the **FIRST FLOOR SLAB drawing.**

You will be left with a polyline that matches the inside perimeter of the first-floor walls.

8. Select the **Slab** icon in the Design menu, RMB, and select **Apply Tool Properties to > Linework and Walls.**

9. Select the polyline you created in Step 6 of this exercise, and press Enter.

10. Enter **Y** (Yes) in the command line to erase the layout geometry, and press Enter.

11. Enter **D** (Direct) in the command line, and press Enter.

12. Enter **B** (Bottom) in the command line, and press Enter to finish the command.

You have now created the first-floor slab, but the slab needs a 30″ turndown to support the edges. To make the turndown do the following:

13. Draw the following closed polyline for the turndown (see the figure below).

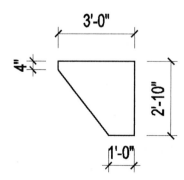

14. Select the polyline, RMB, and select **Convert to > Profile Definition** from the contextual menu.

15. With the **End** Osnap **on,** select the upper right corner of the closed polyline, and press Enter to bring up the **New Profile Definition** dialog box.

Be careful, this insertion point is important!

16. In the New Profile Definition dialog box, enter **FIRST FLOOR SLAB TURNDOWN.** You have now created a Profile.

17. Select **Format > Style Manager** from the Main menu to bring up the **Style Manager.**

18. Under FIRST FLOOR SLAB.dwg select **Architectural Objects > Slab Edge Styles.**

19. Click on Slab Edge Styles, RMB, and select **New** from the contextual menu.

20. Rename the **New Style** to **FIRST FLR SLAB EDGE.**

21. Double-click on FIRST FLR SLAB EDGE to bring up the **Slab Edge Styles** dialog box.

22. Select the **Design Rules** tab.

23. Check the **Fascia** check box, pick **FIRST FLOOR SLAB TURNDOWN** from the Profile drop-down list, and uncheck the A - Auto-Adjust to Edge Height check box (see the figure below).

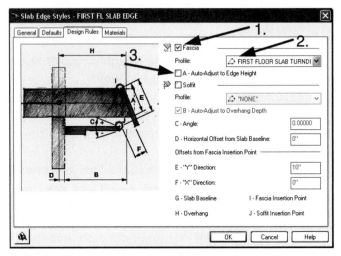

24. Press the **OK** and **Apply** buttons to return to the Drawing Editor.

25. Select the floor slab and move your cursor over the **Properties** palette to open it.

26. Click on the **Edges** icon to bring up the **Slab Edges** dialog box.

27. Select all the edges, select **FIRST FL SLAB EDGE** from the **Edge Style** column, and then press OK (see the figure below).

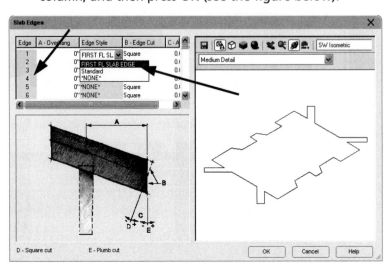

Your first-floor slab now has a turndown. Save the edge style for use on future projects (see the figure below). Save the First Floor Slab file.

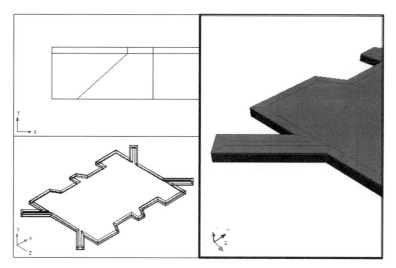

Hands-On

The Column Structure

1. In the **Project Navigator,** in the **Constructs** tab, select the **Constructs** icon, RMB, and select **New > Construct** from the contextual menu.

2. Name the New Construct **FIRST FLOOR COLUMN STRUCTURE,** check the **Level 1** check box, and press OK to return to the Drawing Editor.

3. Double-click **FIRST FLOOR COLUMN STRUCTURE** to bring up the drawing in the Drawing Editor.

4. From the Project navigator, drag **FIRST FLOOR MAIN WALLS** into the FIRST FLOOR COLUMN STRUCTURE drawing that is in the Drawing Editor. (This will automatically Xref the FIRST FLOOR MAIN WALLS into the new FIRST FLOOR COLUMN STRUCTURE drawing.)

The columns are going to be composite W8 × 31 steel columns encased in 16″ × 16″ concrete.

5. Select the **Content Browser** icon on the **Main** menu to bring up the **Content Browser.**

6. In the Content Browser, select the **Architectural Desktop Design Tool Catalog – Imperial > Structural > Members.**

7. Drag the **Concrete Encased Steel W8 16x16** icon into your **Design** palette.

To quickly load a column into the properties palette, select the Concrete Encased Steel W8 16x16 icon, press Enter and place one column in your drawing. You can then erase the column after placing it.

8. Select the **Column Grid** icon from the **Design** tool palette, and move your cursor over the **Properties** palette to open it.

9. Set the following:

    a. Shape = **Rectangular**
    b. Specify on screen = **No**
    c. X - Width = **175'**
    d. Y - depth = **100'**
    e. X Axis Layout type = **Repeat**
    f. X Bay size = **25'-0"**
    g. Y Axis Layout type = **Repeat**
    h. Y Bay size = **25'-0"**
    i. Column Style = **Concrete Encased Steel W8 16x16**

10. Place the Column Grid from the lower left corner of the First Floor main walls.

The Column grid will appear with columns at each node. The Grid will need adjustment.

11. Select the Column Grid, and move your cursor over the **Properties** palette to open it.
12. Change the **Y Axis Layout type** to **Manual.**
13. Click on the **Y Axis Bays** icon to bring up the **Bays along the Y Axis** dialog box.
14. Select the **Add** icon and add two grid lines.
15. In the Bays along the Y Axis dialog box set the grid lines to the following figure.

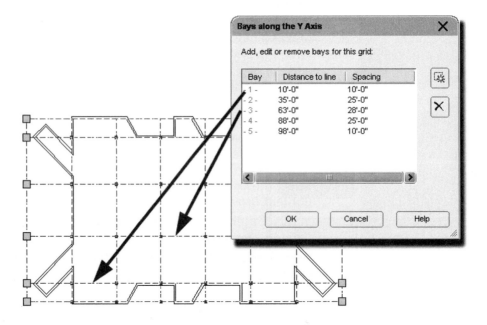

16. Repeat for the X Axis. In the **Bays along the X Axis** dialog box set the grid lines to the following figure.

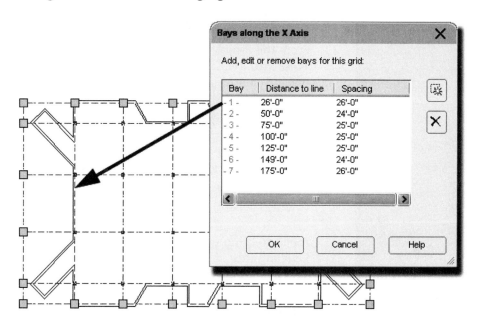

17. Delete the columns shown in the following figure.

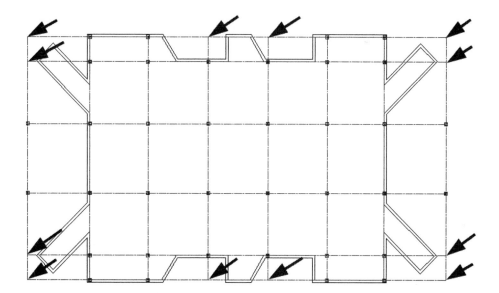

18. Press the **Manage Xrefs** icon to bring up the **Xref Manager** dialog box, and **Detach** the **FIRST FLOOR MAIN WALLS drawing** from the **FIRST FLOOR COLUMN STRUCTURE drawing.**

19. Save the **FIRST FLOOR COLUMN STRUCTURE.dwg.**

You will need to use the column grid separately so do the following:

20. In the **Project Navigator,** in the **Constructs** tab, select the **Constructs** icon, RMB, and select **New > Construct** from the contextual menu.

21. Name the New Construct **COLUMN GRID,** check the **Level 1** check box, and press OK to return to the Drawing Editor.

22. Double-click **COLUMN GRID** to bring up the drawing in the Drawing Editor.

23. From the Project navigator, drag the **FIRST FLOOR COLUMN STRUC-TURE** into the COLUMN GRID drawing in the Drawing Editor. (This will automatically Xref the FIRST FLOOR COLUMN STRUCTURE into the new COLUMN GRID drawing.)

24. Press the **Manage Xrefs** icon to bring up the **Xref Manager** dialog box.

25. Select the **FIRST FLOOR COLUMN STRUCTURE** and then select the **Bind** button to bind it to the COLUMN GRID.dwg.

26. In the COLUMN GRID.dwg, explode the column grid, and delete the columns leaving only the grid.

27. Select the column grid, RMB, and select **Label** from the contextual menu to bring up the **Column Grid Labeling** dialog box. Select the **Y - Labeling** tab.

28. Set the Column Grid Labeling dialog box per the figure below.

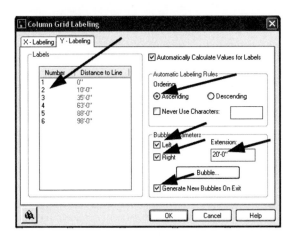

29. Change to the **X - Labeling** tab; set the Column Grid Labeling dialog box per the following figure.

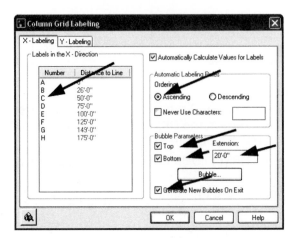

30. Press OK in the Column Grid Labeling dialog box to return to the Drawing Editor.

31. To show the dimensions for the grid, select **Format > AEC Dimension Styles** to bring up the **Style Manager.**

32. Select **Documentation Objects > AEC Dimension Styles > 1 Chain.**

33. Double-click on **1 Chain** to bring up the **AEC Dimension Style Properties** dialog box. Select the **Display Properties** tab.

34. Double-click on **Plan** to bring up the **Display Properties - AEC Dimension Plan Display Representation** dialog box.

35. Select the **Contents** tab.

36. Select **Grid** from the **Apply to** list.

37. Check the **All Grids Lines** check box in the **Grid** area, and press the OK buttons to return to the Drawing editor.

38. Select the grid, RMB, select AEC Dimension from the contextual menu, and drag dimensions down. Repeat for the right side.

39. Save the **COLUMN GRID.dwg** shown in the following figure.

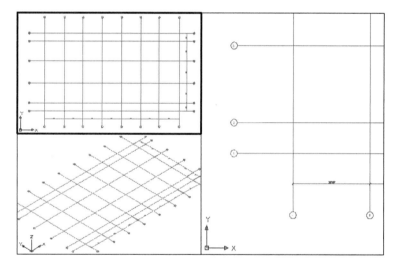

Hands-On

The CORE

The Core includes the elevator shafts, mechanical rooms, and bathrooms.

1. In the **Project Navigator,** in the **Constructs** tab, select the **Constructs** icon, RMB, and select **New > Construct** from the contextual menu.

2. Name the New Construct **CORE,** check the **Level 1** check box, and press OK to return to the Drawing Editor.

3. Double-click **CORE** to bring up the drawing in the Drawing Editor.

4. From the Project Navigator, drag the **FIRST FLOOR MAIN WALLS** and the **FIRST FLOOR COLUMN STRUCTURE** into the CORE drawing that is in the Drawing Editor. (This will automatically Xref the FIRST FLOOR MAIN WALLS and FIRST FLOOR COLUMN STRUCTURE into the new CORE drawing.)

The Core will need 12″ CMU (concrete block walls). ADT 2004 does not come with this type of wall, so you will need to create it by doing the following:

5. Select the **CMU 8** from the **Walls** tool palette and place a **4′-0″** section of wall in the drawing.

6. Select **Format > Style Manager** from the **Main** menu to bring up the **Style Manager.**

7. Select **CORE.dwg > Architectural Objects > WallStyles.**

8. RMB on the **CMU-8** in the Wall Styles folder and select **Copy** from the contextual menu. (CMU-8 exists in CORE.dwg because you placed it there in Step 5 of this exercise.)

9. RMB on **CMU-8** again and select **Paste** from the contextual menu to automatically create a new wall style called **CMU-8 (2).**

10. Rename CMU-8 (2) to **CMU-12.**

11. Double-click on CMU-12 to bring up its **Wall Style Properties** dialog box.

12. Select the **Components** tab.

13. Change the **Width** to **1′-0″, Edge Offset** to **−12″**, and press the **OK** and **Apply** buttons to return to the Drawing Editor.

CMU-12 is now available in the Properties palette.

14. Place the walls **14′-6″** high as shown in the following figure.

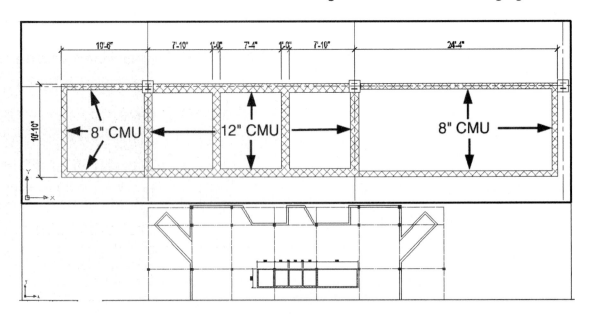

The Bathrooms and Elevators

15. Select the **Content Browser** icon from the Main menu to bring up the Content Browser.

16. Locate the elevators in the **Architectural Desktop Design Tool Catalog - Imperial > Conveying > Elevators** folder.

17. From the **Elevators** folder, drag the **Square Elevator** into your **Design** tool palette.

18. In the Content Browser locate the **Layouts** in the **Architectural Desktop Design Tool Catalog - Imperial > Mechanical > Plumbing Fixtures** folder.

19. From the **Layouts** folder, drag the **Rest Room (Men)** and **Rest Room (Women)** to your **Design** tool palette.

20. Drag the Square elevator from the Design tool palette and place it as shown in the following figure.

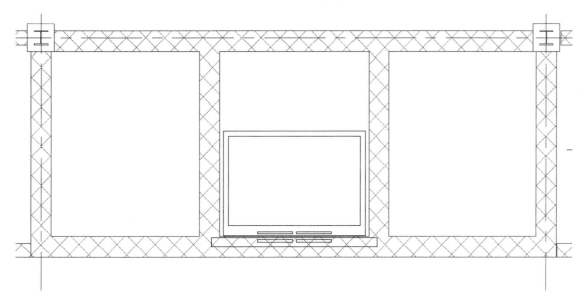

21. Select the wall in front of the elevator, RMB, and select **Insert > Opening** from the contextual menu.

22. Move your cursor over the Properties palette and make the opening 3′-8″ wide and 7′-0″ high.

23. Copy the opening and the elevator to either side of the original (see the figure below).

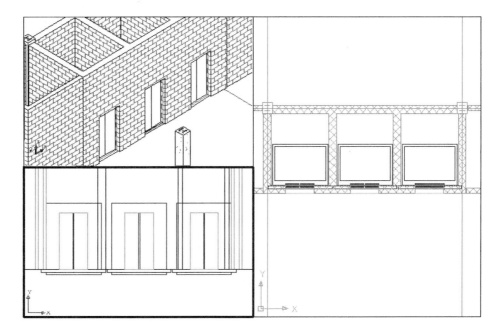

24. Drag the **Rest Room (Men)** from the **Design** tool palette, and place it in the enclosure to the right of the elevators.

25. Mirror the Core so that there is a 7'-0" corridor, and add the **Rest Room (Women)** to the other side.

You may have to select the **Rest Room (Men)** and **Rest Room (Women),** RMB, and **Edit Block in Place.**

26. Add doors, detach the **FIRST FLOOR MAIN WALLS** and **FIRST FLOOR COLUMN STRUCTURE,** and save the **CORE file** (see the figure below).

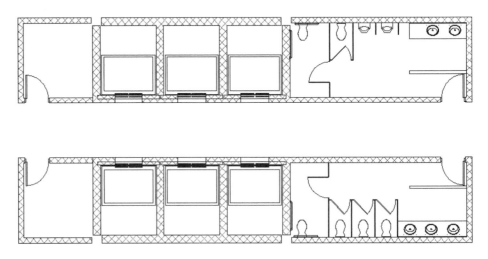

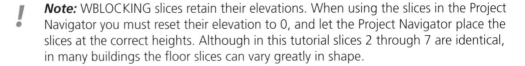

Hands-On

The Second-Floor Walls and Slab

The second- through seventh-floor Walls and Slabs are similar. Create them from the polyline second-floor slice that you WBLOCKED from the mass model in Step 21 of "Creating Slice Plates from the Massing Model."

! **Note:** WBLOCKING slices retain their elevations. When using the slices in the Project Navigator you must reset their elevation to 0, and let the Project Navigator place the slices at the correct heights. Although in this tutorial slices 2 through 7 are identical, in many buildings the floor slices can vary greatly in shape.

1. In the **Project Navigator,** in the **Constructs** tab, select the **Constructs** icon, RMB, and select **New > Construct** from the contextual menu.

2. Name the New Construct **SECOND FLOOR SLAB,** check the **Level 2** check box, and press OK to return to the Drawing Editor.

3. Repeat this process and create the **SECOND FLOOR WALLS** construct.

4. Double-click **SECOND FLOOR WALLS** to bring up the drawing in the Drawing Editor.

5. Select **Insert > Block** from the **Main** menu to bring up the **Insert** dialog box.

6. In the Insert dialog box browse and find the **SECOND FLOOR POLY** that you WBLOCKED in "Creating Slice Plates from the Massing Model."

7. *Uncheck* the **Specify On-screen** check box, check the **Explode** check box, and press OK to place SECOND FLOOR POLY in your SECOND FLOOR SLAB drawing.

8. **Explode** the drawing twice, and erase the rectangular slice indicator.

9. Select Trim and trim the slice as necessary (see the figure below).

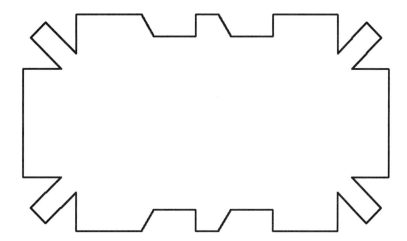

10. Select the slice and move your cursor over the **Properties** palette to open it.

11. In the Properties palette set the **Elevation** of the slice to **0**″ (see the note at the beginning of this exercise).

12. Select the Wall icon in the Design tool palette, RMB, and select Apply Tool Properties to > Linework and Walls from the contextual menu.

13. While the walls are still selected, move your cursor over the **Properties** palette to open it.

14. In the Properties palette set the following:

    a. Style = **Standard**
    b. Width = **12″**
    c. Base Height = **9′-4″**
    d. Justify = **Right**

You have now created the second-floor walls (SECOND FLOOR WALLS .dwg). Save the file.

15. In the **Project Navigator,** in the **Constructs** tab, double-click the **SECOND FLOOR SLAB** icon to bring up the drawing in the Drawing Editor.

16. In the **Project Navigator,** from the **Constructs** tab, drag the **SECOND FLOOR WALLS** into the **SECOND FLOOR SLAB.dwg** in the Drawing Editor.

17. Select the **Slab** icon in the **Design** tool palette, RMB, and select **Apply Tool Properties to > Linework and Walls** from the contextual menu.

18. Select all walls, and press Enter.

19. Enter **N** (N) in the command line, and press Enter.

20. Enter **T** (Top) in the command line, and press Enter to complete the command and create the slab.

21. Enter **L** (Left) in the command line, and press Enter to complete the command and create the slab.

22. With the new slab still selected, move your cursor over the **Properties** palette to open it.

23. Set the **Thickness** of the slab to **6″**, and the Elevation to **−6″**.

You have now created the second-floor slab (SECOND FLOOR SLAB.dwg) Save the file.

You will now need to adjust the second-floor slab to meet the landings of the First Floor Stairs.

24. From the Project navigator, drag **FIRST FLOOR STAIRS** into the **SECOND FLOOR SLAB.dwg** that is in the Drawing Editor.

25. Select the second-floor slab, and adjust the slab to meet the stair landings by moving the slab grips (see the following figure).

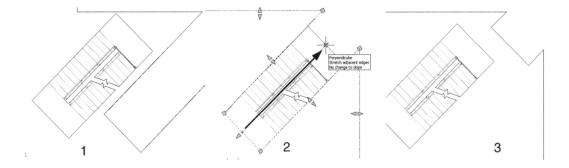

26. Repeat at all four stairways.

27. Detach the **FIRST FLOOR STAIRS.dwg.**

28. Select **File > Save** from the Main menu and save the file (see the figure below).

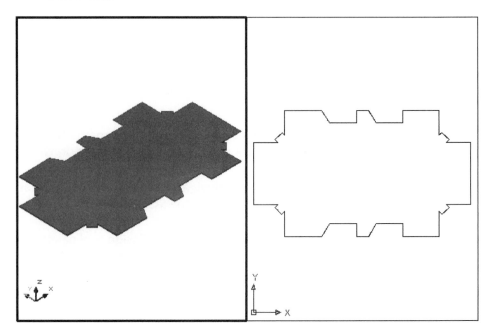

Hands-On

The Third-Floor Slab

1. In the **Project Navigator,** in the **Constructs** tab, select the **SECOND FLOOR SLAB,** RMB, and select **Copy Construct to levels** from the contextual menu to bring up the **Copy Construct to levels** dialog box.

2. Check the check boxes for Level **3,** and then press OK to return to the Drawing Editor.

3. In the **Constructs** tab **Rename** the slab you just created to **THIRD FLOOR SLAB.**

4. Double-click the THIRD FLOOR SLAB icon to bring up the **THIRD FLOOR SLAB.dwg.**

5. Drag the FIRST FLOOR STAIRS.dwg into the **THIRD FLOOR SLAB.dwg.**

6. Change to the Top View.

7. Select the **Stair** icon from the **Design** menu, move your cursor over the **Properties** palette to open it, and place a stair in one stairwell with the following parameters:

    a. Style = **Standard**
    b. Shape = **U Shaped**
    c. Turn Type = **1/2 Landing**
    d. Horizontal Orientation = **Clockwise**
    e. Vertical Orientation = **Up**
    f. Width =**3′-8″**
    g. Base Height = **9′-4″**
    h. Justify = **Left**
    i. Terminate with = **Riser**
    j. Elevation = **0″**

This stair will meet the lower stair at its riser as shown in the figure below.

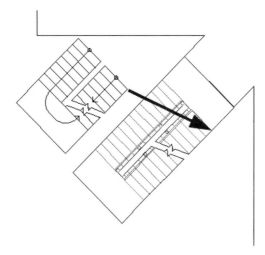

8. Mirror the new stairs to all four corners of the third-floor slab.

9. Adjust the third-floor slab to meet the second-floor stairs in the same manner that you adjusted the second-floor slab to meet the first-floor stairs in "The Column Structure" exercise, Step 27.

10. Select the **Xref Manager** and **Detach** the **FIRST FLOOR STAIR.dwg.**

11. Select **Edit > Cut** from the **Main** menu, and select all four new 9'4"-high stairs that you created in Step 7 of this exercise.

12. Select **File > Save** to save the **THIRD FLOOR SLAB.dwg.**

Hands-On

Making the Second-Floor Stair Construct

1. In the **Project Navigator,** in the **Constructs** tab, select the **Constructs** icon, RMB, and select **New > Construct** from the contextual menu.

2. Name the New Construct **SECOND FLOOR STAIRS,** check the **Level 2** check box, and press OK to return to the Drawing Editor.

3. Double-click **SECOND FLOOR STAIRS** to bring up the drawing in the Drawing Editor.

4. Select **Edit > Paste to Original Coordinates** from the **Main** menu to paste the stairs you cut in Step 11 of this exercise into the **SECOND FLOOR STAIRS.dwg.**

5. Select the Railing icon from the Design menu. Move your cursor over the **Properties** palette to open it, and place a railing on each stair with the following parameters.

   a. Style = **Standard**
   b. Attached to = **Stair**
   c. Side offset = **1-1/2"**
   d. Automatic Placement = **Yes**

6. Select **File > Save** to save the **SECOND FLOOR STAIRS.dwg.**

Hands-On

Making the Fourth-, Fifth-, Sixth-, and Seventh-Floor Slabs

1. In the **Project Navigator,** in the **Constructs** tab, select the **THIRD FLOOR SLAB** icon, RMB, and select **Copy Construct to Levels** from the contextual menu to bring up the **Copy Construct to Levels** dialog box.

2. In the Copy Construct to Levels dialog box check the Level 4, 5, 6, and 7 check boxes, and then press OK to return to the Drawing Editor.

3. In the **Project Navigator,** in the **Constructs** tab the new constructs that you just created will be labeled **THIRD FLOOR SLAB (4)** through

THIRD FLOOR SLAB (7). Rename them **FOURTH FLOOR SLAB** through **SEVENTH FLOOR SLAB,** respectively (see the figure below).

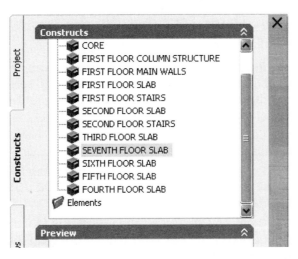

Hands-On

Making the Third-, Fourth-, Fifth-, Sixth-, and Seventh-Floor Walls

1. In the **Project Navigator,** in the **Constructs** tab, select the **SECOND FLOOR WALLS** icon, RMB, and select **Copy Construct to Levels** from the contextual menu to bring up the **Copy Construct to Levels** dialog box.

2. In the Copy Construct to Levels dialog box check the Level 3, 4, 5, 6, and 7 check boxes, and then press OK to return to the Drawing Editor.

3. In the **Project Navigator,** in the **Constructs** tab the new constructs that you just created will be labeled **SECOND FLOOR WALLS (3)** through **SECOND FLOOR WALLS (7).** Rename them **THIRD FLOOR WALLS** through **SEVENTH FLOOR WALLS,** respectively.

Hands-On

Making the Third-, Fourth-, Fifth-, and Sixth-Floor Stairs

1. In the **Project Navigator,** in the **Constructs** tab, select the **SECOND FLOOR STAIR** icon, RMB, and select **Copy Construct to Levels** from the contextual menu to bring up the **Copy Construct to Levels** dialog box.

2. In the Copy Construct to Levels dialog box check the Level 4, 5, and 6 check boxes, and then press OK to return to the Drawing Editor.

3. In the **Project Navigator,** in the **Constructs** tab the new constructs that you just created will be labeled **SECOND FLOOR STAIRS (3)** through **SECOND FLOOR STAIRS (6).** Rename them **THIRD FLOOR STAIRS** through **SIXTH FLOOR STAIRS,** respectively.

Hands-On

Making the Third-, Fourth-, Fifth-, Sixth-, and Seventh-Floor Columns

1. In the **Project Navigator**, in the **Constructs** tab, select the **FIRST FLOOR COLUMN STRUCTURE** icon, RMB, and select **Copy Construct to Levels** from the contextual menu to bring up the **Copy Construct to Levels** dialog box.

2. In the Copy Construct to Levels dialog box check the Level 2 check box, and then press OK to return to the Drawing Editor.

3. In the **Project Navigator**, in the **Constructs** tab the new construct that you just created will be labeled **FIRST FLOOR COLUMN STRUCTURE (2)**. Rename it **SECOND FLOOR COLUMN STRUCTURE.**

4. In the **Project Navigator**, in the **Constructs** tab, double-click the **FIRST FLOOR COLUMN STRUCTURE** icon to bring up the **FIRST FLOOR COLUMN STRUCTURE.dwg** in the Drawing Editor.

5. Using **Quick Select**, select all the columns, move your cursor over the **Properties** palette to open it, and change the logical length to **9'-4"**.

6. Again in the **Project Navigator**, in the **Constructs** tab, select the **SECOND FLOOR COLUMN STRUCTURE** icon, RMB, and select **Copy Construct to Levels** from the contextual menu to bring up the **Copy Construct to Levels** dialog box.

7. Check the Level 3, 4, 5, 6, and 7 check boxes, and then press OK to return to the Drawing Editor.

8. In the **Project Navigator**, in the **Constructs** tab the new constructs that you just created will be labeled **SECOND FLOOR COLUMN STRUCTURE (3)** through **SECOND FLOOR COLUMN STRUCTURE (7)**. Rename them **THIRD FLOOR COLUMN STRUCTURE** through **SEVENTH FLOOR COLUMN STRUCTURE,** respectively.

Hands-On

Making the Second- through Seventh-Floor CORE

Using the methods shown in the previous exercises, make and rename the SECOND through SEVENTH FLOOR Cores.

Hands-On

Creating a View (Showing All the Components Together)

Creating a view will allow you to see all the parts of the building assembled together. You can modify the view to show different components and variations and save those views under different names. It a good idea to create a view as soon as possible in the Documentation phase so that you can see if you need to make modifications.

1. In the **Project Navigator,** change to the **VIEWS** tab.
2. Select the **Views** icon, RMB, and select **New > View** from the contextual menu to bring up the **Add View** dialog box.
3. Enter **TOTAL SW ISOMERTIC VIEW** in the **Name** field, and press the **Next** button to move to the **Context** screen.
4. Check all seven **Level** check boxes, and press the **Next** button to move to the **Content** screen.
5. Check the **Constructs** check box to check all the Constructs, and press the **Next** button to move to the **Viewport Defaults** screen.
6. Check the **Constructs** check box, select **SW Isometric** from the View Direction drop-down list, and set the Viewport Scale to 1/8″ = 1′-0″, press the **Finish** button to return to the Drawing Editor.
7. In the **Project Navigator,** in the **Views** tab, double-click on the **TOTAL SW ISOMERTIC VIEW** icon to bring up the **TOTAL SW ISOMERTIC VIEW.dwg.**
8. Select the **SW Isometric** icon from the **Views** tool bar to change the view to **SW Isometric.**
9. Select the **Hidden** icon in the **Shading** toolbar.

Don't be surprised if the machine takes about 90 seconds to bring up this view. It is generating all your components in 3D (see the figure below).

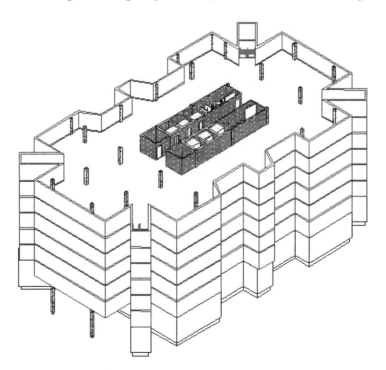

Make a TOTAL TOP VIEW and TOTAL FRONT VIEW in the same manner that you made the TOTAL SW ISOMETRIC VIEW. The only difference is the View Direction you set in the Viewports Defaults screen.

Making the Roof Structure

Before making the roof structure, you will need to modify the height of the seventh-floor walls, and the height of the seventh-floor columns. In the Project Navigator, in the Constructs tab double-click on the SEVENTH FLOOR WALLS.dwg and SEVENTH FLOOR COLUMNS.dwg. Make the Walls 13' high, and the columns 11'-0" high. Save the files after making the changes.

1. In the **Project Navigator,** in the **Constructs** tab, select the **Constructs** icon, RMB, and select **New > Construct** from the contextual menu to bring up the **Add Construct** dialog box.

2. Enter **ROOF STRUCTURE** in the **Name** fields, and check the **Level 7** check box.

3. In the **Project Navigator,** in the **Constructs** tab double-click on the **ROOF STRUCTURE** icon to bring up the **ROOF STRUCTURE.dwg.**

4. In the **Project Navigator,** in the **Constructs** tab, drag the **SEVENTH FLOOR WALLS.dwg** and **SEVENTH FLOOR COLUMN STRUCTURE.dwg** into the **ROOF STRUCTURE.dwg.**

5. Change to the **SW Isometric View,** and with the **Node** Osnap on, place lines at the top of the columns. We will soon convert these lines into **24"-deep bar joists** (see the figure below).

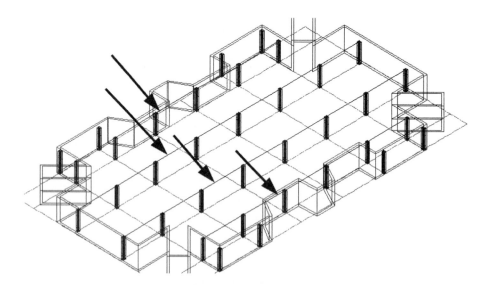

6. Place lines going perpendicular to the first lines (these will become the **12" perlin (cross beam) bar joists).**

7. Select all the lines you just placed, and move your cursor over the Properties palette to open it.

8. Set the **Start Z** and **End Z** to **11'-2-1/2"** (This will raise the perlin lines because they will be sitting on top of the 24" bar joists, and the top of the bar joist is 2½" above its base plate surface.)

9. Select the **Content Browser** icon from the main menu to bring up the **Content Browser.**

10. In the Content Browser locate the **Autodesk Architectural Desktop Design Tool Catalog - Imperial** catalog.

11. Locate the **Bar Joists** in the **structural** folder.

12. From the Bar Joists folder, drag the **Steel Joist 24** and **Steel Joist 12** into the **Design** tool palette.

13. Select the **Steel Joist 24** icon you placed in the design menu, RMB, and select **Apply Tool Properties to > Linework.** Select the first lines you placed, and press Enter.

14. Enter **Y** (Yes) in the command line, and press Enter.

15. Press the Esc key to clear the grips.

You have just created the main 24″ joist beams for the roof structure (see the figure below).

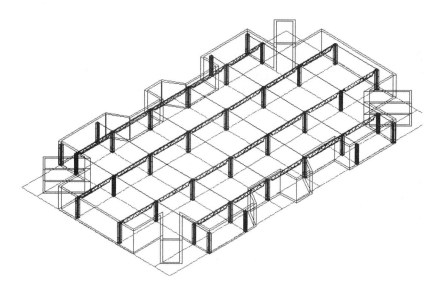

16. Change to the Top view and **array** the perlin lines at 48″ on center (see the following figure).

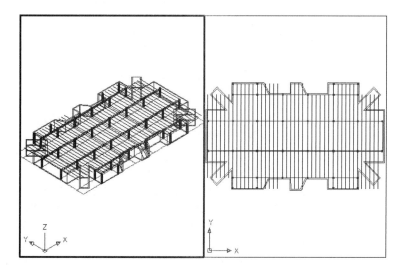

17.   Trim, adjust, and add any lines as necessary.

18.   Select the **Steel Joist 12** icon you placed in the design menu, RMB, and select **Apply Tool Properties to > Linework.** Select the first lines you placed, and press Enter.

19.   Enter **Y** (Yes) in the command line, and press Enter.

20.   Press the Esc key to clear the grips.

You have just created the 12″ perlin cross joist beams for the roof structure (see the figure below).

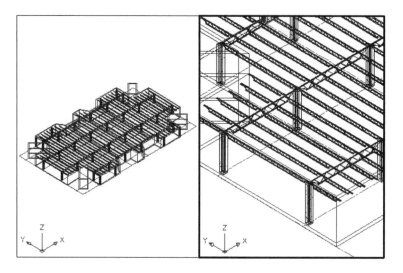

Hands-On

Making the Roof Slab and Roof Cant

1.   In the **Project Navigator** in the **Constructs** tab create a new Construct called **ROOF SLAB,** and place it on **Level 7.**

2.   Double-click the ROOF SLAB icon you just made to bring up the **ROOF SLAB.dwg** in the Drawing Editor.

3.   Drag the **SEVENTH FLOOR WALLS** into the Drawing Editor.

4.   Place lines across the stair ways as shown in the following figure.

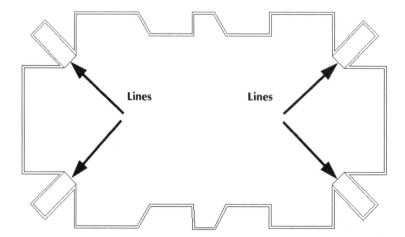

5. Enter **BPOLY** in the command line, and press Enter.
6. Pick a point in the center of the roof walls, and press Enter to make a polyline of the inside of the walls.
7. Select the **Manage Xrefs** icon, and **Detach** the SEVENTH FLOOR WALLS.dwg leaving just the polyline, and the lines in front of the stairways.
8. Select the **Slab** icon from the **Design** tool palette, RMB, and select **Apply Tool Properties to > Linework and Walls** from the contextual menu.
9. Select the polyline, and press Enter.
10. Enter **Y** (Yes) in the command line, and press Enter.
11. Enter **P** (Projected) in the command line, and press Enter.

"Projected" will create the elevation for the slab.

12. Enter **11'-5"** for the base height, and press Enter.

11'-5" is the top of the perlins (cross bar joists).

13. Enter **B** (Bottom), and press Enter to create the slab.

"Bottom" means elevation will be to bottom of slab.

14. For the **Cant,** change to the Front View and zoom close to an edge. Using that edge as a guide, create a polyline in the shape, size, and direction shown in the figure below.

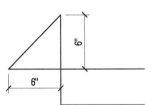

15. Select the polyline you just created, RMB, and select **Convert To > Profile Definition** from the contextual menu.
16. Click at the lower right hand corner of the polyline, enter **CANT PRO-FILE** in the new Profile Definition dialog box that appears, and press OK.

You have now created the CANT profile that you will place at the edges of your roof slab, but first you have to create a Slab Edge Style.

17. Select **Format > Style Manager** to bring up the Style Manager.
18. Select **Architectural Objects > Slab Edge Styles,** RMB, and select New from the contextual menu to create a new Slab Edge Style.
19. Name the New Style **CANT EDGE.**
20. Double-click on CANT EDGE to bring up the **Slab Edge Styles** dialog box.
21. Change to the **Design Rules** tab.

22. Check the **Fascia** check box. Select **CANT PROFILE** from the **Profile** drop-down list, *un*check the **A - Auto-Adjust to Edge Height** check box and press OK.
23. Press the Apply button to return to the Drawing Editor.
24. Select the slab, and move your cursor over the **Properties** palette to open it.
25. Click the **Edges** icon to bring up the **Slab Edges** dialog box.
26. In the Properties palette select all the Edges; select CANT EDGE from the Edge Style drop-down list, and press OK.

Your slab is now complete with a cant at its edges (see the figure below).

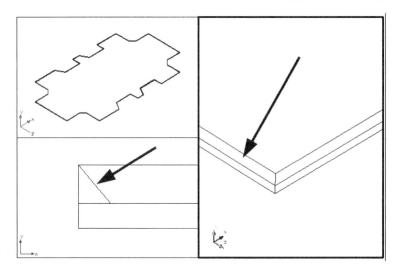

27. Remove any lines you don't need, and save the file.

Hands-On

Making the Rooftop Structure

The roof structure sits on top of the roof slab so it can be an element of the roof slab. We will use the CORE construct, change it to Element, modify it, and add a roof slab.

1. Use the **ROOF SLAB.dwg** from the previous exercise.
2. In the **Project Navigator,** in the **Constructs** tab, select the **CORE.dwg,** RMB, and **Copy** then **Paste** to create **CORE (2).**
3. Rename CORE2 to **ROOF TOP STRUCTURE.**
4. Drag ROOF TOP STRUCTURE into the **Elements** folder to convert it into an **Element.**
5. Select **ROOF TOP STRUCTURE,** RMB, and select **Attach Element To Constructs...** from the contextual menu to bring up the **Attach Element to Construct** dialog box.
6. Check the **ROOF SLAB** check box.

This connects the ROOF TOP STRUCTURE to the ROOF SLAB.

7. In the **Project Navigator,** in the **Constructs** tab in the **Elements** folder, double-click on the **ROOF TOP STRUCTURE** to bring it into the Drawing Editor.

8. In the **ROOF TOP STRUCTURE.dwg,** remove the elevators, wall openings, and close all walls where they met the columns in the original CORE.dwg.

9. Select the perimeter walls, and change their height to 16'-0".

10. Using the same technique used to add the roof slab and cant, create a roof slab over the rooftop structure.

11. Save the **ROOF TOP STRUCTURE.dwg.**

12. In the **Project Navigator,** in the **Constructs** tab drag the **ROOF TOP STRUCTURE** into the **ROOF SLAB.dwg.**

13. In the ROOF SLAB drawing, change to the Front View.

14. Select the **ROOF TOP STRUCTURE** and move your cursor over the **Properties** palette to open it.

15. Set the **Insertion point y** to 11'-9" (top of the slab).

16. Change back to the Top View.

The ROOF TOP STRUCTURE doesn't appear in the Top view—that is because it is above the Cut Plane. To set the Cut Plane do the following:

a. Select **Format > Display Manager** from the **Main** menu to bring up the **Display Manager.**

b. Select the **Configurations** folder, and double-click on **Medium** detail to bring up the **Cut Plane** tab.

c. Set the Display Above Range to **18'-0",** and the **Cut Height** to **12'-0".**

d. Press the **Apply** and **OK** buttons to return to the Drawing Editor.

Now you can see the ROOF TOP STRUCTURE.

17. Save the ROOF SLAB.dwg.

Hands-On

Adding the ROOF STRUCTURE.dwg and ROOF SLAB to Your VIEW

1. In the **Project Navigator,** change to the **Views** tab.

2. In the Views tab, select **TOTAL SW ISOMETRIC VIEW,** RMB, and select **Properties** from the contextual menu to bring up the **Modify View** dialog box.

3. Select **Content,** check the **ROOF STRUCTURE** and **ROOF SLAB** check boxes to add these drawings to the View, and press OK to return to the Drawing Editor.

4. In the **Project Navigator,** in the Views tab, double-click on **TOTAL SW ISOMETRIC VIEW** to bring it up in the Drawing Editor (see the figure below).

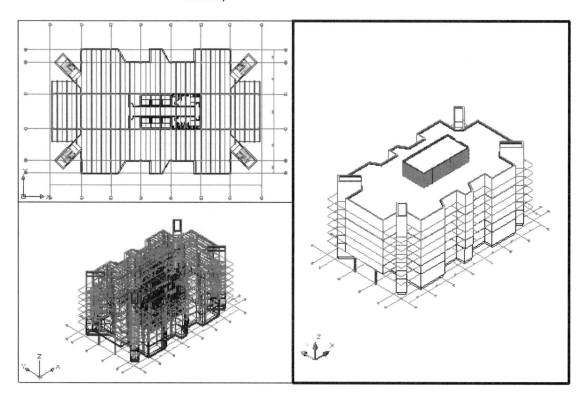

Note: I have raised the Stairway walls and added slabs to them, but this was not documented.

When doing big buildings, generating 3D views can be very processor intensive. It is best to work in wireframe, and use Hidden or Flat Shade only if absolutely necessary. This will change as the processors become increasingly more powerful.

Hands-On

Making a Section and Elevation

1. Use the **TOTAL SW ISOMETRIC VIEW.dwg.**
2. Change to the **Model** Layout.
3. Change to **Top** View.
4. Select the **Section** icon from the **Design** tool palette.
5. Click two horizontal points across your top view of the building, and press Enter.

6. Enter **60'-0"** in the command line, and press Enter to create the Section Object (see the figure below).

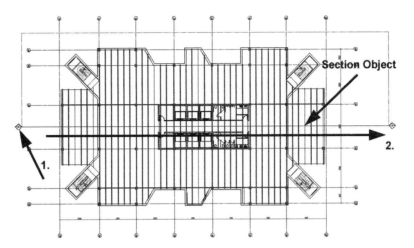

7. Pan the view to the left side to give you more room in the Drawing Editor.

8. Select the Section Object, RMB, and select Generate Section from the contextual menu to bring up the **Generate Section/Elevation** dialog box (see the figure below).

9. Press the **Pick Point** icon, and pick a point for the section adjacent to the building in the Drawing Editor.

10. Select **Section_Elevation** for the **Display Set.**

11. Select the **Select Objects** icon, type **All** in the command line, and press Enter twice to return to the **Generate Section/Elevation** dialog box.

12. In the Generate Section/Elevation dialog box, press OK to generate the section.

13. Repeat this process using the Elevation icon from the Design tool palette to create an elevation (see the figure below).

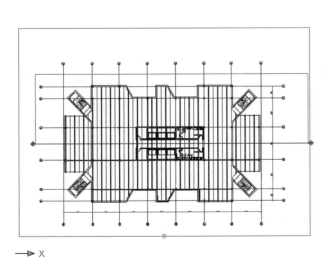

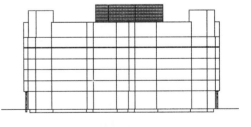

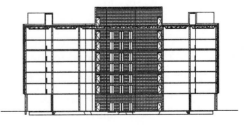

14. Erase all the Sections and Elevations you created and resave the file.

Making SW Isometric and Elevation and Section Plotting Sheets

1. In the **Project Navigator** change to the Sheets tab.
2. Select the **Sheets** icon, RMB, and select **New > Sheet** from the contextual menu.
3. Name the new sheet **SW ISOMETRIC PLOT SHEET.**
4. Double-click on **SW ISOMETRIC PLOT SHEET** to bring up the drawing in the Drawing Editor.
5. In the **SW ISOMETRIC PLOT SHEET.dwg,** change to the **Plot** layout.
6. Return to the Views tab.
7. Drag the **TOTAL SW ISOMETRIC VIEW.dwg** (without the sections) into the ELEVATIONS_and_SECTIONS.dwg.

A Paperspace viewport with a SW Isometric View of your building will be created in the **SW ISOMETRIC PLOT SHEET.**

8. In the **Project Navigator** change to the Sheets tab.
9. Select the **Sheets** icon, RMB, and select **New > Sheet** from the contextual menu.
10. Name the new sheet **ELEVATIONS_and_SECTIONS.**
11. Double-click on **ELEVATIONS_and_SECTIONS** icon to bring up the drawing in the Drawing Editor.
12. In the **ELEVATIONS_and_SECTIONS.dwg,** change to the **Plot** layout
13. Return to the Views tab.
14. Drag the **TOTAL SW ISOMETRIC VIEW.dwg** (without the sections) into the ELEVATIONS_and_SECTIONS.dwg.

A Paperspace viewport with a SW Isometric View of your building will be created in the **ELEVATIONS_and_SECTIONS.dwg.**

15. In the ELEVATIONS_and_SECTIONS.dwg, in the Plot layout, erase the viewport.
16. Select **View > Viewports > 3 Viewports** from the main menu.
17. Enter **H** (Horizontal) in the command line, and press Enter.
18. Press Enter twice to create two new Paperspace viewports.
19. Change to the **Model** layout.
20. Generate a Section, and Front and Side Elevations using the methods learned in the previous exercise.
21. Change back to the **Plot** layout.
22. Double-click in one viewport to enter Model Space, and move the elevation into place.
23. Double-click in the other viewport and move the section into place.

24. Double-click in the third viewport and move the other elevation into place.

25. Double-click outside the viewports to enter Paperspace. Select each viewport border, and move your cursor over the Properties palette to open it.

26. In the Properties palette, set the Standard scale to 1/8" = 1'-0". The Paperspace viewport layer doesn't show (see the figure below).

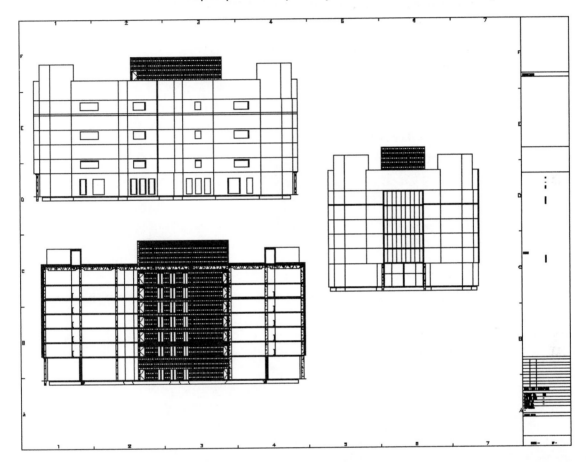

Now any changes made in the constructs can be updated in the Plot sheets. You can add windows, doors, and so on and modify the building. Remember to save each file after you make changes. An easy trick is to press the X icon at the right corner of your drawing. If you have made any changes, the program will ask if you want to save before exiting that drawing. Finally, if you refresh the sections in the construct, you can reload the Plotting sheets, and they will update your changes.

Offices, which are Elements, can be added. Feel free to use this tutorial as a basis to test your other skills learned from the exercises in this book.

Be patient, this tutorial was developed on a 2-GHz Pentium 4 with 1/2 GHz of Ram, and regeneration times for the 3D model were very high. Although not tested by me, a dual Intel XEON process may be necessary for large buildings.

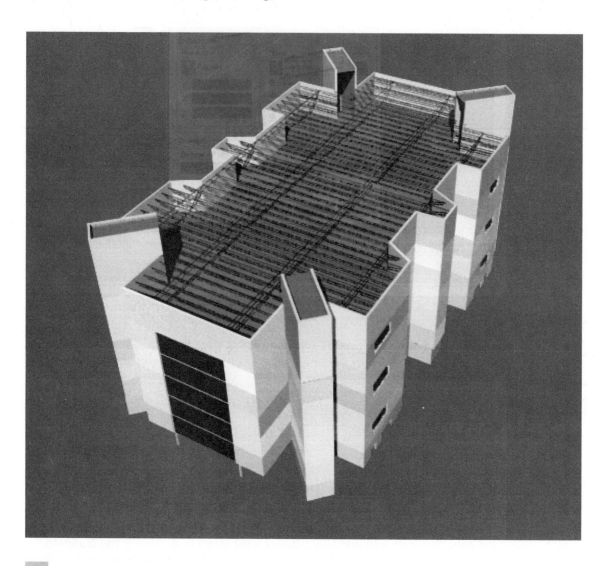

Index

A

Activate a field, 21
Activate a viewport, 21
Add Property Sets, 58–59
ADT 2004, 21 (*See also* Autodesk Architectural
    Desktop 2004)
AEC dimension chains, 246–48
AEC Dimension Style:
    creating, 238–39
    doors and window, 241–44
    using and modifying, 239–41
AEC Dimension Wizard, 235, 248–49
AEC dimensions, 235–49
    concepts, 235
    creating Dimension Style, 237–38
    detaching objects from, 245–46
    manual, 236, 244–45
    setting Text Style, 236–37
AEC objects, 1, 21 (*See also* Objects)
    Live Sectioned, 270
Ancillary, defined, 21
Appliances, add using DesignCenter, 316–17
Apply Tool Properties:
    to roof slabs, 197–98
    to roofs, 195–96
    to slabs, 209–10
Architectural Studio, publish to, 36
ArchVision, 346
Autodesk Architectural Desktop 2004:
    AEC objects, 1
    compatibility, 11–13
    contextual menus, 4
    3D, 11
    2D functionality, 11
    documentation, 13
    export to AutoCAD feature support, 9
    improvements in, 9
    interface, 23
    Multi-View Blocks, 2
    network version, 10
    Styles, 2
    Subscription Program, 14
    support and training, 13
    tool palettes, 3
Auto-hide, 26
AutoCAD dimensions, compared to AEC
    Dimensions, 235–36
Autodesk AEC Object Enabler, 9
Autodesk Revit files, 9
Autodesk VIZ
    VIZ Render and, 10
Autodesk VIZ Render (*See* VIZ Render)
Autodesk Website icon, creating, 283
Automatic Property Source, 299

B

Bar joists:
    adding, 224–27
    tutorial project for, 404–6
Bathroom, tutorial project for, 394–96
Beams, 217 (*See also* Structural members)
Bionatics EASYnat plug-in, 367, 371
Body modifiers, walls, 82–83
Boolean subtraction, 48–49
Braces, 217 (*See also* Structural members)
Browse, defined, 21

C

Catalog Library, 31–32
Chain1, 246–48
Chain2, 246–48
Check boxes, 3
CIRCLE SCHEDULE, 298
Cleanups, walls, 88–89
Column grid:
    defined, 217
    labeling, 227–28

Column grid, *continued*
    placing, 219–20
    tutorial project for, 389–93
Columns, 217 (*See also* Structural members)
    creating concrete and steel, 223–24
    grid for, 219–20
    placing, 219
    tutorial project for, 389–93
    upper-floor, 402
Compatibility of Autodesk Architectural Desktop
    2004, 11–13
Concrete and steel columns, 223–24
Content browser, 31–33
    bringing up, 31
    Catalog Library, 31–32
    functions of, 31
Content browser icon, 31
Contextual menus, defined, 4, 21
Contour massing models, 52–53
CORE:
    tutorial project, 393–96
    upper-floor, 402
Counters, kitchen:
    add using DesignCenter, 318–20
    splash edge style, 318–20
Create AEC Content, to place light fixture, 279–80
Curtain wall property tool palette, 124
Curtain walls, 123–41
    Applying Tool Properties to elevation sketch,
      132–34
    Applying Tool Properties to layout grid, 130–32
    creating new tool palette, 125
    editing grid in place, 134–37
    editing styles, 137–40
    miter angles, 126–28
    placing, 126
    Roof/Floor Line selections, 128–30
Curves, layout
    concepts, 230
    creating and using, 231
    using wall as, 231–32
Custom installation, 17–19
Custom schedules:
    Property Set Definitions, 298–300
    table style, 300–303
    using, 303–5
Customizing:
    schedules, 298–305
    windows and doors, 150
Cutting boundary, 270
    inside, 270
    outside, 270

D

2D building:
    creating with detailer, 307–12
    labeling with detailer, 312–13
2D elevations, 256–57
2D layout grid, adding and labeling, 229–30
3D mesh, creating content from, 285–87
Design content, 316
DesignCenter, 315–24
    adding appliances, 316–17
    adding counters, 318–20
    adding sink, 320–23
    concepts, 315–16
    Create AEC Content, 279–80
    light fixtures, 279–81
    sections and elevations, 323–24
Detailer, 307–13
    creating 2D building with, 307–12
    labeling 2D building with, 312–13
Dialog box, defined, 21
Dimension Style:
    AEC (*See* AEC Dimension style)
    creating, 237–38
Display tree, defined, 21
Docking, allow, 27
Documentation for Autodesk Architectural
    Desktop 2004, 13
Door, 107–22
    adding a profile, 113–14
    changing size, 110–11
    dimensioning with AEC Dimension Style,
      241–44
    editing styles, 118–19
    material tab, 119–22
    moving, 117–18
    placing using Offset/Center, 109–10
    placing using reference, 109
    swing angle, 112–13
    swing location, 110–11
Door assemblies, 141–50
    adding sidelites, 146–48
    changing sidelites, 149
    creating a primary grid, 142–43
    creating style for double doors, 144
    Door/Window Assembly Infill, 144–45
    sills, 149
    sizing frame, 148
    testing partially complete, 146
    using custom, 150
Door knob, adding, 114–17
Door objects, 107

Door property tool palette, 108
Door tags, placing, 292–94
Door/Window Assembly Infill, 144–45
Double doors, door assembly for, 144
Drape Tool, 52–53
Drawing Editor, 3, 21, 26
Drawing management, 10, 325–44
    assigning constructs and elements in Project
        Navigator, 333–36
    concepts, 326
    creating constructs and elements in Project
        Navigator, 329–30
    creating plotting sheets in Project Navigator,
        338–44
    creating views in Project Navigator, 336–38
    using Project Browser, 326–29
    working with constructs and elements in Project
        Navigator, 331–33
Drawing Setup, 36
Drop-down list, defined, 21
DWG (drawing), defined, 21

E

EASYnat content, 367, 371
Edit Property Sets, 58–59
Elevation plotting sheets, 412–14
Elevation sketch, Applying Tool Properties to,
        132–34
Elevation view, defined, 21
Elevations, 251–63
    creating new tool palette, 251–52
    creating sample building, 252–54
    2D, 256–57
    in DesignCenter, 323–24
    making, 254–56
    subdivisions, 257–62
    tutorial project for, 410–12
Elevators, tutorial project for, 394–96
End miters, 126–28
Enter button, 21
Enter key, 21
etransmit, 37
Exporting:
    to AutoCAD feature support, 9
    schedules to databases, 295

F

Fascia Profile, 199–200

Field, activating, 21
First-floor slab, 386–89
Floor slices (*See* Slice plates)
Free Form, 42–43
Full body:
    inside, 270
    outside, 270

G

Gouraud icon, 53
Grass, in VIZ Render, 365–66
Grid (*See* Layout grid)
Grips:
    changing walls by pulling on, 76–77
    changing window size with, 99
    door swing location using, 110–11
    modifying stairs with, 156–57

H

Hatch, 270

I

Idrop technology, 31–32
Inside cutting boundary, 270
Inside full body, 270
Installation, 15–19
Intelligent architectural objects, 10–11
        (*See also* Objects)
Intelligent building model objects, 10–11
Interface, 23
Interference conditions:
    stairs, 162–63
    walls, 87–88
Isometric plotting sheets, 412–14

J

Joists:
    adding, 224–27
    tutorial project for, 404–6

K

Kitchen:
    adding appliances, 316–17
    counters, 318–20
    sink, 320–23
    splash edge style, 318–20

L

Landings:
    anchoring second stair to, 163–64
    placing multi-landing stairs, 160–61
    railing and support for, 181
    railing for, 180–81
Layout curve:
    concepts, 230
    creating and using, 231
    using wall as, 231–32
Layout grid:
    Applying Tool Properties to, 130–32
    door/window assemblies, 142–43
    editing, 134–37
Layout grid (2D):
    adding and labeling, 229–30
    using, 232–34
Layout Volume Grid (3D), 234
Light fixtures:
    creating, 275–76
    custom fluorescent, 275–76
    placing, 279–80
    testing, 276–79
    testing from DesignCenter, 280–81
Live Sections, 263–64, 269–74
    concepts, 269–70
    creating, 272–73
    modifying, 273–74

M

Manual AEC Dimensions:
    adding, 244–45
    compared to AEC Dimensions, 236
Mask Blocks, 275–82
    creating, 275–76
    defined, 275
    placing, 279–80
    testing, 276–79
    testing from DesignCenter, 280–81

Mass model, concepts, 5
Mass modeling (*See also* Massing)
    concepts, 40
Massing:
    changing slice plates into space boundaries
        and walls, 51
    concepts, 40
    creating object, 40–42
    creating slice plates, 47–48, 380–82
    Drape Tool, 52–53
    joining two objects, 44, 46
    modifying object after applying slice plates,
        48–51
    rendering of, 378–80
    slice markers, 48
    tutorial project for, 373–78
    using slice plates, 383–85
Massing model, 5
Materials:
    door, 119–22
    in VIZ Render, 355–66
Miter angles, 126–28
Multi-landing stairs, 160–61
Multi-View Blocks, 283–90
    concepts, 283
    creating, 288–89
    creating Autodesk Website icon, 283
    creating content from 3D mesh, 285–87
    defined, 2
    testing, 289–90

N

Network version of Autodesk Architectural
        Desktop 2004, 10
Nsight3D website, 284

O

ObjectARX technology, 10–11
Objects, 1, 10–11 (*See also* Specific object)
    curtain wall, 123
    defined, 1, 21
    door, 107
    slab (*See* Slabs)
    space, 60–63
    space Boundary, 55
    stair, 151
    wall, 73